La Corda d'Oro

ARAM PUBLIC LIBRARY
DELAVAN, WIS. 2

Story & Art by Yuki Kure

Kahoko Hino
(General Education School, 2nd year)

The heroine. She knows nothing about music, but she still finds herself participating in the music competition equipped with a magic violin.

Len Tsukimori
(Music School, 2nd year)

A violin major and a cold perfectionist from a musical family of unquestionable talent.

Ryotaro Tsuchiura
(General Education, 2nd year)

A member of the soccer team who seems to be looking after Kahoko as a fellow Gen Ed student.

Keiichi Shimizu
(Music school, 1st year)

A student of the cello who walks to the beat of his own drum and is often lost in the world of music. He is also often asleep.

Kazuki Hihara
(Music school, 3rd year)

An energetic and friendly trumpet major and a fan of anything fun.

Azuma Yunoki
(Music school, 3rd year)

A flute major and the son of a graceful and kind traditional flower arrangement master. He even has a dedicated fan club called the "Yunoki Guard."

Hiroto Kanazawa
(Music teacher)

The contest coordinator whose lazy demeanor suggests he is avoiding any hassle.

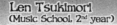

Story

Our story is set at Seisou Academy, which is split into the General Education School and Music School. One day Kahoko, a Gen Ed student, encounters a music fairy named Lili, who gives her a magic violin that anyone can play. All of a sudden, Kahoko finds herself in the school's music competition with good-looking, quirky Music School students as her fellow contestants! Kahoko eventually comes to accept this daunting task and actually finds herself enjoying music. She has just started thinking about the contest in a more positive light when...

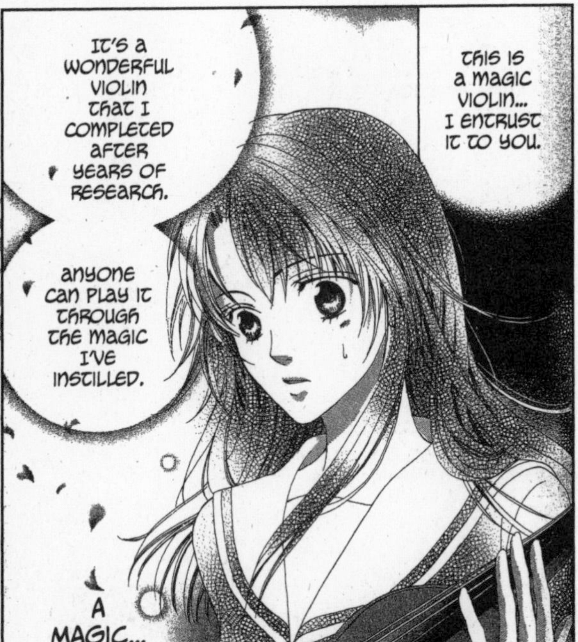
THIS IS A MAGIC VIOLIN... I ENTRUST IT TO YOU.
IT'S A WONDERFUL VIOLIN THAT I COMPLETED AFTER YEARS OF RESEARCH.
ANYONE CAN PLAY IT THROUGH THE MAGIC I'VE INSTILLED.
A MAGIC... VIOLIN?!

Previously...

Kahoko is the only one who can see the music fairy, or *Fata*, named Lili. Lili claims he has been in search of people who are compatible with *Fatas*, and gives Kahoko a magic violin. What will Kahoko do now that Lili has entrusted her with his wish that more people feel closer to music?!

The music fairy Lili, who got Kahoko caught up in this affair. ↓

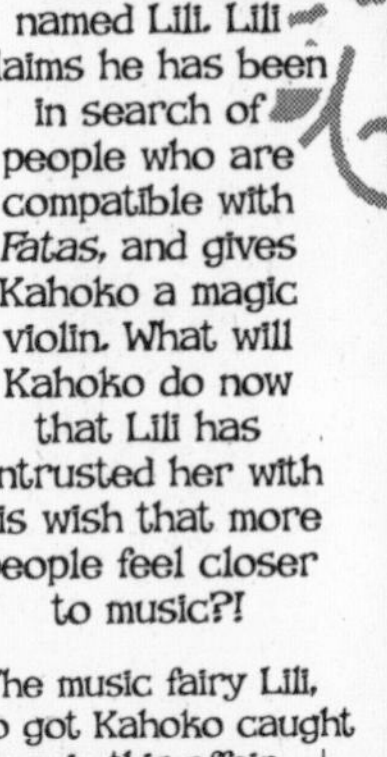

La Corda d'Oro

CONTENTS
Volume 2

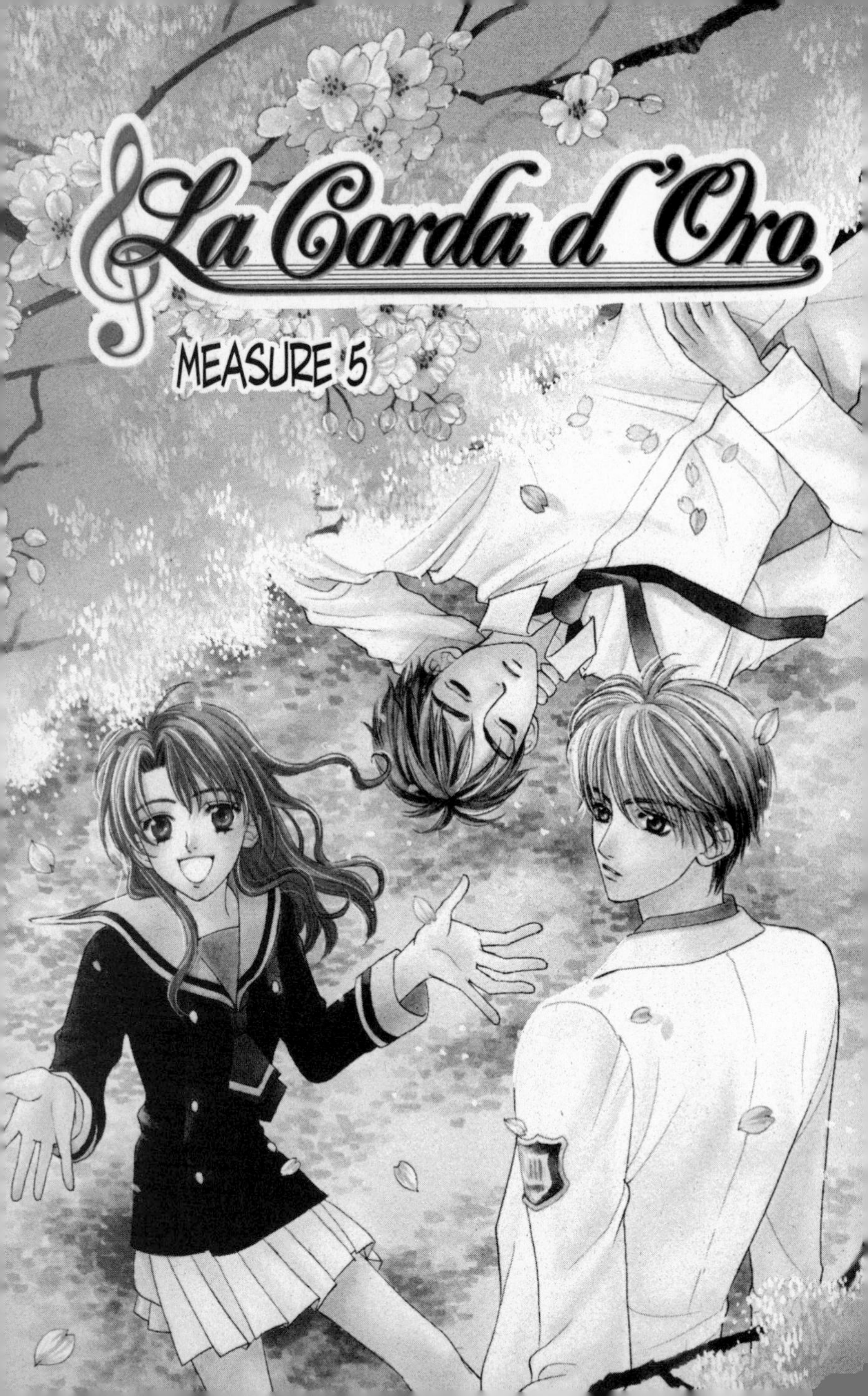
La Corda d'Oro
MEASURE 5

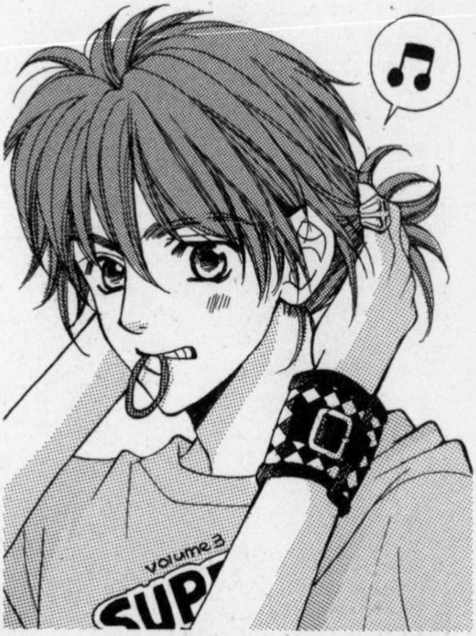

♫
volume 3
SUP

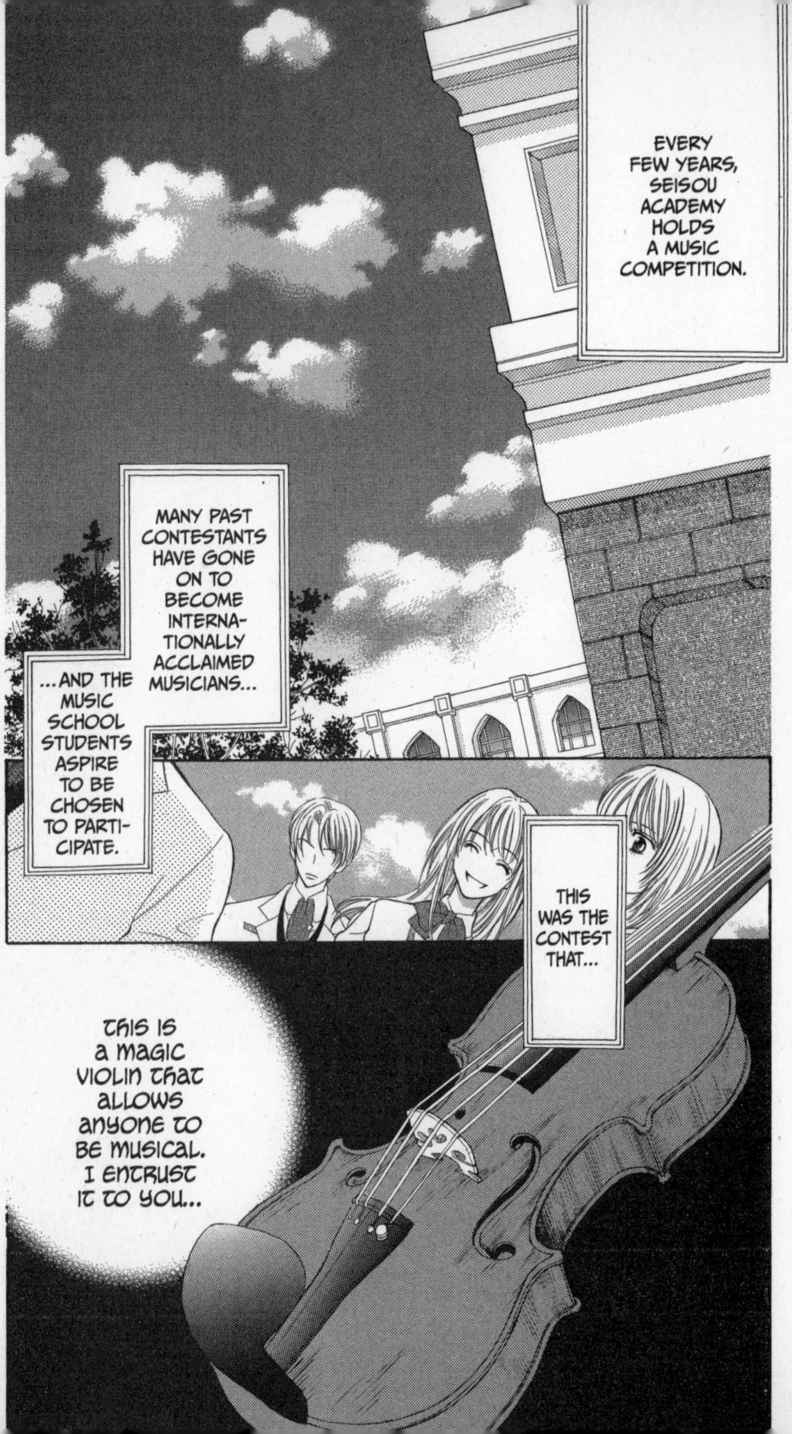
EVERY FEW YEARS, SEISOU ACADEMY HOLDS A MUSIC COMPETITION.
MANY PAST CONTESTANTS HAVE GONE ON TO BECOME INTERNATIONALLY ACCLAIMED MUSICIANS...
...AND THE MUSIC SCHOOL STUDENTS ASPIRE TO BE CHOSEN TO PARTICIPATE.
THIS WAS THE CONTEST THAT...
THIS IS A MAGIC VIOLIN THAT ALLOWS ANYONE TO BE MUSICAL. I ENTRUST IT TO YOU...

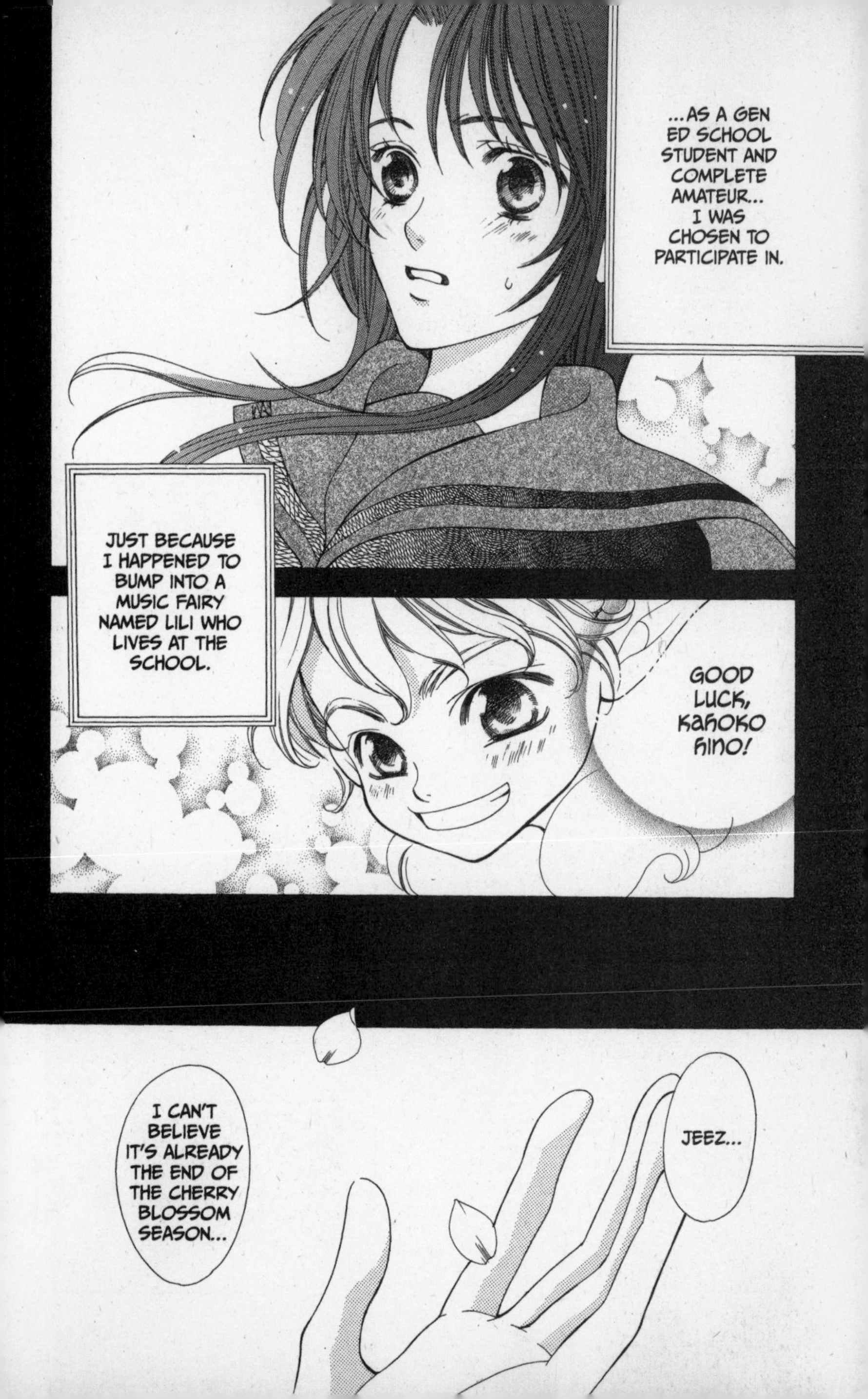
...AS A GEN ED SCHOOL STUDENT AND COMPLETE AMATEUR... I WAS CHOSEN TO PARTICIPATE IN.
JUST BECAUSE I HAPPENED TO BUMP INTO A MUSIC FAIRY NAMED LILI WHO LIVES AT THE SCHOOL.
GOOD LUCK, KAHOKO HINO!
JEEZ...
I CAN'T BELIEVE IT'S ALREADY THE END OF THE CHERRY BLOSSOM SEASON...

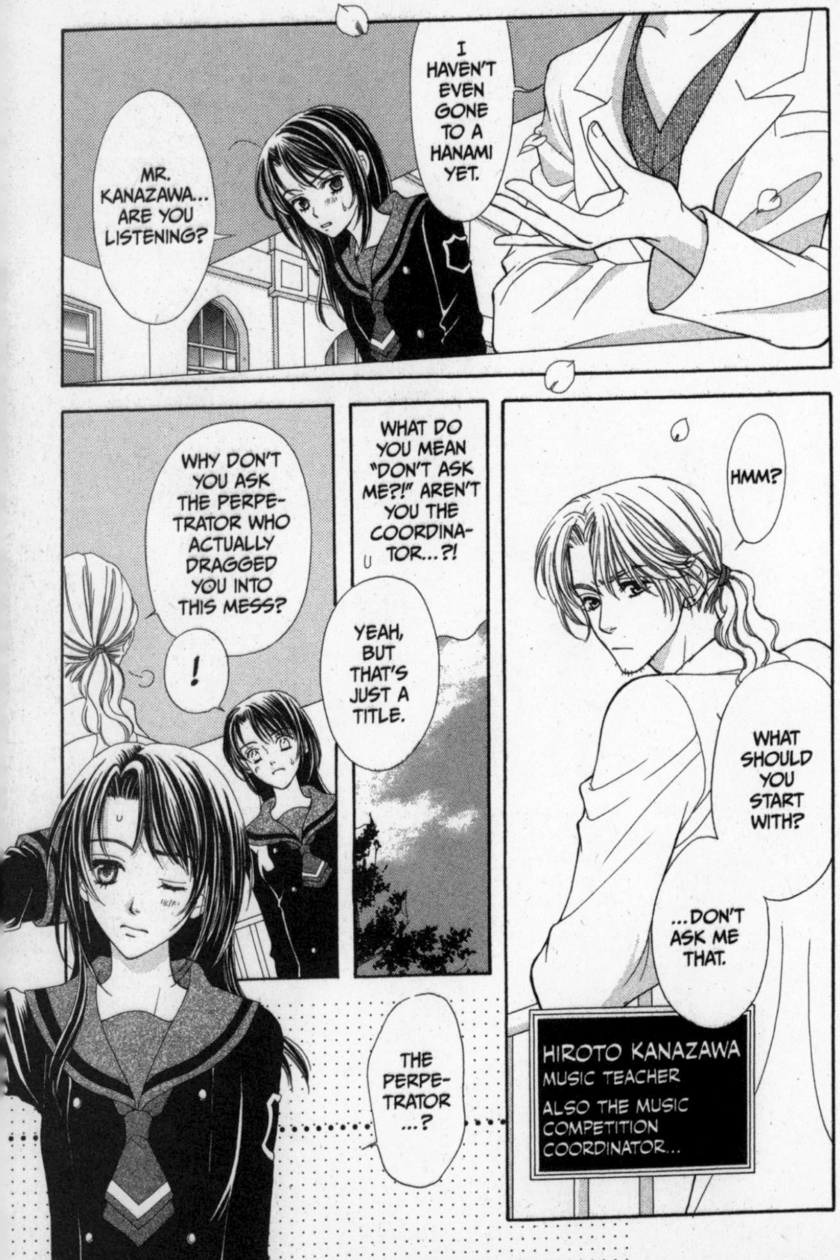
I HAVEN'T EVEN GONE TO A HANAMI YET.
MR. KANAZAWA... ARE YOU LISTENING?
HMM?
WHAT SHOULD YOU START WITH?
...DON'T ASK ME THAT.
HIROTO KANAZAWA
MUSIC TEACHER
ALSO THE MUSIC COMPETITION COORDINATOR...
WHAT DO YOU MEAN "DON'T ASK ME?!" AREN'T YOU THE COORDINATOR...?!
YEAH, BUT THAT'S JUST A TITLE.
WHY DON'T YOU ASK THE PERPETRATOR WHO ACTUALLY DRAGGED YOU INTO THIS MESS?
!
THE PERPETRATOR...?

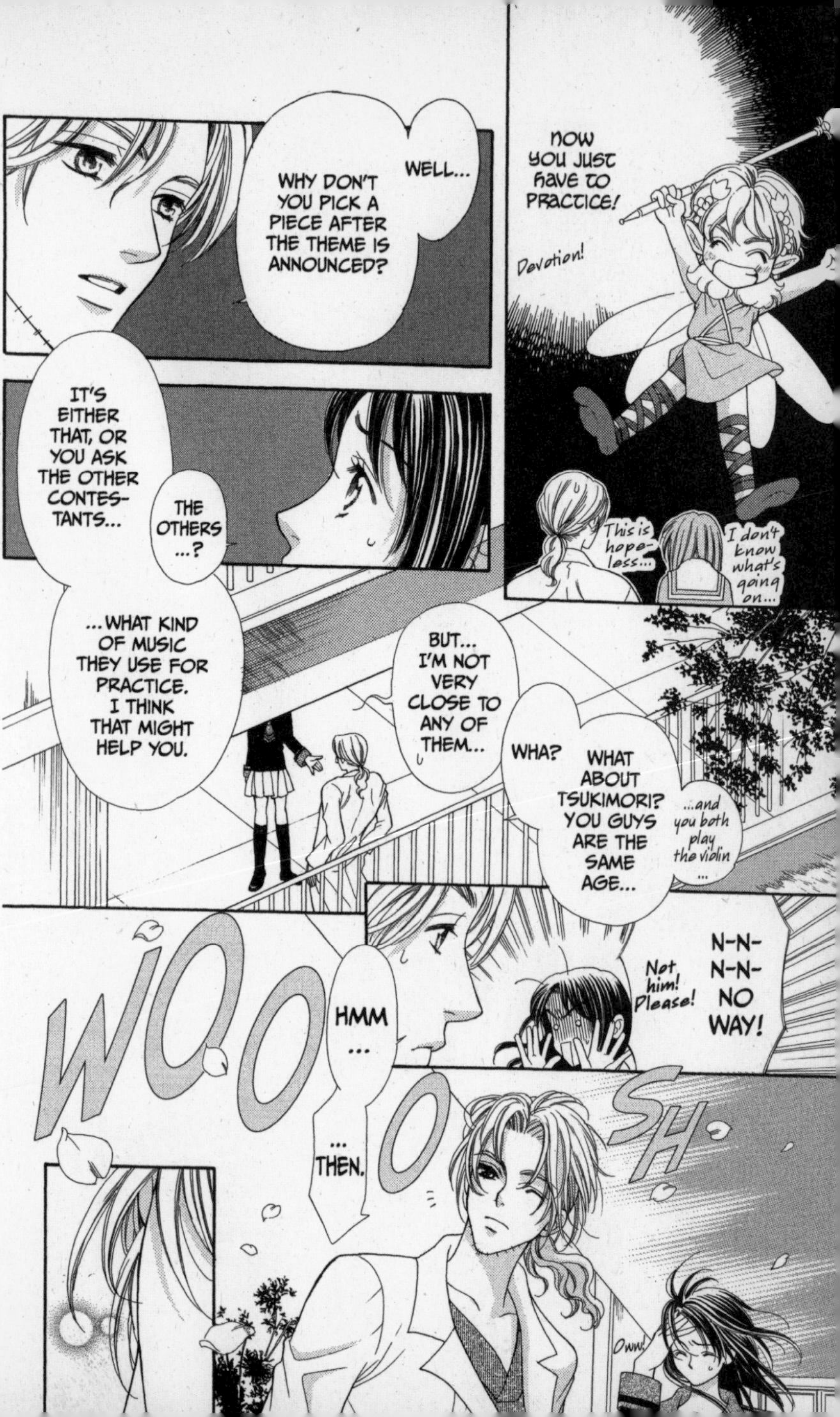
NOW YOU JUST HAVE TO PRACTICE!
Devotion!
This is hope-less...
I don't know what's going on...
WELL...
WHY DON'T YOU PICK A PIECE AFTER THE THEME IS ANNOUNCED?
IT'S EITHER THAT, OR YOU ASK THE OTHER CONTES-TANTS...
THE OTHERS ...?
...WHAT KIND OF MUSIC THEY USE FOR PRACTICE. I THINK THAT MIGHT HELP YOU.
BUT... I'M NOT VERY CLOSE TO ANY OF THEM...
WHA?
WHAT ABOUT TSUKIMORI? YOU GUYS ARE THE SAME AGE...
...and you both play the violin ...
N-N-N-N-NO WAY!
Not him! Please!
HMM ...
... THEN.
WOOOOSH
Oww!

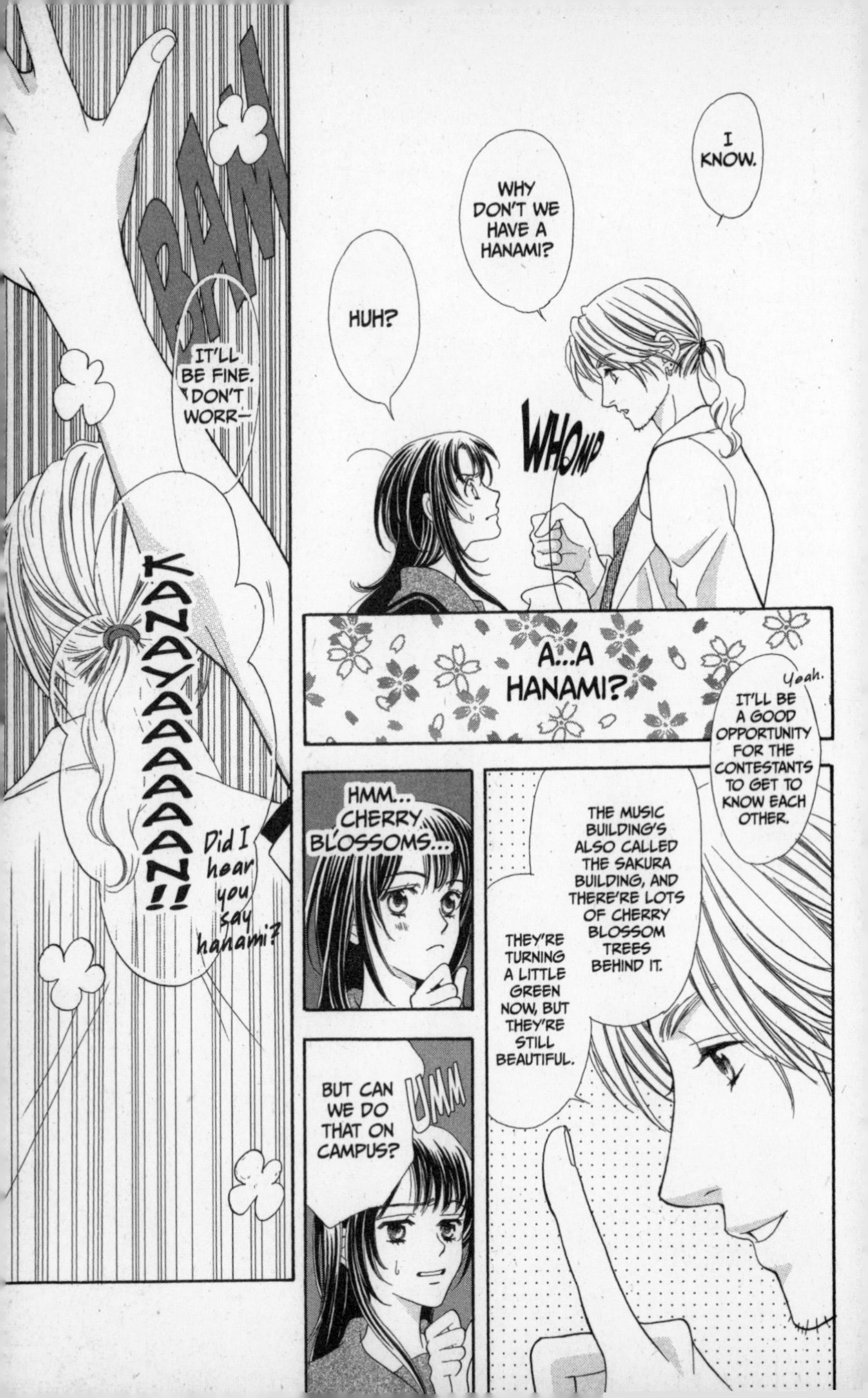
I KNOW.
WHY DON'T WE HAVE A HANAMI?
HUH?
WHOMP
A...A HANAMI?
Yeah.
IT'LL BE A GOOD OPPORTUNITY FOR THE CONTESTANTS TO GET TO KNOW EACH OTHER.
THE MUSIC BUILDING'S ALSO CALLED THE SAKURA BUILDING, AND THERE'RE LOTS OF CHERRY BLOSSOM TREES BEHIND IT.
THEY'RE TURNING A LITTLE GREEN NOW, BUT THEY'RE STILL BEAUTIFUL.
HMM... CHERRY BLOSSOMS...
UMM
BUT CAN WE DO THAT ON CAMPUS?
BAM
IT'LL BE FINE. DON'T WORR–
KANAYAAAAAAAAN!!
Did I hear you say hanami?

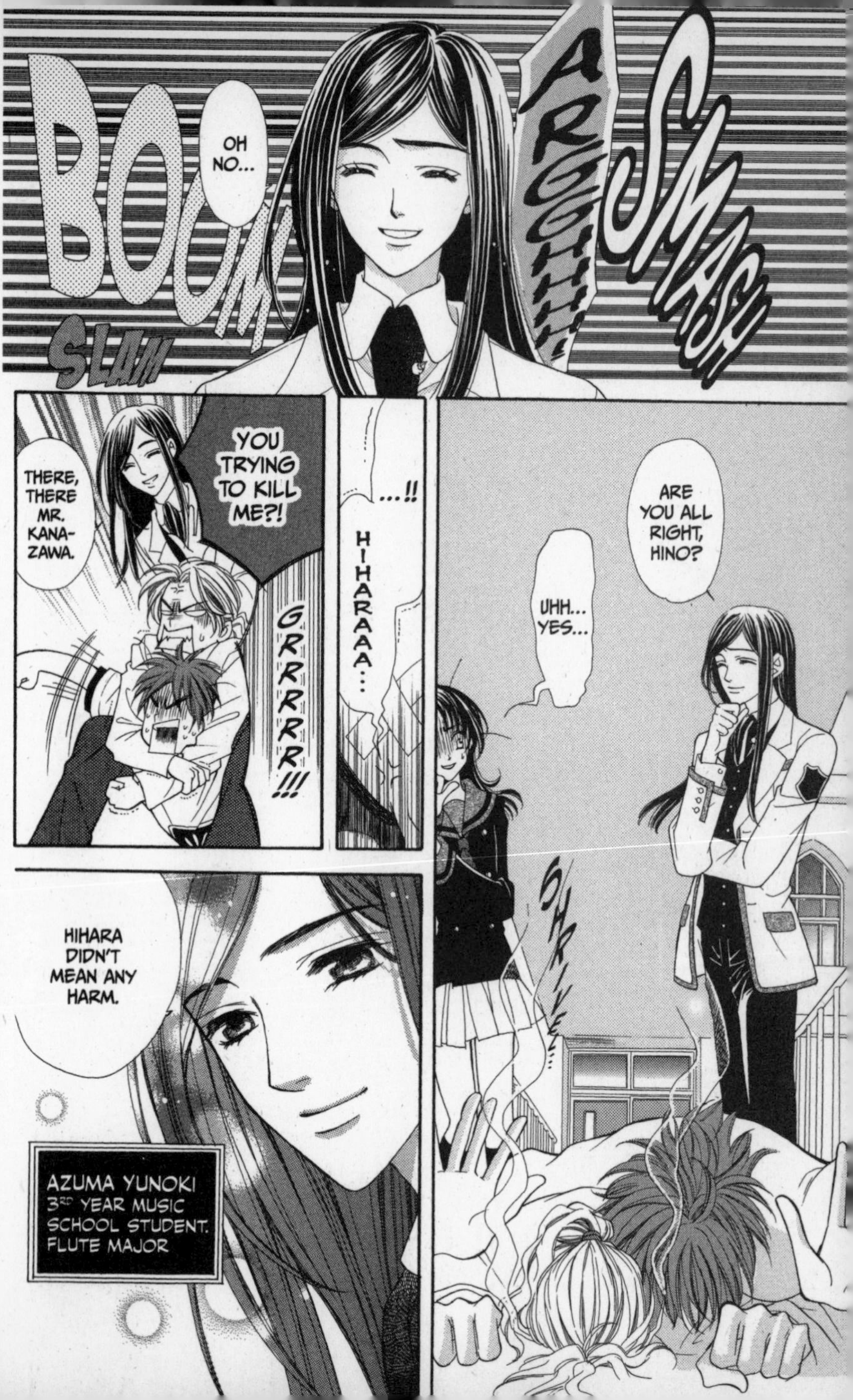
SMASH!
ARGGHHHH!
OH NO...
BOOM
SLAM
ARE YOU ALL RIGHT, HINO?
UHH... YES...
SHRIVEL...
...!!
HIHARAAA...
GRRRRR!!!
YOU TRYING TO KILL ME?!
THERE, THERE MR. KANAZAWA.
HIHARA DIDN'T MEAN ANY HARM.
AZUMA YUNOKI 3RD YEAR MUSIC SCHOOL STUDENT. FLUTE MAJOR

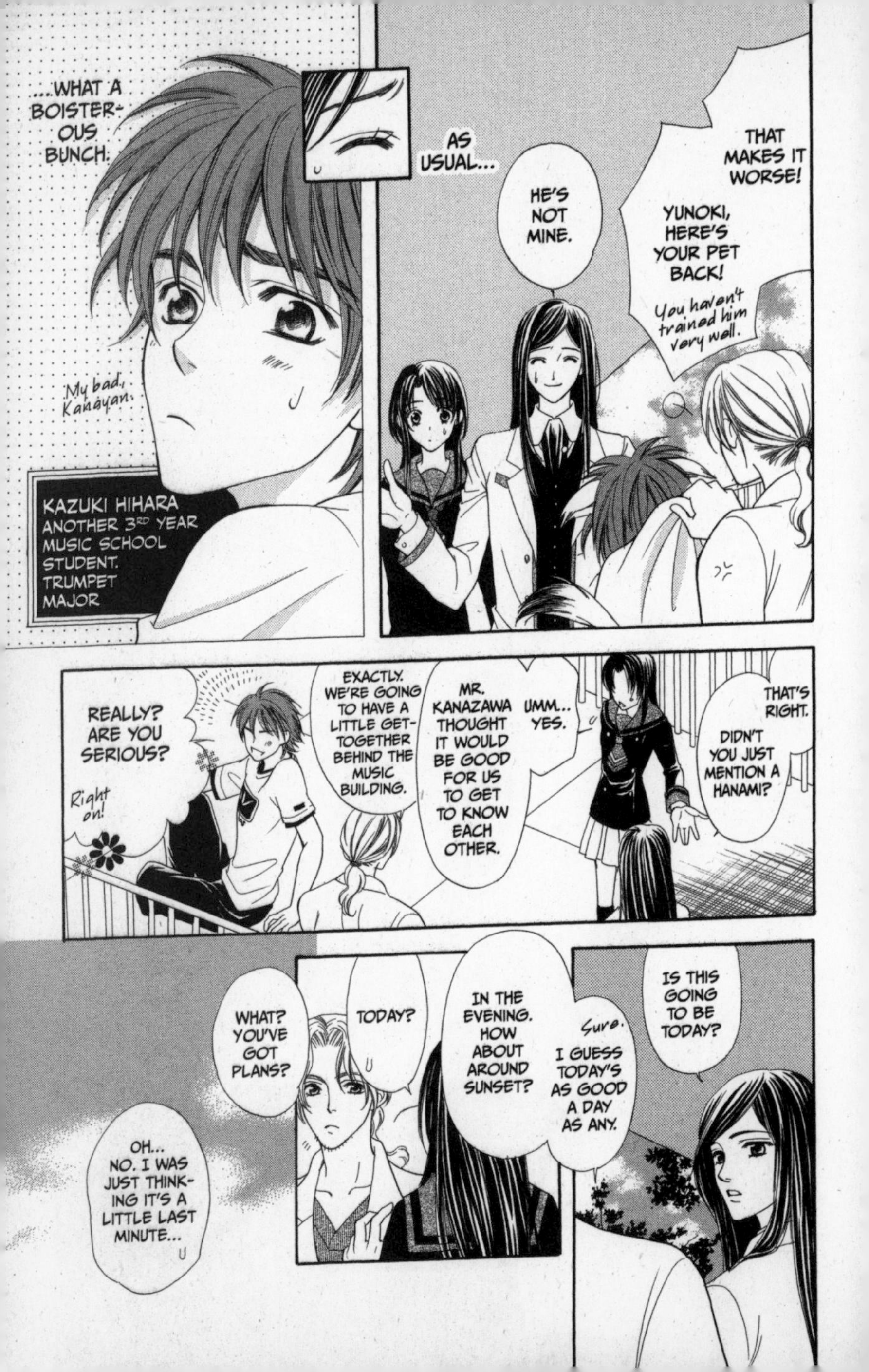
THAT MAKES IT WORSE!
YUNOKI, HERE'S YOUR PET BACK!
You haven't trained him very well.
HE'S NOT MINE.
AS USUAL...
...WHAT A BOISTER-OUS BUNCH.
My bad, Kanayan.
KAZUKI HIHARA ANOTHER 3RD YEAR MUSIC SCHOOL STUDENT. TRUMPET MAJOR
THAT'S RIGHT.
DIDN'T YOU JUST MENTION A HANAMI?
UMM... YES.
MR. KANAZAWA THOUGHT IT WOULD BE GOOD FOR US TO GET TO KNOW EACH OTHER.
EXACTLY. WE'RE GOING TO HAVE A LITTLE GET-TOGETHER BEHIND THE MUSIC BUILDING.
REALLY? ARE YOU SERIOUS?
Right on!
IS THIS GOING TO BE TODAY?
Sure.
I GUESS TODAY'S AS GOOD A DAY AS ANY.
IN THE EVENING. HOW ABOUT AROUND SUNSET?
TODAY?
WHAT? YOU'VE GOT PLANS?
OH... NO. I WAS JUST THINK-ING IT'S A LITTLE LAST MINUTE...

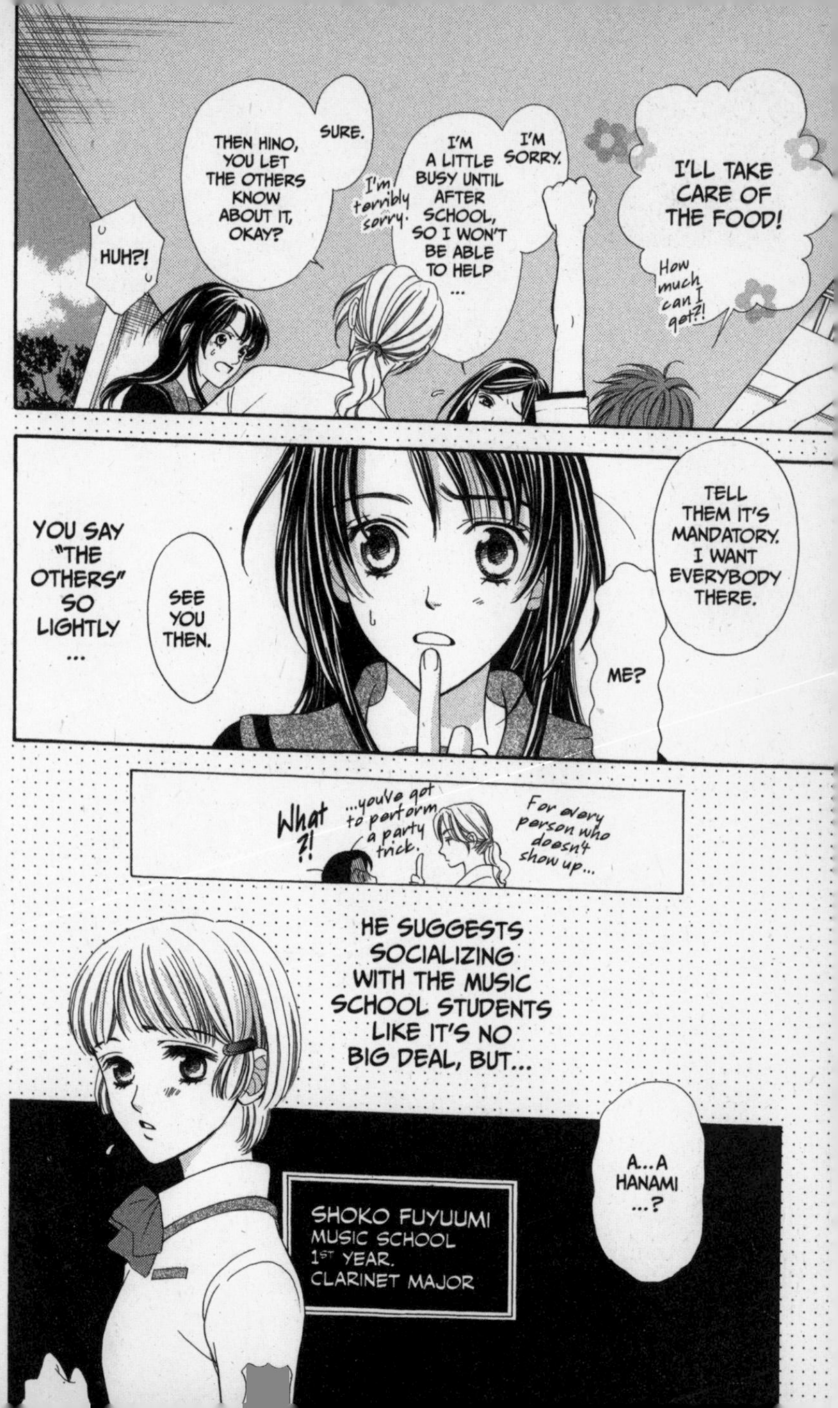
I'LL TAKE CARE OF THE FOOD!
How much can I get?!
I'M SORRY.
I'M A LITTLE BUSY UNTIL AFTER SCHOOL, SO I WON'T BE ABLE TO HELP...
I'm terribly sorry.
SURE.
THEN HINO, YOU LET THE OTHERS KNOW ABOUT IT, OKAY?
HUH?!
TELL THEM IT'S MANDATORY. I WANT EVERYBODY THERE.
ME?
SEE YOU THEN.
YOU SAY "THE OTHERS" SO LIGHTLY...
For every person who doesn't show up...
...you've got to perform a party trick.
What?!
HE SUGGESTS SOCIALIZING WITH THE MUSIC SCHOOL STUDENTS LIKE IT'S NO BIG DEAL, BUT...
A...A HANAMI...?
SHOKO FUYUUMI MUSIC SCHOOL 1ST YEAR. CLARINET MAJOR

UHHH...

KEIICHI SHIMIZU
MUSIC SCHOOL
1ST YEAR.
CELLO MAJOR

Hello.
It's me again (Yuki).
I'd like to express
my gratitude to you
for buying Volume 2
of La Corda. Yes,
it was a rocky road,
but I was able to get
through this second
volume.

• • • • • • • • • • • • •

Volume 2 includes
Movements 5 through 8.
I hope you enjoy it.

SO SORRY
TO SPRING
THIS ON YOU,
BUT PLEA...

?!

RAAH!!

EEK!!

CAN THIS
POSSIBLY
GO WELL?

Z z z

GRR

SHAKE

WHEN IT
COMES TO A
PARTICULAR
SECOND-YEAR
STUDENT...

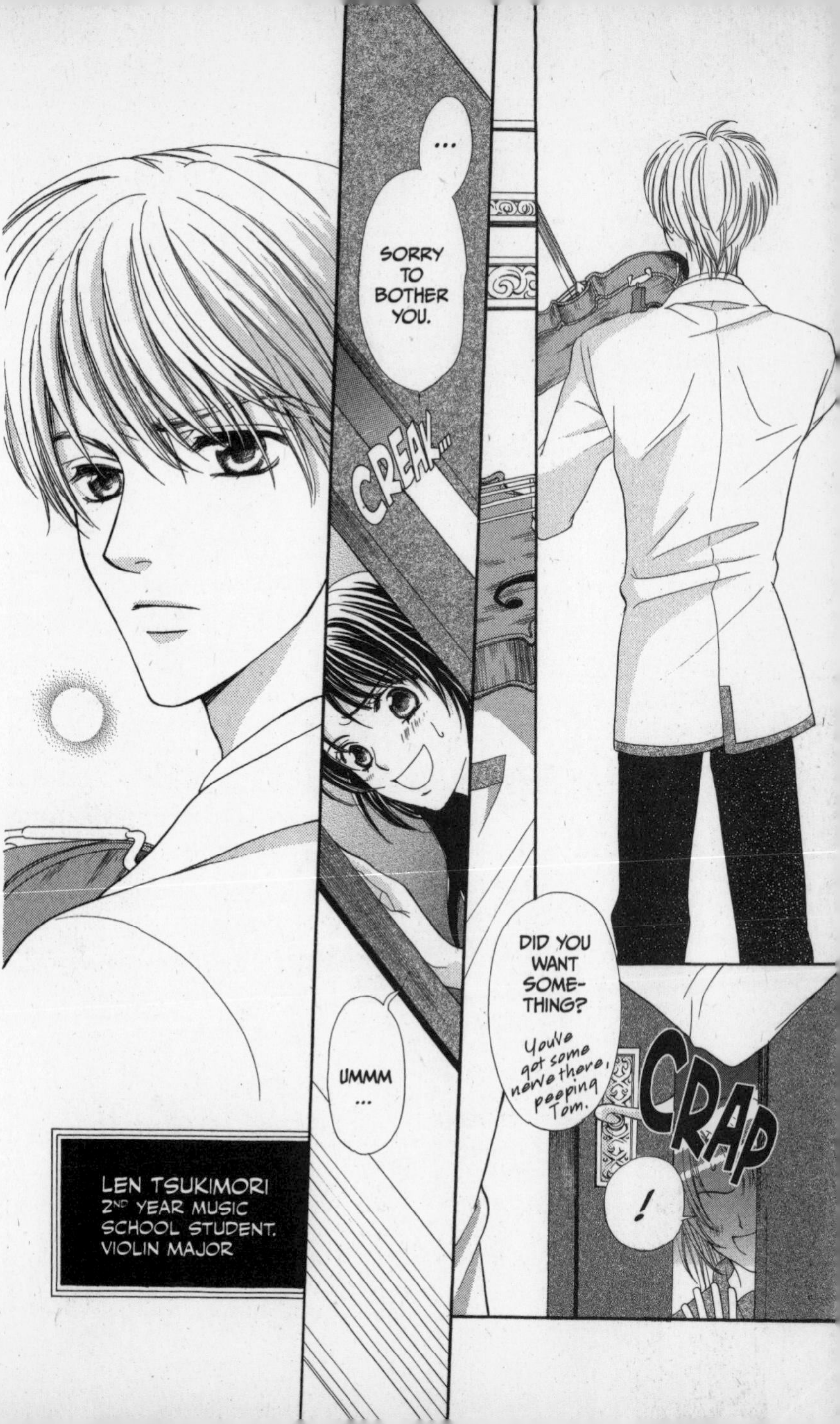
...
SORRY TO BOTHER YOU.
CREAK...
DID YOU WANT SOMETHING?
You've got some nerve there, peeping Tom.
UMMM...
CRAP
!
LEN TSUKIMORI
2ND YEAR MUSIC SCHOOL STUDENT.
VIOLIN MAJOR

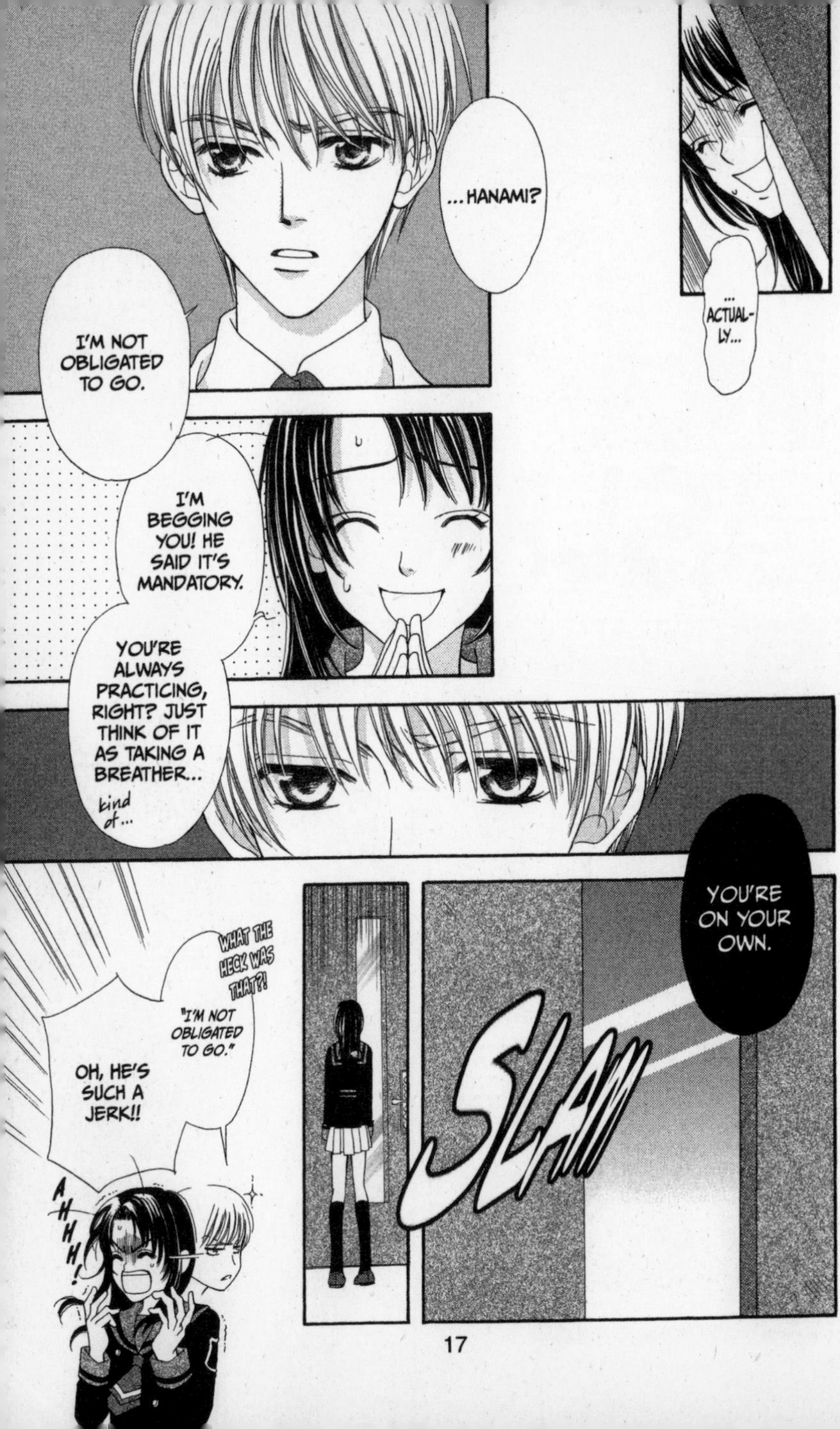

...ACTUAL-LY...
...HANAMI?
I'M NOT OBLIGATED TO GO.
I'M BEGGING YOU! HE SAID IT'S MANDATORY.
YOU'RE ALWAYS PRACTICING, RIGHT? JUST THINK OF IT AS TAKING A BREATHER...
kind of...
YOU'RE ON YOUR OWN.
SLAM
WHAT THE HECK WAS THAT?!
"I'M NOT OBLIGATED TO GO."
OH, HE'S SUCH A JERK!!
AHHH!

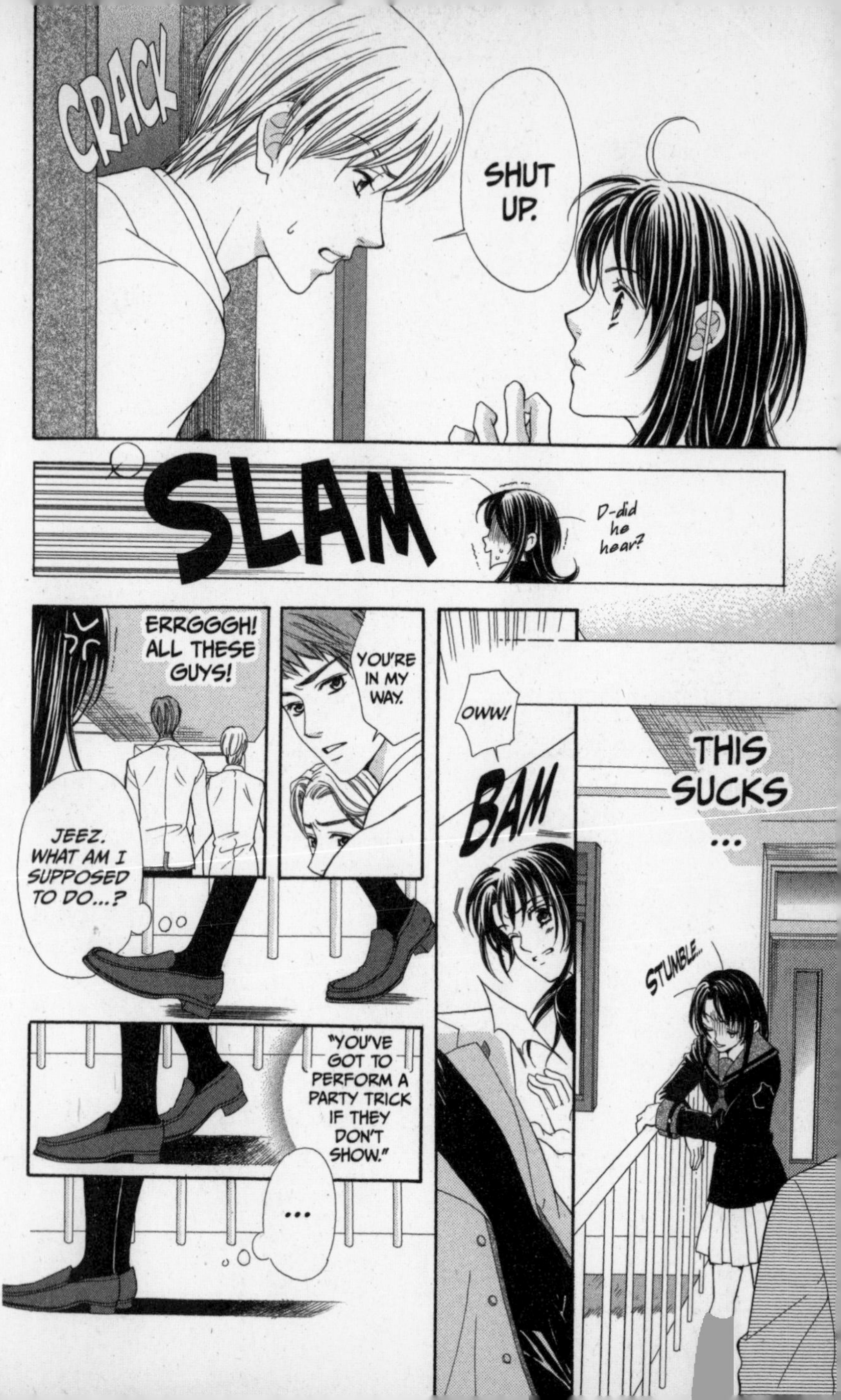
SHUT UP.
CRACK
D-did he hear?
SLAM
THIS SUCKS...
STUMBLE...
OWW!
BAM
YOU'RE IN MY WAY.
ERRGGGH! ALL THESE GUYS!
JEEZ. WHAT AM I SUPPOSED TO DO...?
"YOU'VE GOT TO PERFORM A PARTY TRICK IF THEY DON'T SHOW."
...

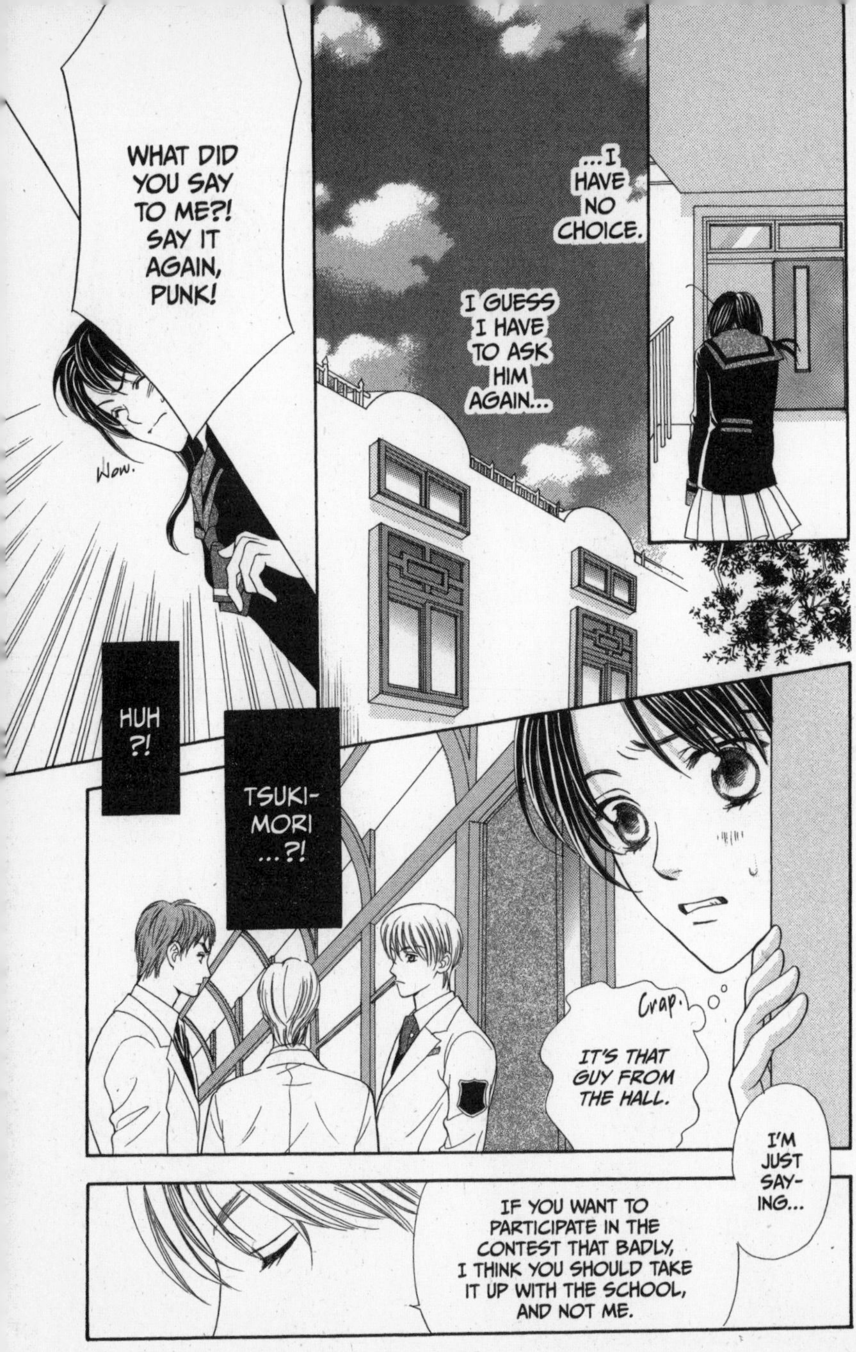

...I HAVE NO CHOICE.
I GUESS I HAVE TO ASK HIM AGAIN...
WHAT DID YOU SAY TO ME?! SAY IT AGAIN, PUNK!
Wow.
HUH?!
Crap.
IT'S THAT GUY FROM THE HALL.
TSUKI-MORI...?!
I'M JUST SAYING...
IF YOU WANT TO PARTICIPATE IN THE CONTEST THAT BADLY, I THINK YOU SHOULD TAKE IT UP WITH THE SCHOOL, AND NOT ME.

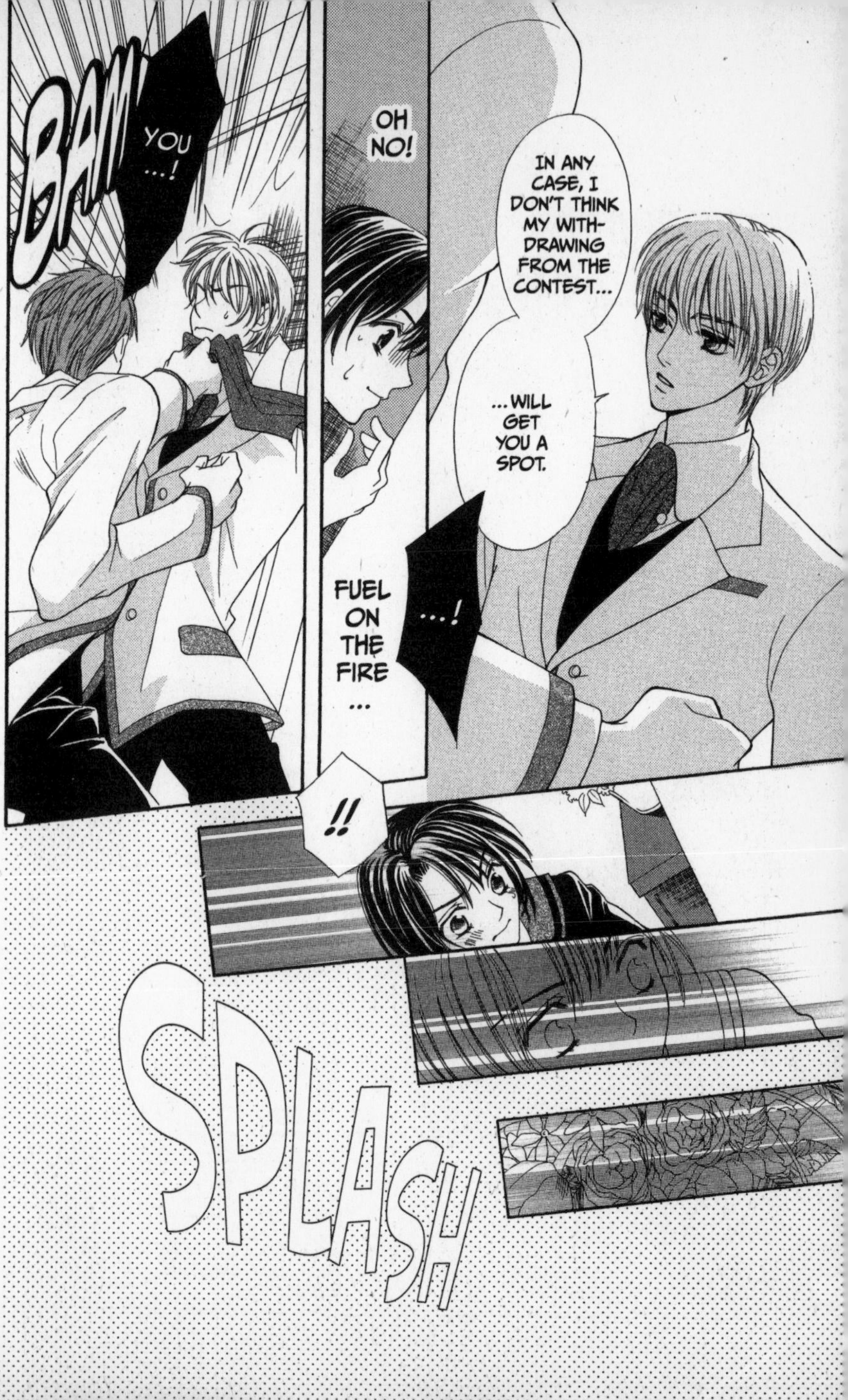
IN ANY CASE, I DON'T THINK MY WITH-DRAWING FROM THE CONTEST...
...WILL GET YOU A SPOT.
...!
OH NO!
FUEL ON THE FIRE ...
BAM
YOU ...!
!!
SPLASH

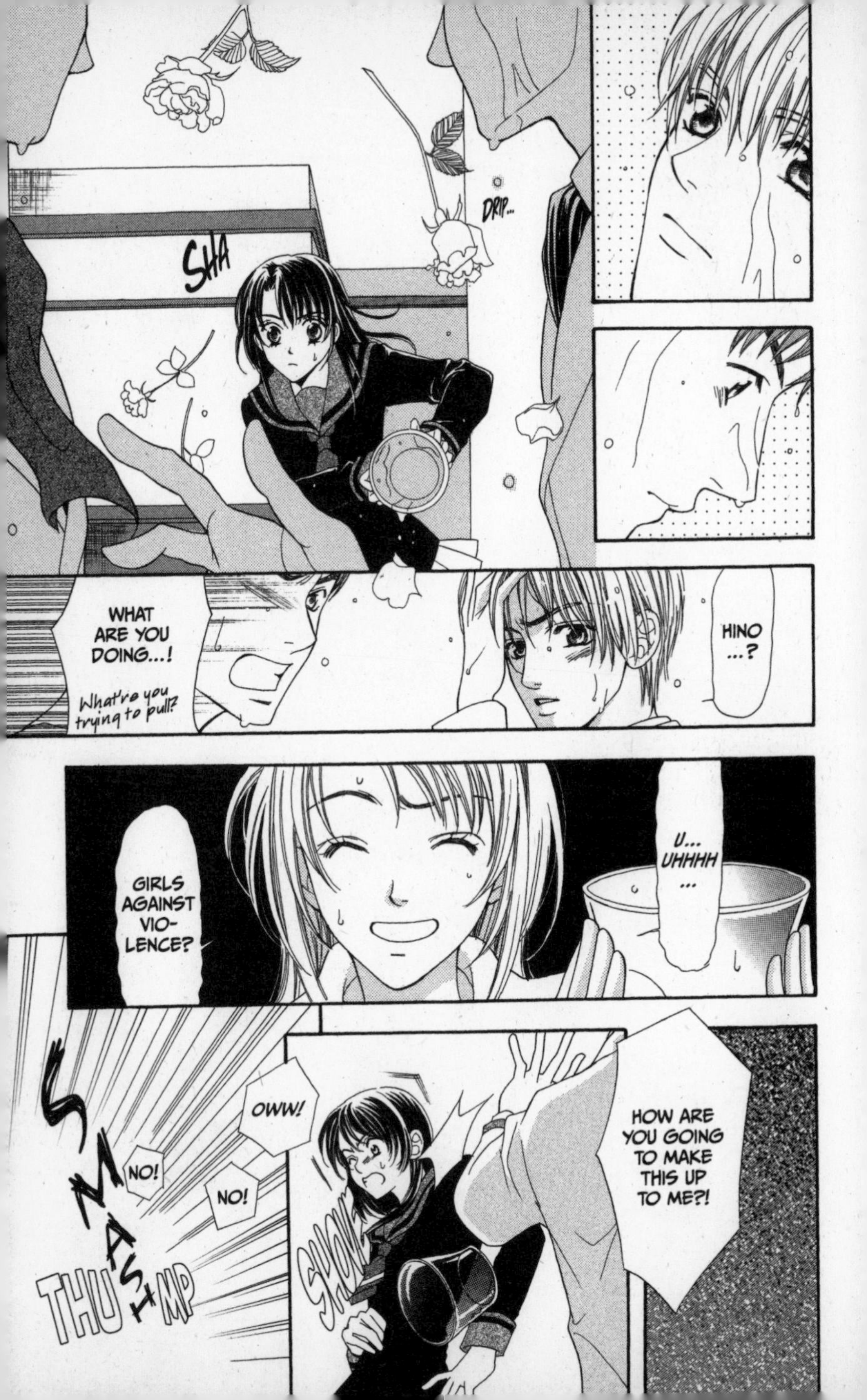
DRIP...
SHA
HINO ...?
WHAT ARE YOU DOING...!
What're you trying to pull!?
U... UHHHH ...
GIRLS AGAINST VIO-LENCE?
HOW ARE YOU GOING TO MAKE THIS UP TO ME?!
OWW!
NO!
NO!
SMASH
THUMP

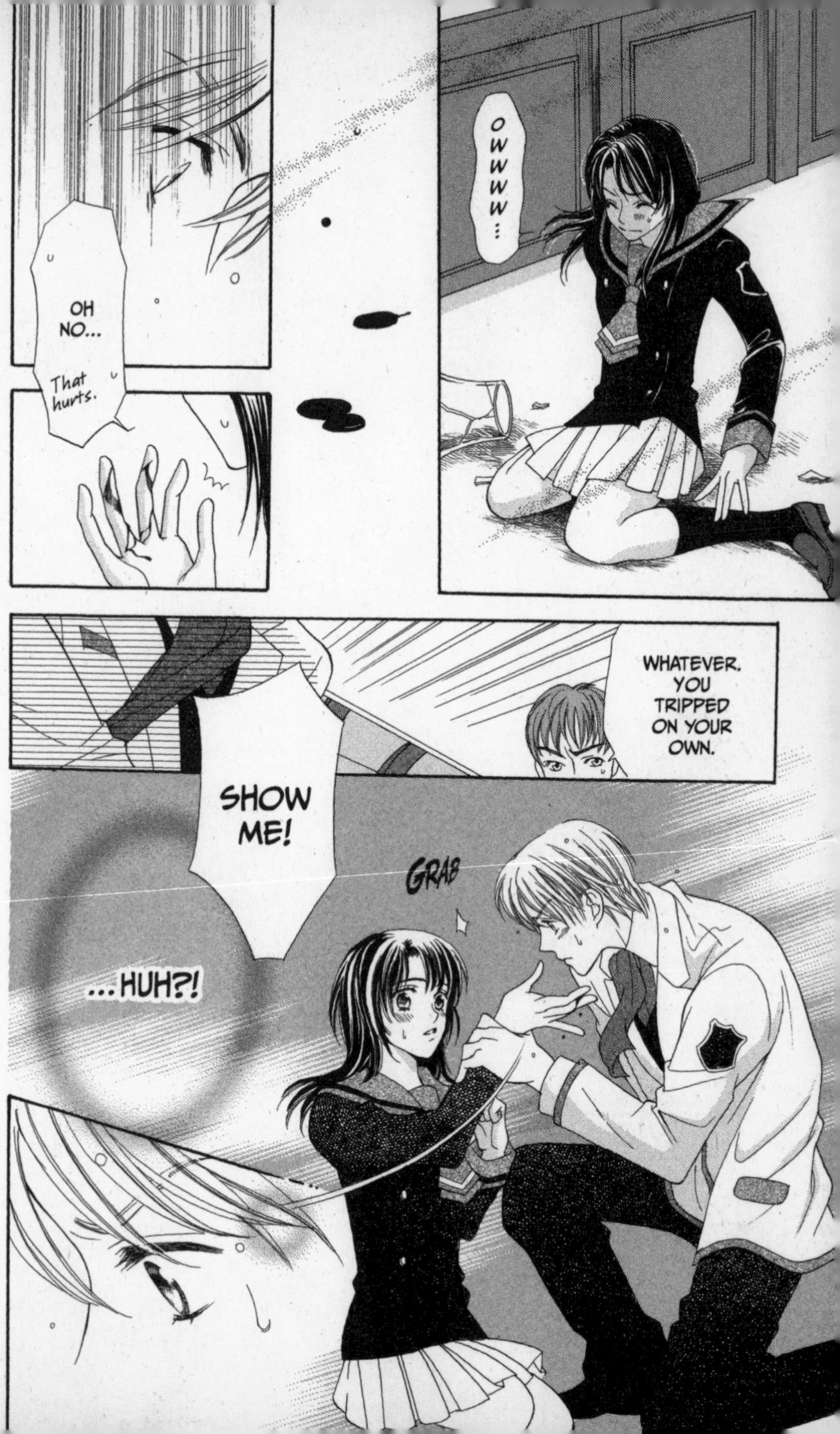
OWWWW...
OH NO...
That hurts.
WHATEVER. YOU TRIPPED ON YOUR OWN.
SHOW ME!
GRAB
...HUH?!

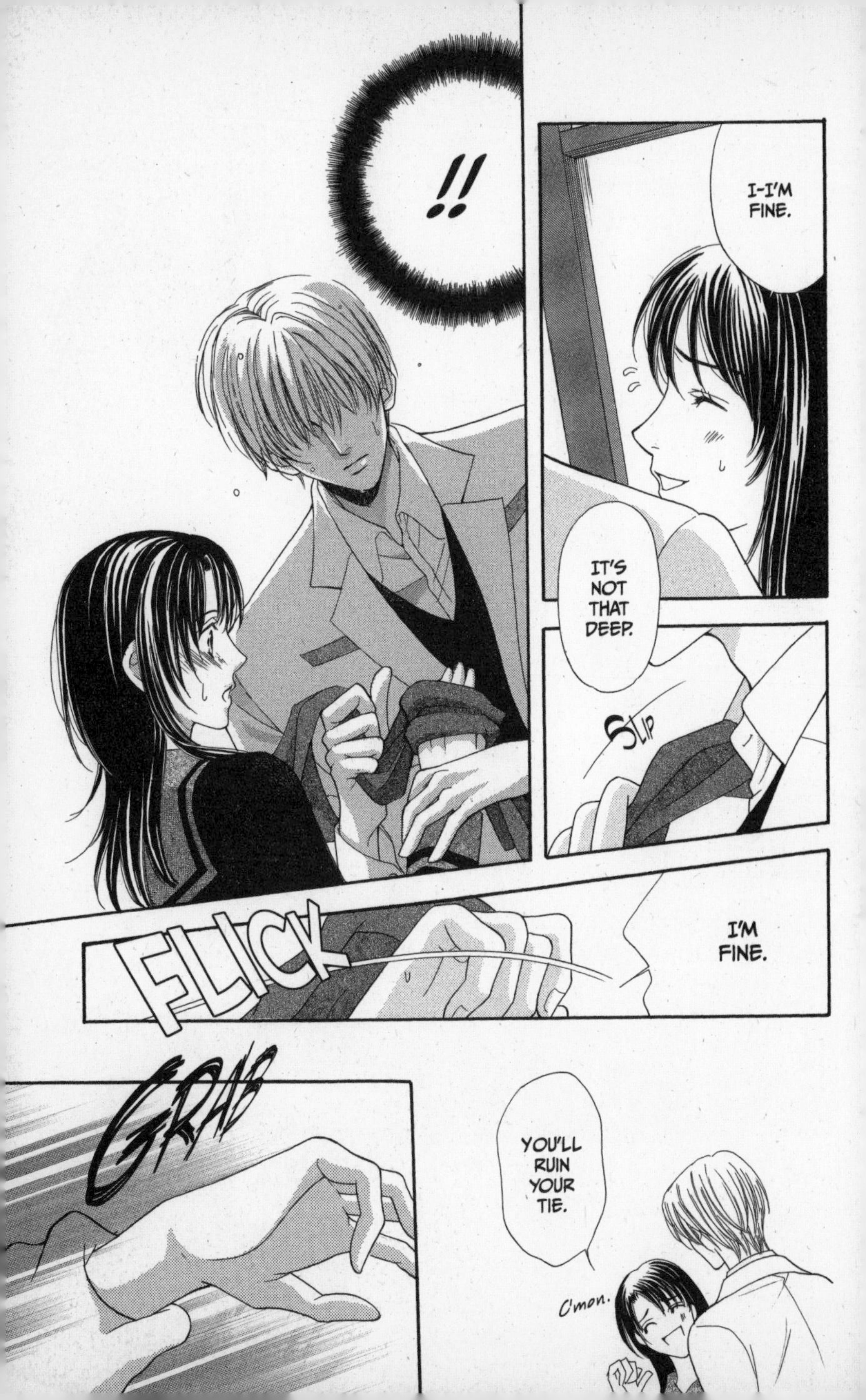
I-I'M FINE.
IT'S NOT THAT DEEP.
SLIP
!!
I'M FINE.
FLICK
YOU'LL RUIN YOUR TIE.
C'mon.
GRAB

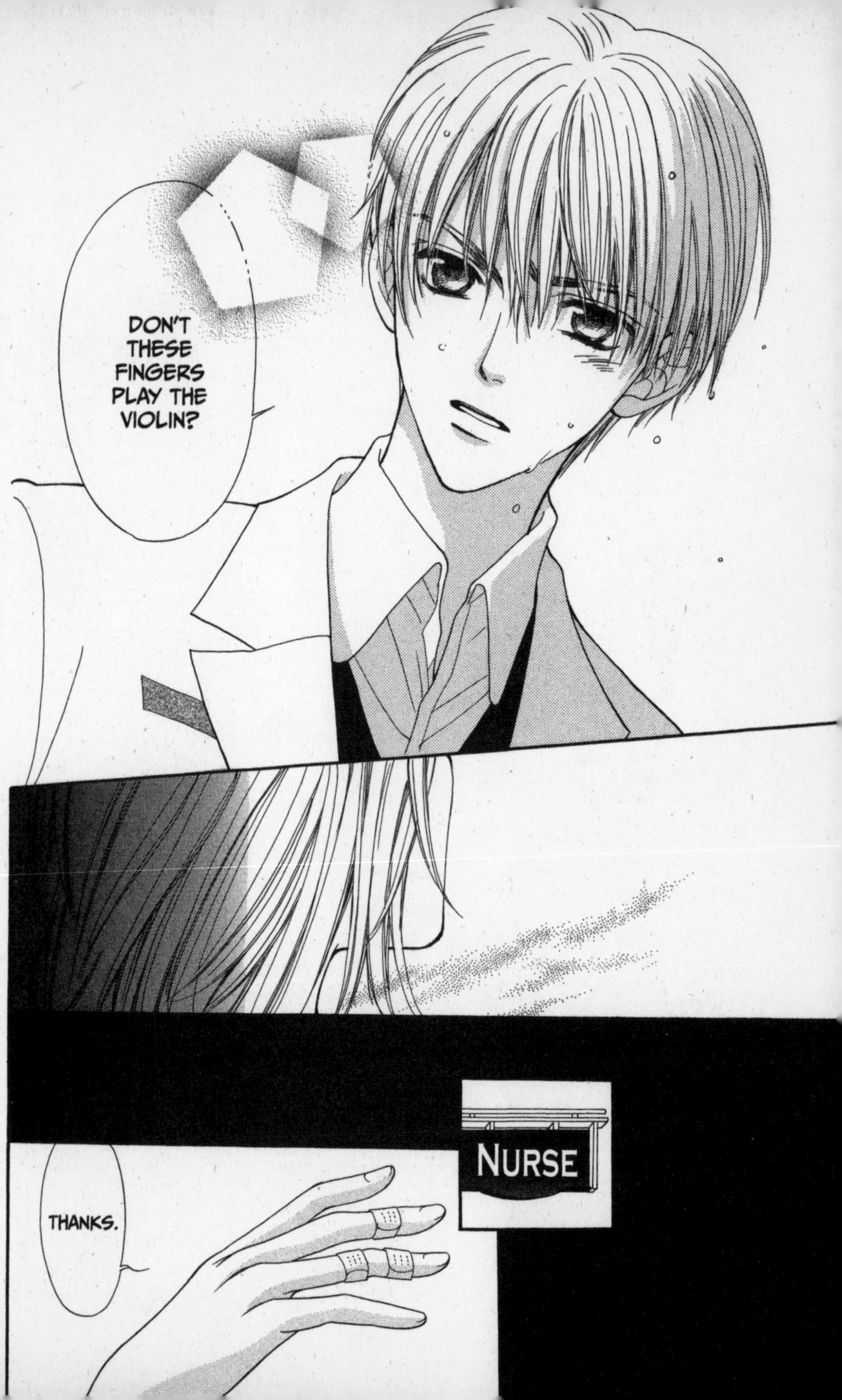
DON'T THESE FINGERS PLAY THE VIOLIN?
NURSE
THANKS.

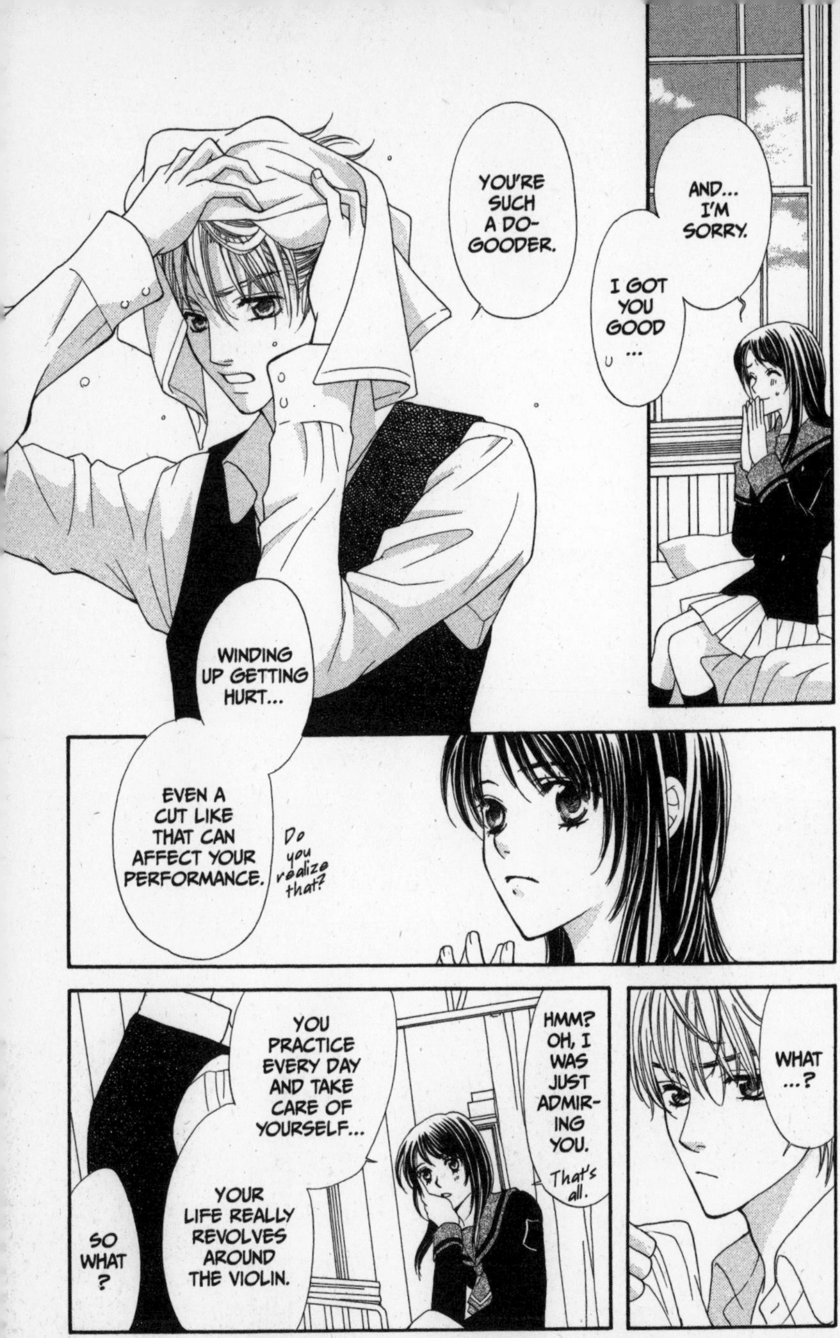
AND... I'M SORRY.
I GOT YOU GOOD ...
YOU'RE SUCH A DO-GOODER.
WINDING UP GETTING HURT...
EVEN A CUT LIKE THAT CAN AFFECT YOUR PERFORMANCE.
Do you realize that?
WHAT ...?
HMM? OH, I WAS JUST ADMIR-ING YOU.
That's all.
YOU PRACTICE EVERY DAY AND TAKE CARE OF YOURSELF...
YOUR LIFE REALLY REVOLVES AROUND THE VIOLIN.
SO WHAT ?

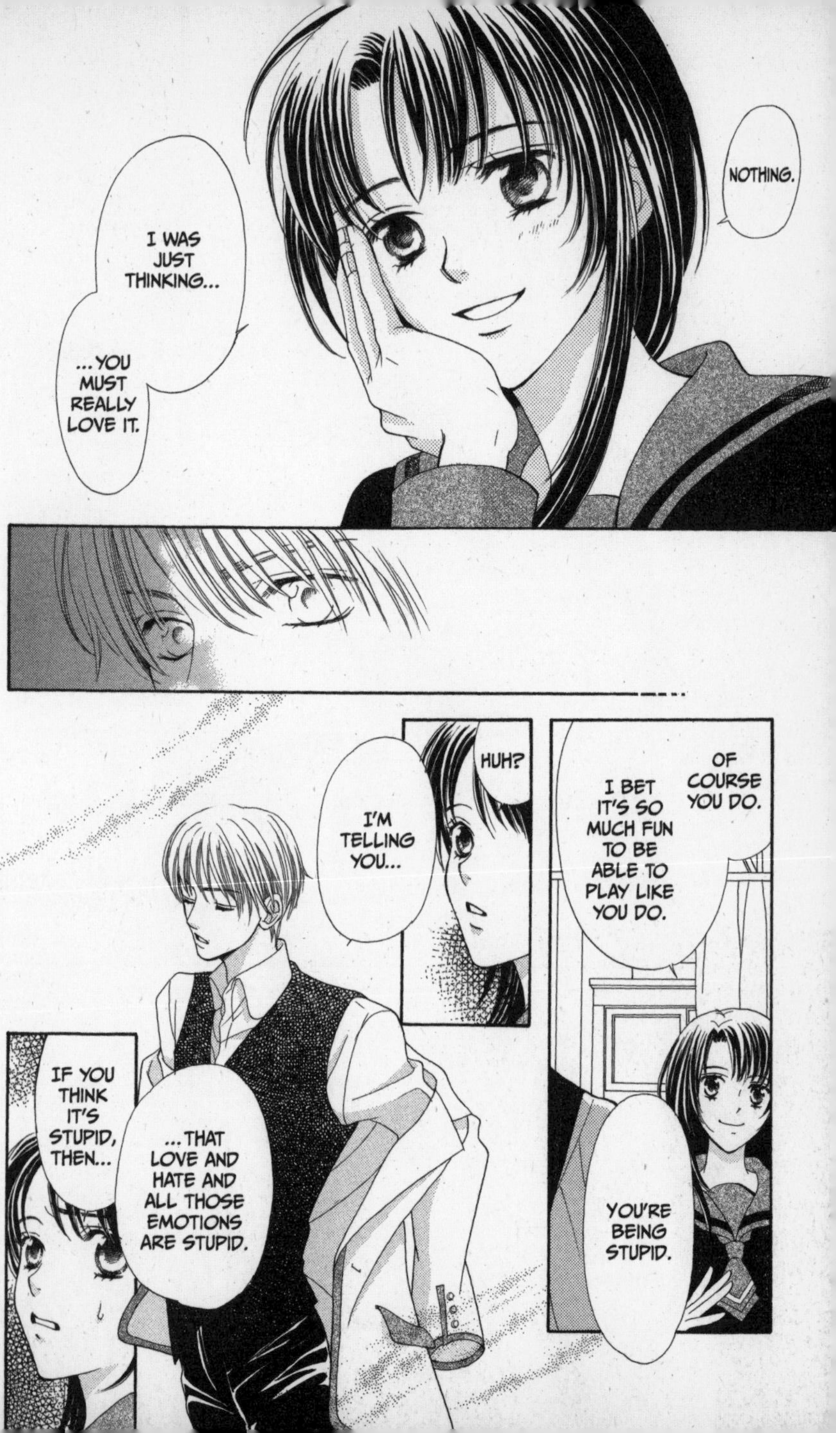
NOTHING.
I WAS JUST THINKING...
...YOU MUST REALLY LOVE IT.
OF COURSE YOU DO.
I BET IT'S SO MUCH FUN TO BE ABLE TO PLAY LIKE YOU DO.
YOU'RE BEING STUPID.
HUH?
I'M TELLING YOU...
...THAT LOVE AND HATE AND ALL THOSE EMOTIONS ARE STUPID.
IF YOU THINK IT'S STUPID, THEN...

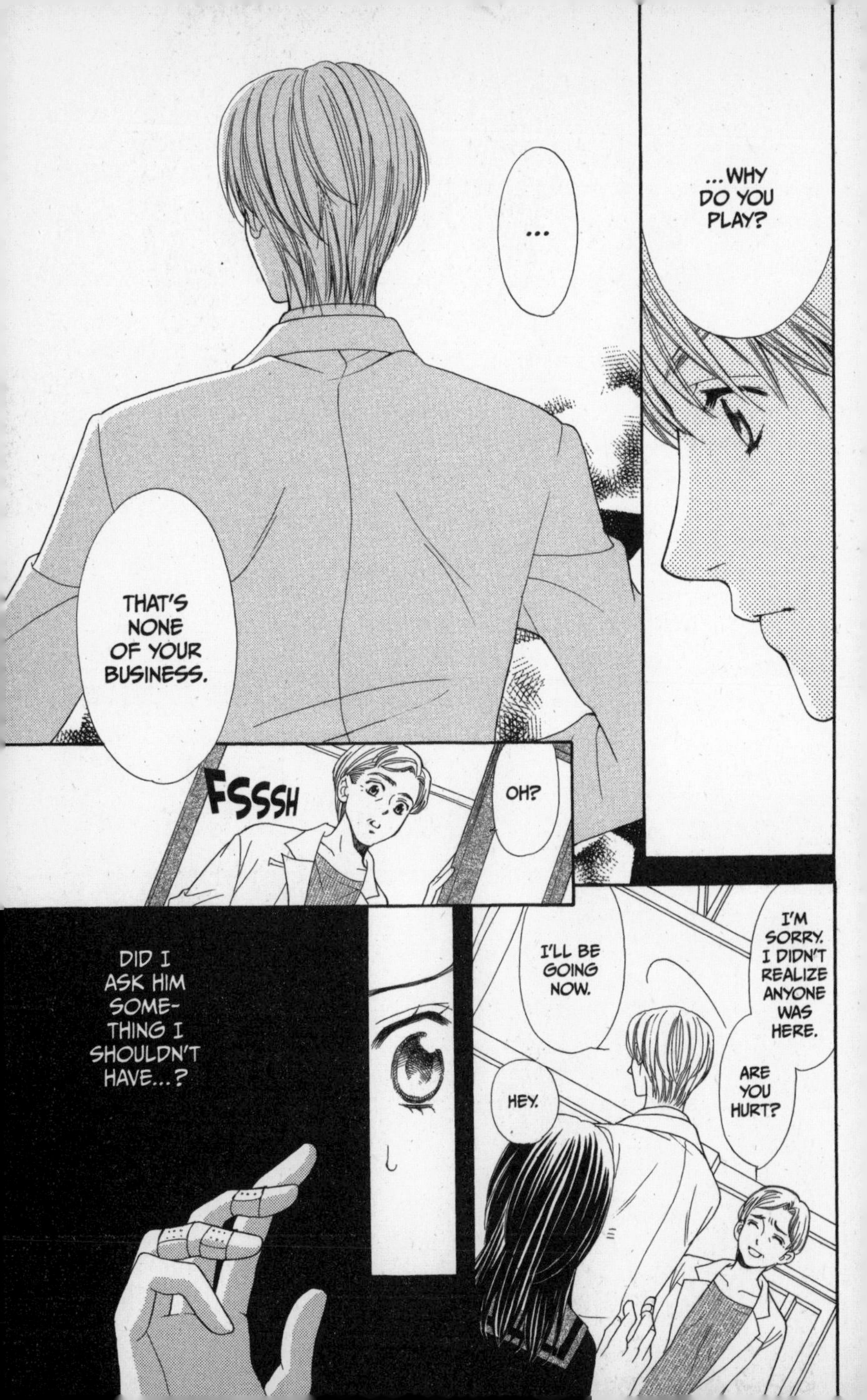
...WHY DO YOU PLAY?
...
THAT'S NONE OF YOUR BUSINESS.
FSSSH
OH?
I'M SORRY. I DIDN'T REALIZE ANYONE WAS HERE.
I'LL BE GOING NOW.
ARE YOU HURT?
HEY.
DID I ASK HIM SOME-THING I SHOULDN'T HAVE...?

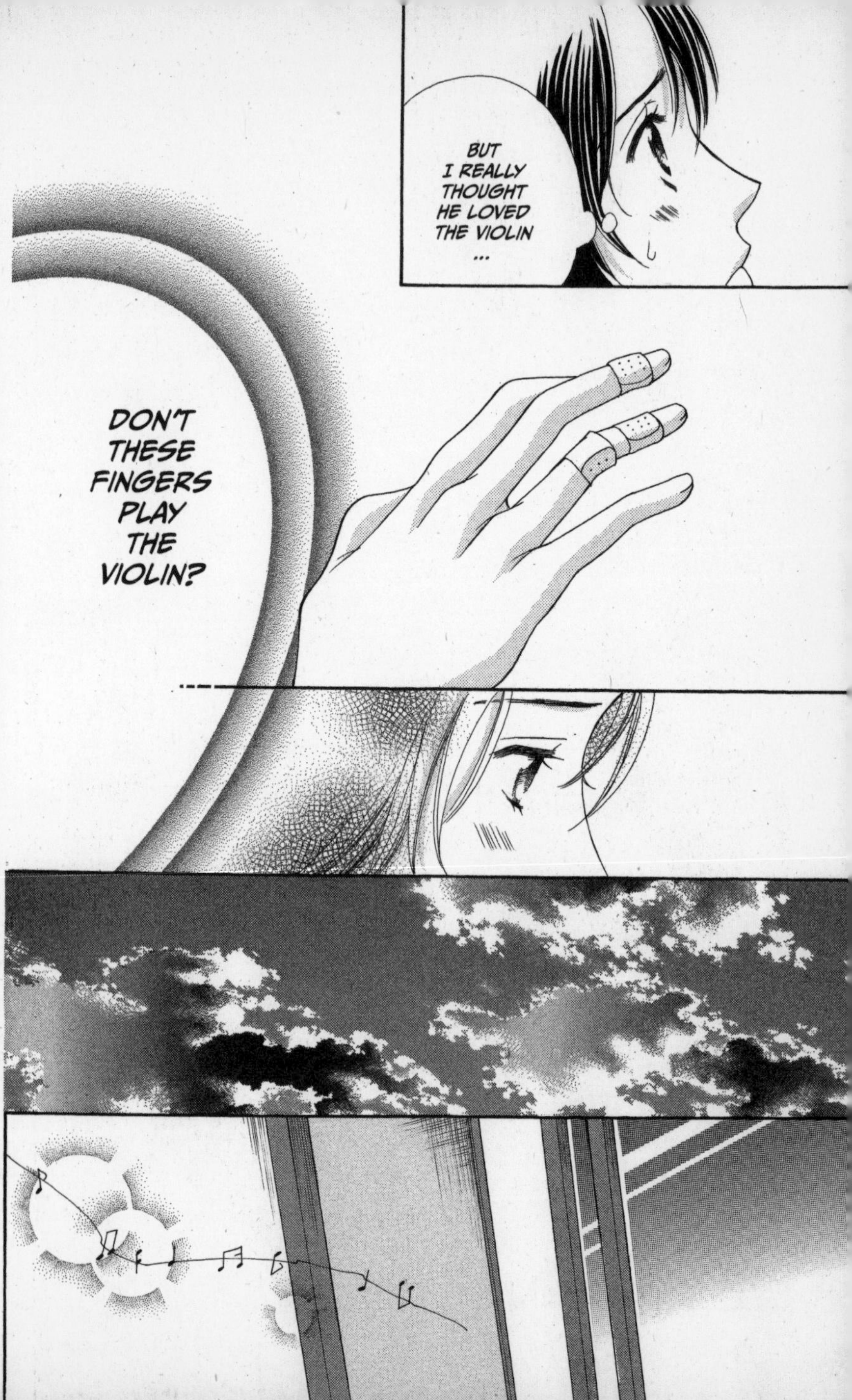
BUT I REALLY THOUGHT HE LOVED THE VIOLIN ...
DON'T THESE FINGERS PLAY THE VIOLIN?

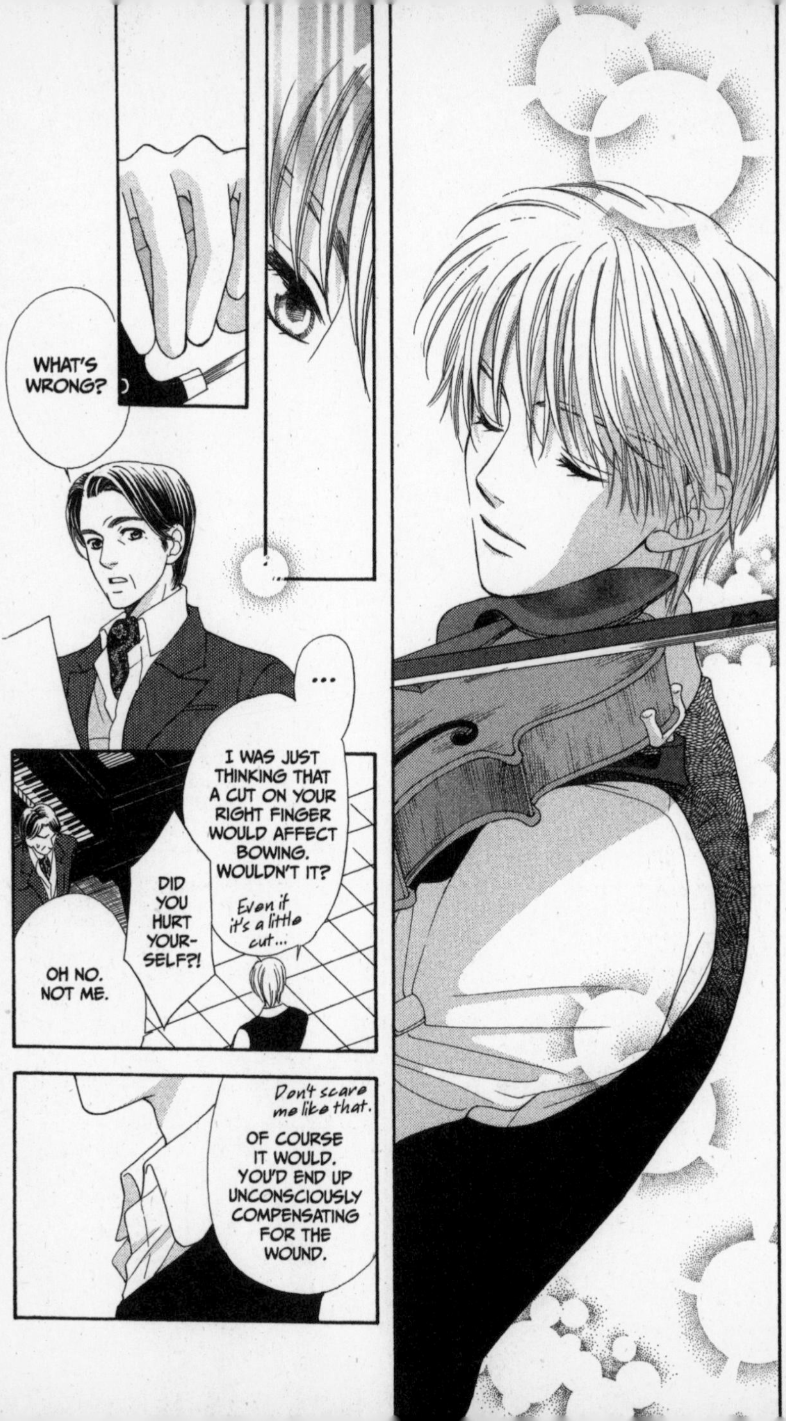
..
WHAT'S WRONG?
...
I WAS JUST THINKING THAT A CUT ON YOUR RIGHT FINGER WOULD AFFECT BOWING. WOULDN'T IT?
Even if it's a little cut...
DID YOU HURT YOURSELF?!
OH NO. NOT ME.
Don't scare me like that.
OF COURSE IT WOULD. YOU'D END UP UNCONSCIOUSLY COMPENSATING FOR THE WOUND.

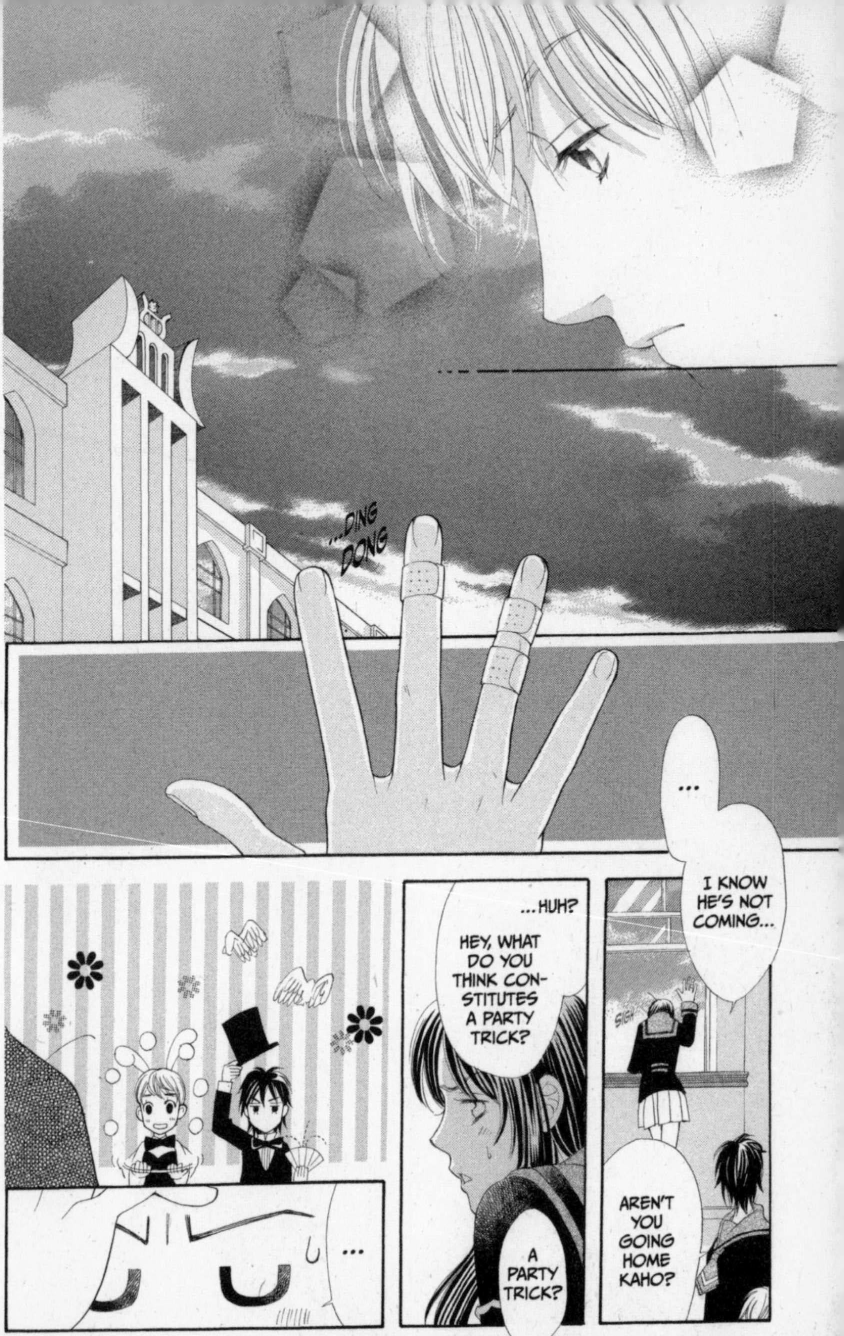
...DING DONG
...
I KNOW HE'S NOT COMING...
SIGH
AREN'T YOU GOING HOME KAHO?
...HUH?
HEY, WHAT DO YOU THINK CON-STITUTES A PARTY TRICK?
A PARTY TRICK?
...

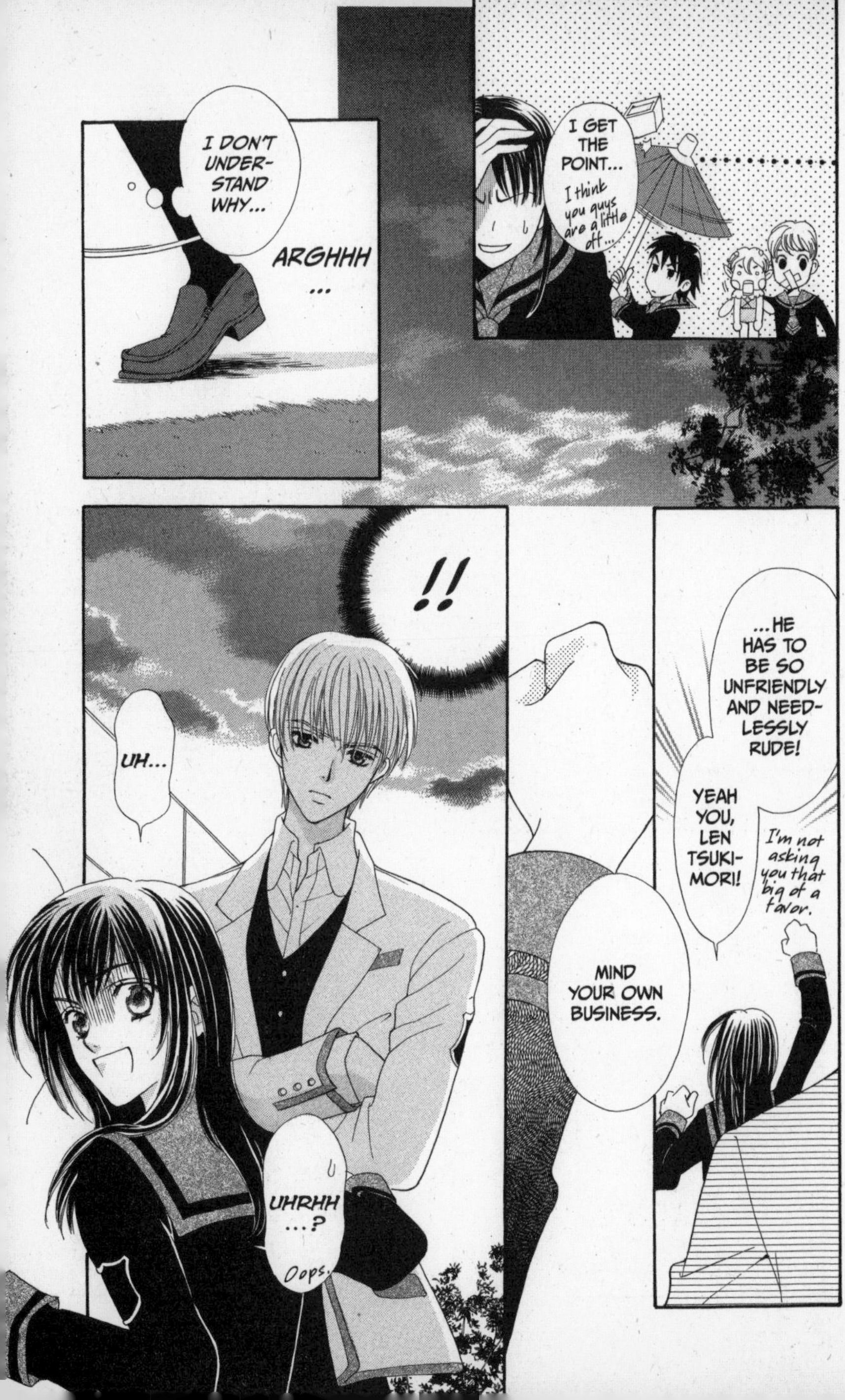
I GET THE POINT...
I think you guys are a little off...
I DON'T UNDER-STAND WHY...
ARGHHH ...
...HE HAS TO BE SO UNFRIENDLY AND NEED-LESSLY RUDE!
YEAH YOU, LEN TSUKI-MORI!
I'm not asking you that big of a favor.
MIND YOUR OWN BUSINESS.
!!
UH...
UHRHH ...?
Oops.

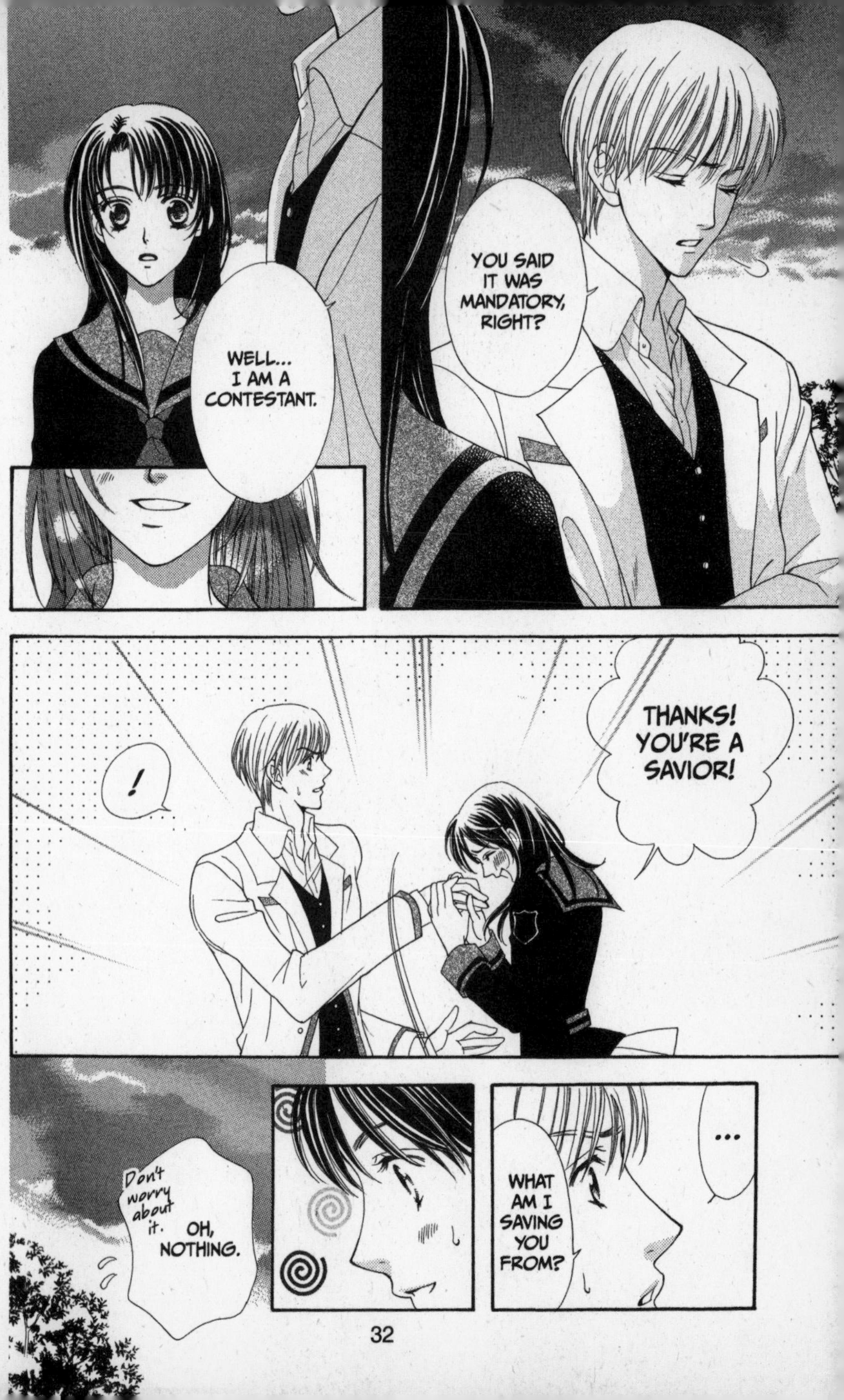
YOU SAID IT WAS MANDATORY, RIGHT?
WELL... I AM A CONTESTANT.
THANKS! YOU'RE A SAVIOR!
!
...
WHAT AM I SAVING YOU FROM?
OH, NOTHING.
Don't worry about it.

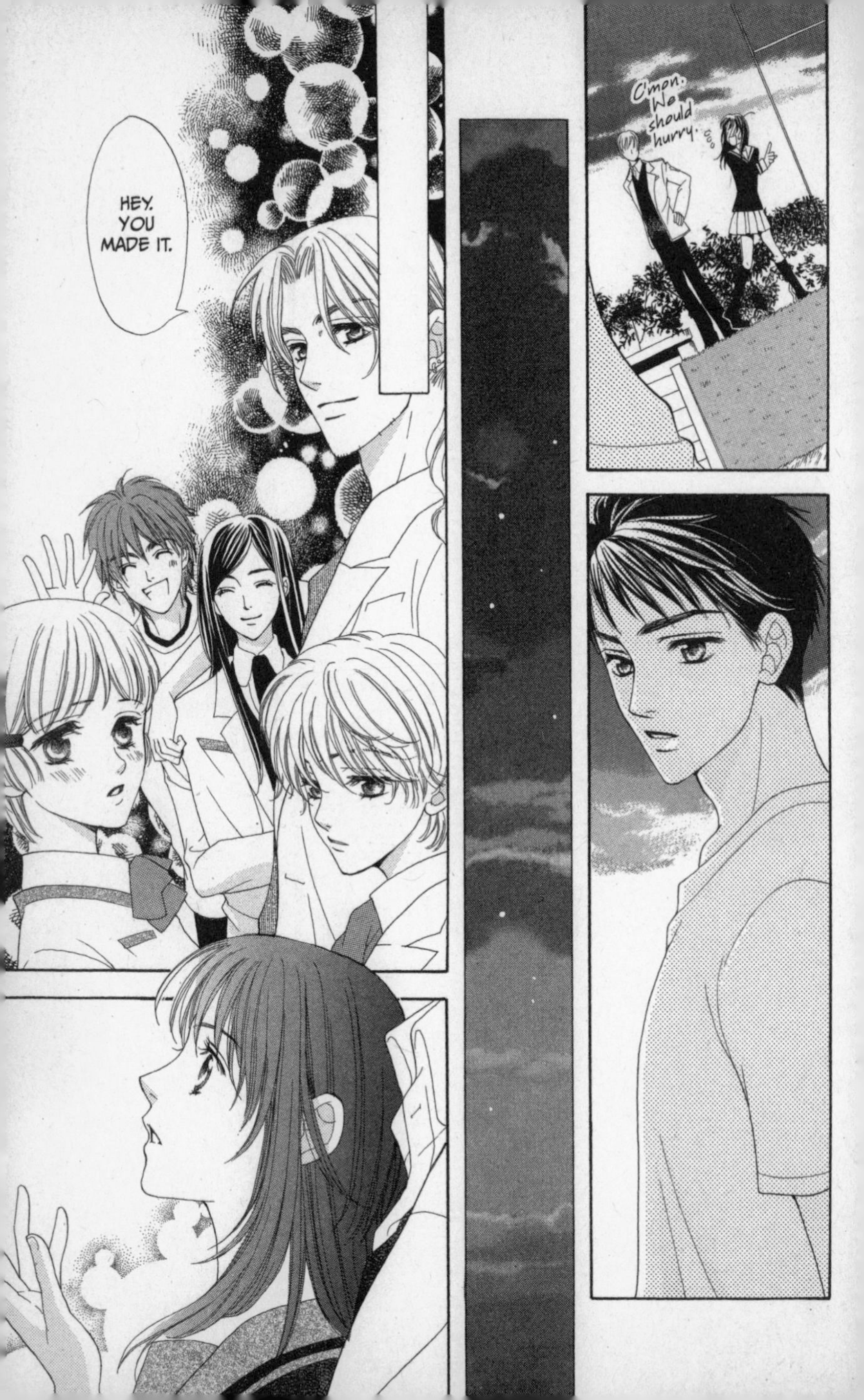
C'mon. We should hurry.
HEY. YOU MADE IT.

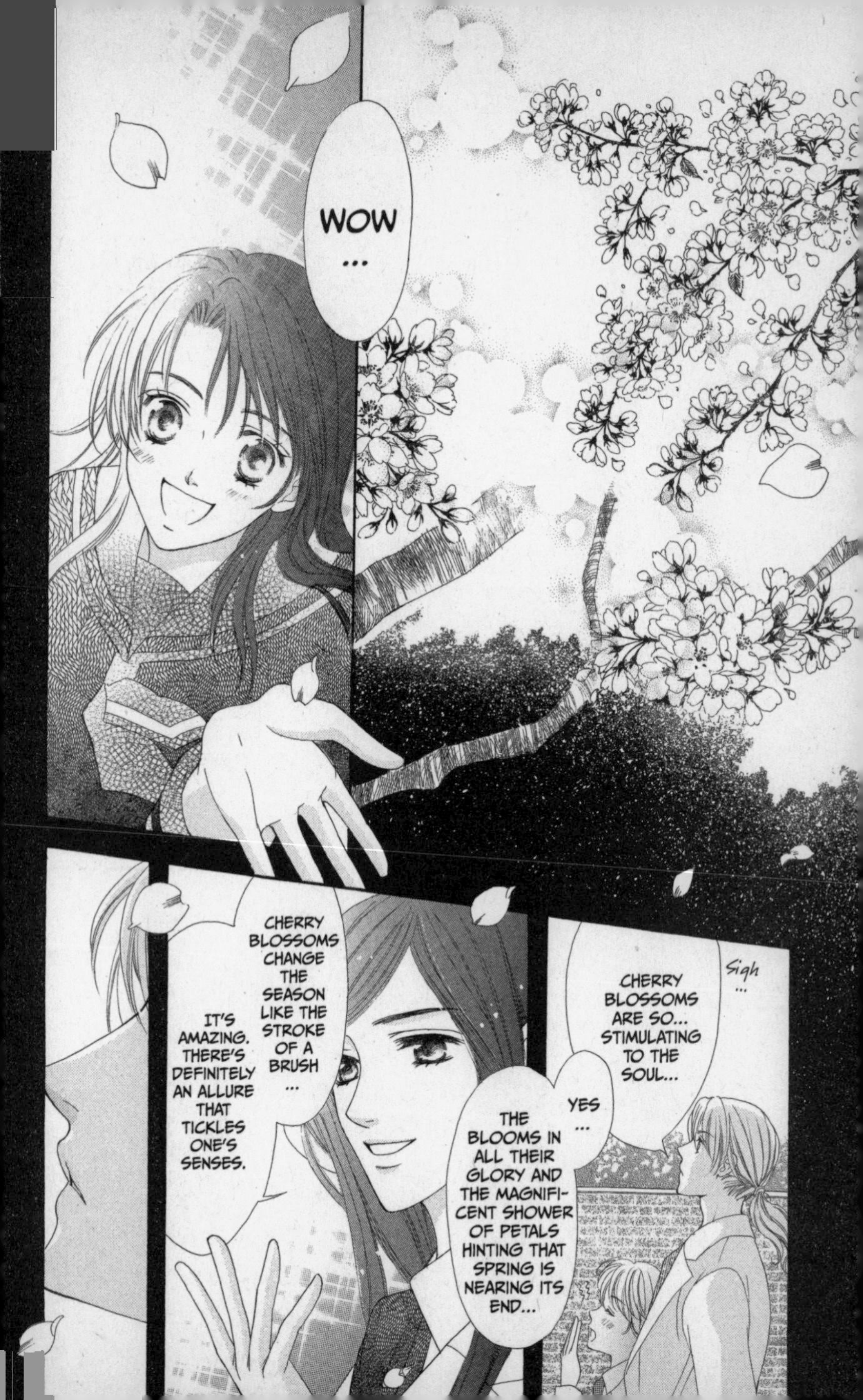
WOW ...
Sigh ...
CHERRY BLOSSOMS ARE SO... STIMULATING TO THE SOUL...
YES ...
THE BLOOMS IN ALL THEIR GLORY AND THE MAGNIFICENT SHOWER OF PETALS HINTING THAT SPRING IS NEARING ITS END...
CHERRY BLOSSOMS CHANGE THE SEASON LIKE THE STROKE OF A BRUSH ...
IT'S AMAZING. THERE'S DEFINITELY AN ALLURE THAT TICKLES ONE'S SENSES.

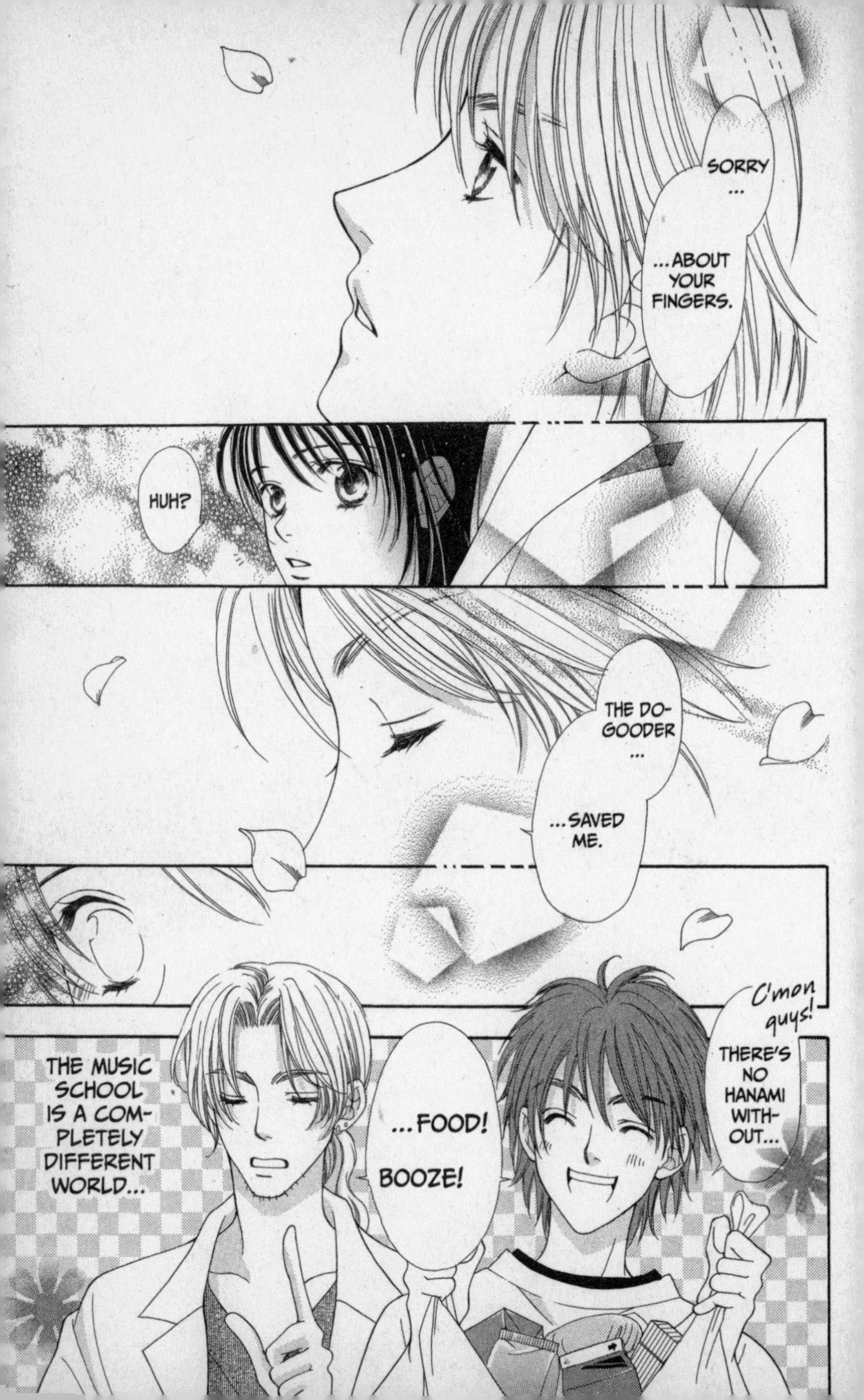
SORRY ...
...ABOUT YOUR FINGERS.
HUH?
THE DO-GOODER ...
...SAVED ME.
C'mon guys!
THERE'S NO HANAMI WITH-OUT...
...FOOD!
BOOZE!
THE MUSIC SCHOOL IS A COM-PLETELY DIFFERENT WORLD...

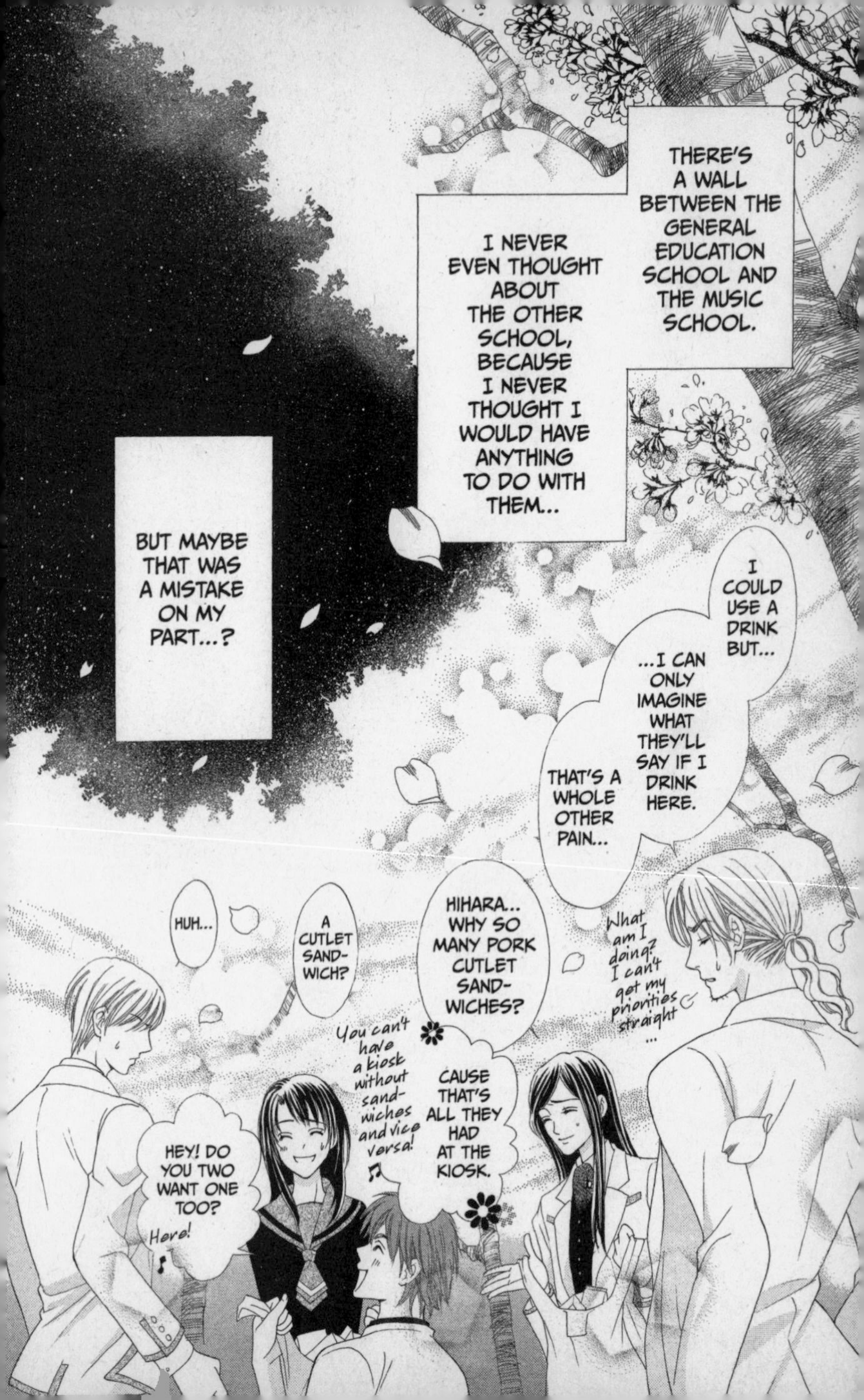
THERE'S A WALL BETWEEN THE GENERAL EDUCATION SCHOOL AND THE MUSIC SCHOOL.
I NEVER EVEN THOUGHT ABOUT THE OTHER SCHOOL, BECAUSE I NEVER THOUGHT I WOULD HAVE ANYTHING TO DO WITH THEM...
BUT MAYBE THAT WAS A MISTAKE ON MY PART...?
I COULD USE A DRINK BUT...
...I CAN ONLY IMAGINE WHAT THEY'LL SAY IF I DRINK HERE.
THAT'S A WHOLE OTHER PAIN...
What am I doing? I can't get my priorities straight...
HIHARA... WHY SO MANY PORK CUTLET SAND-WICHES?
CAUSE THAT'S ALL THEY HAD AT THE KIOSK.
You can't have a kiosk without sand-wiches and vice versa!
A CUTLET SAND-WICH?
HUH...
HEY! DO YOU TWO WANT ONE TOO?
Here!

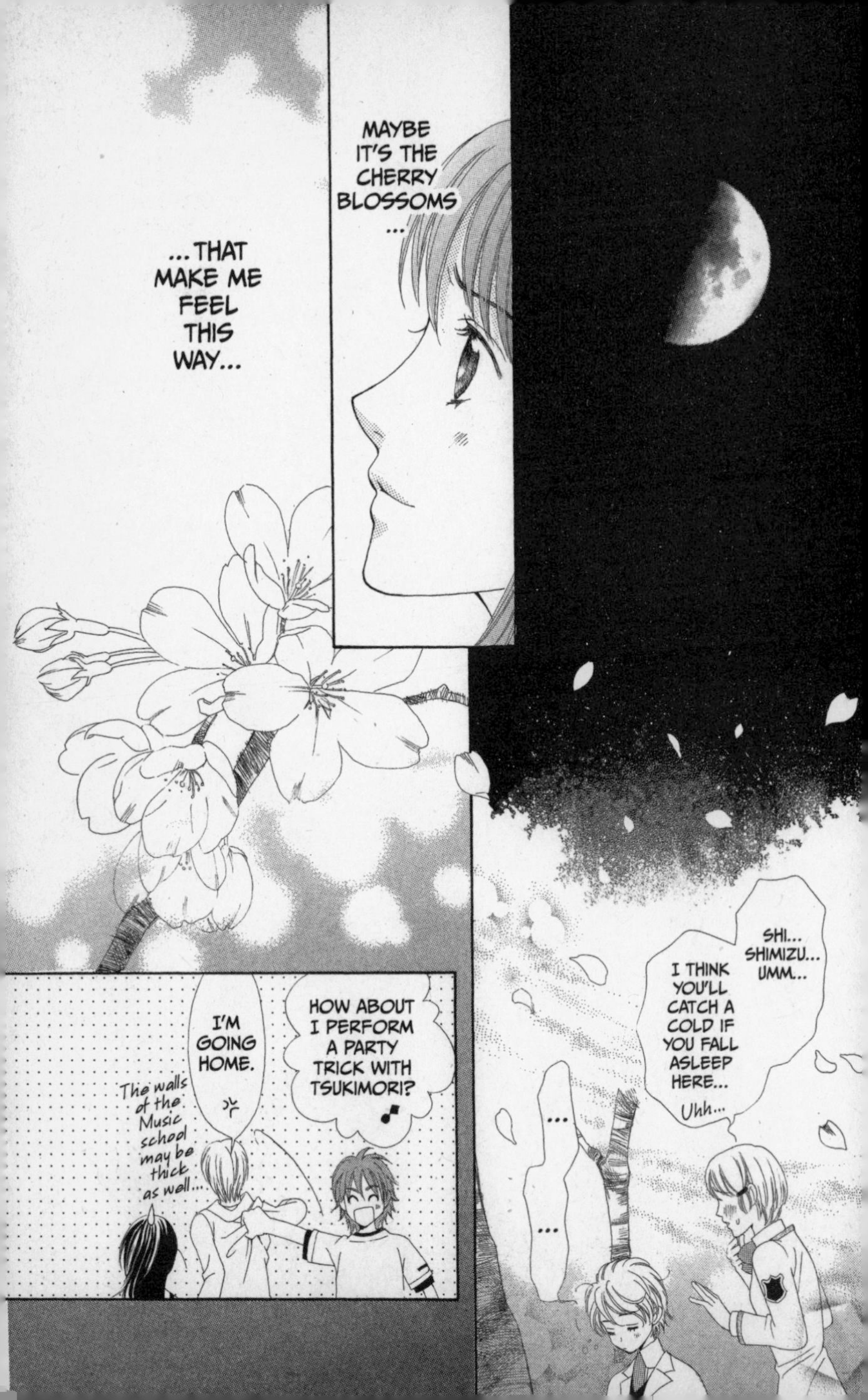
MAYBE IT'S THE CHERRY BLOSSOMS ...
... THAT MAKE ME FEEL THIS WAY...
SHI... SHIMIZU... UMM...
I THINK YOU'LL CATCH A COLD IF YOU FALL ASLEEP HERE...
Uhh...
...
...
HOW ABOUT I PERFORM A PARTY TRICK WITH TSUKIMORI?
I'M GOING HOME.
The walls of the Music school may be thick as well...

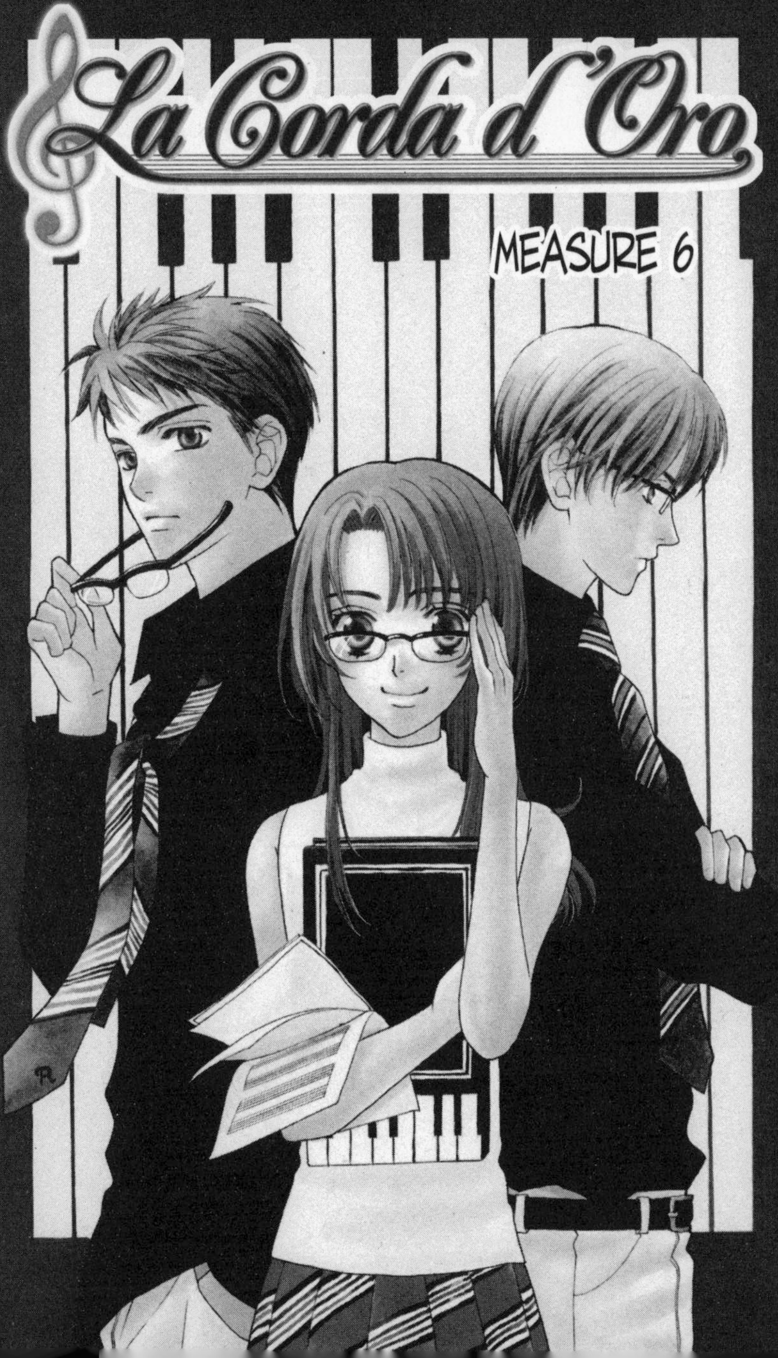
La Corda d'Oro
MEASURE 6

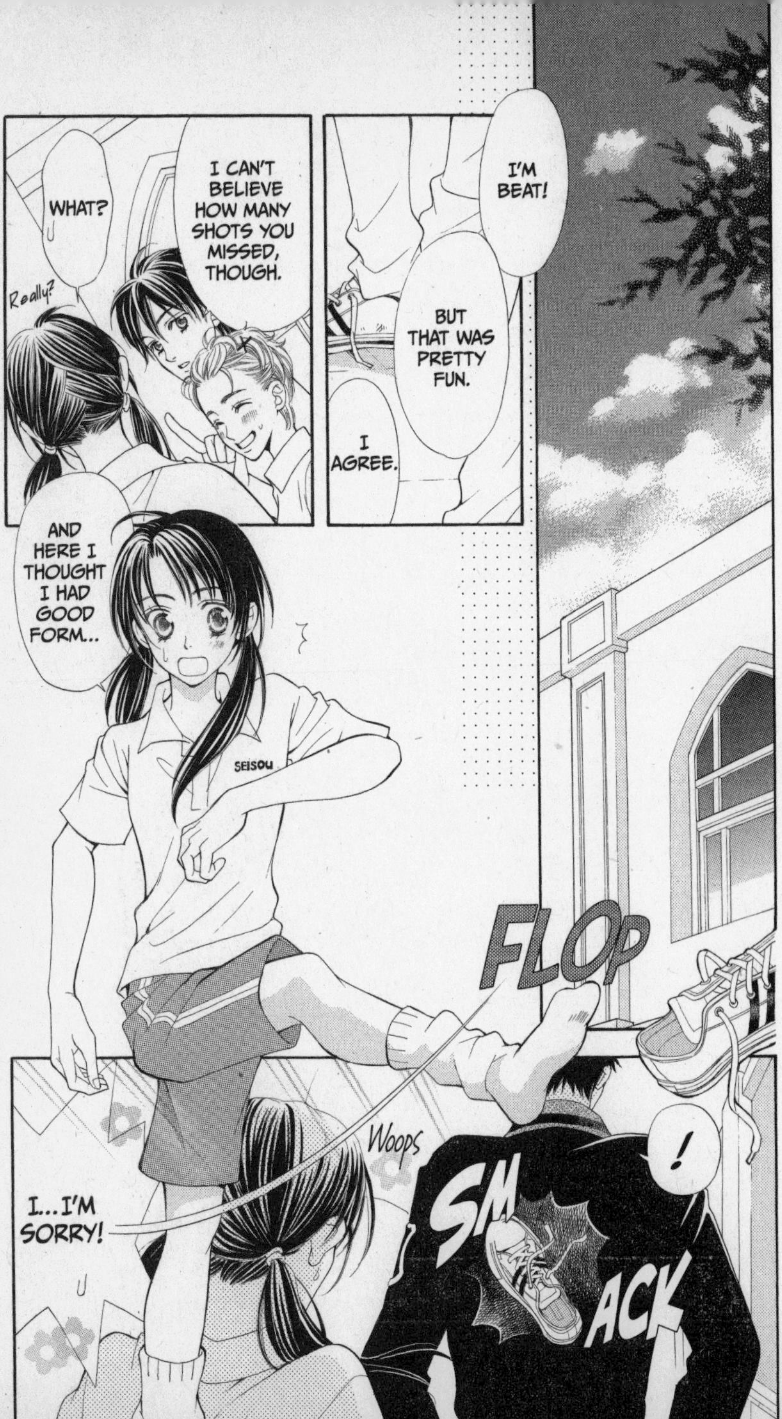
I'M BEAT!
BUT THAT WAS PRETTY FUN.
I AGREE.
I CAN'T BELIEVE HOW MANY SHOTS YOU MISSED, THOUGH.
WHAT?
Really?
AND HERE I THOUGHT I HAD GOOD FORM...
SEISOU
FLOP
!
SMACK
Woops
I...I'M SORRY!

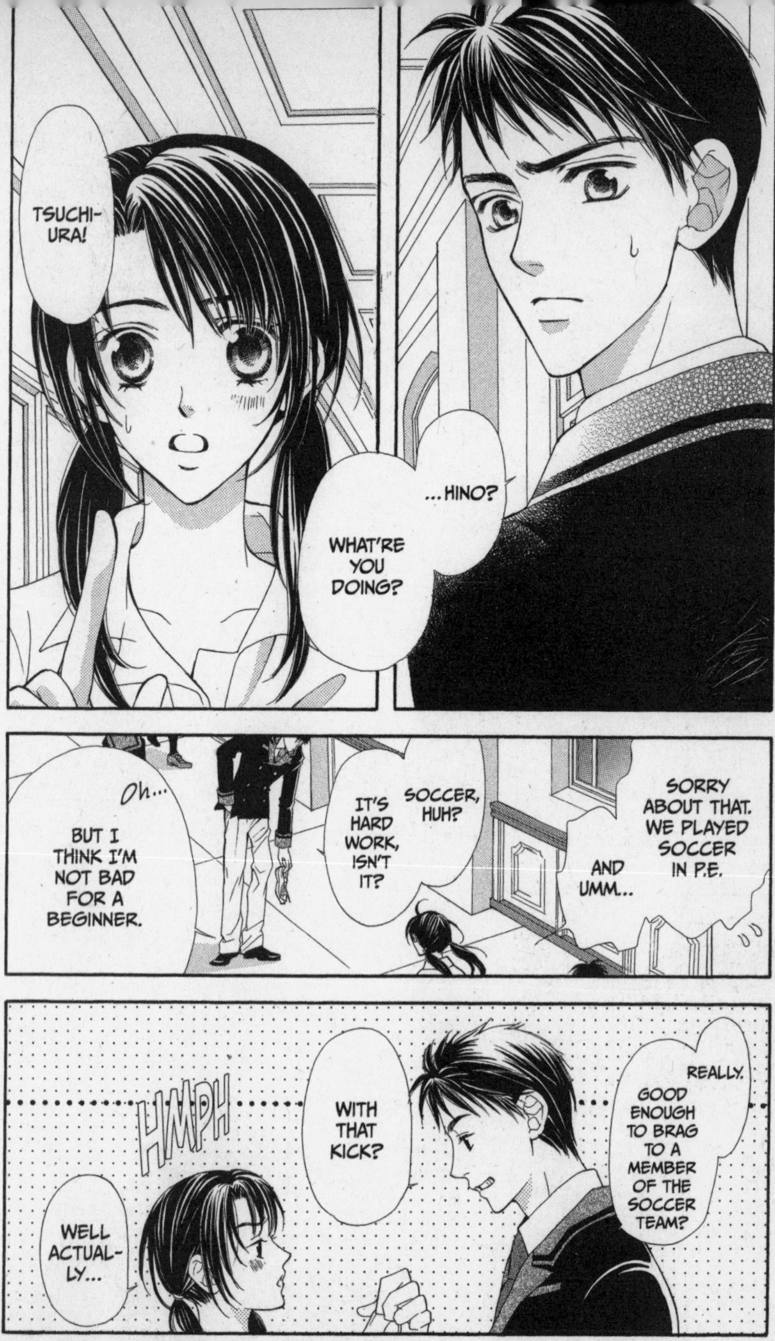
...HINO?
WHAT'RE YOU DOING?
TSUCHIURA!
SORRY ABOUT THAT. WE PLAYED SOCCER IN P.E.
AND UMM...
SOCCER, HUH?
IT'S HARD WORK, ISN'T IT?
Oh...
BUT I THINK I'M NOT BAD FOR A BEGINNER.
REALLY.
GOOD ENOUGH TO BRAG TO A MEMBER OF THE SOCCER TEAM?
WITH THAT KICK?
HMPH
WELL ACTUALLY...

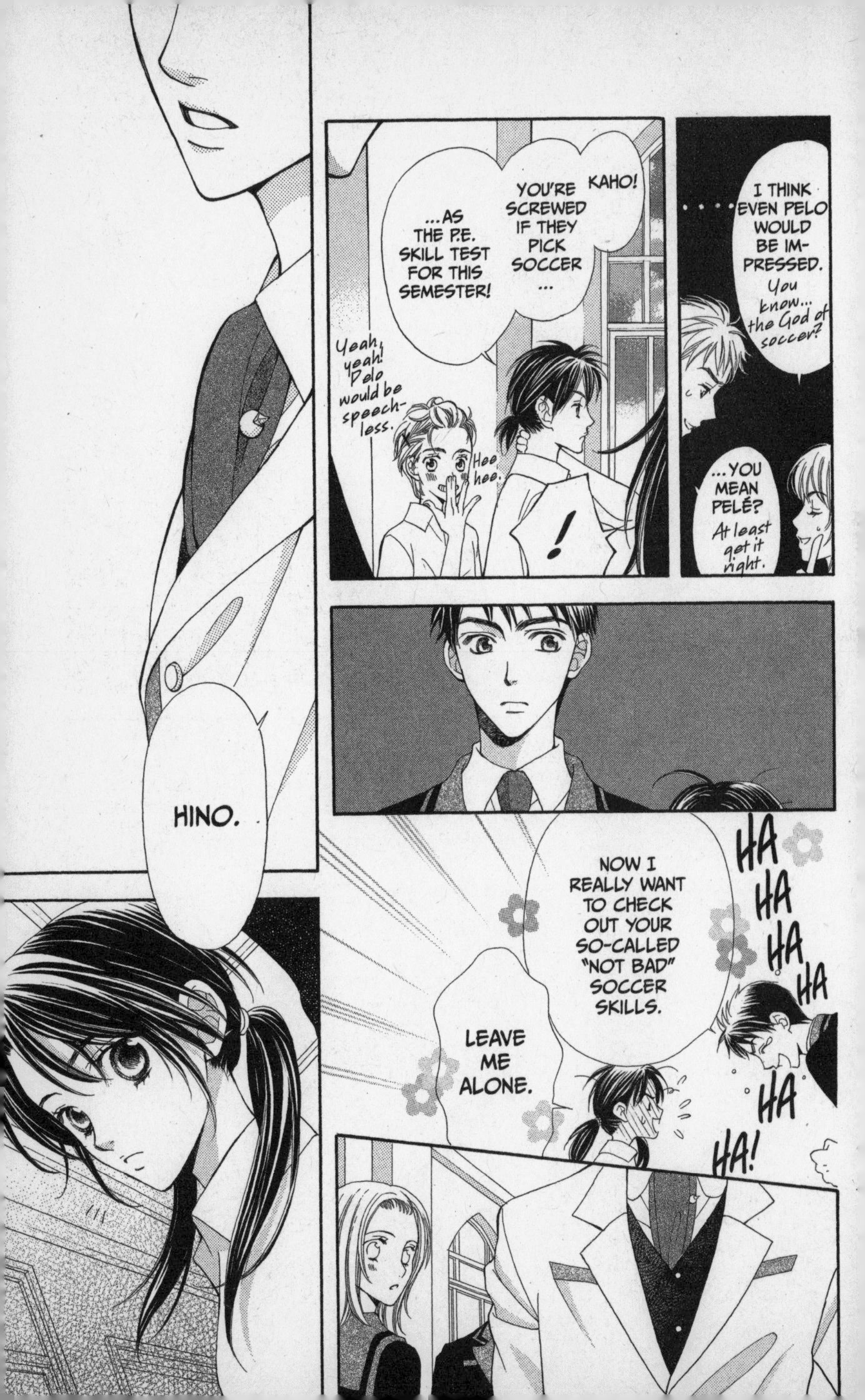

I THINK EVEN PELO WOULD BE IMPRESSED.
You know... the God of soccer?
...
...YOU MEAN PELÉ?
At least get it right.
KAHO!
YOU'RE SCREWED IF THEY PICK SOCCER ...
...AS THE P.E. SKILL TEST FOR THIS SEMESTER!
!
Hee hee.
Yeah, yeah! Pelo would be speechless.
HINO.
HA HA HA HA HA HA!
NOW I REALLY WANT TO CHECK OUT YOUR SO-CALLED "NOT BAD" SOCCER SKILLS.
LEAVE ME ALONE.

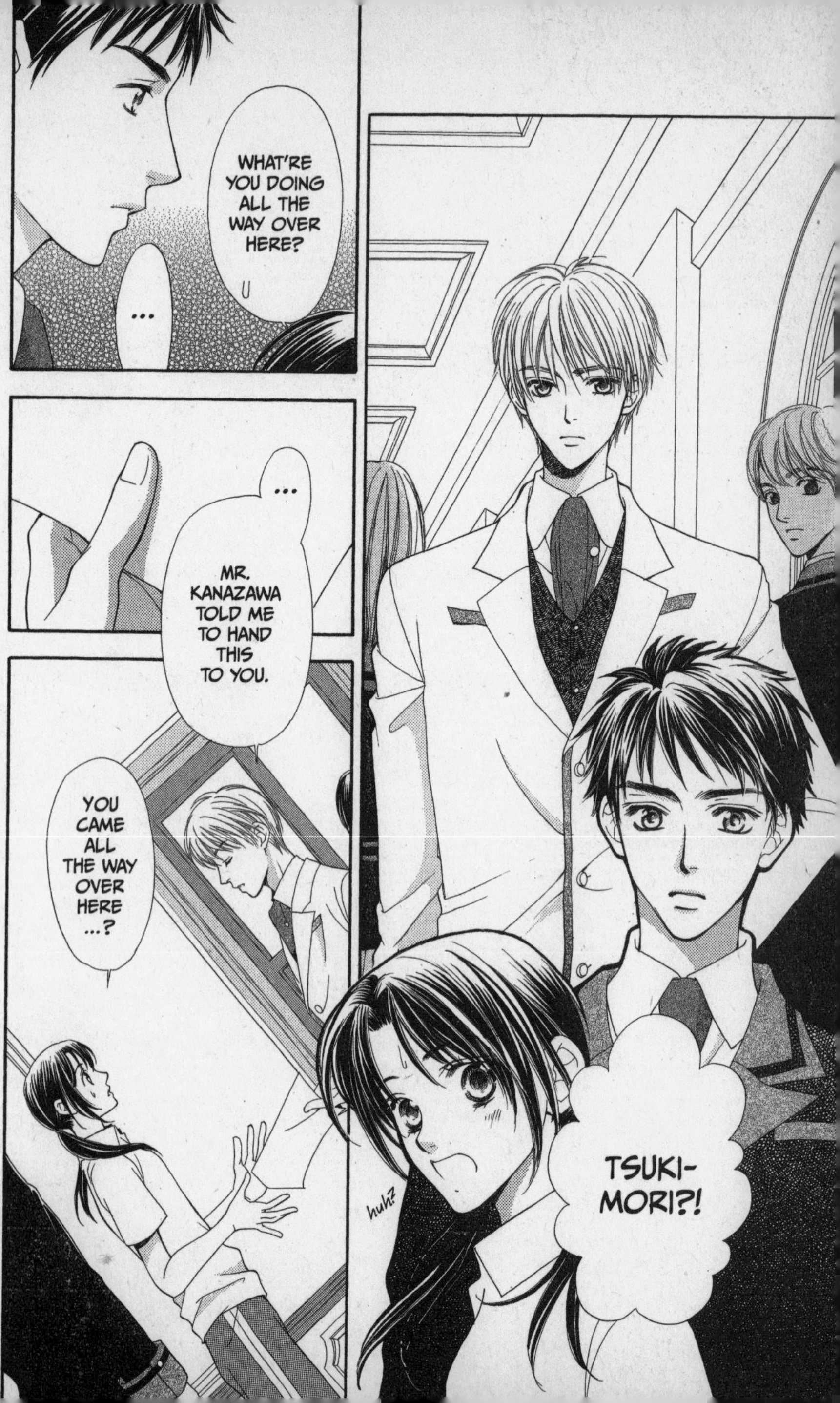
TSUKI-MORI?!
huh?
WHAT'RE YOU DOING ALL THE WAY OVER HERE?
...
...
MR. KANAZAWA TOLD ME TO HAND THIS TO YOU.
YOU CAME ALL THE WAY OVER HERE ...?

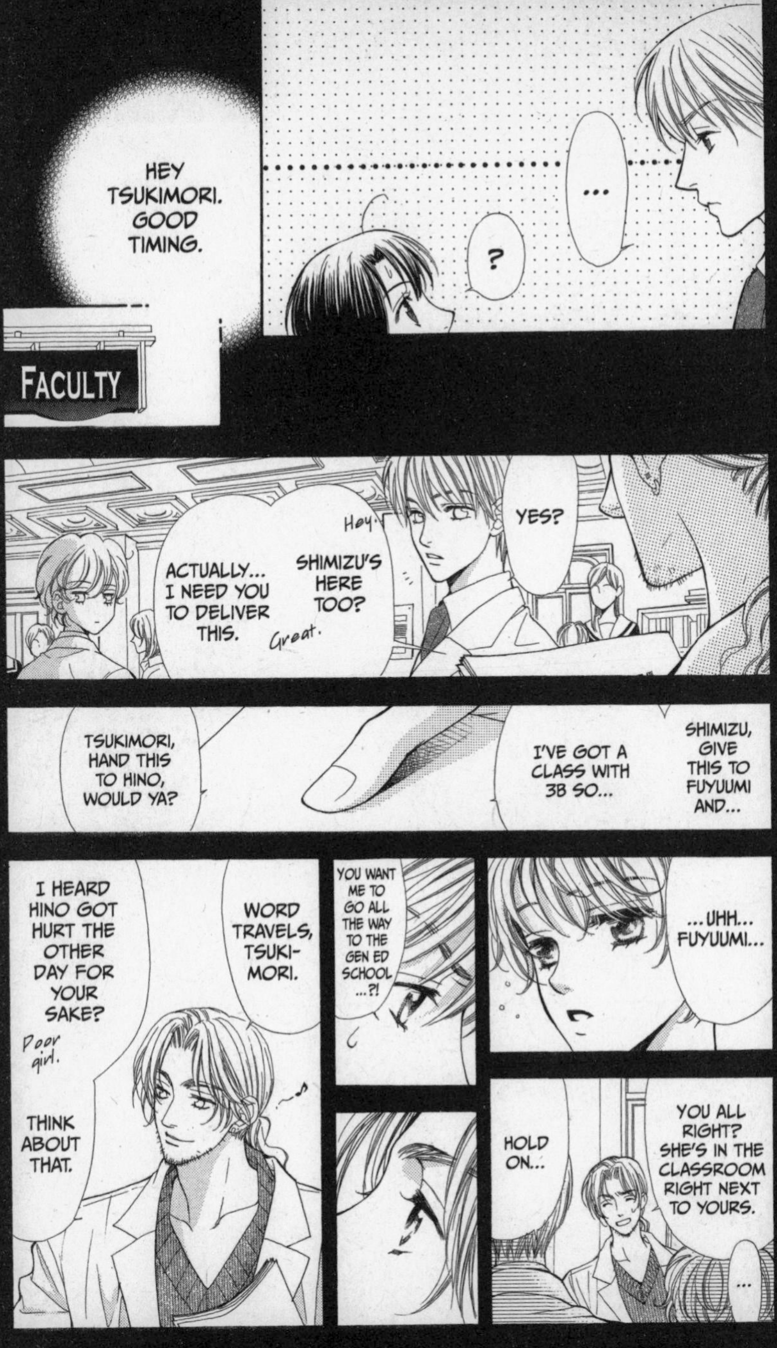
...
?
HEY TSUKIMORI. GOOD TIMING.
FACULTY
YES?
Hey.
SHIMIZU'S HERE TOO?
Great.
ACTUALLY... I NEED YOU TO DELIVER THIS.
SHIMIZU, GIVE THIS TO FUYUUMI AND...
I'VE GOT A CLASS WITH 3B SO...
TSUKIMORI, HAND THIS TO HINO, WOULD YA?
...UHH... FUYUUMI...
YOU ALL RIGHT? SHE'S IN THE CLASSROOM RIGHT NEXT TO YOURS.
HOLD ON...
...
YOU WANT ME TO GO ALL THE WAY TO THE GEN ED SCHOOL ...?!
WORD TRAVELS, TSUKI-MORI.
I HEARD HINO GOT HURT THE OTHER DAY FOR YOUR SAKE?
Poor girl.
THINK ABOUT THAT.

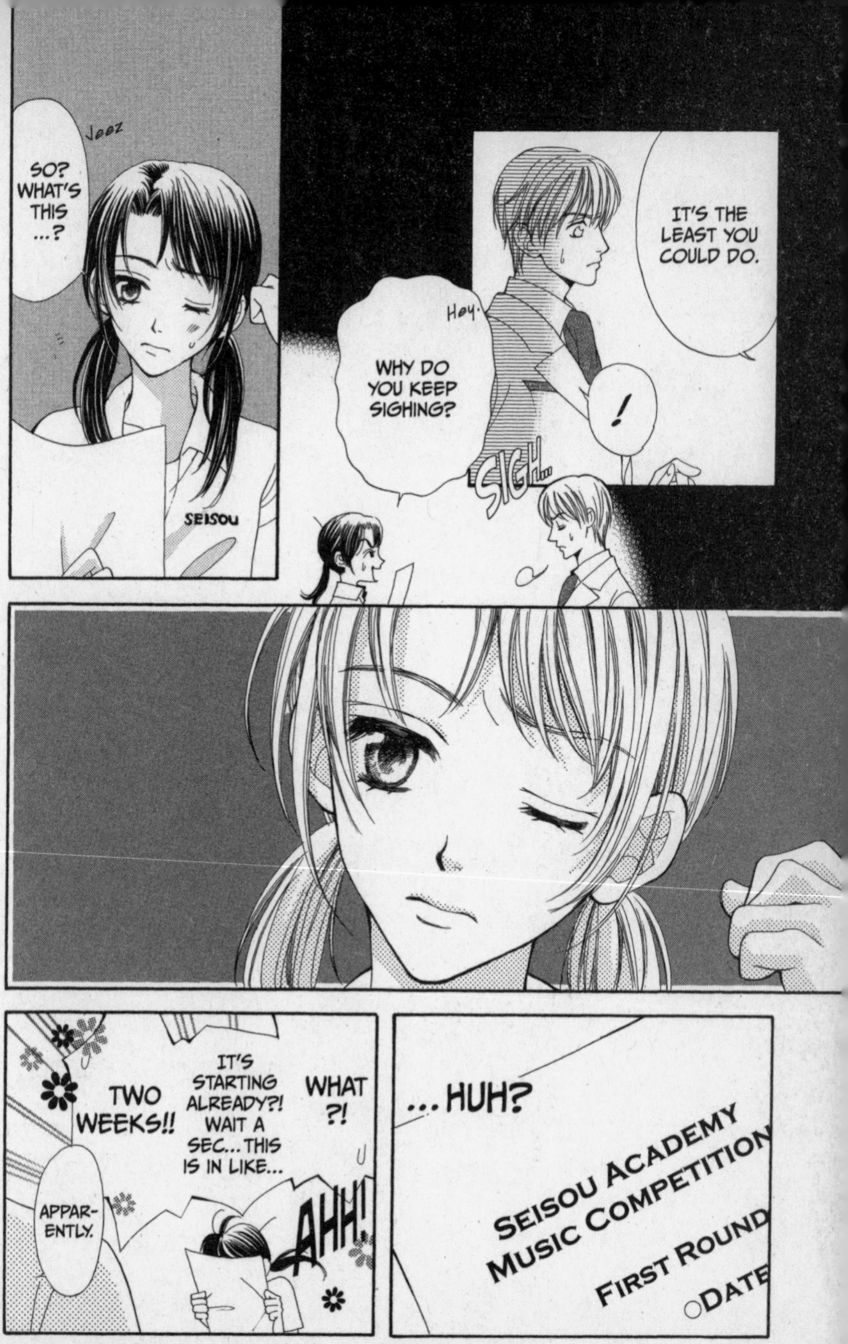
IT'S THE LEAST YOU COULD DO.
!
Hey.
WHY DO YOU KEEP SIGHING?
SIGH...
Jeez
SO? WHAT'S THIS ...?
SEISOU
...HUH?
Seisou Academy
Music Competition
First Round
○Date
WHAT ?!
IT'S STARTING ALREADY?! WAIT A SEC...THIS IS IN LIKE...
TWO WEEKS!!
AHH!
APPAR-
ENTLY.

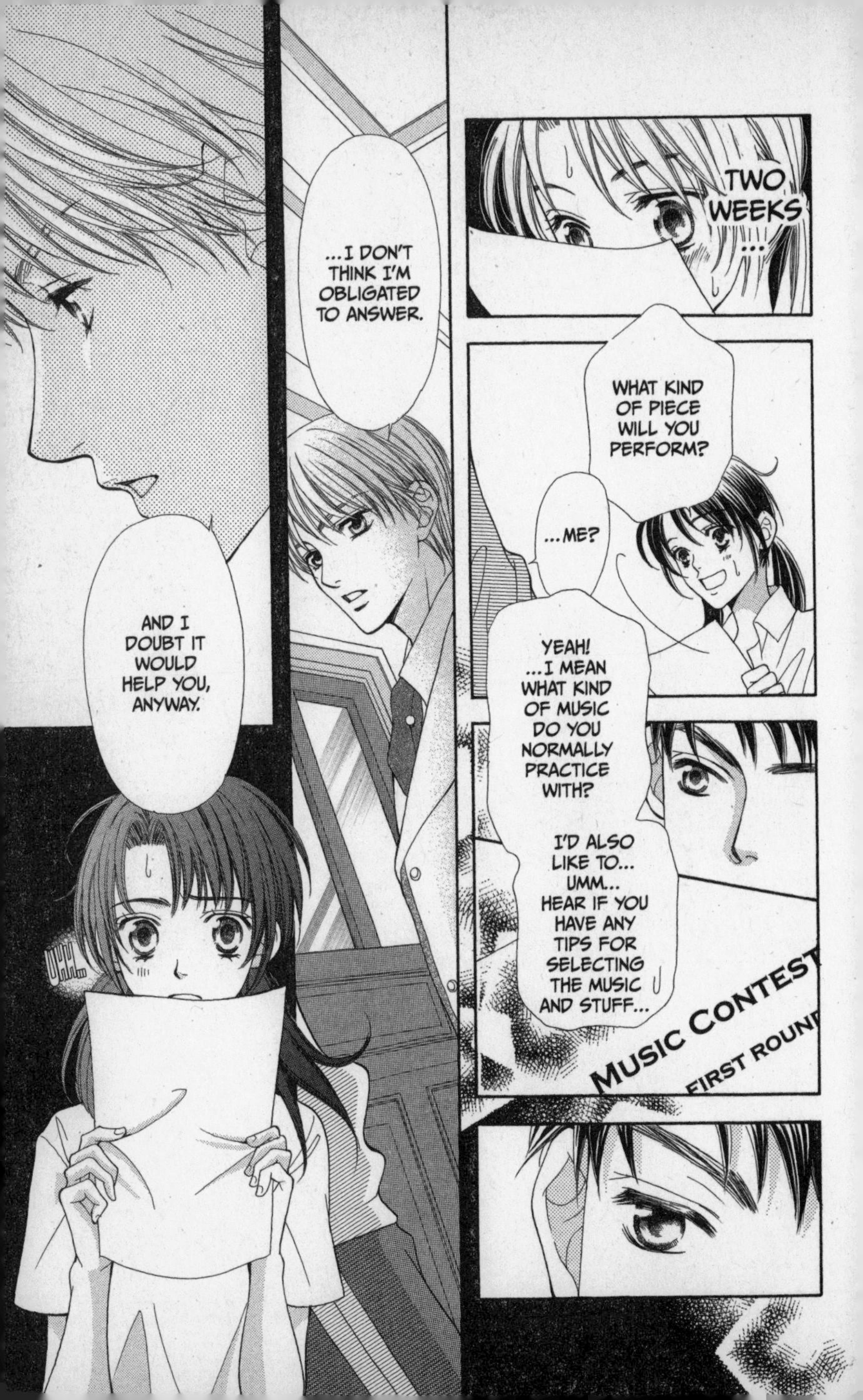
TWO WEEKS...
WHAT KIND OF PIECE WILL YOU PERFORM?
...ME?
YEAH! ...I MEAN WHAT KIND OF MUSIC DO YOU NORMALLY PRACTICE WITH?
I'D ALSO LIKE TO... UMM... HEAR IF YOU HAVE ANY TIPS FOR SELECTING THE MUSIC AND STUFF...
MUSIC CONTEST
FIRST ROUN
...I DON'T THINK I'M OBLIGATED TO ANSWER.
AND I DOUBT IT WOULD HELP YOU, ANYWAY.
UHH...

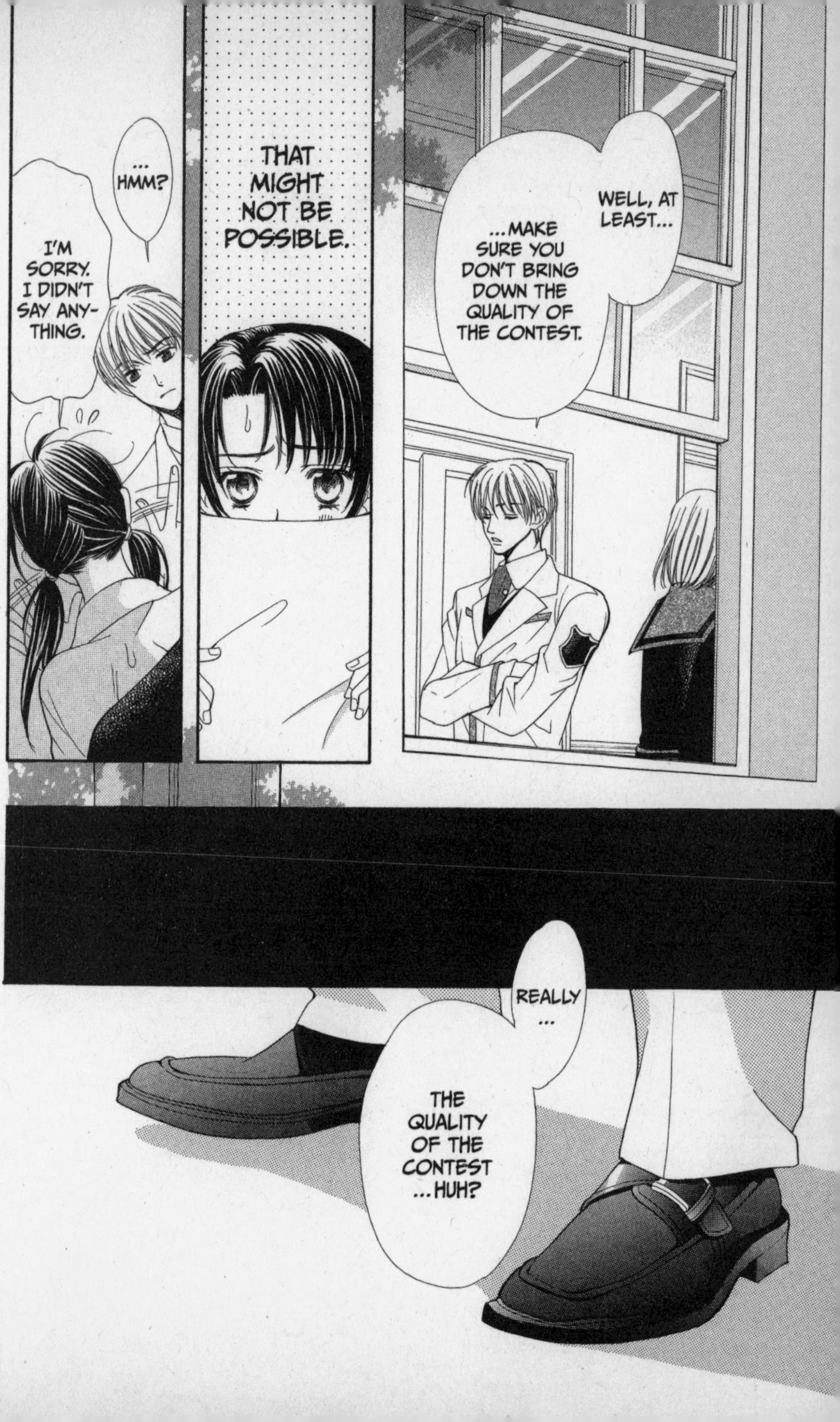
WELL, AT LEAST...
...MAKE SURE YOU DON'T BRING DOWN THE QUALITY OF THE CONTEST.
THAT MIGHT NOT BE POSSIBLE.
...HMM?
I'M SORRY. I DIDN'T SAY ANY-THING.
REALLY...
THE QUALITY OF THE CONTEST ...HUH?

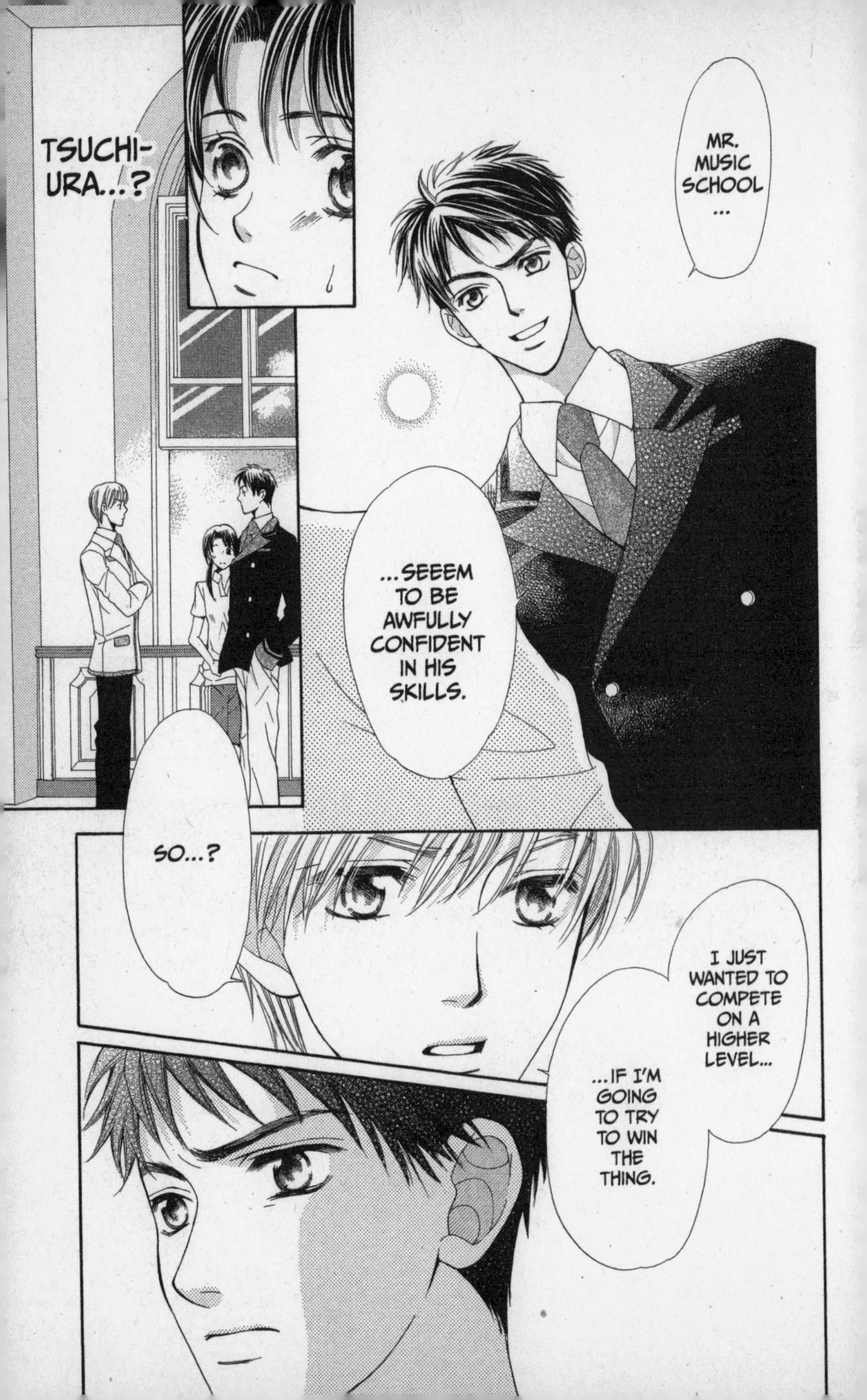
MR. MUSIC SCHOOL ...
...SEEEM TO BE AWFULLY CONFIDENT IN HIS SKILLS.
TSUCHI-URA...?
SO...?
I JUST WANTED TO COMPETE ON A HIGHER LEVEL...
...IF I'M GOING TO TRY TO WIN THE THING.

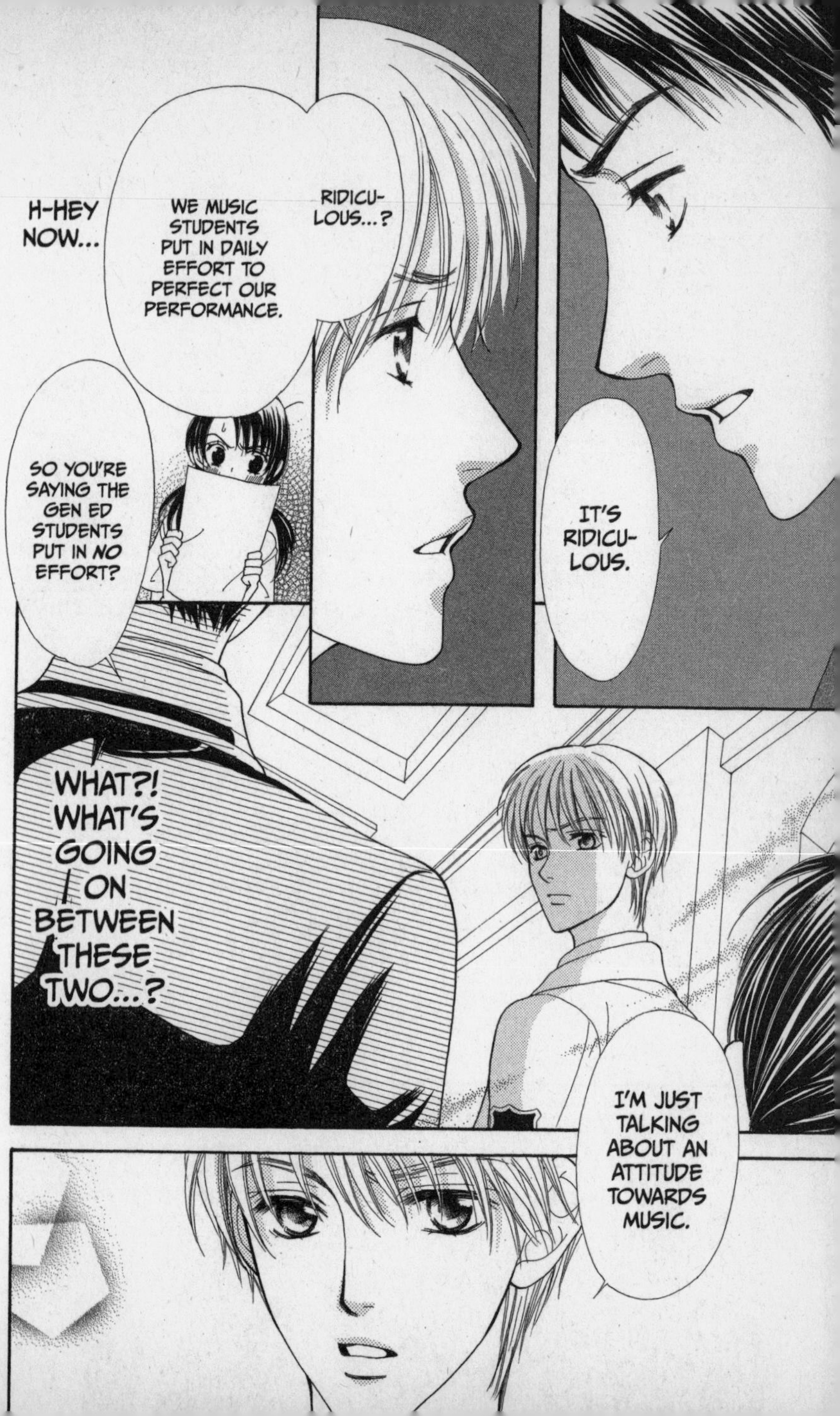

IT'S RIDICULOUS.
RIDICULOUS...?
WE MUSIC STUDENTS PUT IN DAILY EFFORT TO PERFECT OUR PERFORMANCE.
H-HEY NOW...
SO YOU'RE SAYING THE GEN ED STUDENTS PUT IN *NO* EFFORT?
WHAT?! WHAT'S GOING ON BETWEEN THESE TWO...?
I'M JUST TALKING ABOUT AN ATTITUDE TOWARDS MUSIC.

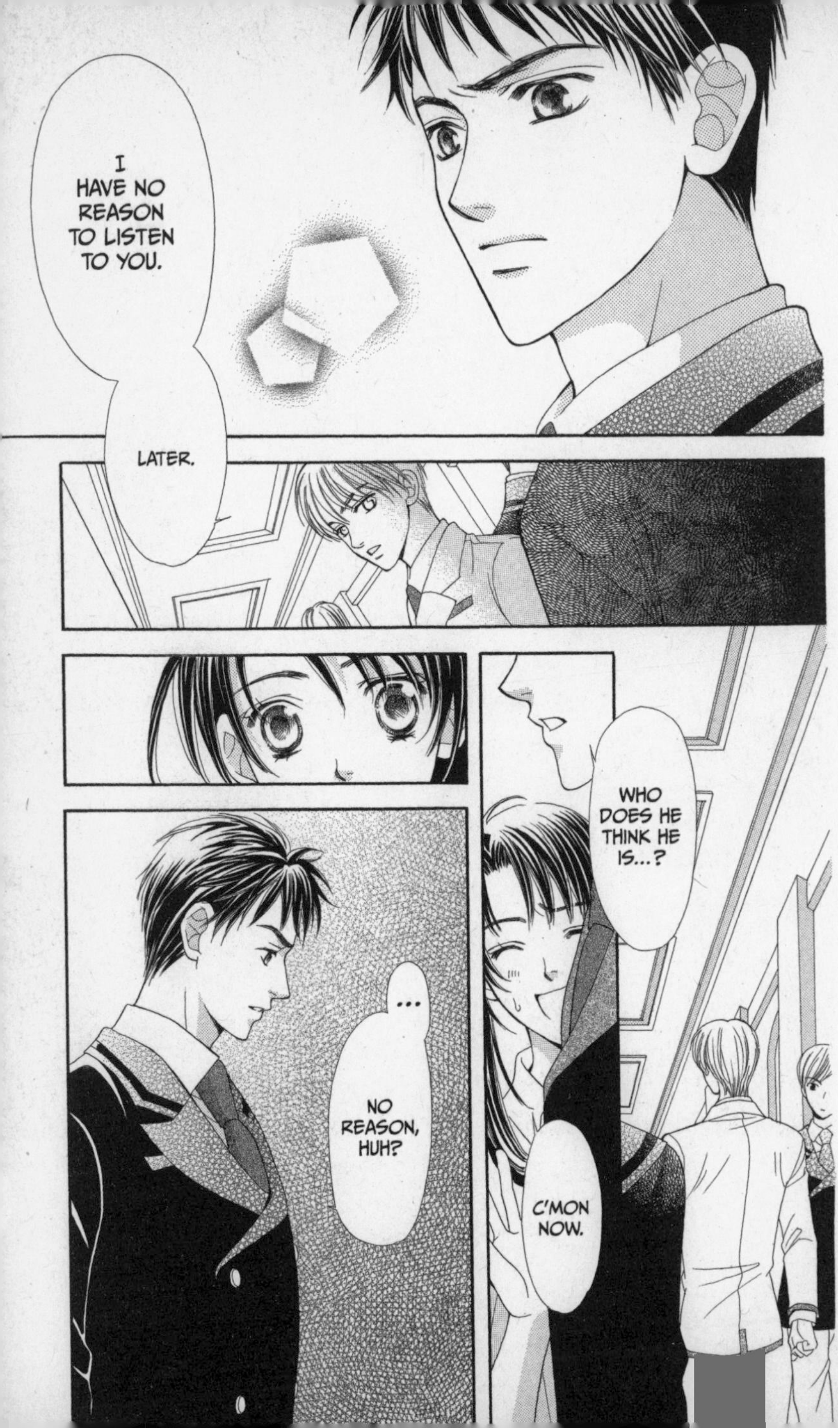
I HAVE NO REASON TO LISTEN TO YOU.
LATER.
WHO DOES HE THINK HE IS...?
C'MON NOW.
...
NO REASON, HUH?

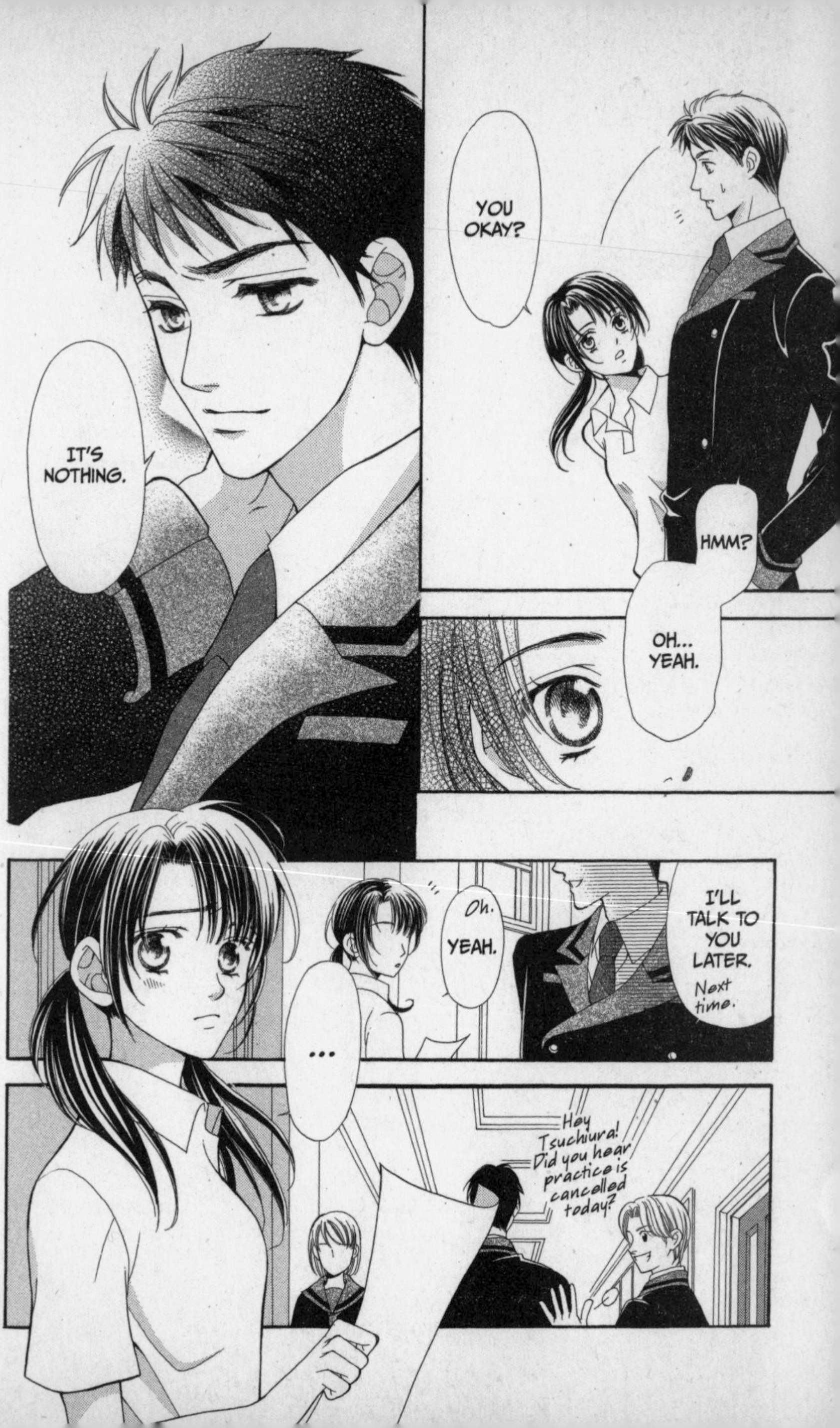
YOU OKAY?
HMM?
OH... YEAH.
IT'S NOTHING.
I'LL TALK TO YOU LATER.
Next time.
Oh.
YEAH.
...
Hey Tsuchiura! Did you hear practice is cancelled today?

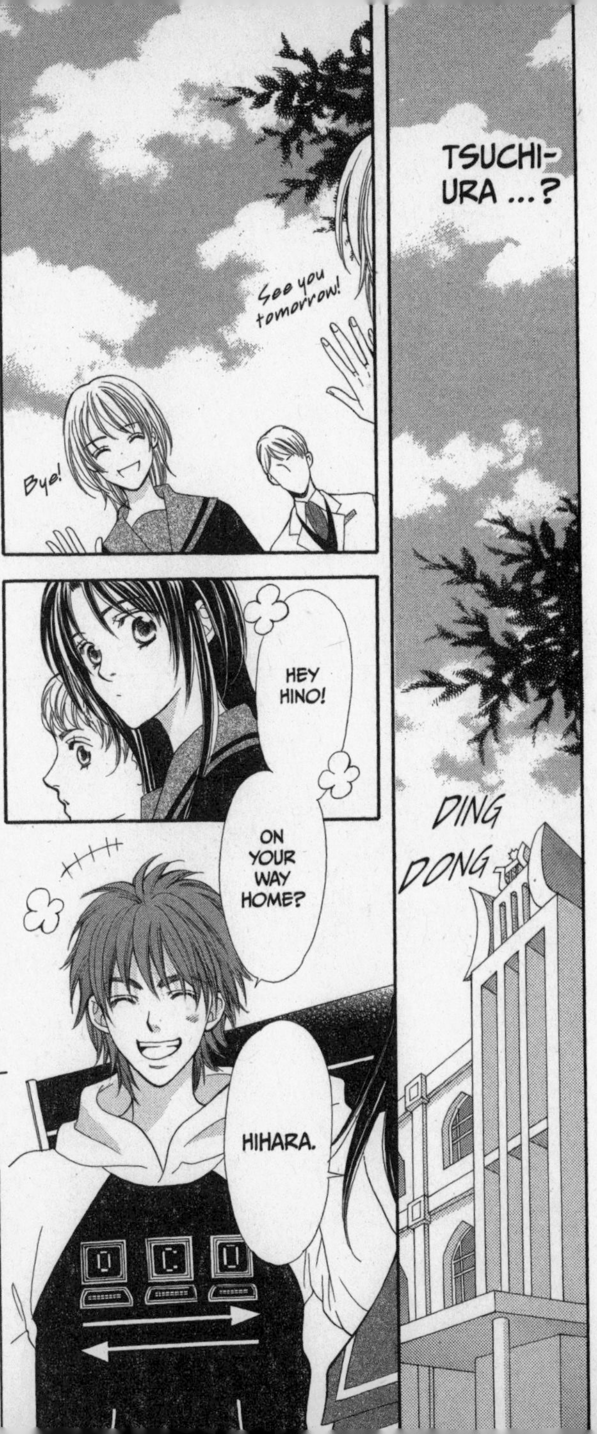
TSUCHI-URA ...?
DING DONG
See you tomorrow!
Bye!
HEY HINO!
ON YOUR WAY HOME?
HIHARA.

Measure 5 was published in the April magazine, so I decided to include a hanami. I actually hadn't decided on anything when I finished the cover (you turn in color prints before the deadline for the b&w script), but I was able to somehow make a connection...

From Measure 6, our story will head into the first selection. Drawing the sketch on the cover with the glasses was fun and refreshing. I was planning on making Ren and Ryotaro's shirts white, but they ended up looking like businessmen, so I decided against it...
I told you, [redacted]-kun.

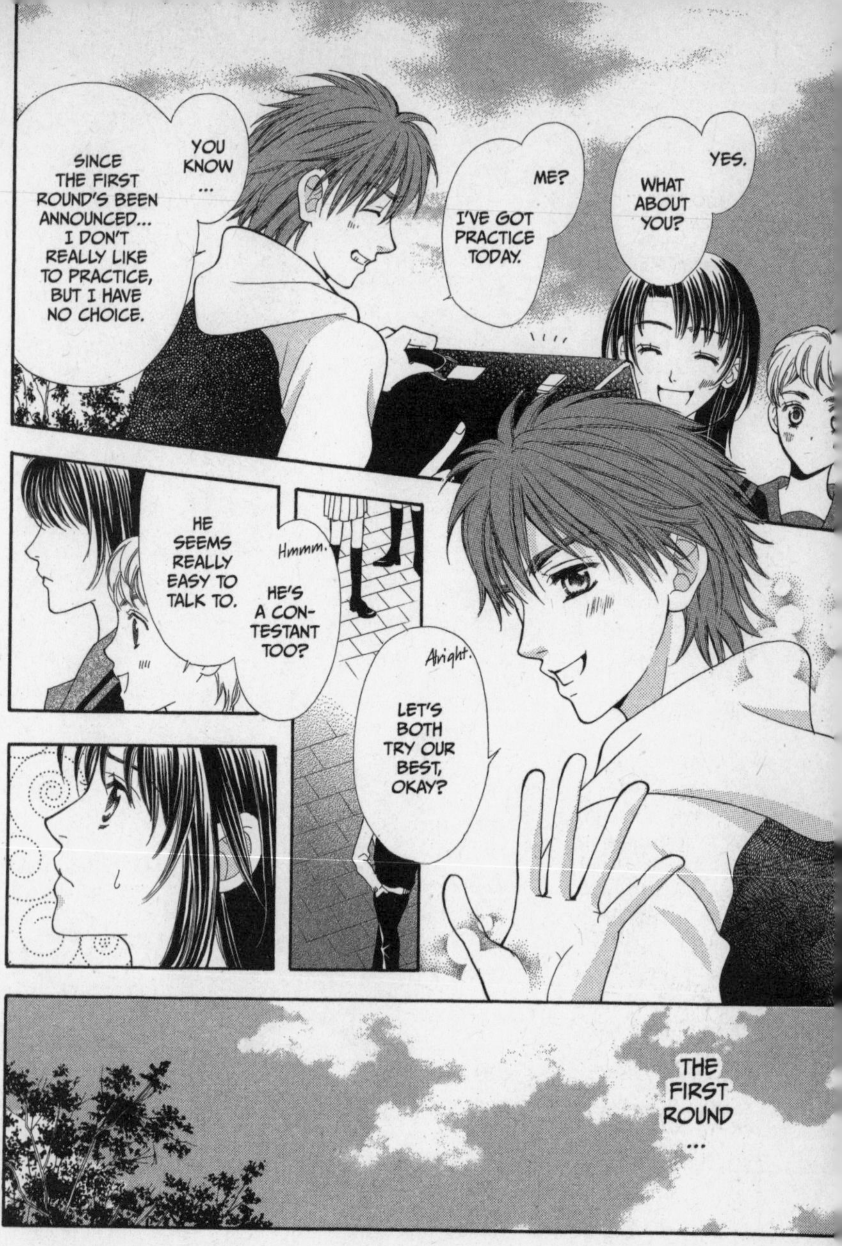
YES.
WHAT ABOUT YOU?
ME?
I'VE GOT PRACTICE TODAY.
YOU KNOW ...
SINCE THE FIRST ROUND'S BEEN ANNOUNCED... I DON'T REALLY LIKE TO PRACTICE, BUT I HAVE NO CHOICE.
Alright.
LET'S BOTH TRY OUR BEST, OKAY?
Hmmm.
HE'S A CON-TESTANT TOO?
HE SEEMS REALLY EASY TO TALK TO.
THE FIRST ROUND ...

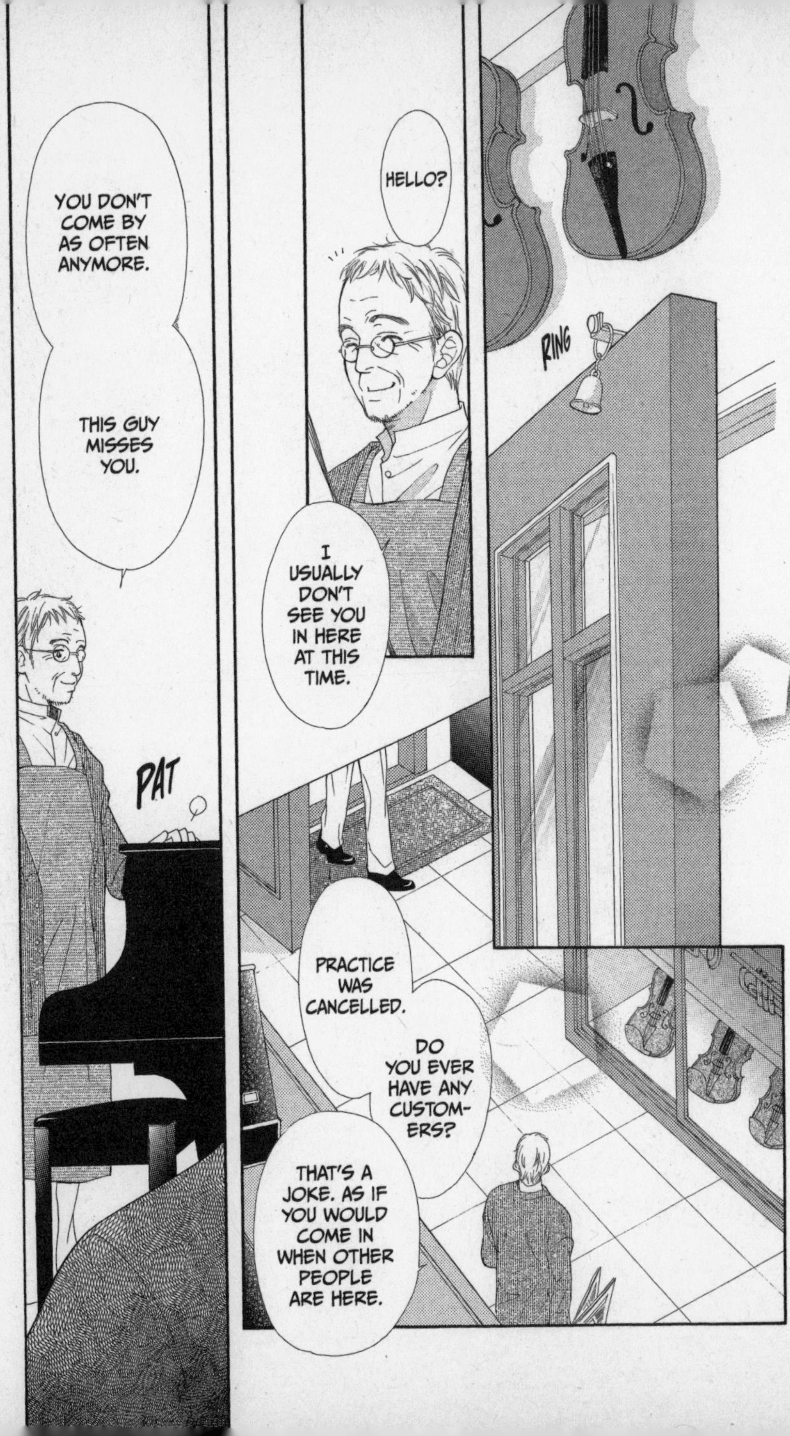
RING
HELLO?
I USUALLY DON'T SEE YOU IN HERE AT THIS TIME.
PRACTICE WAS CANCELLED.
DO YOU EVER HAVE ANY CUSTOM-ERS?
THAT'S A JOKE. AS IF YOU WOULD COME IN WHEN OTHER PEOPLE ARE HERE.
YOU DON'T COME BY AS OFTEN ANYMORE.
THIS GUY MISSES YOU.
PAT

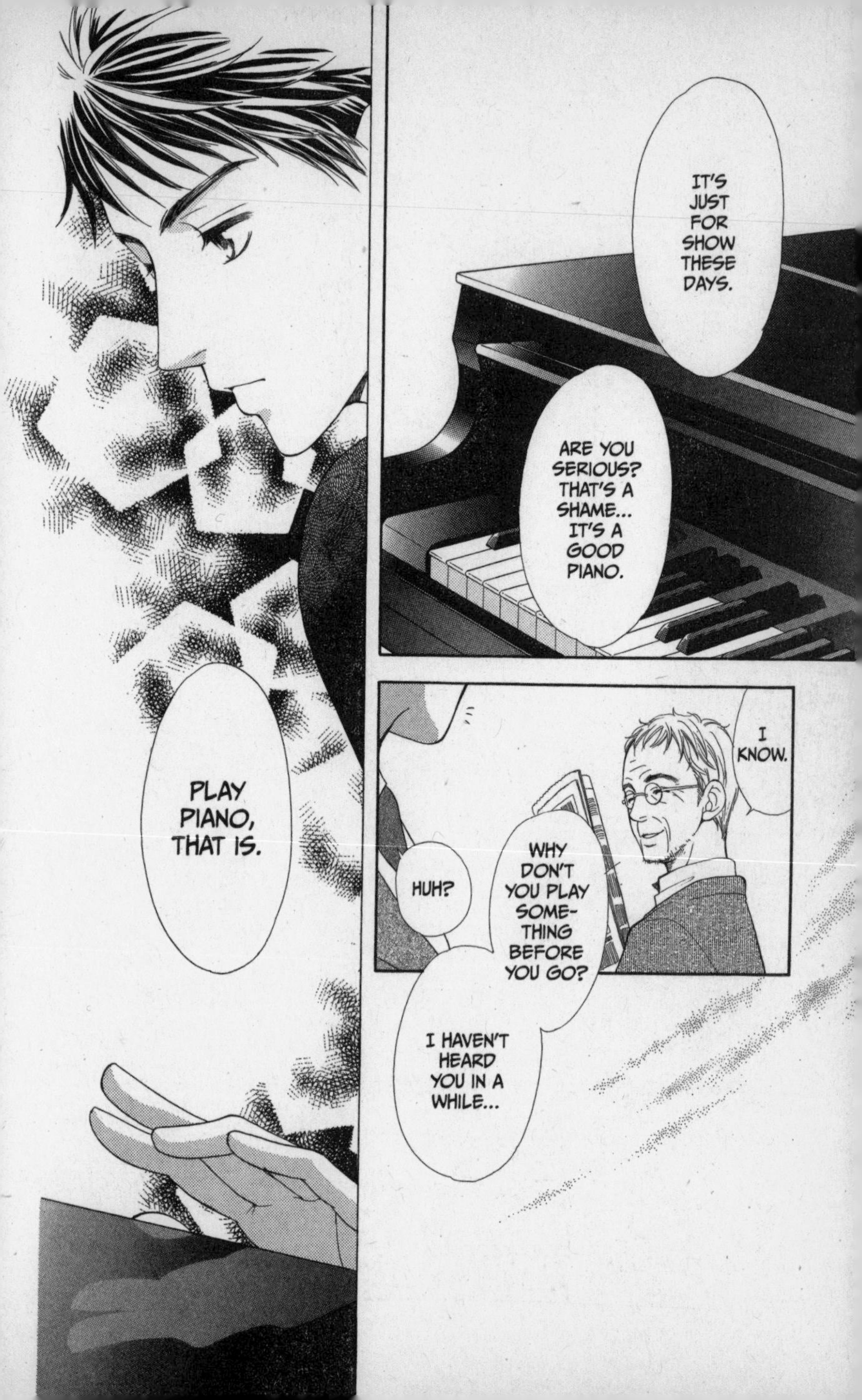
IT'S JUST FOR SHOW THESE DAYS.
ARE YOU SERIOUS? THAT'S A SHAME... IT'S A GOOD PIANO.
I KNOW.
WHY DON'T YOU PLAY SOME-THING BEFORE YOU GO?
HUH?
I HAVEN'T HEARD YOU IN A WHILE...
PLAY PIANO, THAT IS.

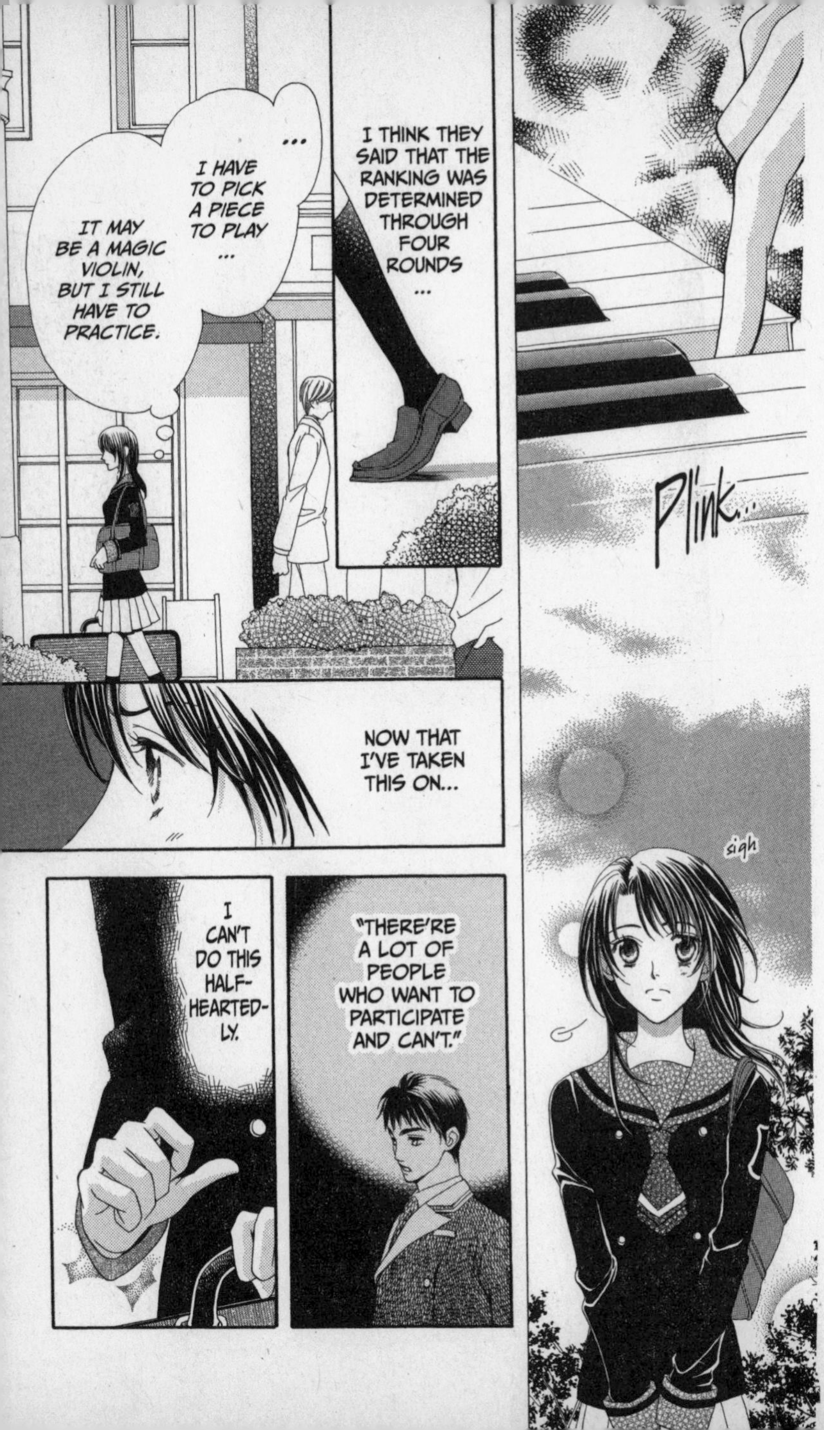
Plink...
sigh
I THINK THEY SAID THAT THE RANKING WAS DETERMINED THROUGH FOUR ROUNDS ...
...
I HAVE TO PICK A PIECE TO PLAY ...
IT MAY BE A MAGIC VIOLIN, BUT I STILL HAVE TO PRACTICE.
NOW THAT I'VE TAKEN THIS ON...
"THERE'RE A LOT OF PEOPLE WHO WANT TO PARTICIPATE AND CAN'T."
I CAN'T DO THIS HALF-HEARTED-LY.

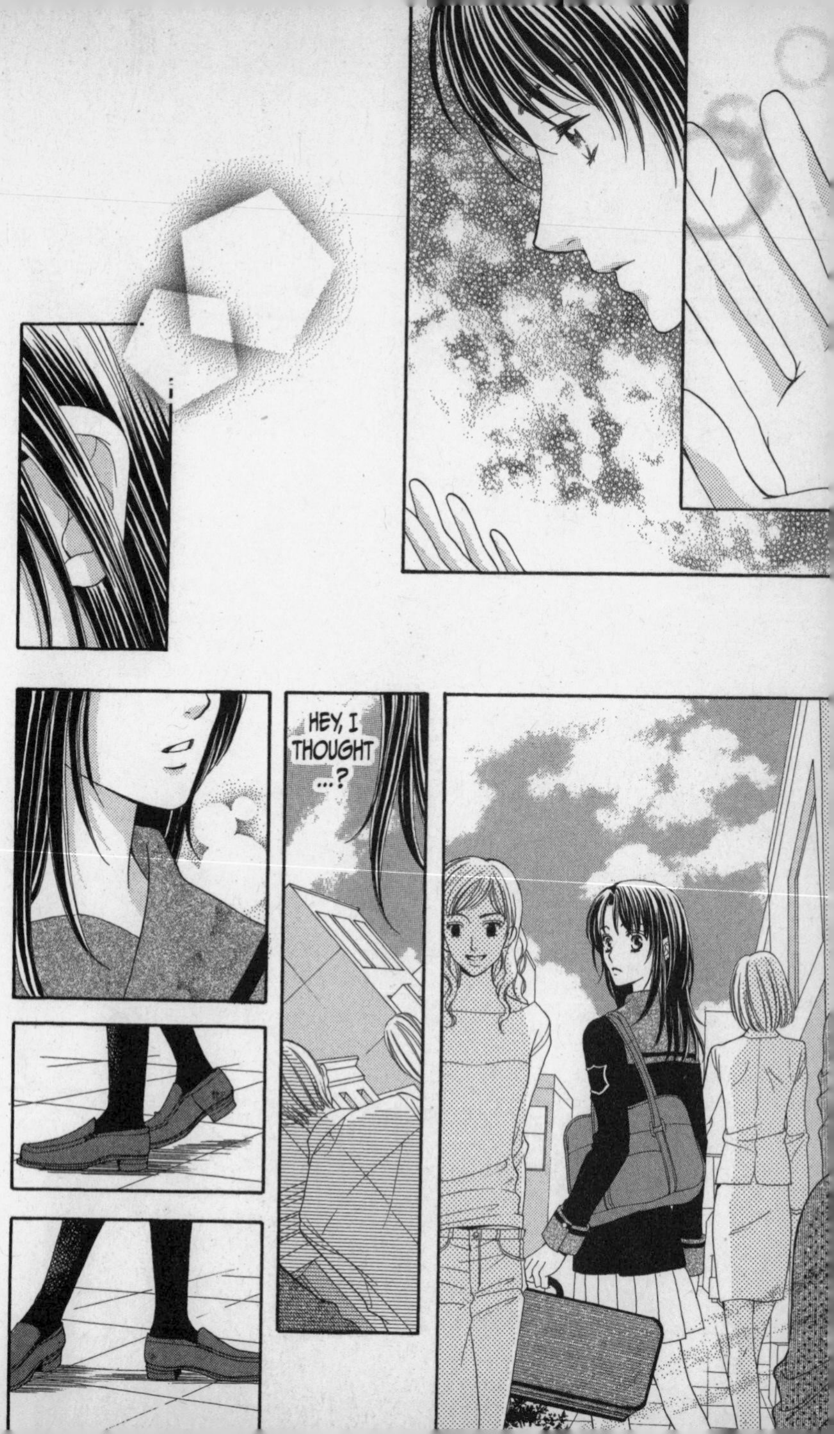
HEY, I THOUGHT ...?

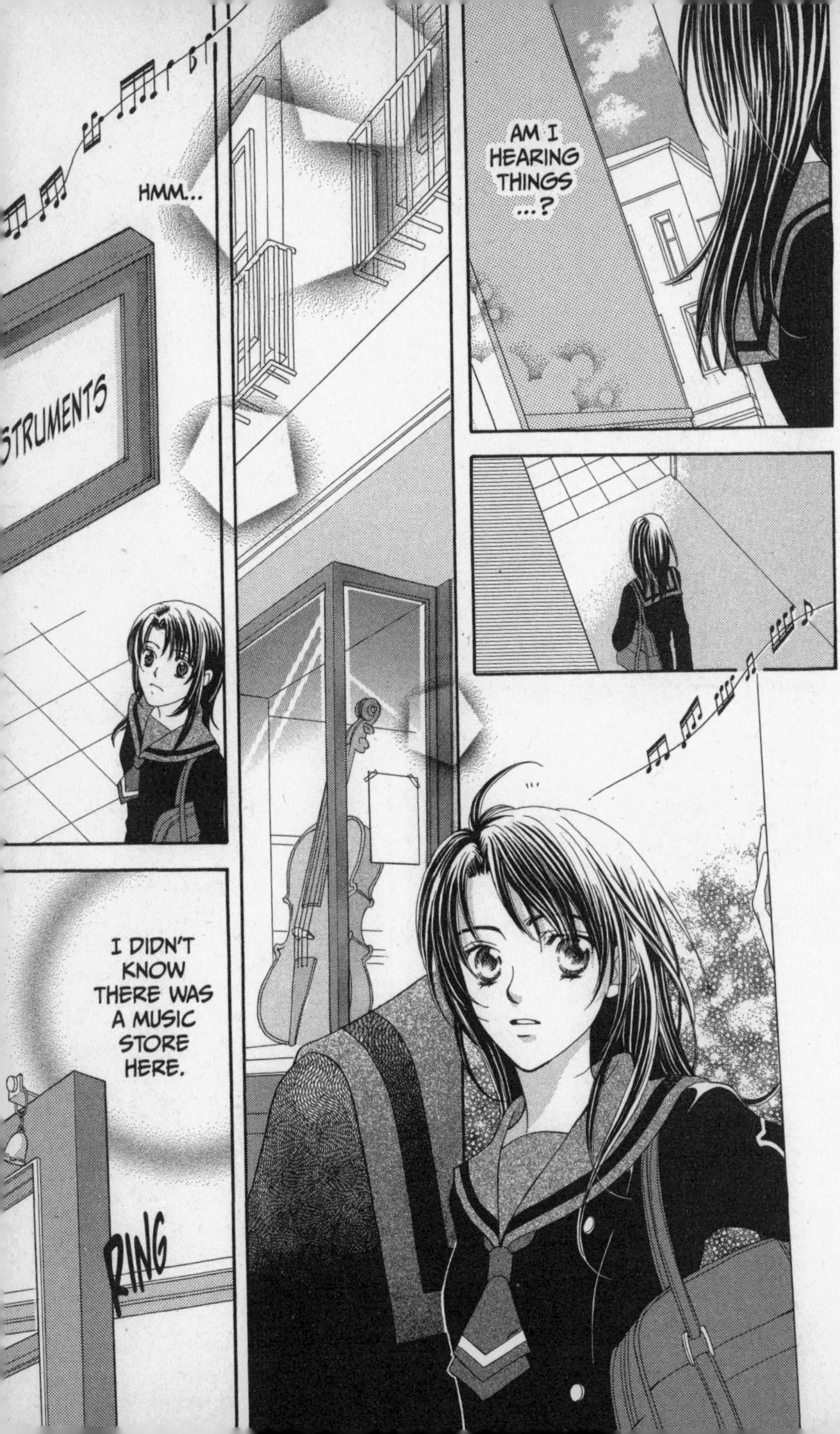
AM I HEARING THINGS ...?
...
HMM...
STRUMENTS
I DIDN'T KNOW THERE WAS A MUSIC STORE HERE.
RING

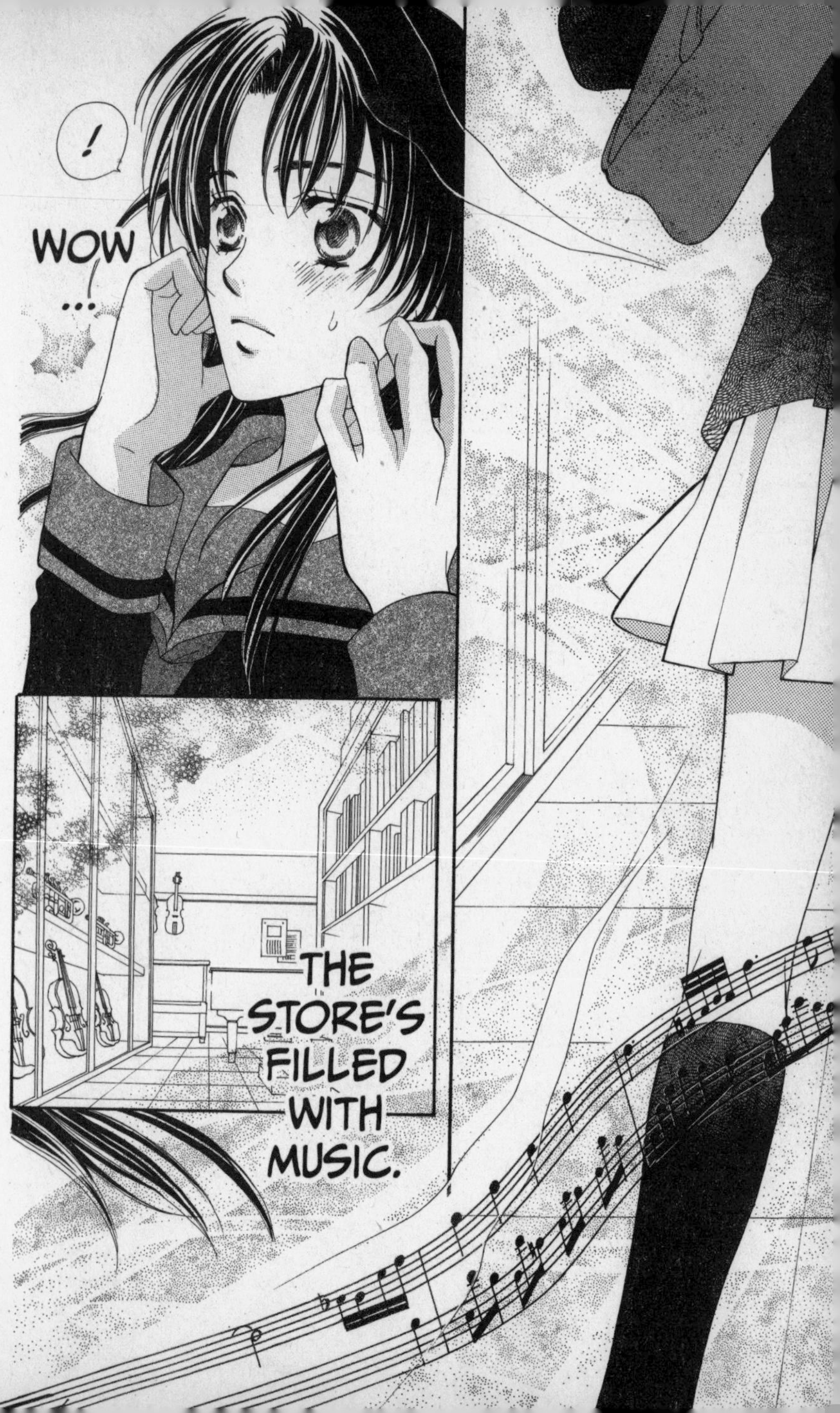
!
WOW...
THE STORE'S FILLED WITH MUSIC.

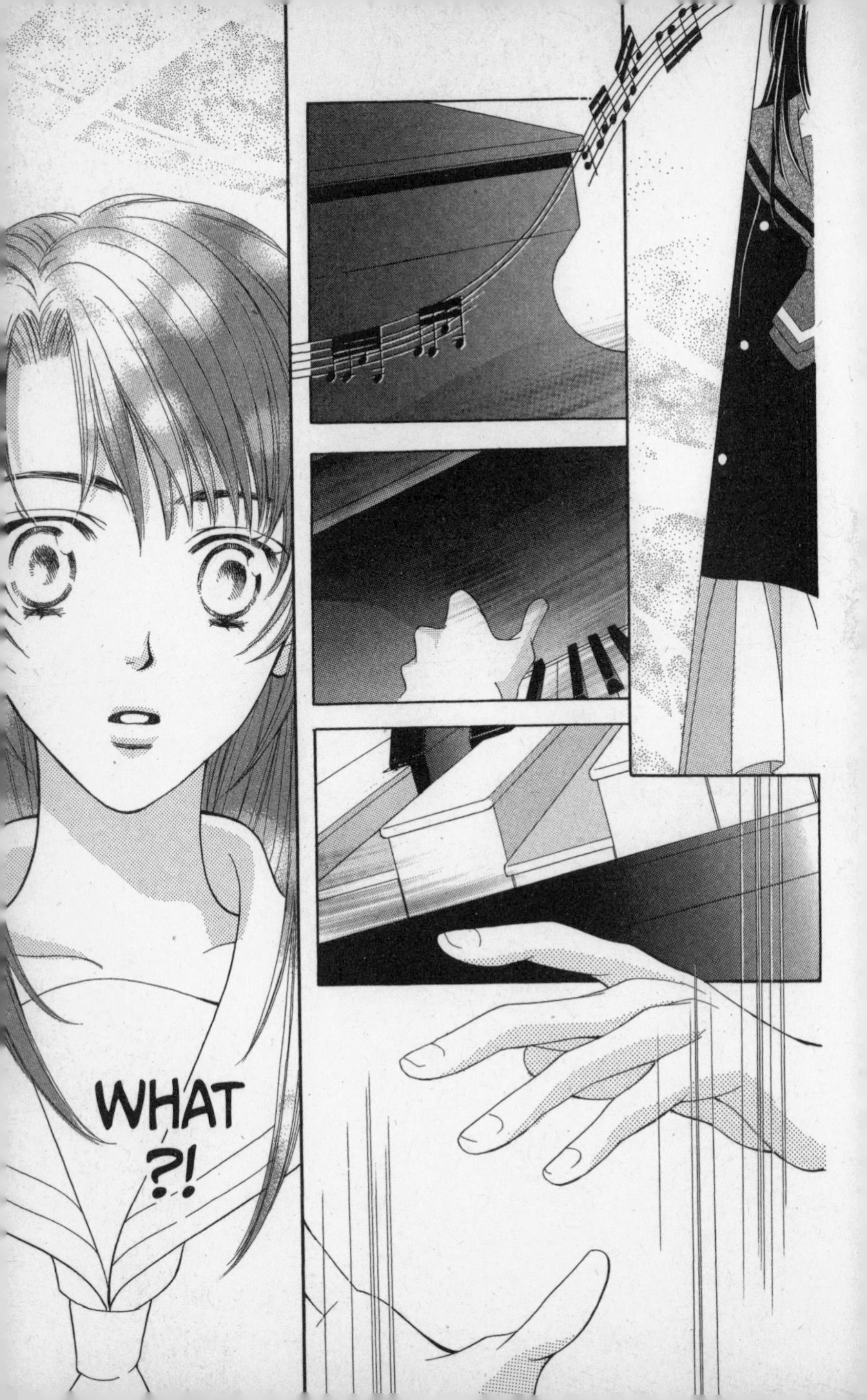
WHAT ?!

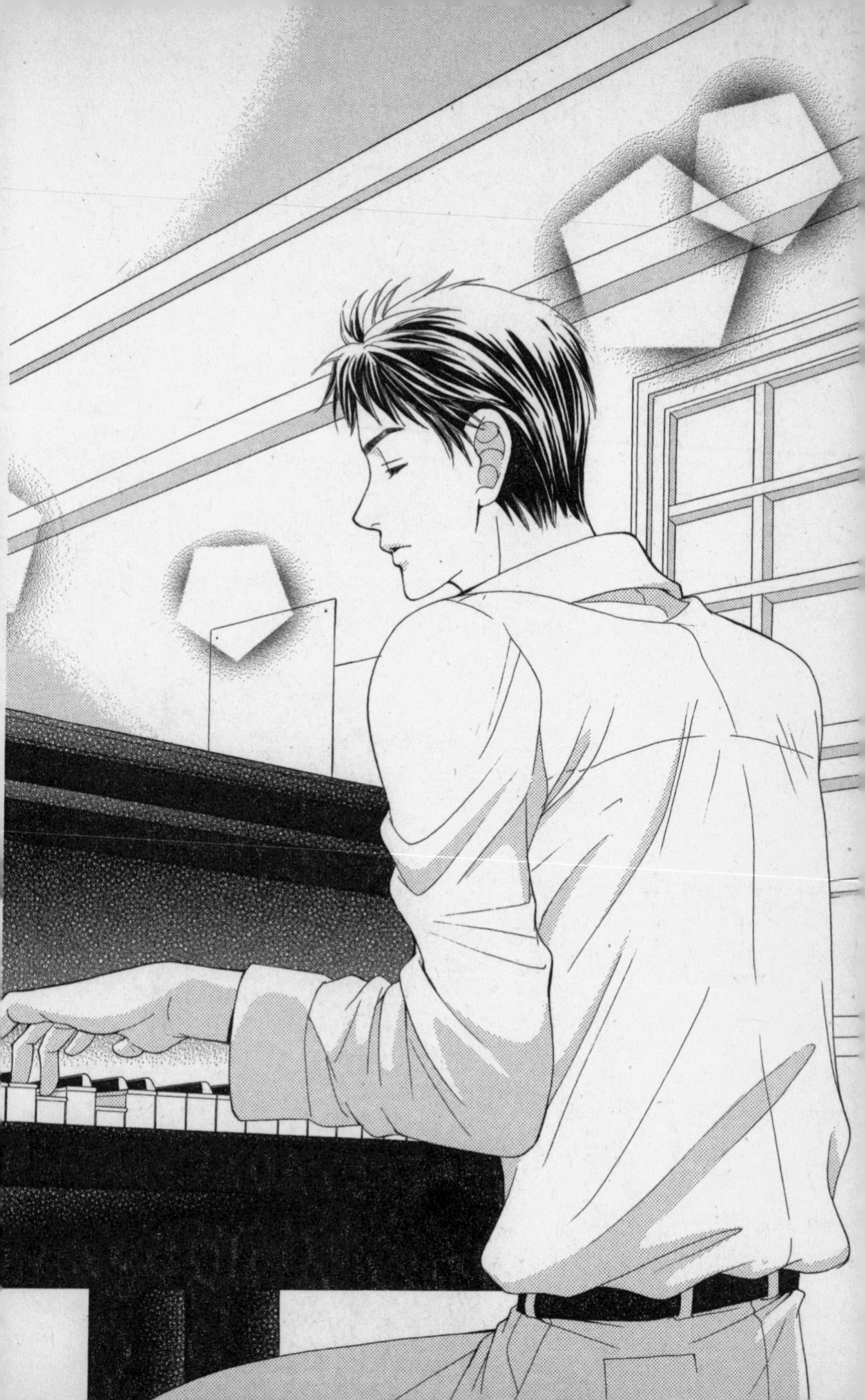

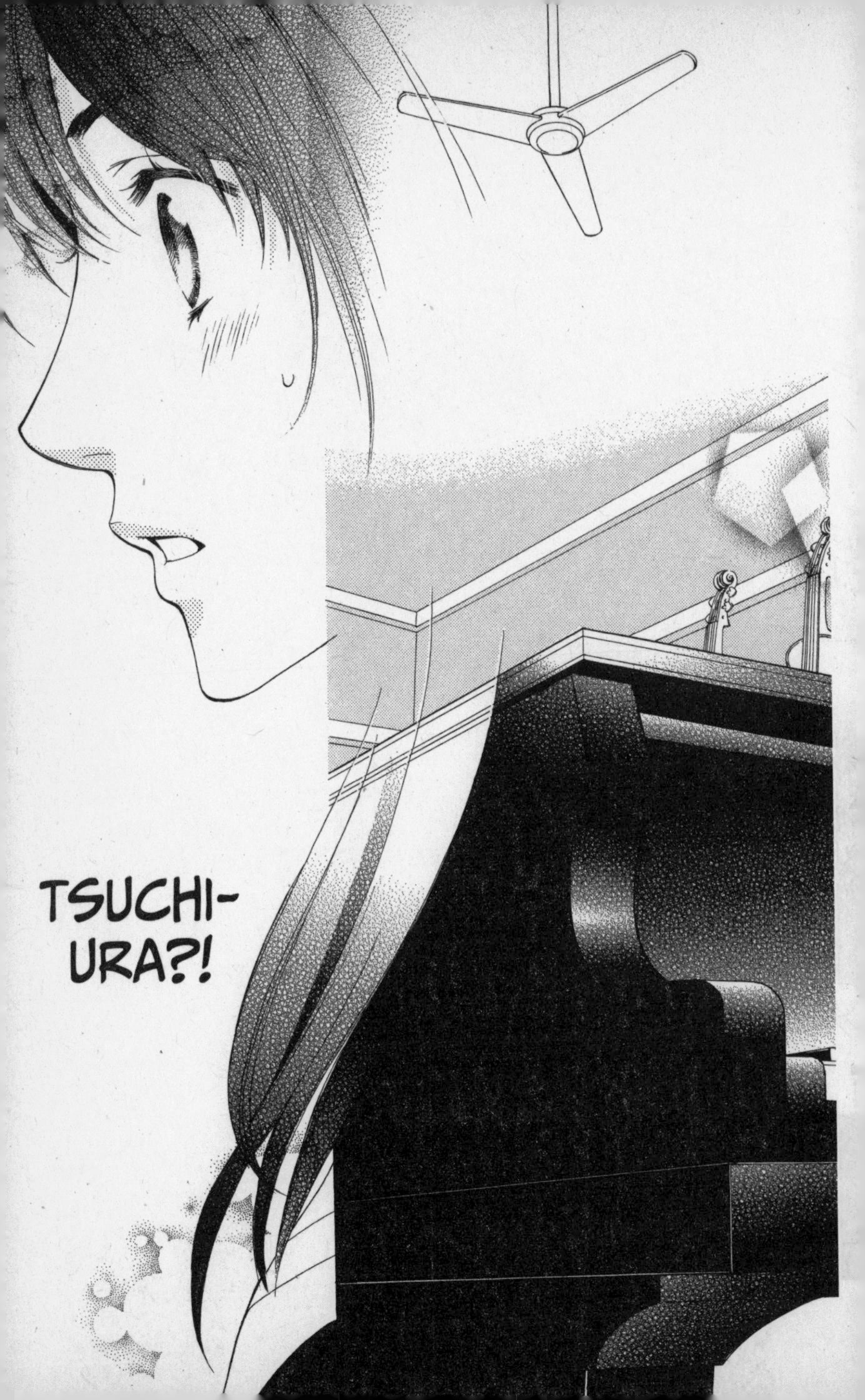
TSUCHI-
URA?!

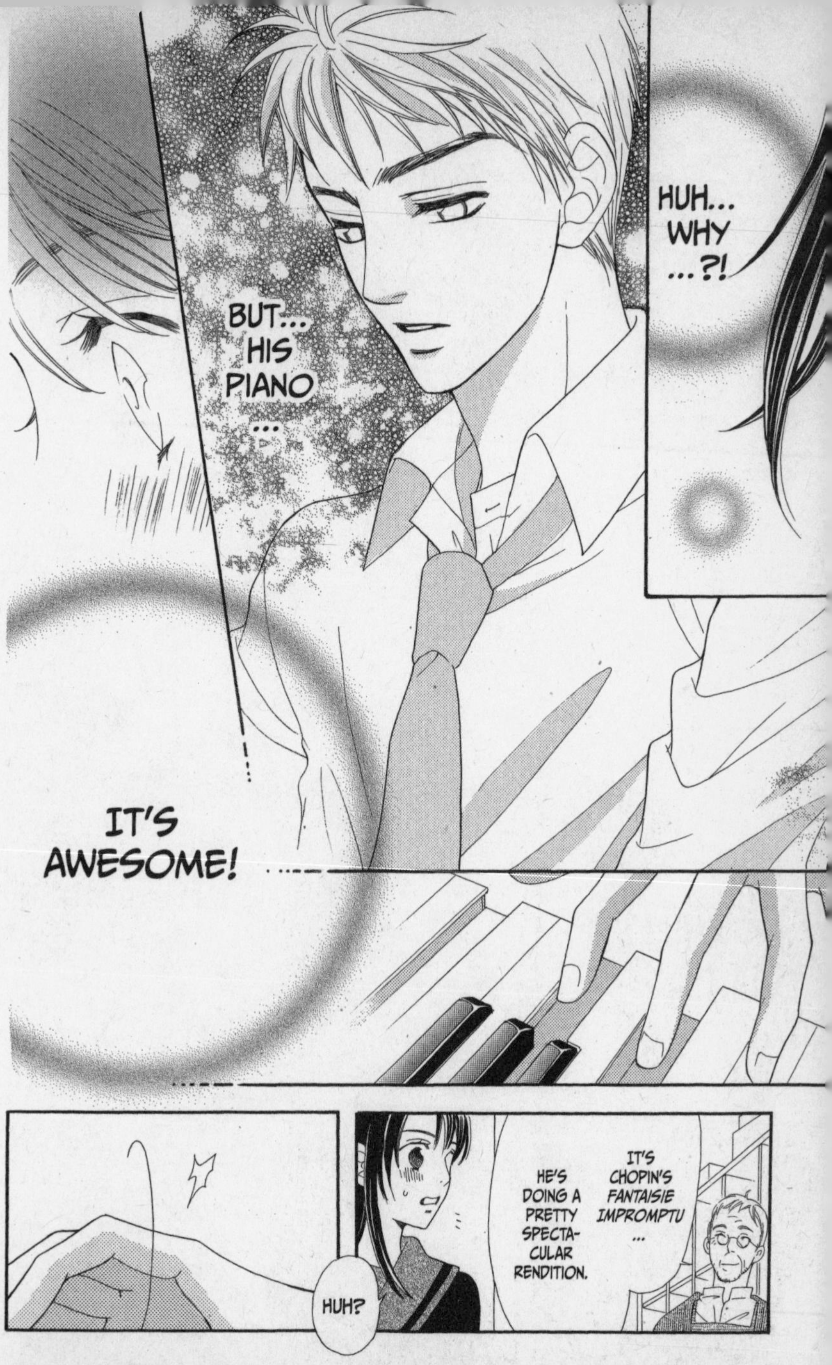
HUH... WHY ...?!
BUT... HIS PIANO ...
IT'S AWESOME!
IT'S CHOPIN'S FANTAISIE IMPROMPTU ...
HE'S DOING A PRETTY SPECTA-CULAR RENDITION.
HUH?

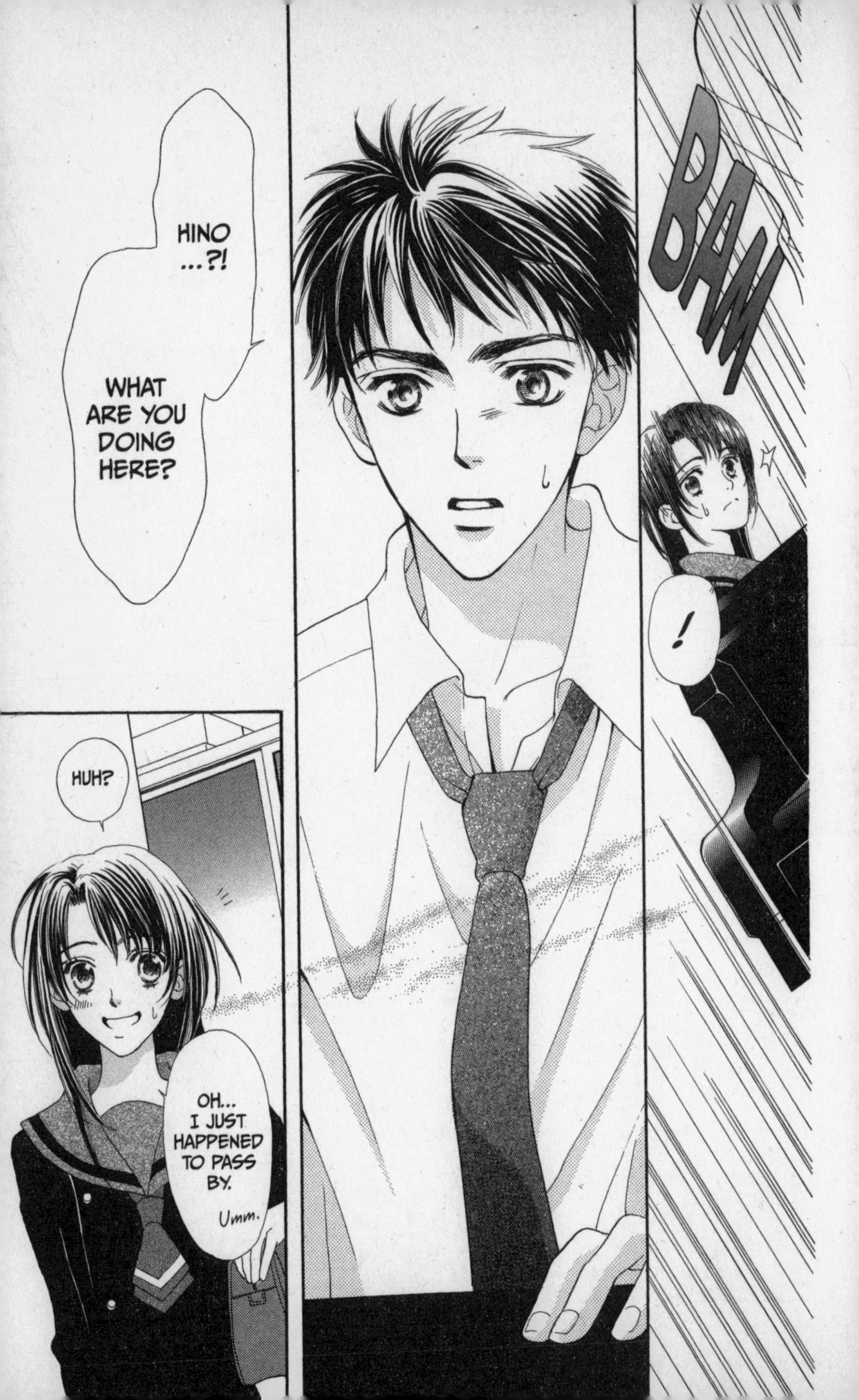
BAM
!
HINO ...?!
WHAT ARE YOU DOING HERE?
HUH?
OH... I JUST HAPPENED TO PASS BY.
Umm.

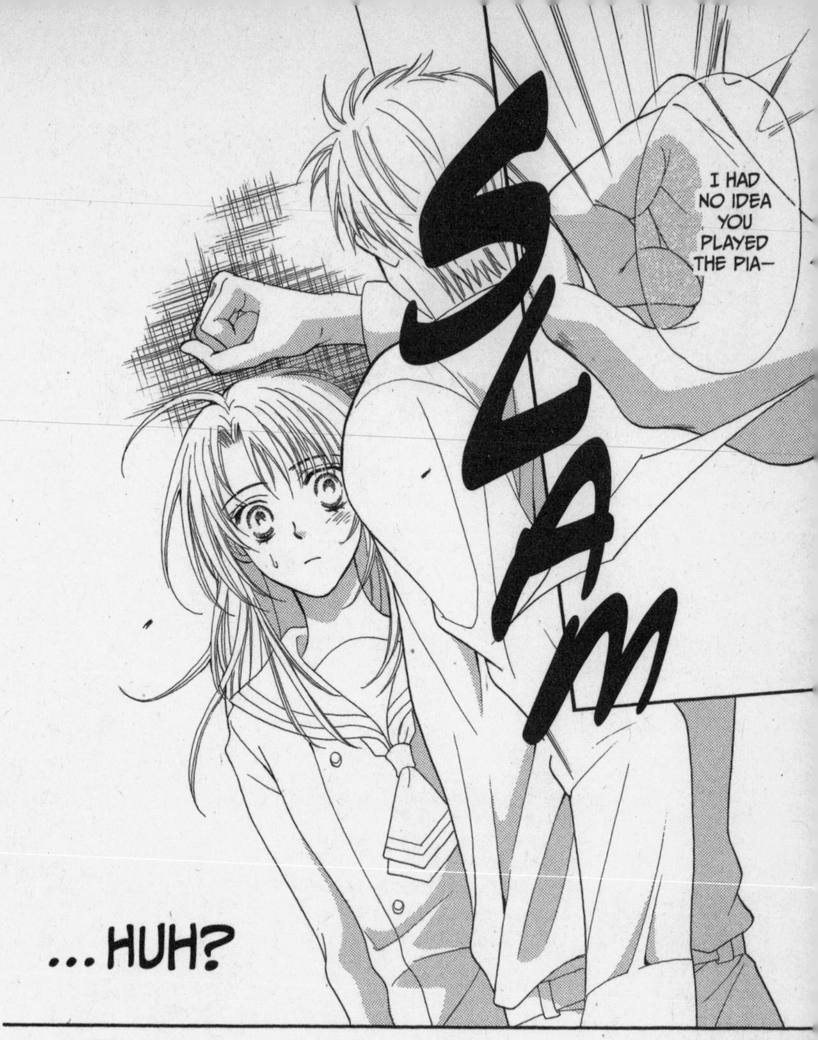
I HAD NO IDEA YOU PLAYED THE PIA—
SLAM
...HUH?
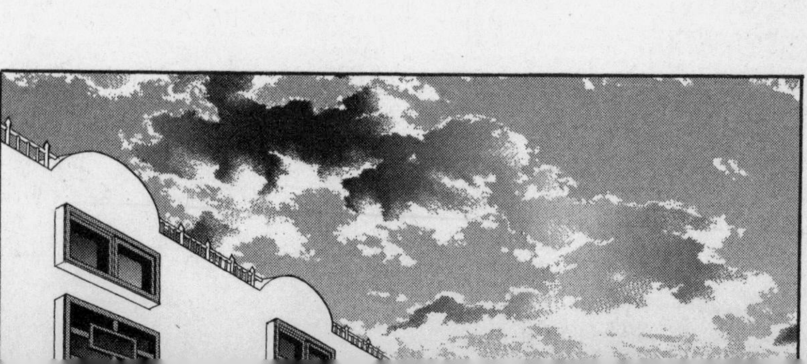

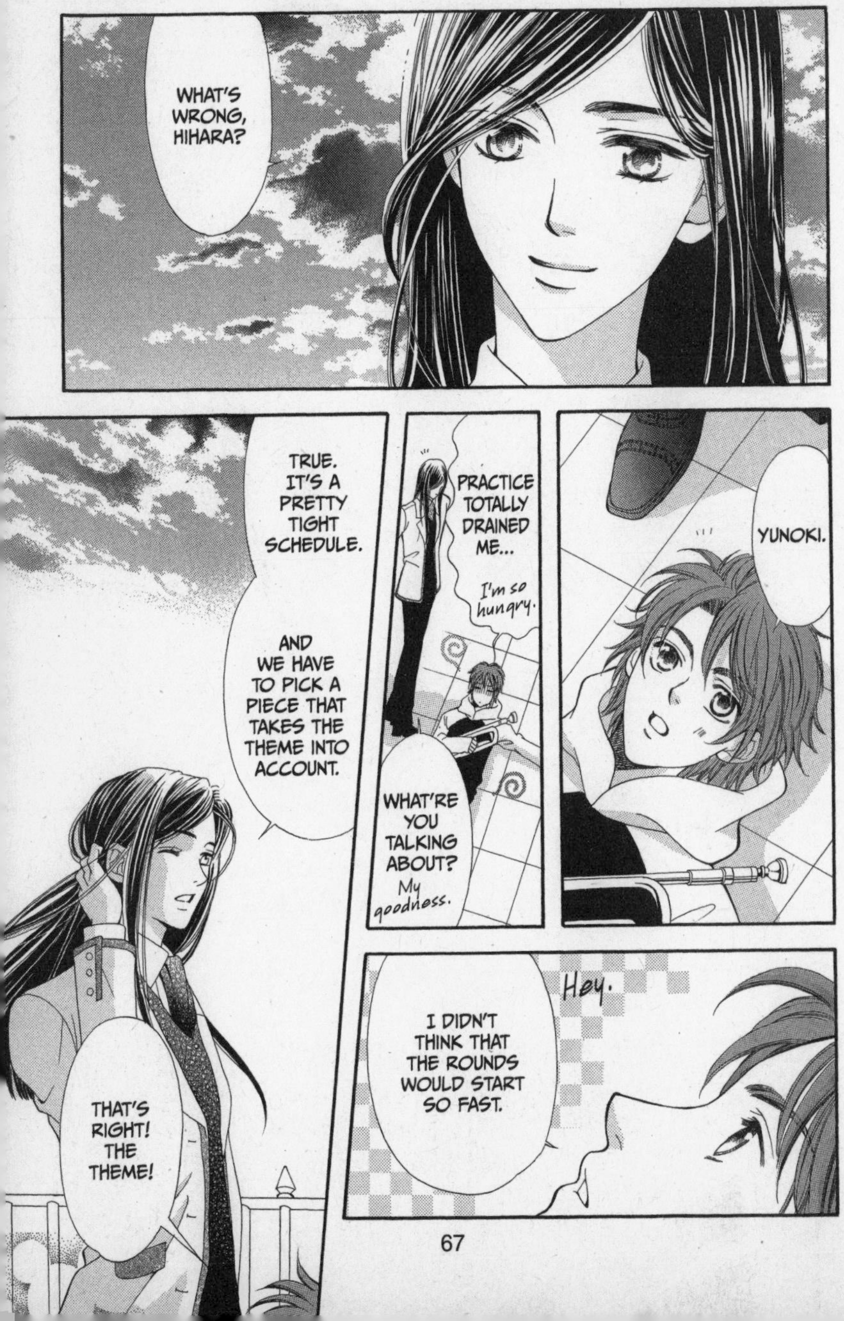
WHAT'S WRONG, HIHARA?
YUNOKI.
PRACTICE TOTALLY DRAINED ME...
I'm so hungry.
WHAT'RE YOU TALKING ABOUT?
My goodness.
Hey.
I DIDN'T THINK THAT THE ROUNDS WOULD START SO FAST.
TRUE. IT'S A PRETTY TIGHT SCHEDULE.
AND WE HAVE TO PICK A PIECE THAT TAKES THE THEME INTO ACCOUNT.
THAT'S RIGHT! THE THEME!

"A BEGINNING"...

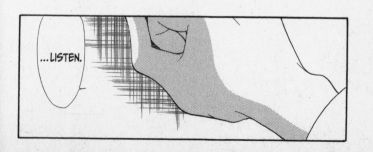

...LISTEN.

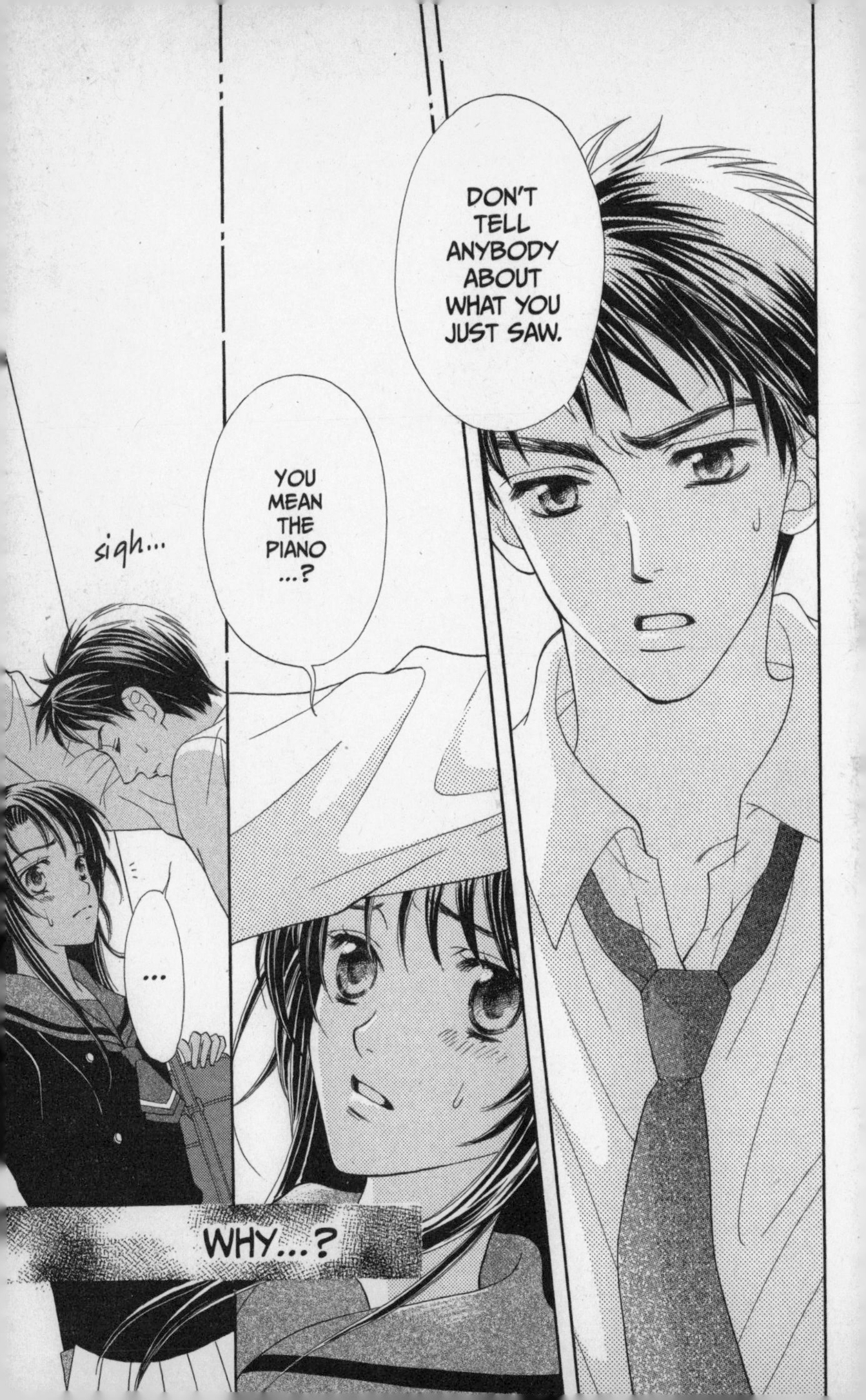
DON'T TELL ANYBODY ABOUT WHAT YOU JUST SAW.
YOU MEAN THE PIANO ...?
sigh...
...
WHY...?

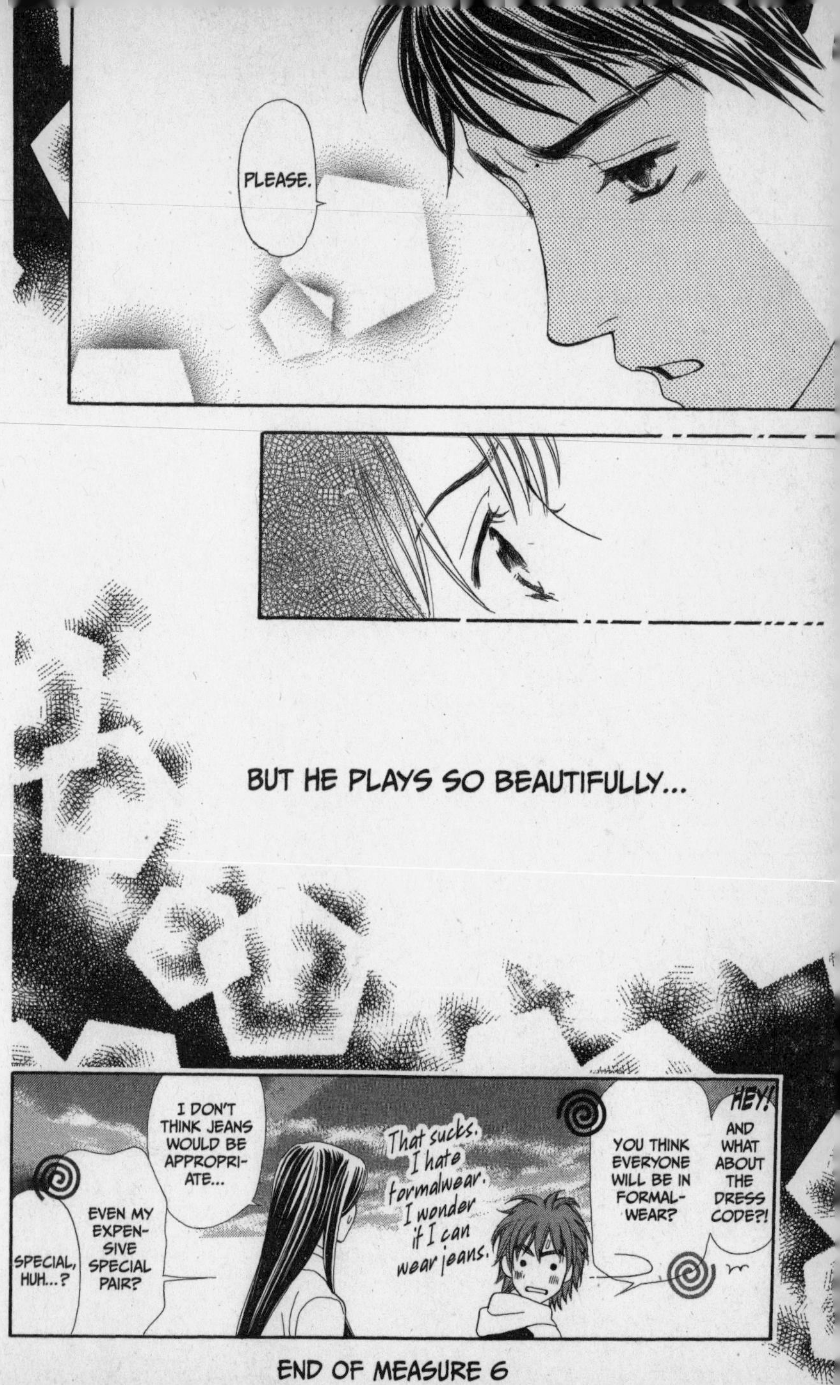
PLEASE.
BUT HE PLAYS SO BEAUTIFULLY...
HEY! AND WHAT ABOUT THE DRESS CODE?!
YOU THINK EVERYONE WILL BE IN FORMALWEAR?
That sucks. I hate formalwear. I wonder if I can wear jeans.
I DON'T THINK JEANS WOULD BE APPROPRIATE...
EVEN MY EXPENSIVE SPECIAL PAIR?
SPECIAL, HUH...?

END OF MEASURE 6

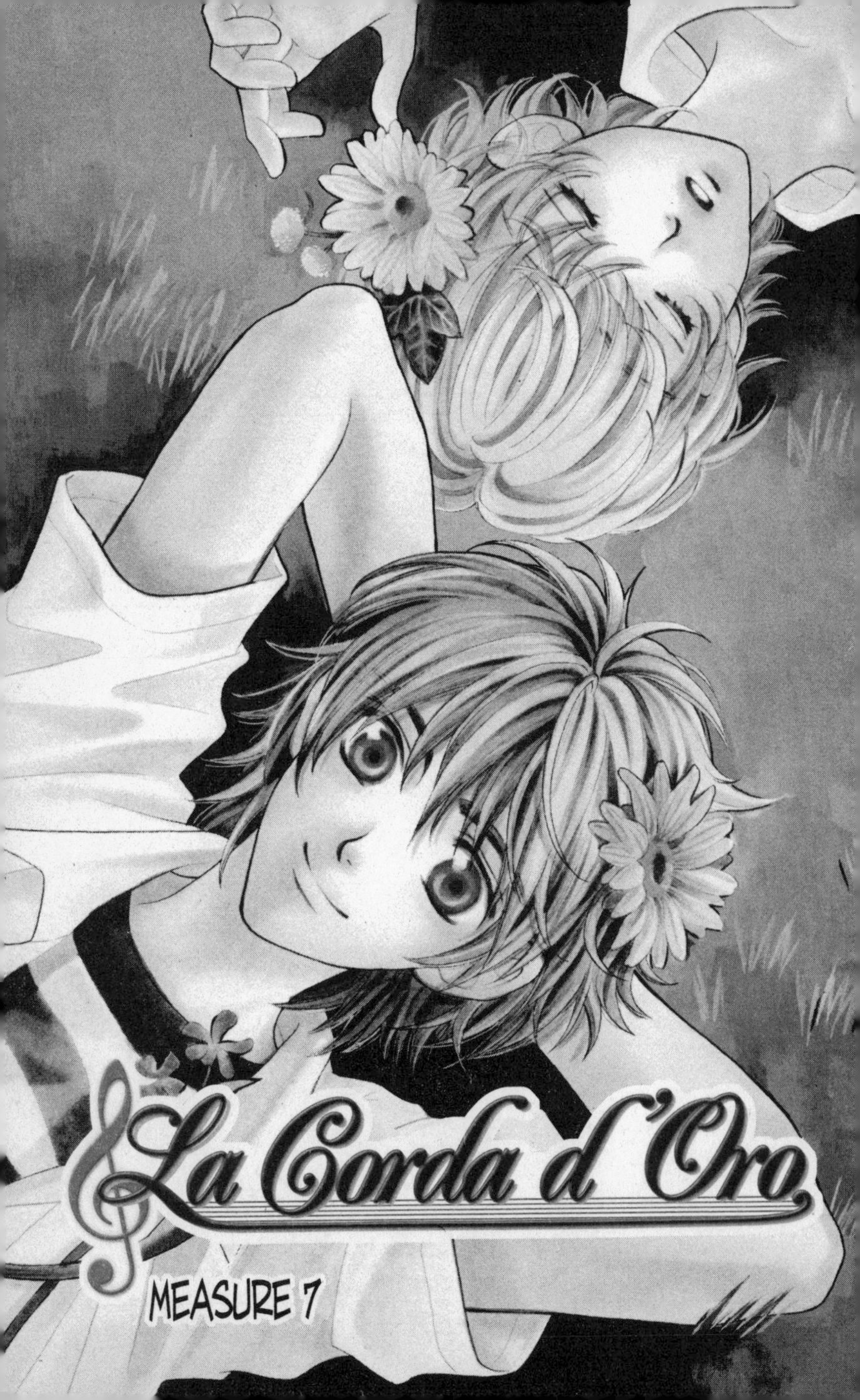
La Corda d'Oro
MEASURE 7

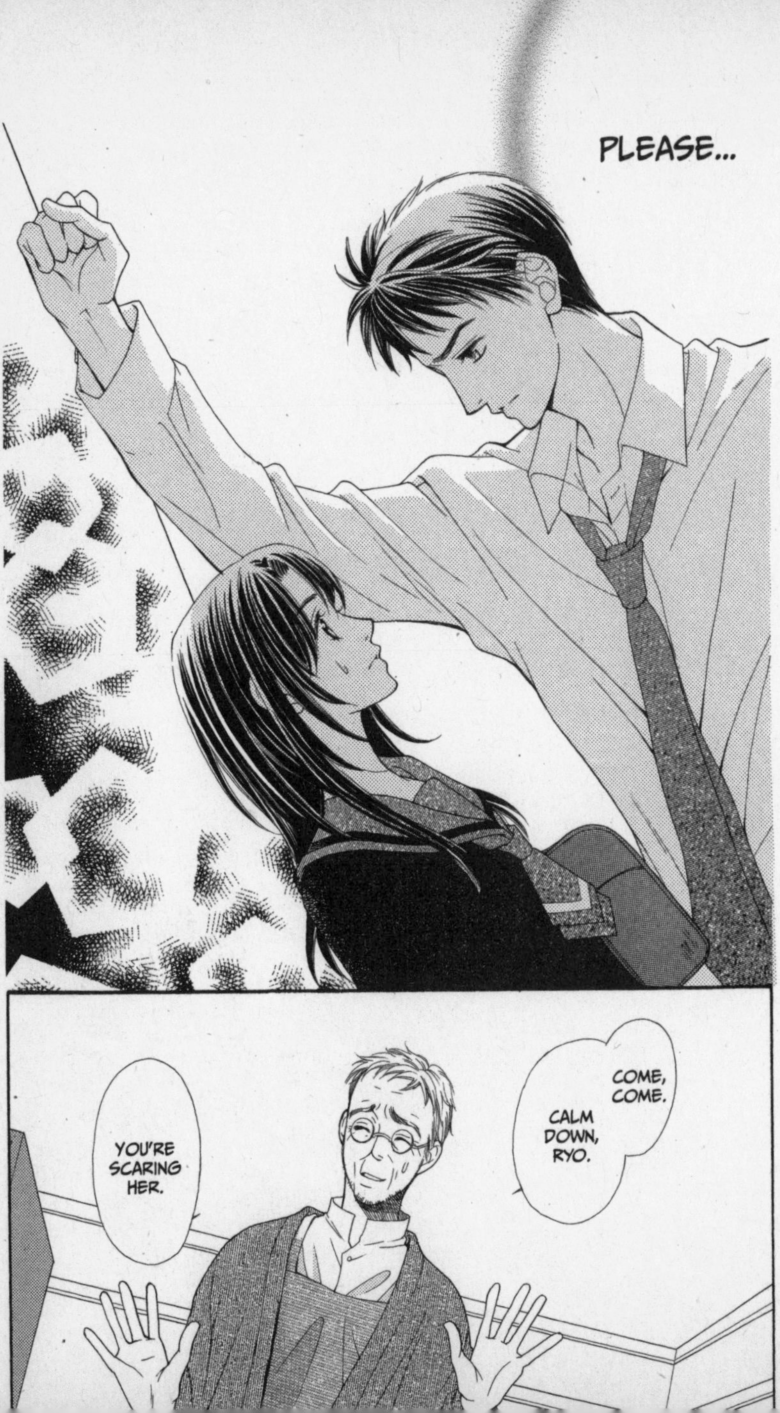
PLEASE...
COME, COME.
CALM DOWN, RYO.
YOU'RE SCARING HER.

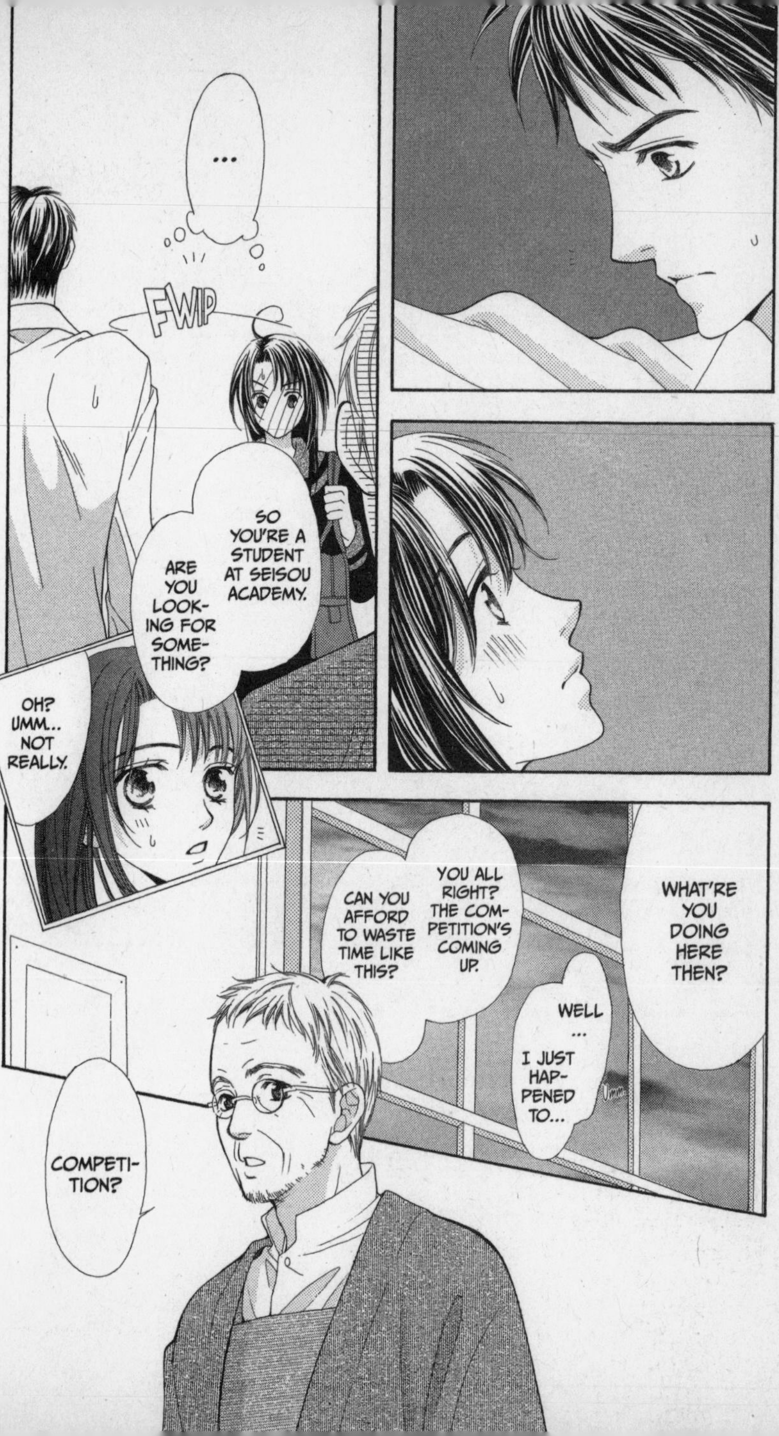
...
FWIP
SO YOU'RE A STUDENT AT SEISOU ACADEMY.
ARE YOU LOOKING FOR SOMETHING?
OH? UMM... NOT REALLY.
WHAT'RE YOU DOING HERE THEN?
WELL ... I JUST HAP-PENED TO...
Umm
YOU ALL RIGHT? THE COM-PETITION'S COMING UP.
CAN YOU AFFORD TO WASTE TIME LIKE THIS?
COMPETI-TION?

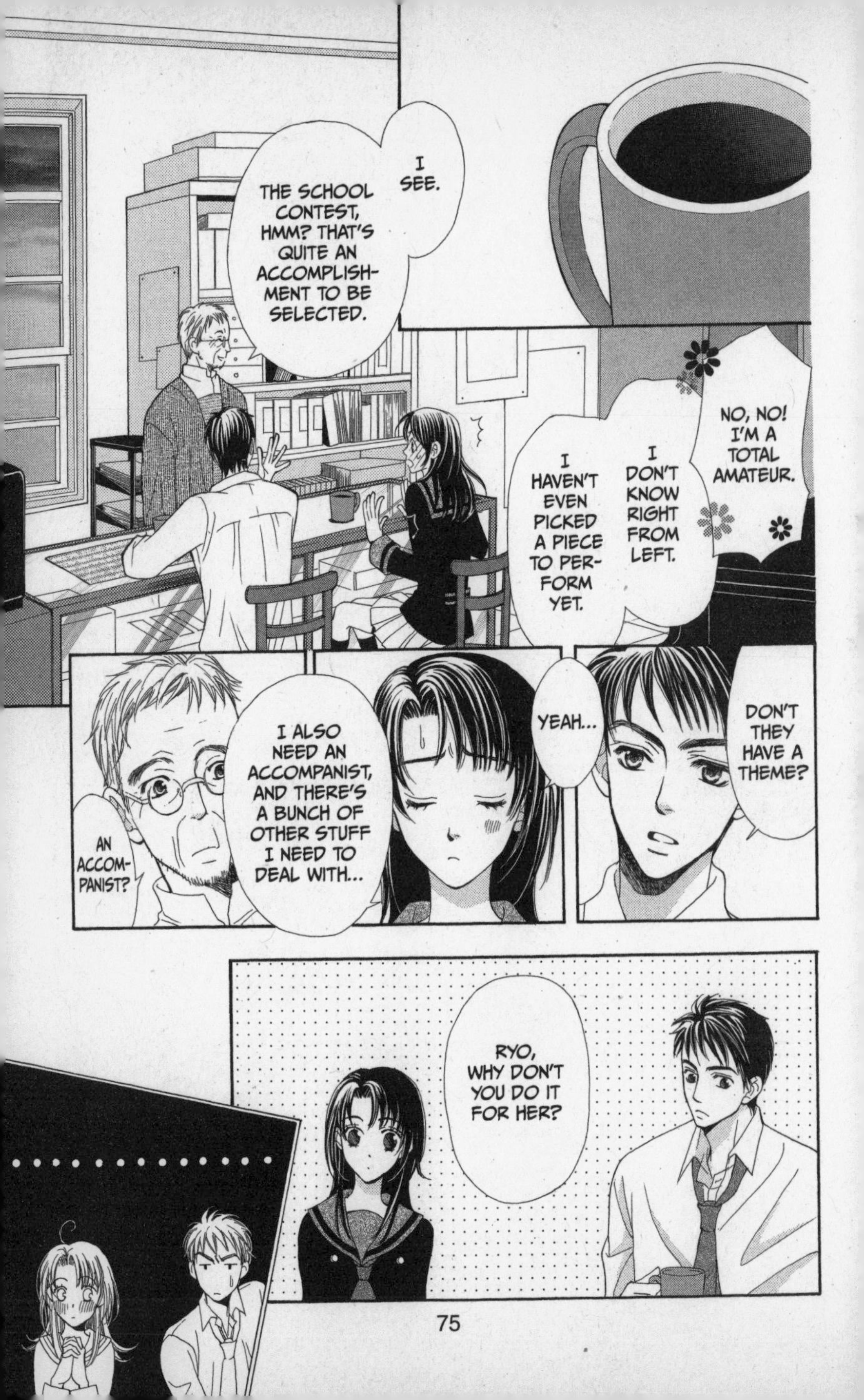
NO, NO! I'M A TOTAL AMATEUR.
I DON'T KNOW RIGHT FROM LEFT.
I HAVEN'T EVEN PICKED A PIECE TO PER-FORM YET.
I SEE.
THE SCHOOL CONTEST, HMM? THAT'S QUITE AN ACCOMPLISH-MENT TO BE SELECTED.
DON'T THEY HAVE A THEME?
YEAH...
I ALSO NEED AN ACCOMPANIST, AND THERE'S A BUNCH OF OTHER STUFF I NEED TO DEAL WITH...
AN ACCOM-PANIST?
RYO, WHY DON'T YOU DO IT FOR HER?
• • • • • • • • • • • • •

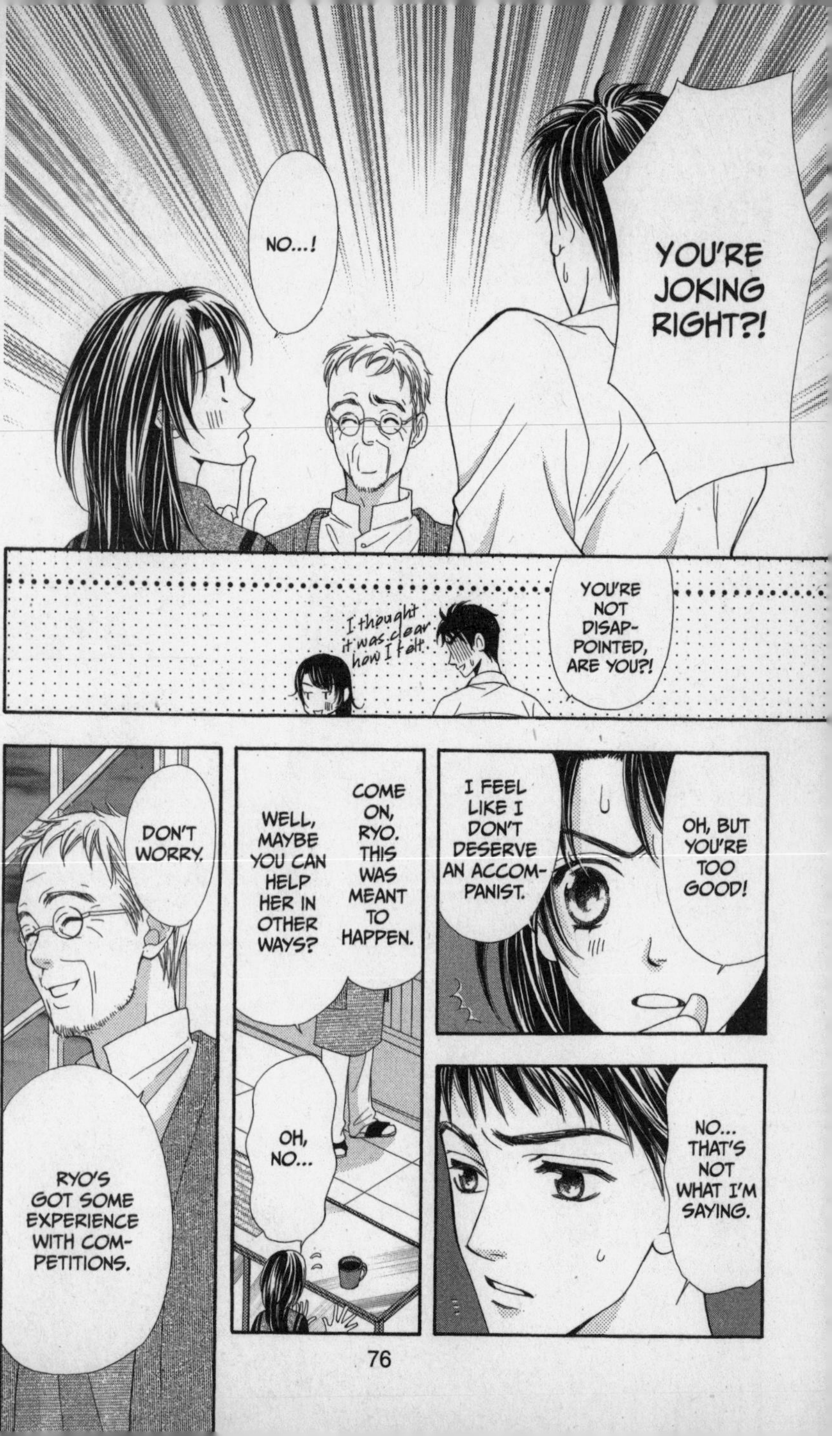
YOU'RE JOKING RIGHT?!
NO...!
YOU'RE NOT DISAP-POINTED, ARE YOU?!
I thought it was clear how I felt.
OH, BUT YOU'RE TOO GOOD!
I FEEL LIKE I DON'T DESERVE AN ACCOM-PANIST.
NO... THAT'S NOT WHAT I'M SAYING.
COME ON, RYO. THIS WAS MEANT TO HAPPEN.
WELL, MAYBE YOU CAN HELP HER IN OTHER WAYS?
OH, NO...
DON'T WORRY.
RYO'S GOT SOME EXPERIENCE WITH COM-PETITIONS.

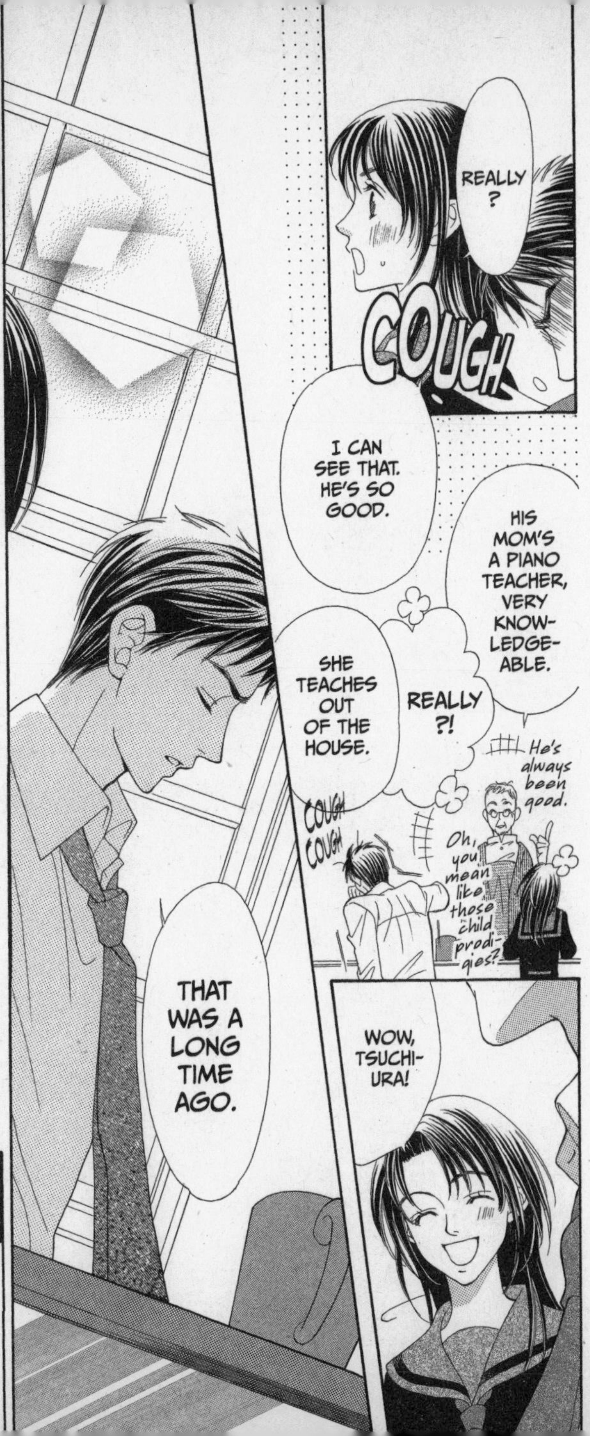
REALLY?
COUGH
I CAN SEE THAT. HE'S SO GOOD.
HIS MOM'S A PIANO TEACHER, VERY KNOW-LEDGE-ABLE.
REALLY?!
SHE TEACHES OUT OF THE HOUSE.
He's always been good.
Oh, you mean like those child prodi-gies?
COUGH COUGH
WOW, TSUCHI-URA!
THAT WAS A LONG TIME AGO.

Moving right along into Measure 7. Kazuki and Keiichi are on the cover. Unlike the second-years, a frame with these two was so carefree and I really liked it. A precious pair.

The story progresses, focusing on Ryotaro and Kahoko. The cover pair only have minor roles...

So Kazuki/Keiichi fans are rightfully enraged (profuse apologies).

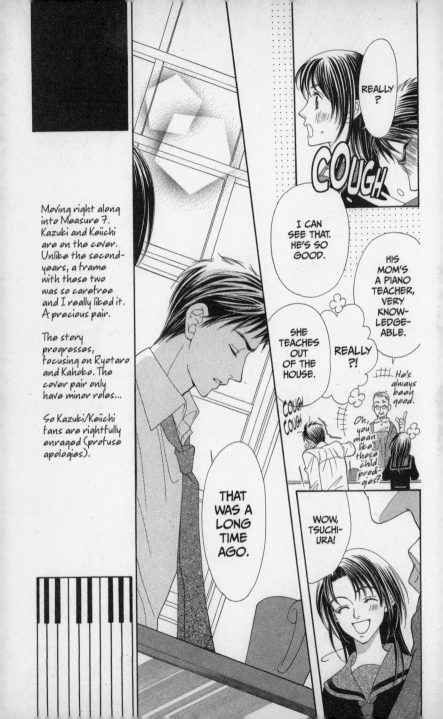

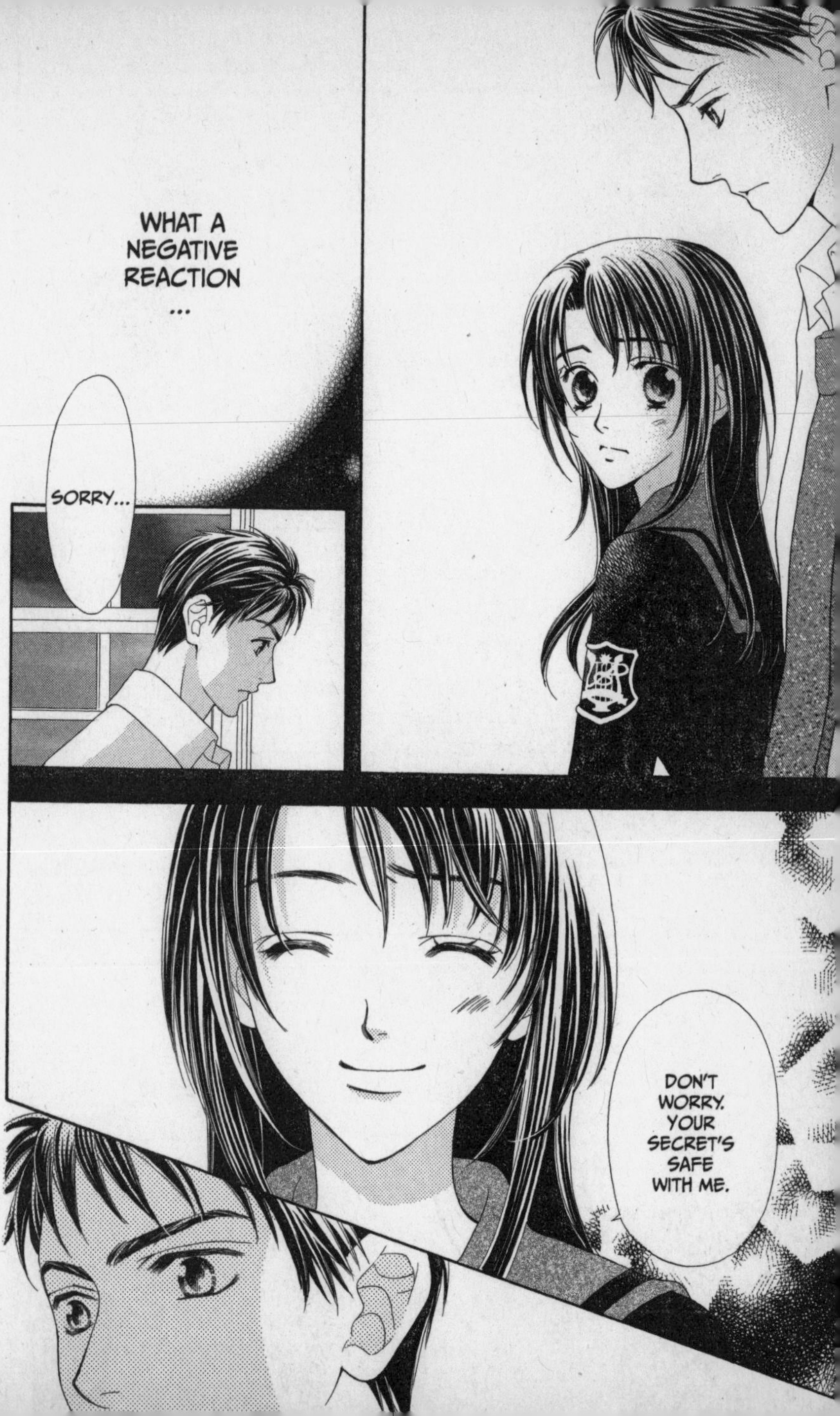
WHAT A NEGATIVE REACTION ...
SORRY...
DON'T WORRY. YOUR SECRET'S SAFE WITH ME.

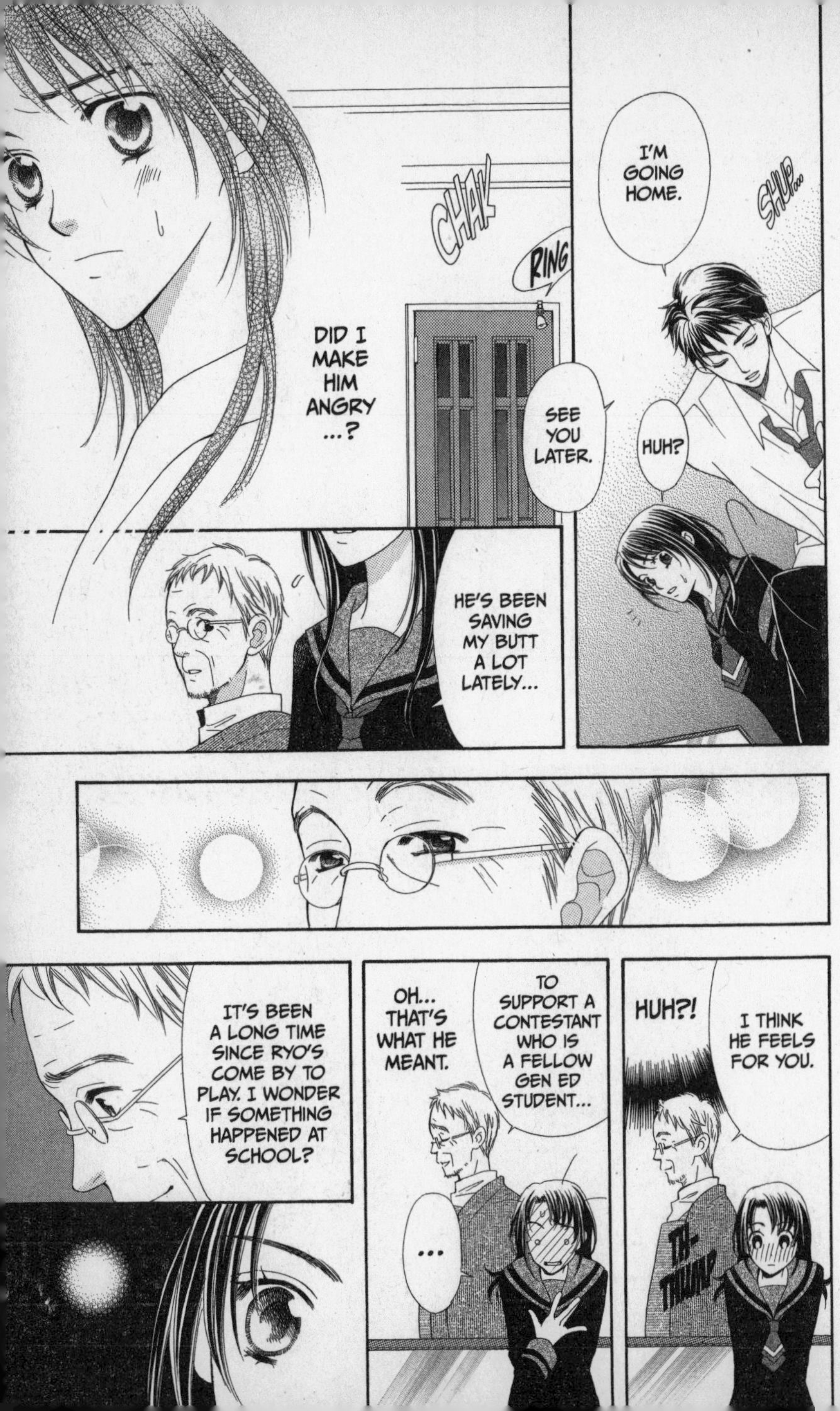
I'M GOING HOME.
SHUP...
HUH?
CHAK
RING
SEE YOU LATER.
DID I MAKE HIM ANGRY ...?
HE'S BEEN SAVING MY BUTT A LOT LATELY...
I THINK HE FEELS FOR YOU.
HUH?!
TH-THUMP
TO SUPPORT A CONTESTANT WHO IS A FELLOW GEN ED STUDENT...
OH... THAT'S WHAT HE MEANT.
...
IT'S BEEN A LONG TIME SINCE RYO'S COME BY TO PLAY. I WONDER IF SOMETHING HAPPENED AT SCHOOL?

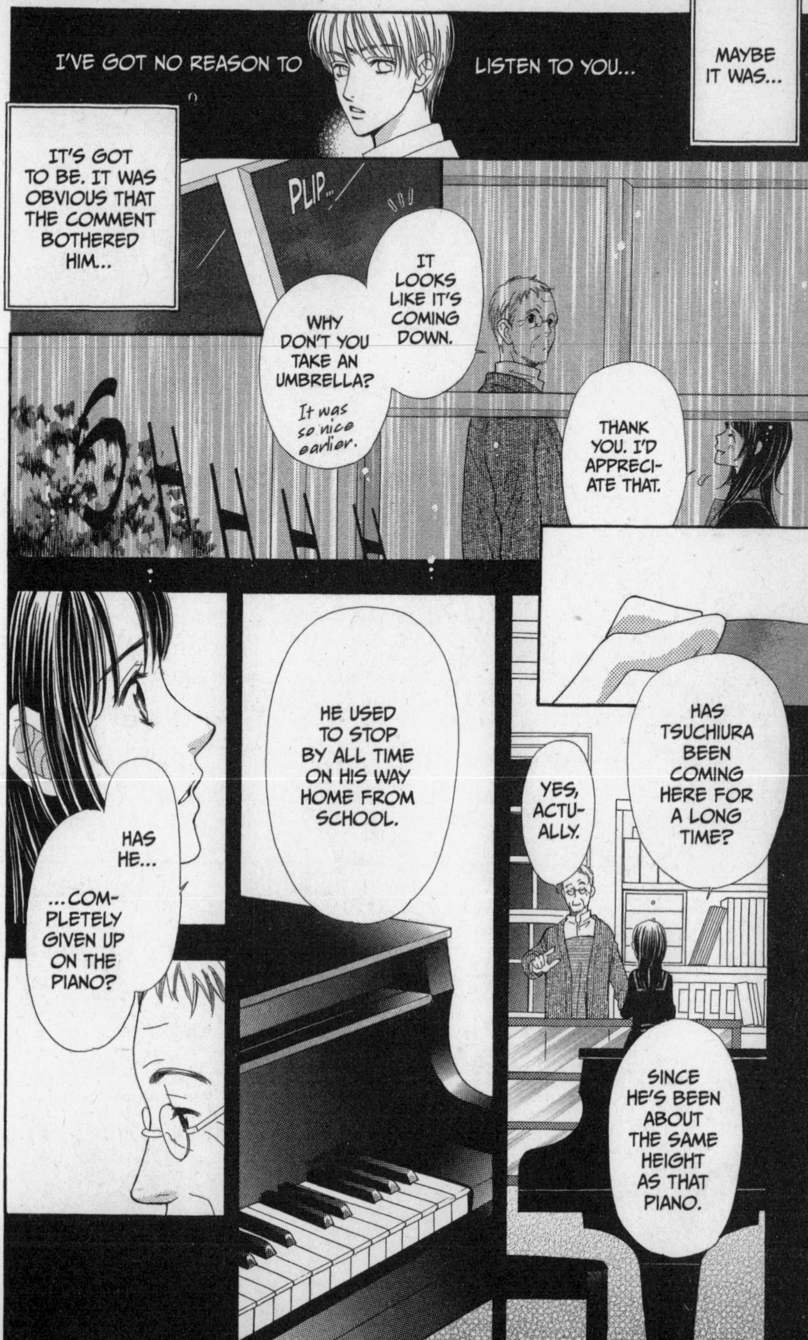
MAYBE IT WAS...
I'VE GOT NO REASON TO
LISTEN TO YOU...
IT'S GOT TO BE. IT WAS OBVIOUS THAT THE COMMENT BOTHERED HIM...
PLIP...
IT LOOKS LIKE IT'S COMING DOWN.
WHY DON'T YOU TAKE AN UMBRELLA?
It was so nice earlier.
THANK YOU. I'D APPRECIATE THAT.
HAS TSUCHIURA BEEN COMING HERE FOR A LONG TIME?
YES, ACTUALLY.
SINCE HE'S BEEN ABOUT THE SAME HEIGHT AS THAT PIANO.
HE USED TO STOP BY ALL TIME ON HIS WAY HOME FROM SCHOOL.
HAS HE...
...COMPLETELY GIVEN UP ON THE PIANO?

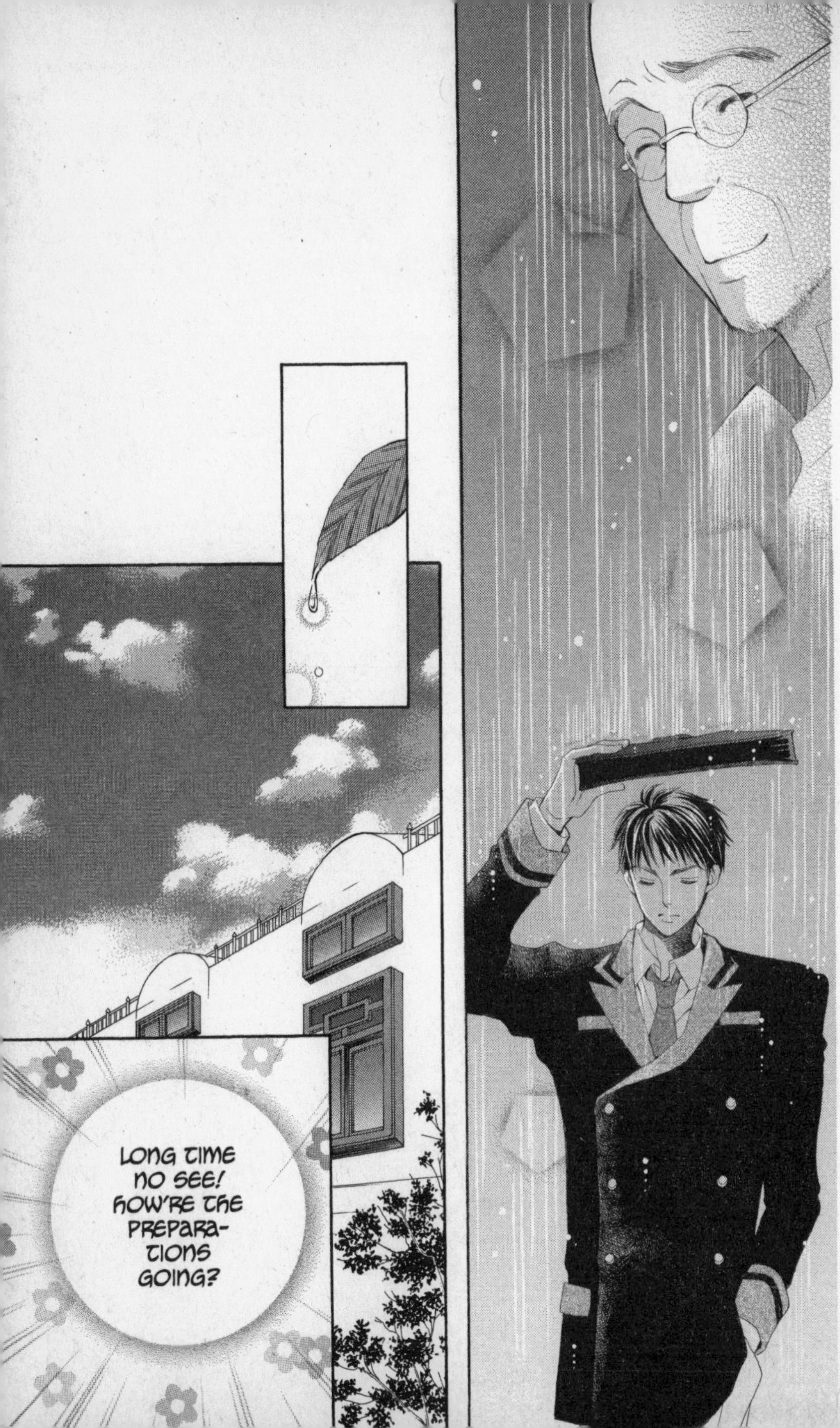
LONG TIME NO SEE! HOW'RE THE PREPARA-TIONS GOING?

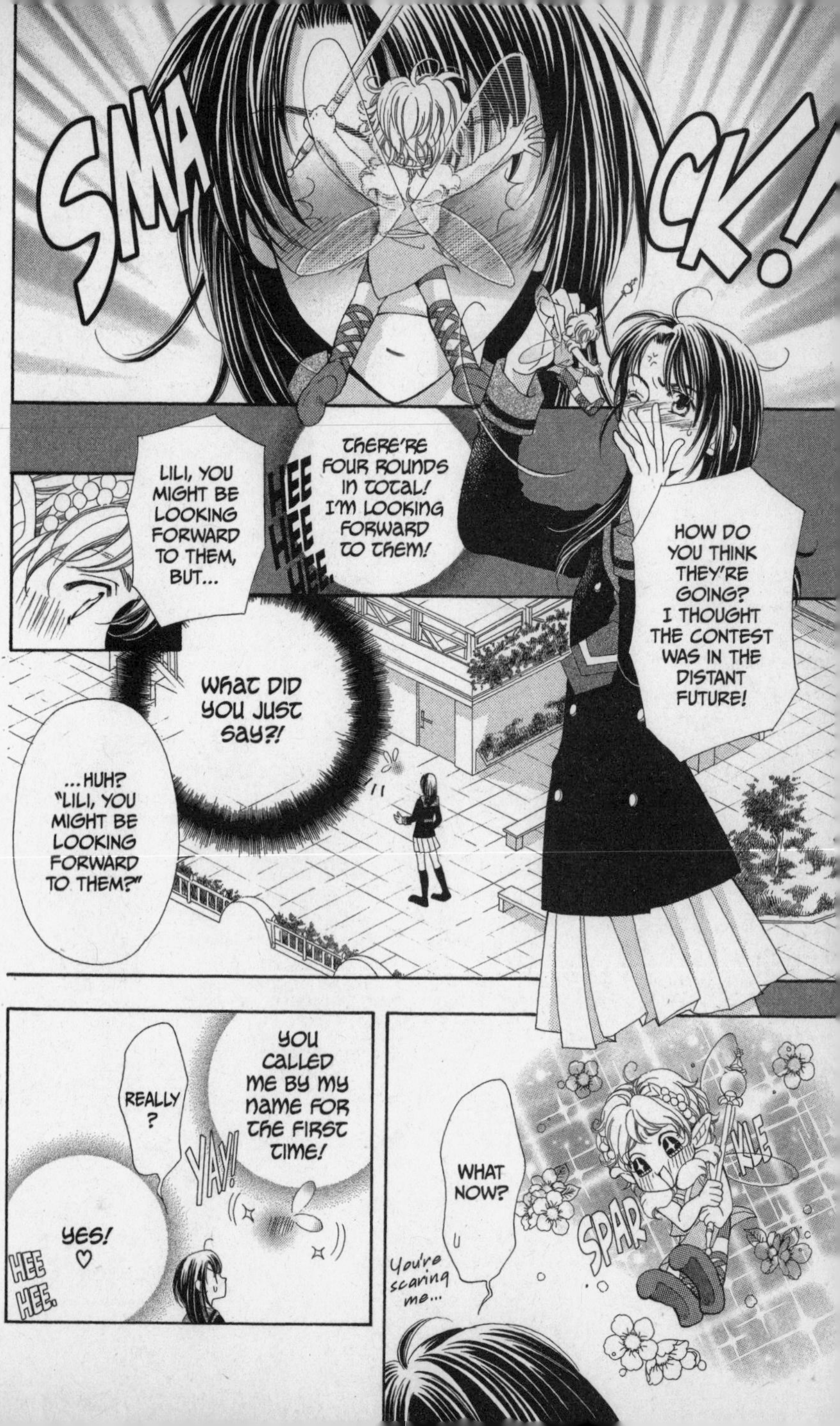
SMACK!!
HOW DO YOU THINK THEY'RE GOING? I THOUGHT THE CONTEST WAS IN THE DISTANT FUTURE!
THERE'RE FOUR ROUNDS IN TOTAL! I'M LOOKING FORWARD TO THEM!
HEE HEE HEE.
LILI, YOU MIGHT BE LOOKING FORWARD TO THEM, BUT...
WHAT DID YOU JUST SAY?!
...HUH? "LILI, YOU MIGHT BE LOOKING FORWARD TO THEM?"
SPARKLE
WHAT NOW?
You're scaring me...
YOU CALLED ME BY MY NAME FOR THE FIRST TIME!
YAY!
REALLY?
YES! ♡
HEE HEE.

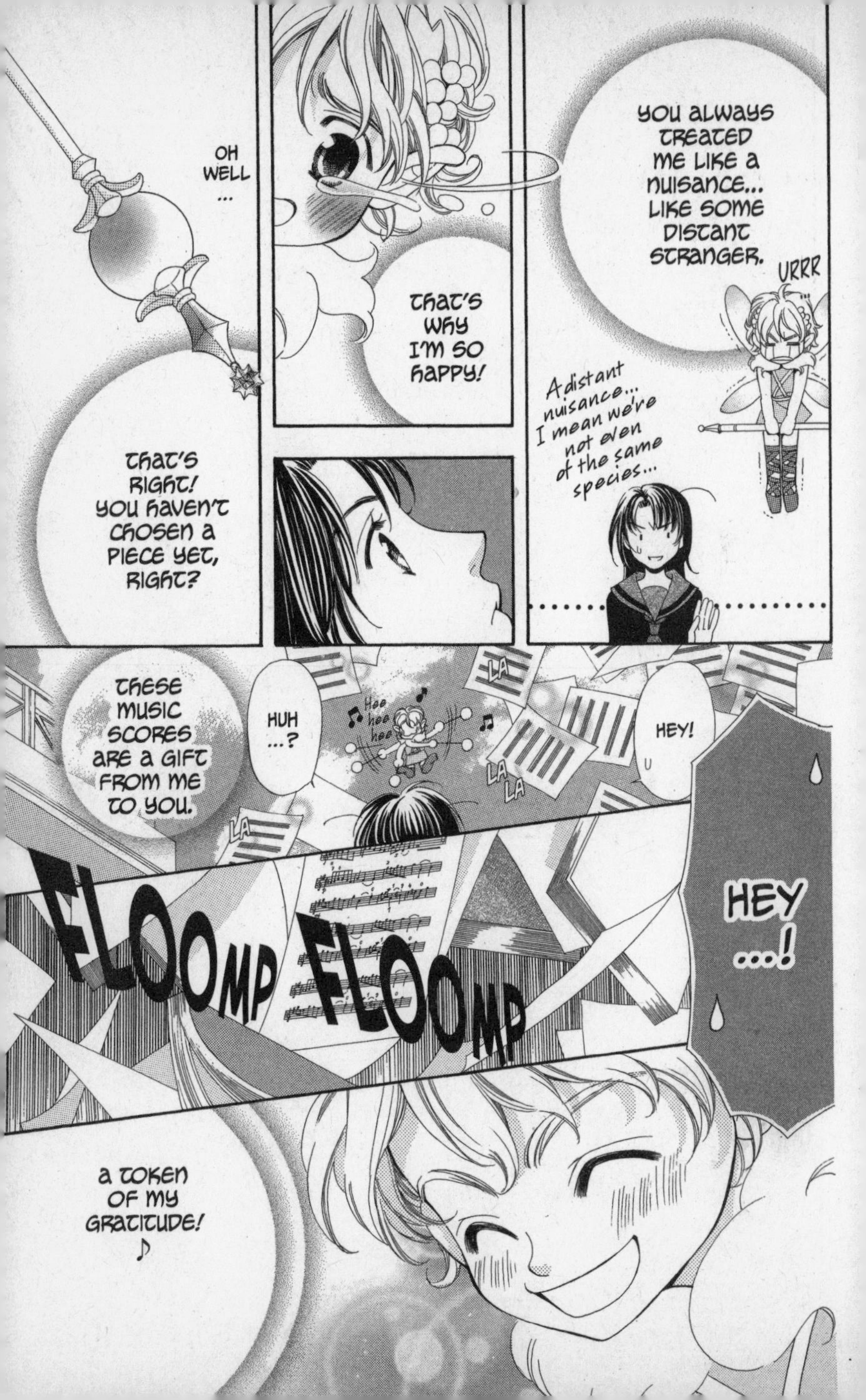
YOU ALWAYS TREATED ME LIKE A NUISANCE... LIKE SOME DISTANT STRANGER.
URRR...
A distant nuisance... I mean we're not even of the same species...
THAT'S WHY I'M SO HAPPY!
OH WELL...
THAT'S RIGHT! YOU HAVEN'T CHOSEN A PIECE YET, RIGHT?
HEY!
LA
LA LA
Hee hee hee
HUH...?
THESE MUSIC SCORES ARE A GIFT FROM ME TO YOU.
LA
HEY...!
FLOOMP FLOOMP
A TOKEN OF MY GRATITUDE! ♪

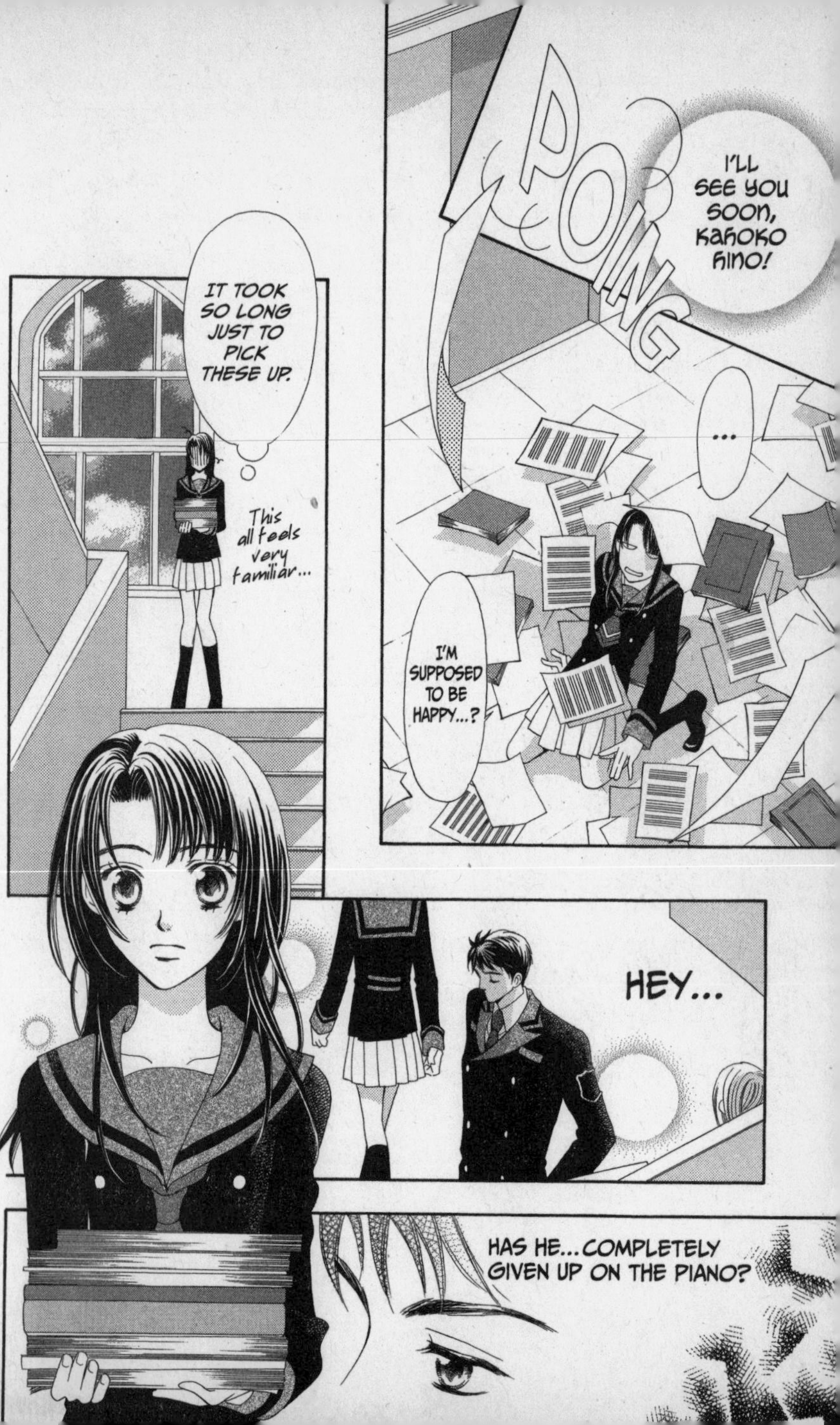
I'LL SEE YOU SOON, KAHOKO HINO!
POING
...
I'M SUPPOSED TO BE HAPPY...?
IT TOOK SO LONG JUST TO PICK THESE UP.
This all feels very familiar...
HEY...
HAS HE...COMPLETELY GIVEN UP ON THE PIANO?

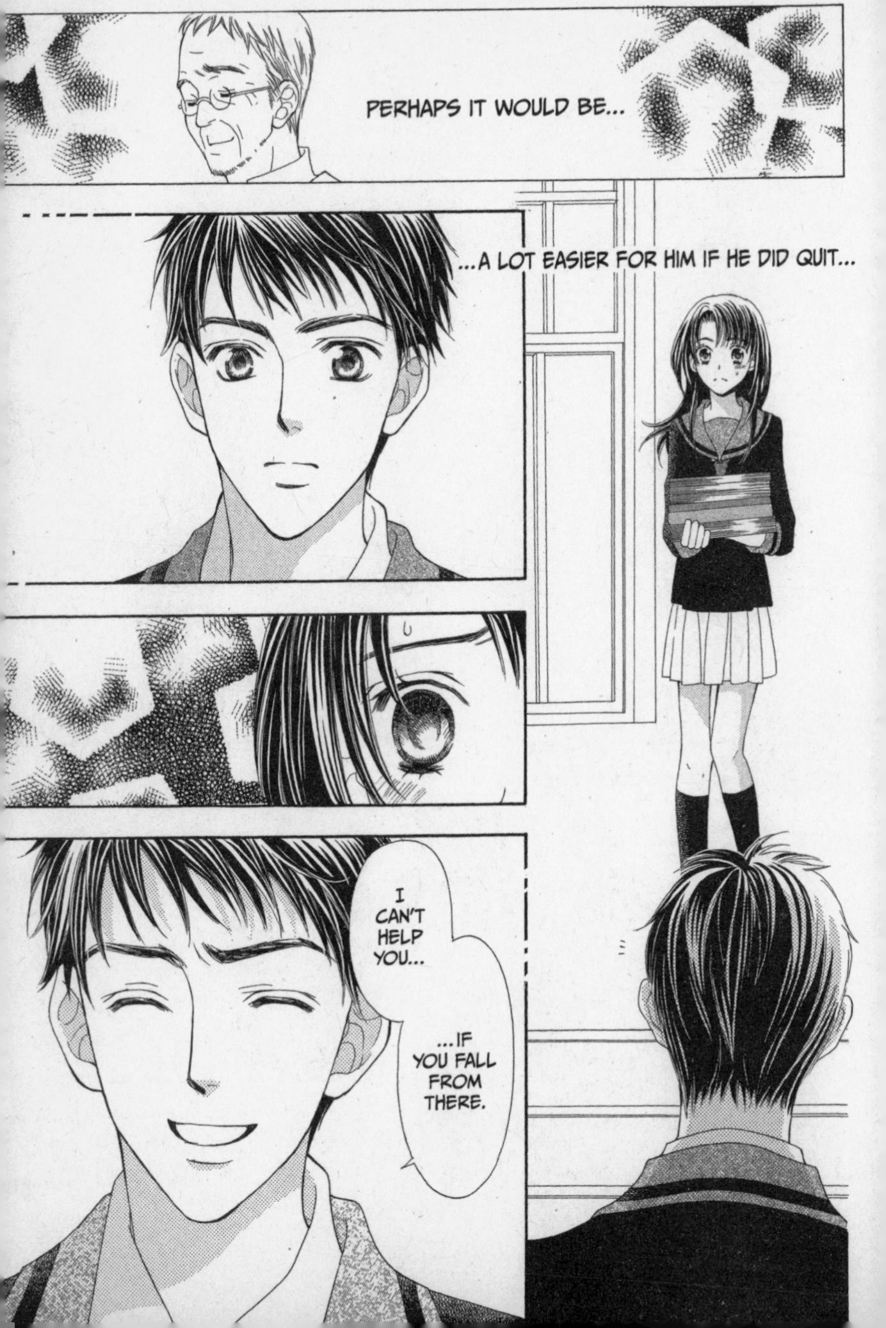
PERHAPS IT WOULD BE...
...A LOT EASIER FOR HIM IF HE DID QUIT...
I CAN'T HELP YOU...
...IF YOU FALL FROM THERE.

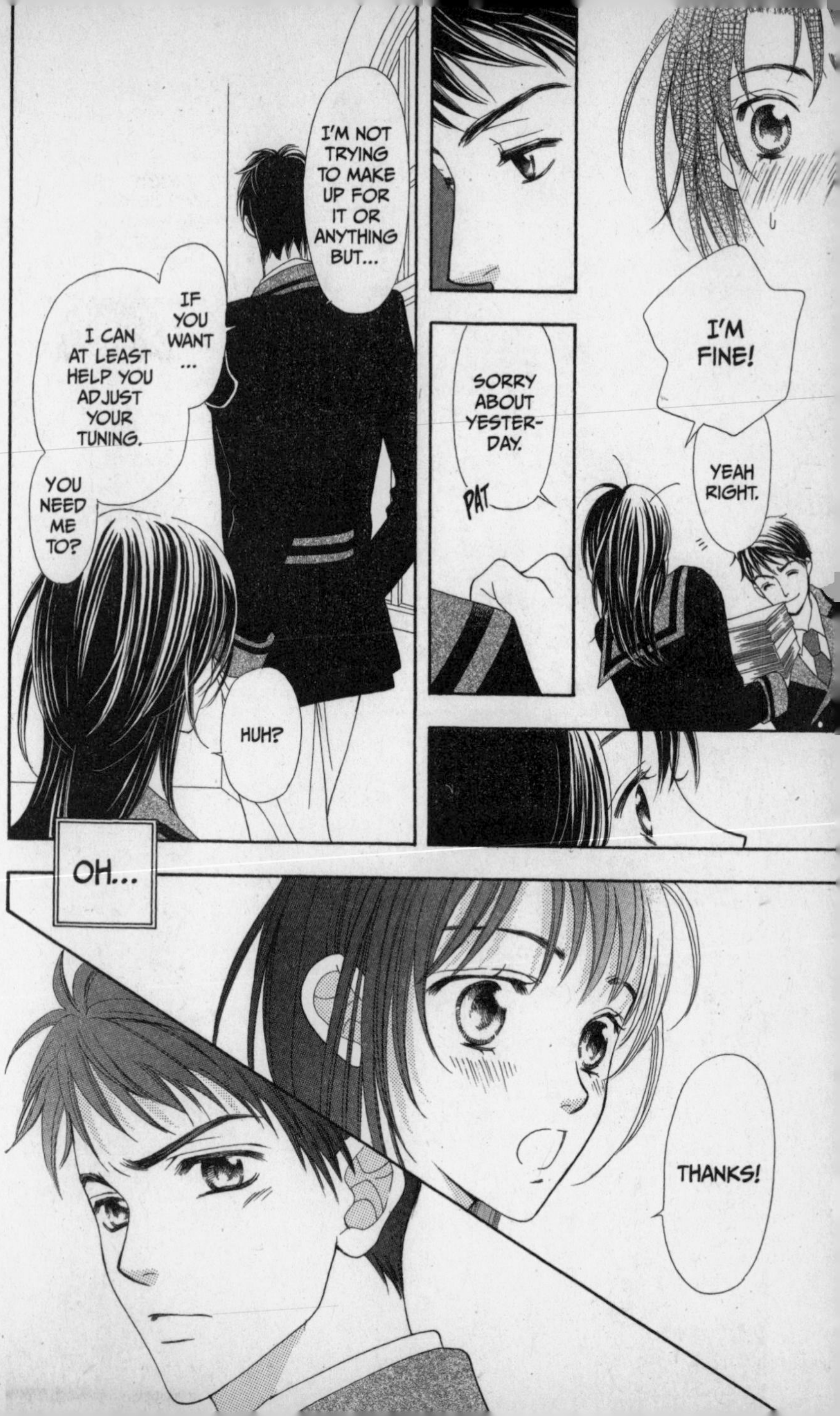
I'M FINE!
YEAH RIGHT.
SORRY ABOUT YESTER-DAY.
PAT
I'M NOT TRYING TO MAKE UP FOR IT OR ANYTHING BUT...
IF YOU WANT ...
I CAN AT LEAST HELP YOU ADJUST YOUR TUNING.
YOU NEED ME TO?
HUH?
OH...
THANKS!

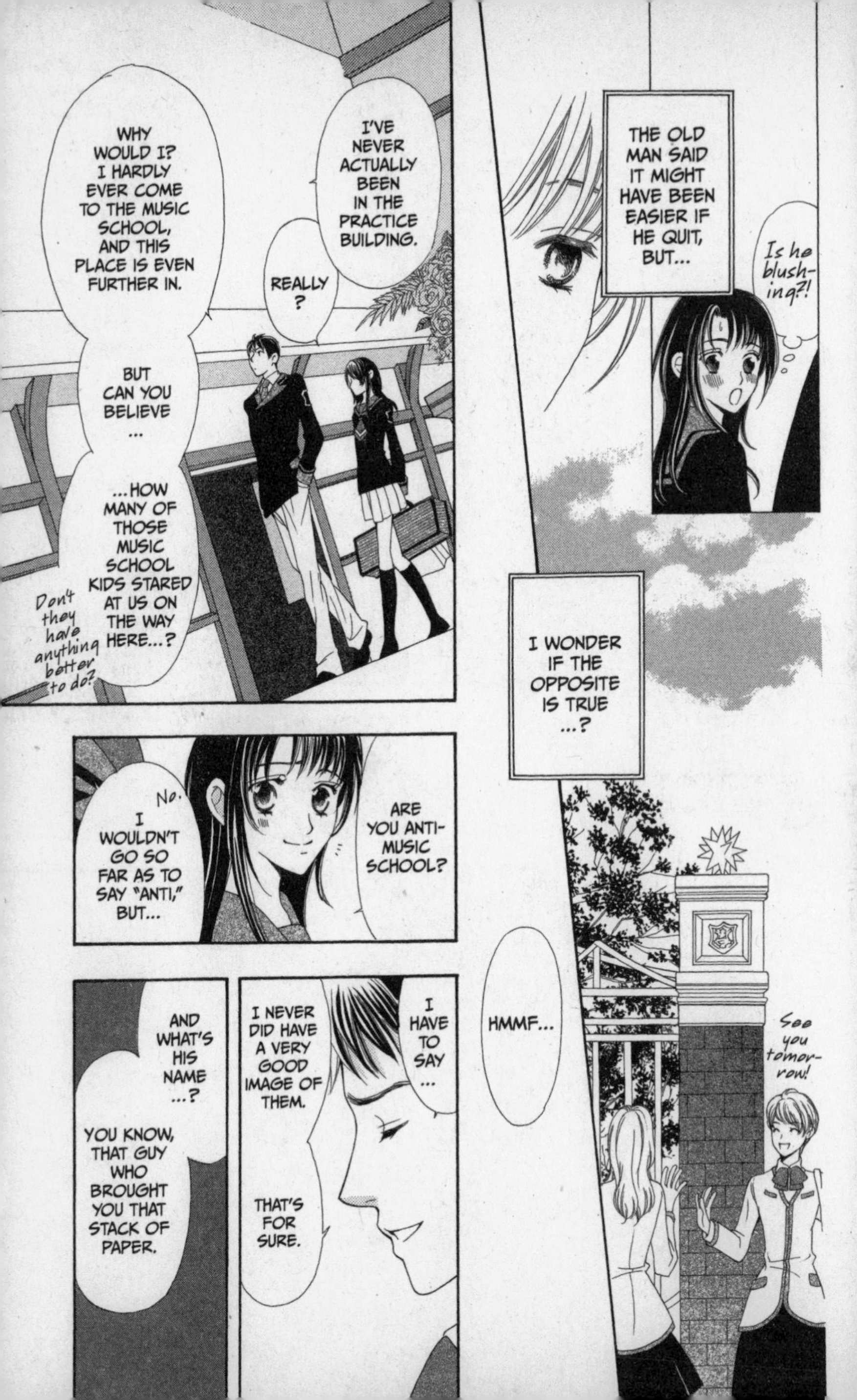
THE OLD MAN SAID IT MIGHT HAVE BEEN EASIER IF HE QUIT, BUT...
Is he blushing?!
I WONDER IF THE OPPOSITE IS TRUE ...?
See you tomorrow!
HMMF...
I'VE NEVER ACTUALLY BEEN IN THE PRACTICE BUILDING.
REALLY ?
WHY WOULD I? I HARDLY EVER COME TO THE MUSIC SCHOOL, AND THIS PLACE IS EVEN FURTHER IN.
BUT CAN YOU BELIEVE ...
...HOW MANY OF THOSE MUSIC SCHOOL KIDS STARED AT US ON THE WAY HERE...?
Don't they have anything better to do?
ARE YOU ANTI-MUSIC SCHOOL?
No.
I WOULDN'T GO SO FAR AS TO SAY "ANTI," BUT...
I HAVE TO SAY ...
I NEVER DID HAVE A VERY GOOD IMAGE OF THEM.
THAT'S FOR SURE.
AND WHAT'S HIS NAME ...?
YOU KNOW, THAT GUY WHO BROUGHT YOU THAT STACK OF PAPER.

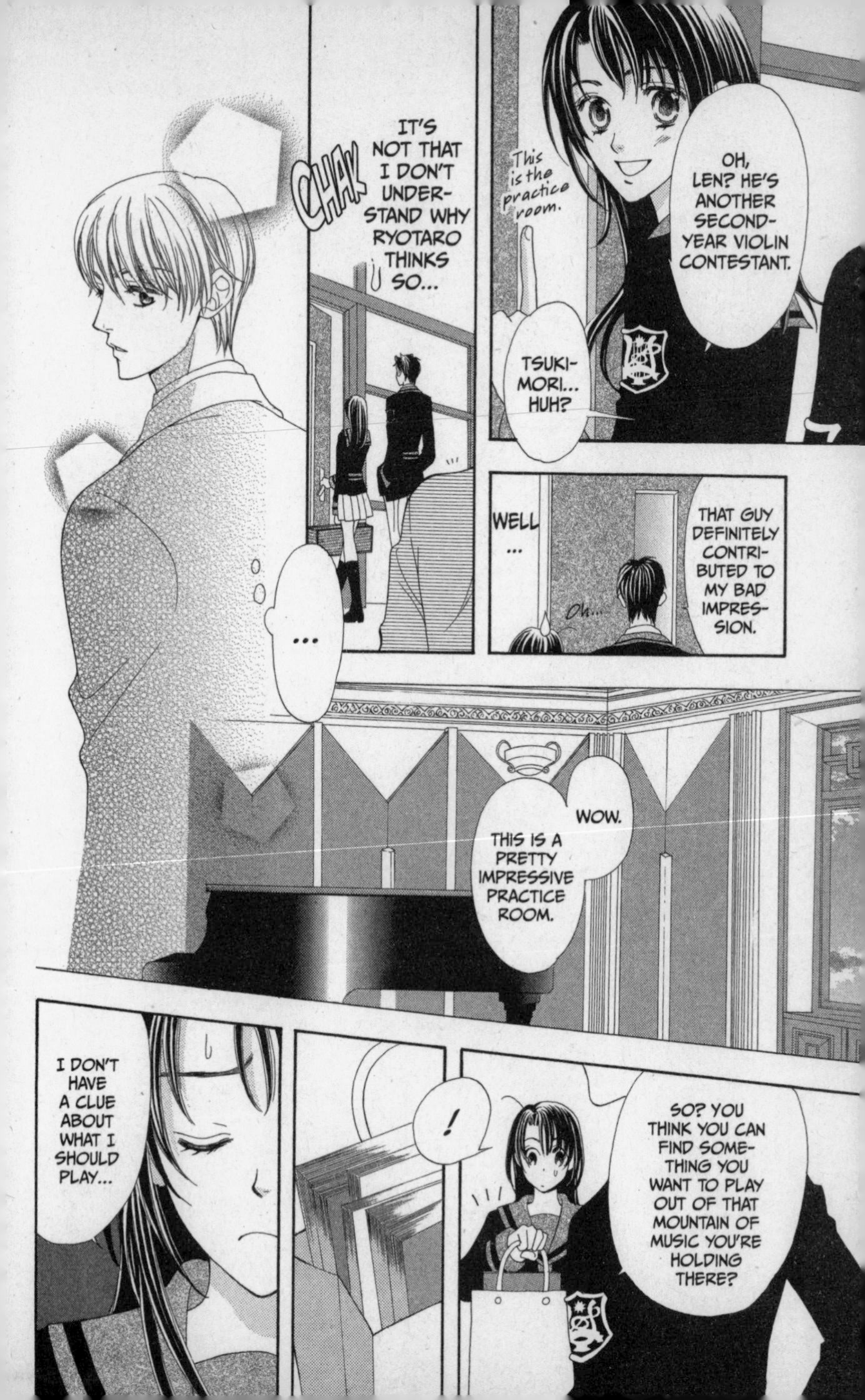

OH, LEN? HE'S ANOTHER SECOND-YEAR VIOLIN CONTESTANT.
This is the practice room.
TSUKI-MORI... HUH?
THAT GUY DEFINITELY CONTRI-BUTED TO MY BAD IMPRES-SION.
WELL...
Oh...
IT'S NOT THAT I DON'T UNDER-STAND WHY RYOTARO THINKS SO...
CHAK
...
WOW.
THIS IS A PRETTY IMPRESSIVE PRACTICE ROOM.
SO? YOU THINK YOU CAN FIND SOME-THING YOU WANT TO PLAY OUT OF THAT MOUNTAIN OF MUSIC YOU'RE HOLDING THERE?
!
I DON'T HAVE A CLUE ABOUT WHAT I SHOULD PLAY...

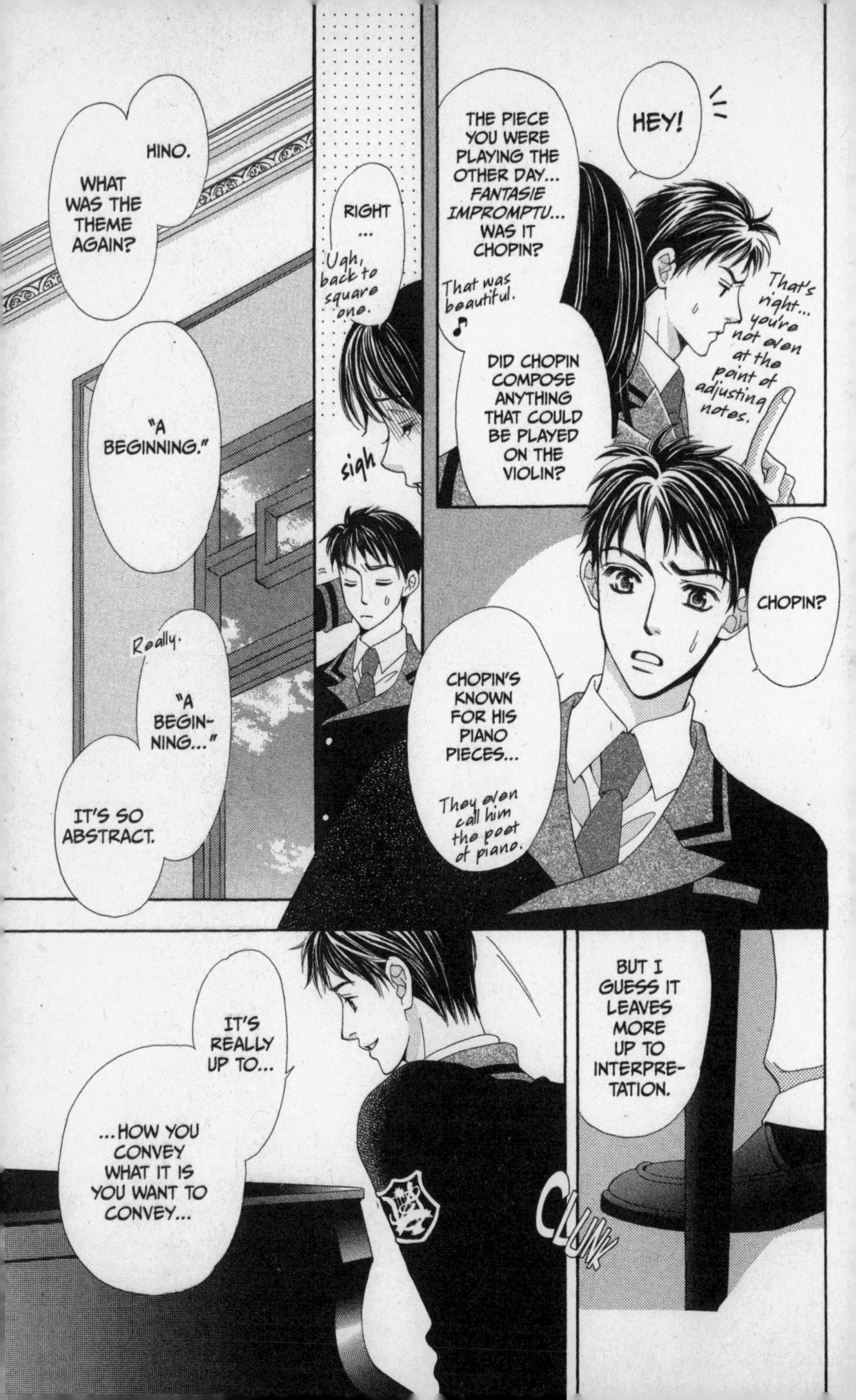
HEY!
THE PIECE YOU WERE PLAYING THE OTHER DAY... *FANTASIE IMPROMPTU*... WAS IT CHOPIN?
That was beautiful. ♪
DID CHOPIN COMPOSE ANYTHING THAT COULD BE PLAYED ON THE VIOLIN?
That's right... you're not even at the point of adjusting notes.
CHOPIN?
CHOPIN'S KNOWN FOR HIS PIANO PIECES...
They even call him the poet of piano.
RIGHT...
Ugh, back to square one.
sigh
HINO.
WHAT WAS THE THEME AGAIN?
"A BEGINNING."
Really.
"A BEGIN-NING..."
IT'S SO ABSTRACT.
BUT I GUESS IT LEAVES MORE UP TO INTERPRE-TATION.
CLUNK
IT'S REALLY UP TO...
...HOW YOU CONVEY WHAT IT IS YOU WANT TO CONVEY...

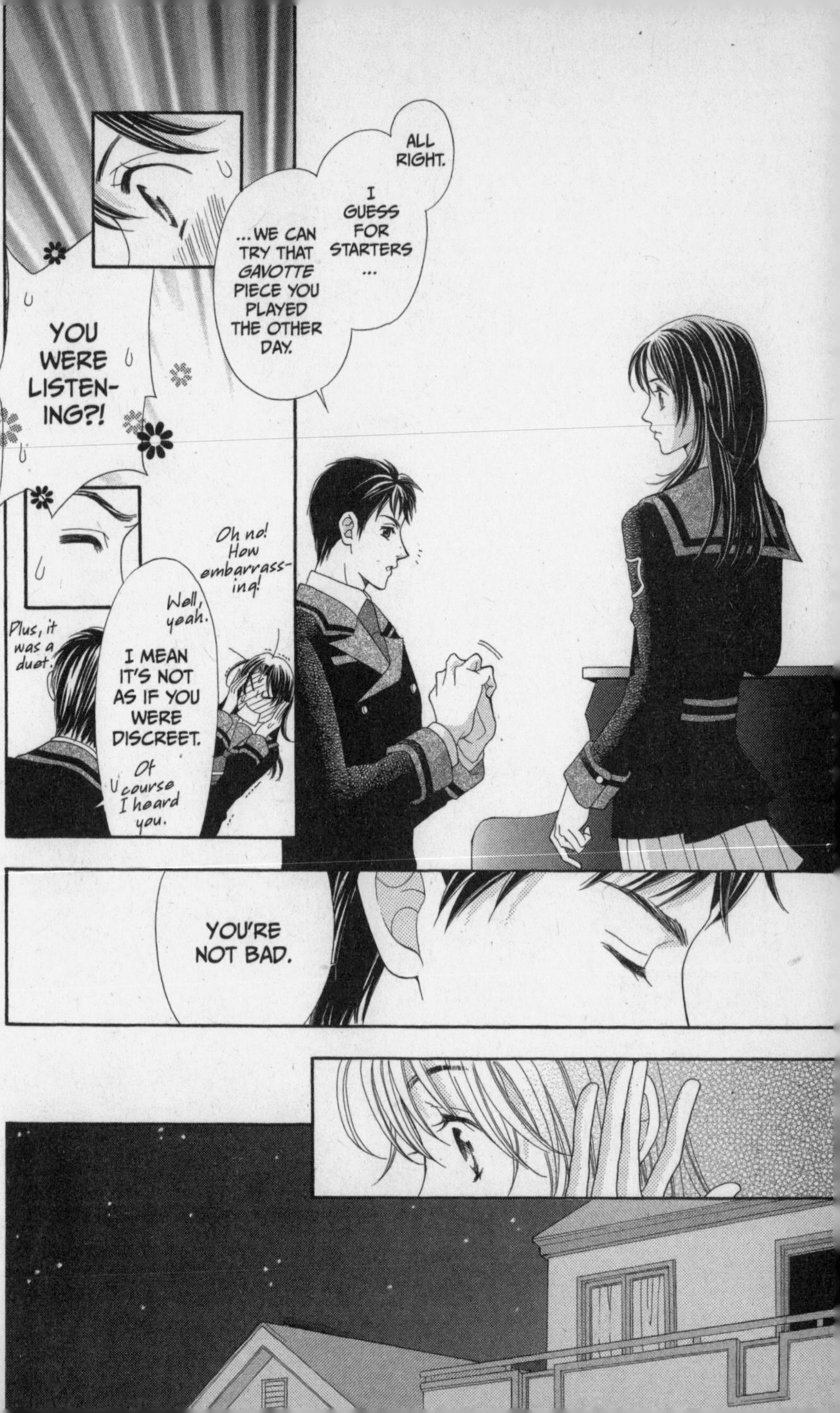
ALL RIGHT.
I GUESS FOR STARTERS ...
...WE CAN TRY THAT GAVOTTE PIECE YOU PLAYED THE OTHER DAY.
YOU WERE LISTEN-ING?!
Oh no! How embarrass-ing!
Well, yeah.
I MEAN IT'S NOT AS IF YOU WERE DISCREET.
Of course I heard you.
Plus, it was a duet.
YOU'RE NOT BAD.

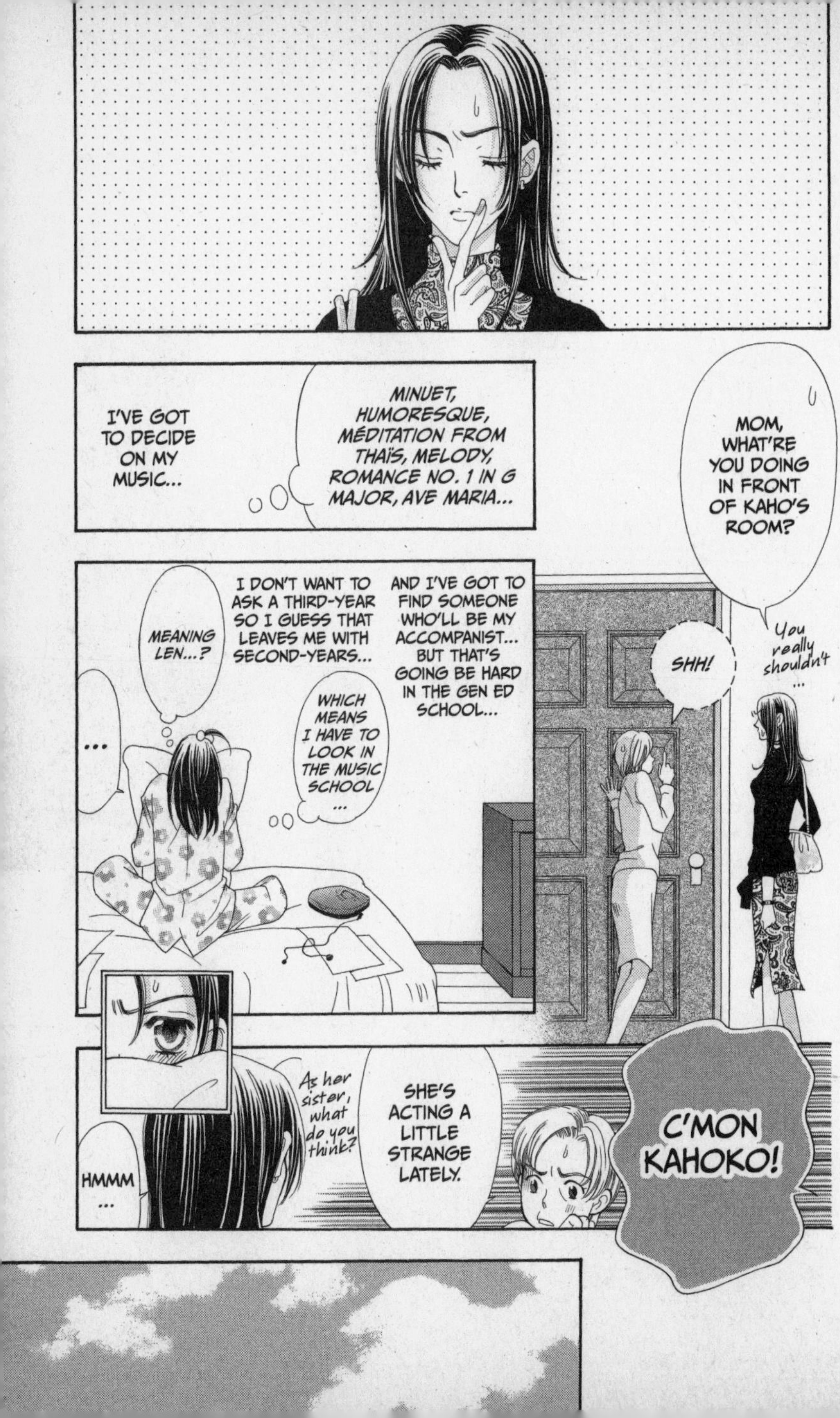
MINUET, HUMORESQUE, MÉDITATION FROM THAÏS, MELODY, ROMANCE NO. 1 IN G MAJOR, AVE MARIA...
I'VE GOT TO DECIDE ON MY MUSIC...
MOM, WHAT'RE YOU DOING IN FRONT OF KAHO'S ROOM?
You really shouldn't ...
SHH!
AND I'VE GOT TO FIND SOMEONE WHO'LL BE MY ACCOMPANIST... BUT THAT'S GOING BE HARD IN THE GEN ED SCHOOL...
I DON'T WANT TO ASK A THIRD-YEAR SO I GUESS THAT LEAVES ME WITH SECOND-YEARS...
WHICH MEANS I HAVE TO LOOK IN THE MUSIC SCHOOL ...
MEANING LEN...?
...
C'MON KAHOKO!
SHE'S ACTING A LITTLE STRANGE LATELY.
As her sister, what do you think?
HMMM ...

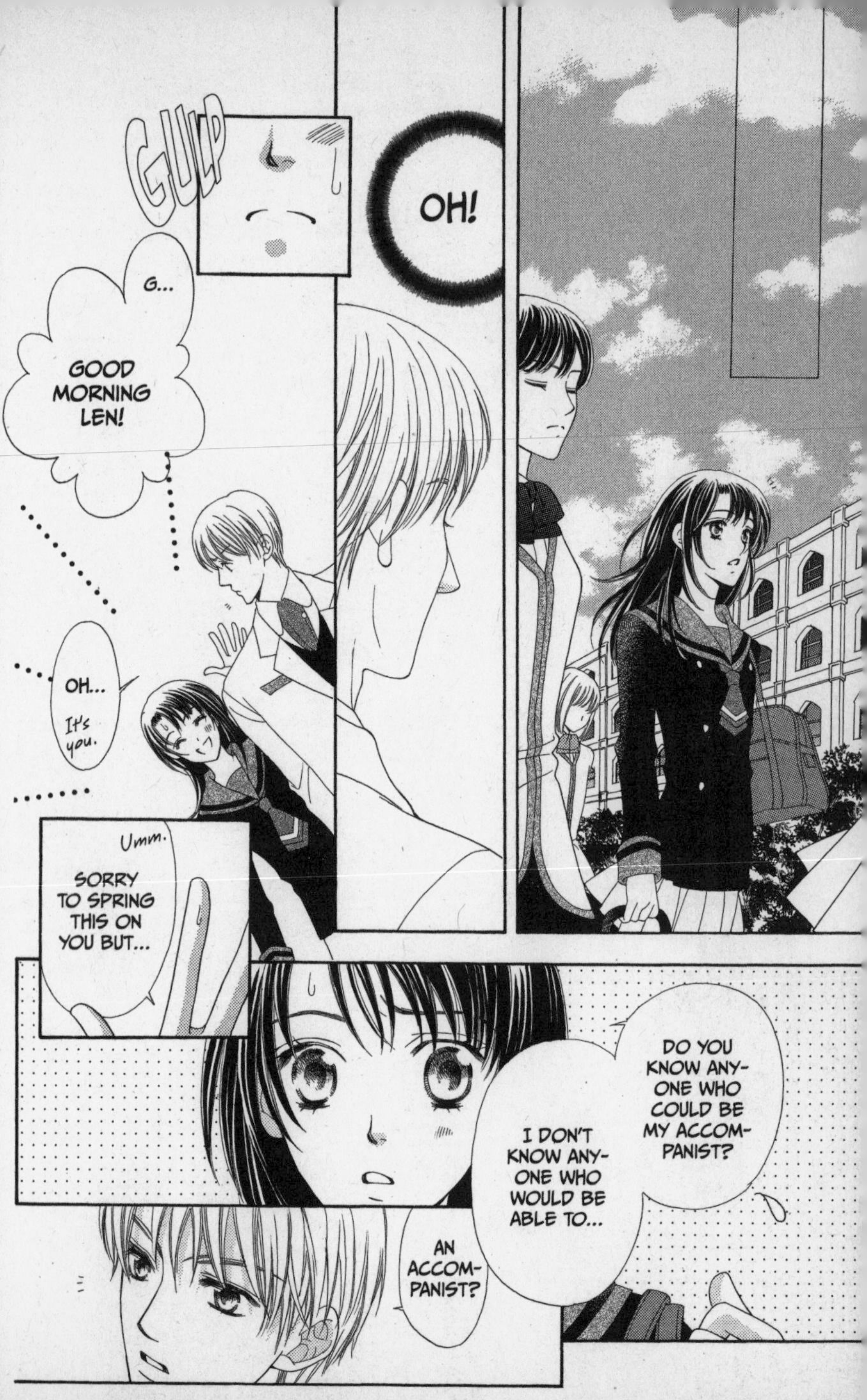
OH!
GULP
G...
GOOD MORNING LEN!
OH...
It's you.
Umm.
SORRY TO SPRING THIS ON YOU BUT...
DO YOU KNOW ANY-ONE WHO COULD BE MY ACCOM-PANIST?
I DON'T KNOW ANY-ONE WHO WOULD BE ABLE TO...
AN ACCOM-PANIST?

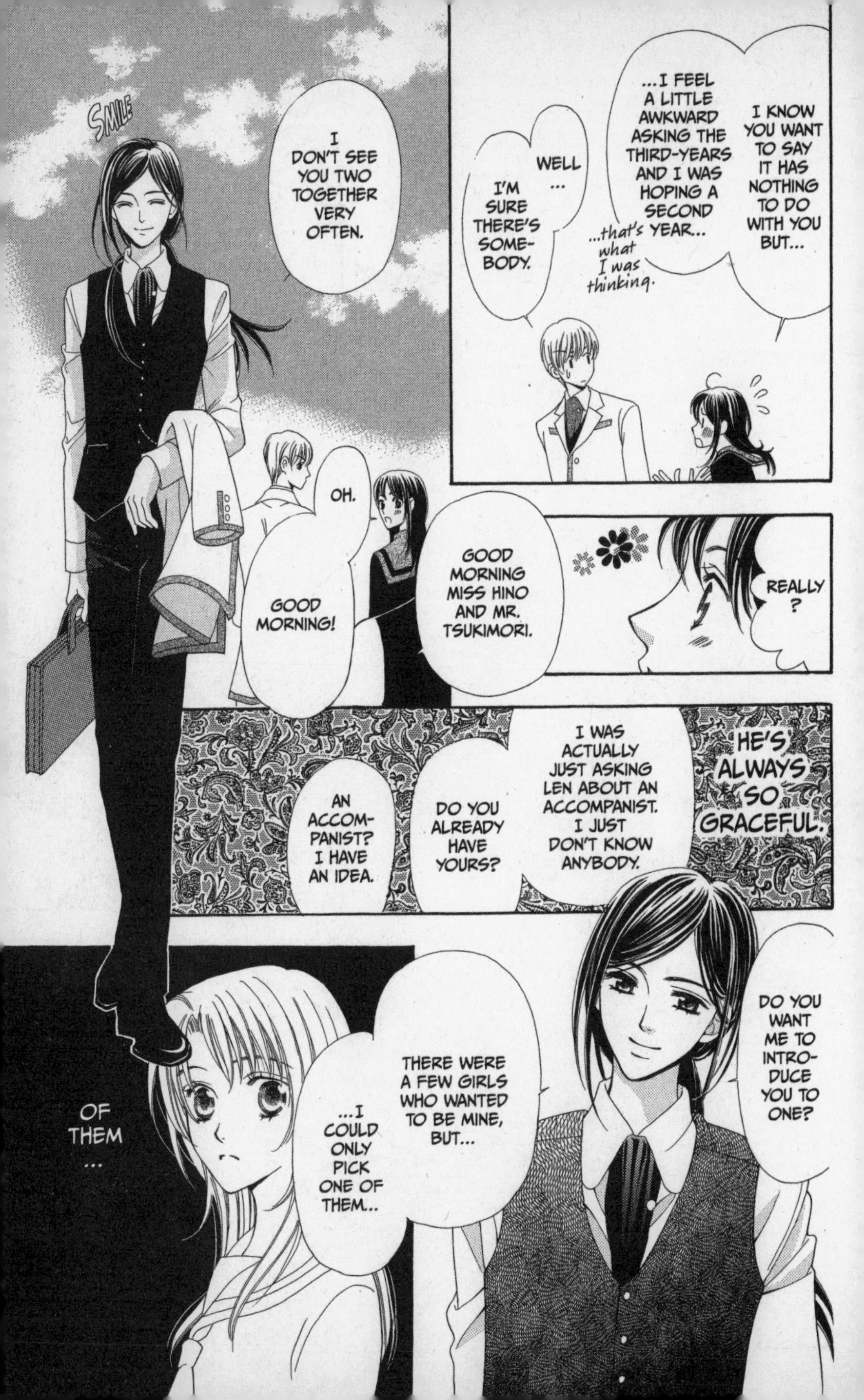
I KNOW YOU WANT TO SAY IT HAS NOTHING TO DO WITH YOU BUT...
...I FEEL A LITTLE AWKWARD ASKING THE THIRD-YEARS AND I WAS HOPING A SECOND YEAR...
...that's what I was thinking.
WELL...
I'M SURE THERE'S SOME-BODY.
REALLY?
GOOD MORNING MISS HINO AND MR. TSUKIMORI.
OH.
GOOD MORNING!
SMILE
I DON'T SEE YOU TWO TOGETHER VERY OFTEN.
HE'S ALWAYS SO GRACEFUL.
I WAS ACTUALLY JUST ASKING LEN ABOUT AN ACCOMPANIST. I JUST DON'T KNOW ANYBODY.
DO YOU ALREADY HAVE YOURS?
AN ACCOM-PANIST? I HAVE AN IDEA.
DO YOU WANT ME TO INTRO-DUCE YOU TO ONE?
THERE WERE A FEW GIRLS WHO WANTED TO BE MINE, BUT...
...I COULD ONLY PICK ONE OF THEM...
OF THEM...

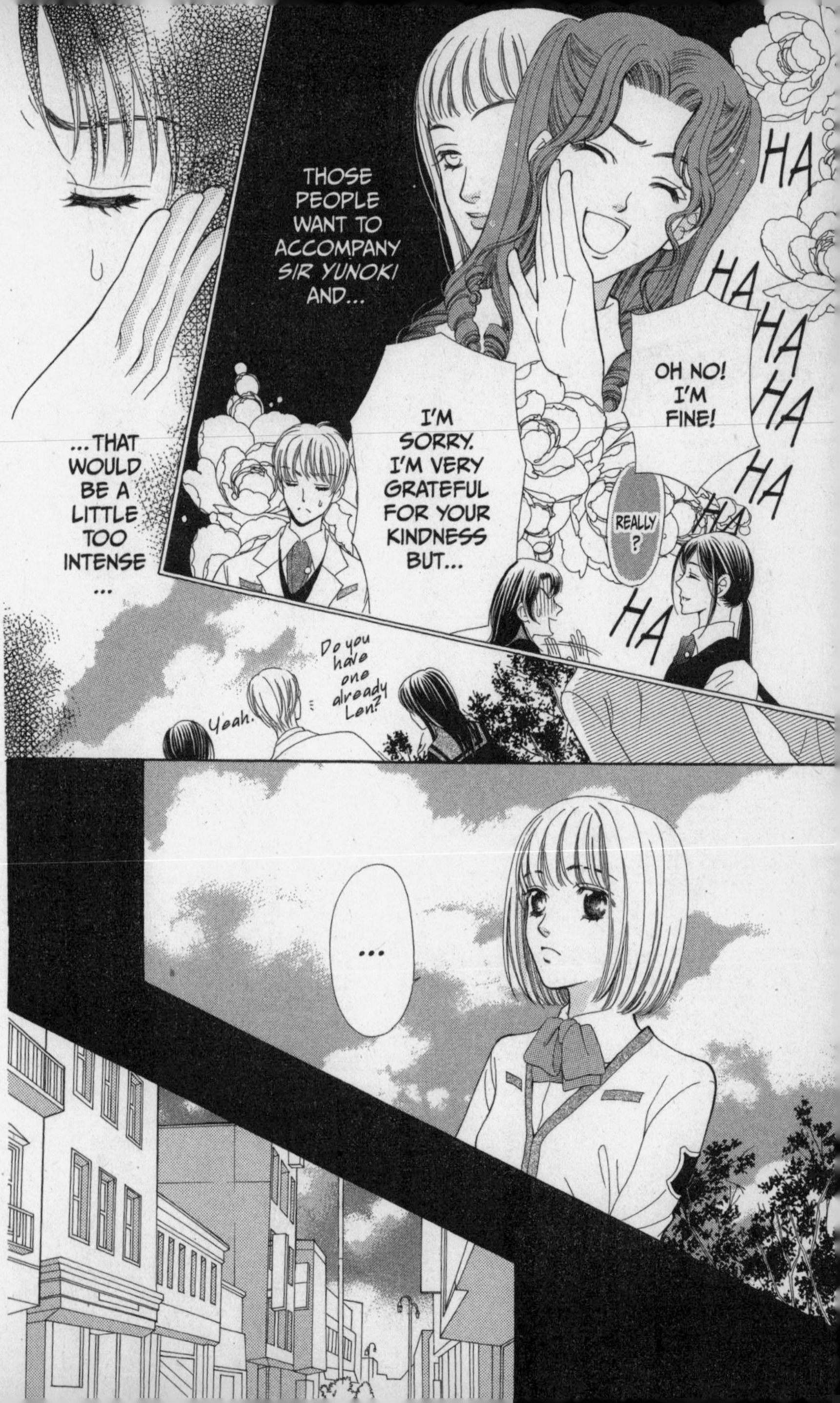
HA HA HA HA HA HA HA HA
THOSE PEOPLE WANT TO ACCOMPANY SIR YUNOKI AND...
OH NO! I'M FINE!
REALLY?
I'M SORRY. I'M VERY GRATEFUL FOR YOUR KINDNESS BUT...
...THAT WOULD BE A LITTLE TOO INTENSE ...
Do you have one already Len?
Yeah.
...

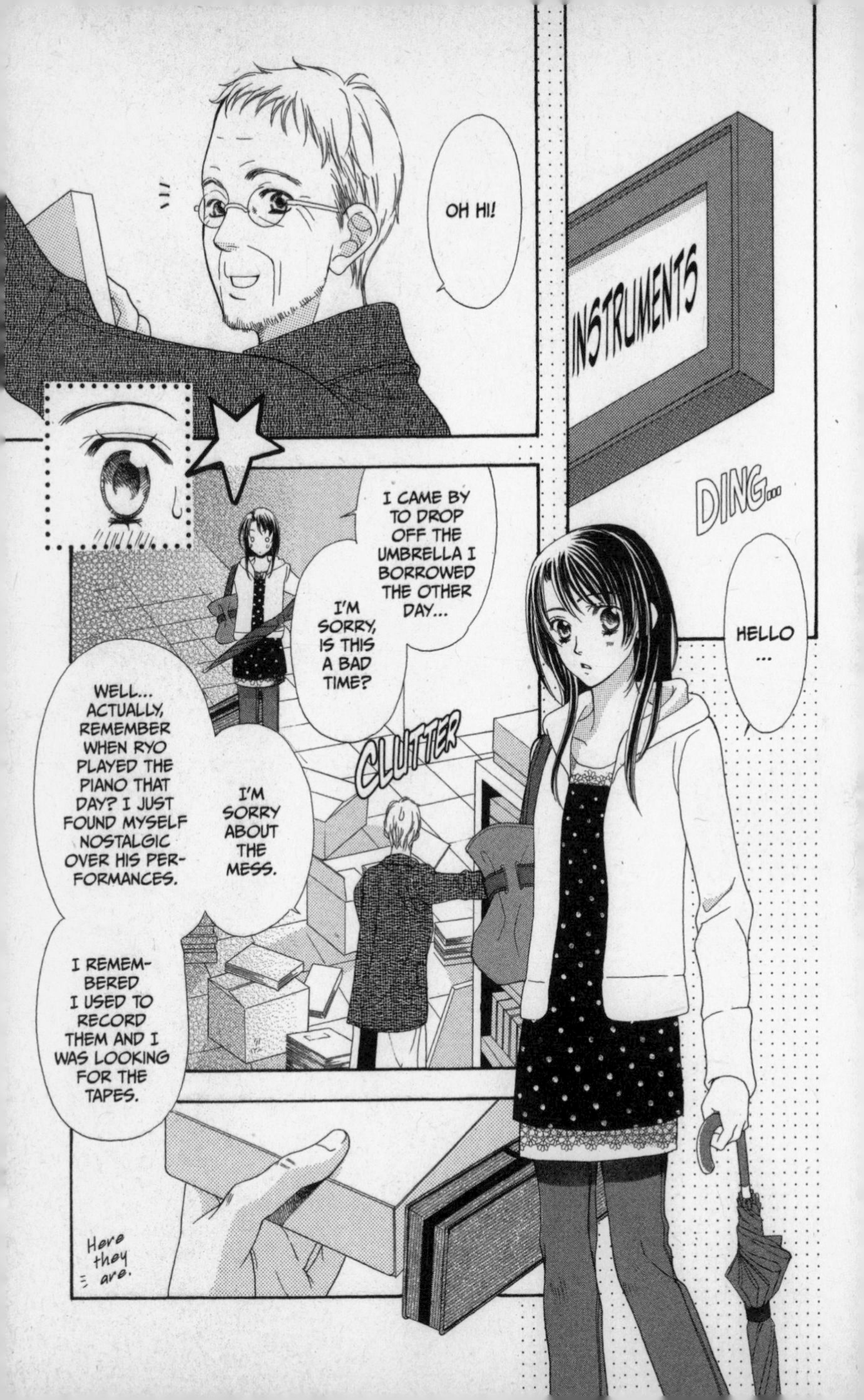
INSTRUMENTS
DING...
OH HI!
HELLO ...
I CAME BY TO DROP OFF THE UMBRELLA I BORROWED THE OTHER DAY...
I'M SORRY, IS THIS A BAD TIME?
CLUTTER
I'M SORRY ABOUT THE MESS.
WELL... ACTUALLY, REMEMBER WHEN RYO PLAYED THE PIANO THAT DAY? I JUST FOUND MYSELF NOSTALGIC OVER HIS PER-FORMANCES.
I REMEM-BERED I USED TO RECORD THEM AND I WAS LOOKING FOR THE TAPES.
Here they are.

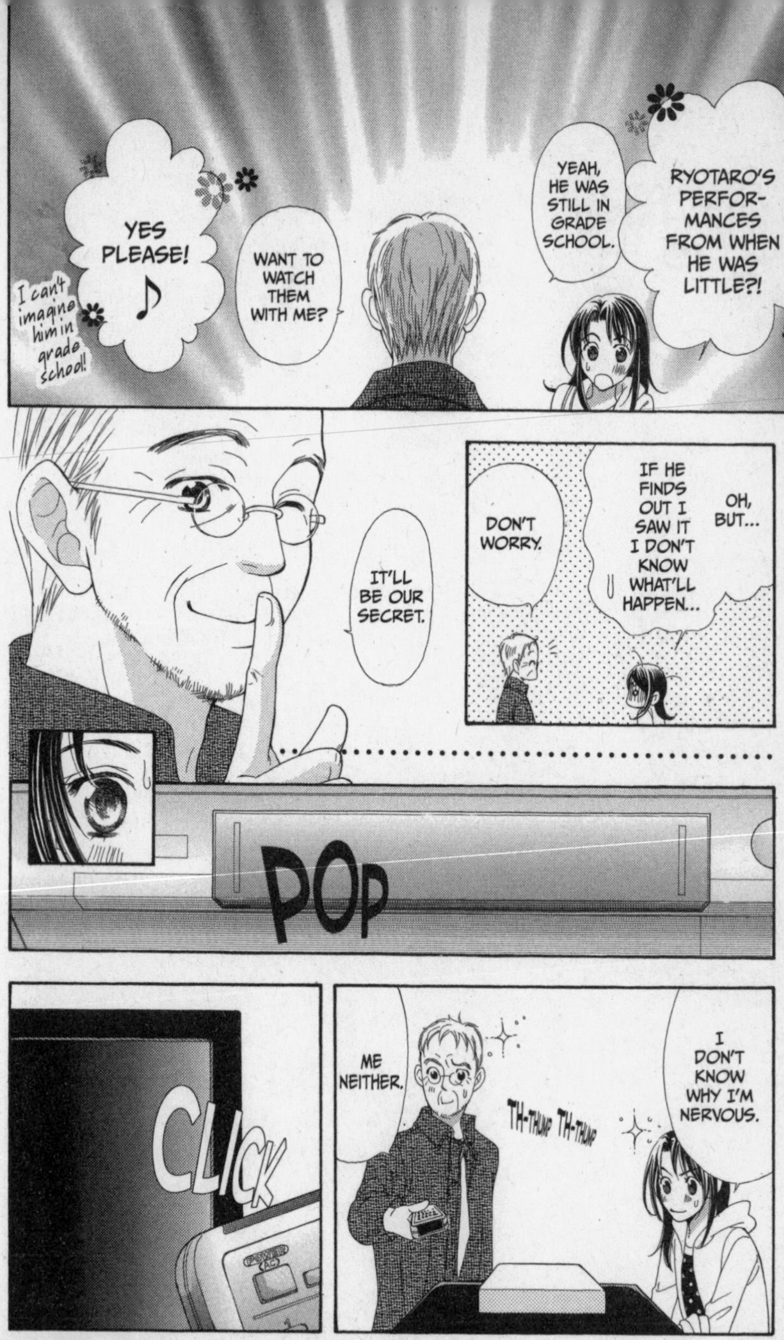
RYOTARO'S PERFORMANCES FROM WHEN HE WAS LITTLE?!
YEAH, HE WAS STILL IN GRADE SCHOOL.
WANT TO WATCH THEM WITH ME?
YES PLEASE! ♪
I can't imagine him in grade school!
OH, BUT...
IF HE FINDS OUT I SAW IT I DON'T KNOW WHAT'LL HAPPEN...
DON'T WORRY.
IT'LL BE OUR SECRET.
POP
I DON'T KNOW WHY I'M NERVOUS.
TH-THUMP TH-THUMP
ME NEITHER.
CLICK
POWER (AC)

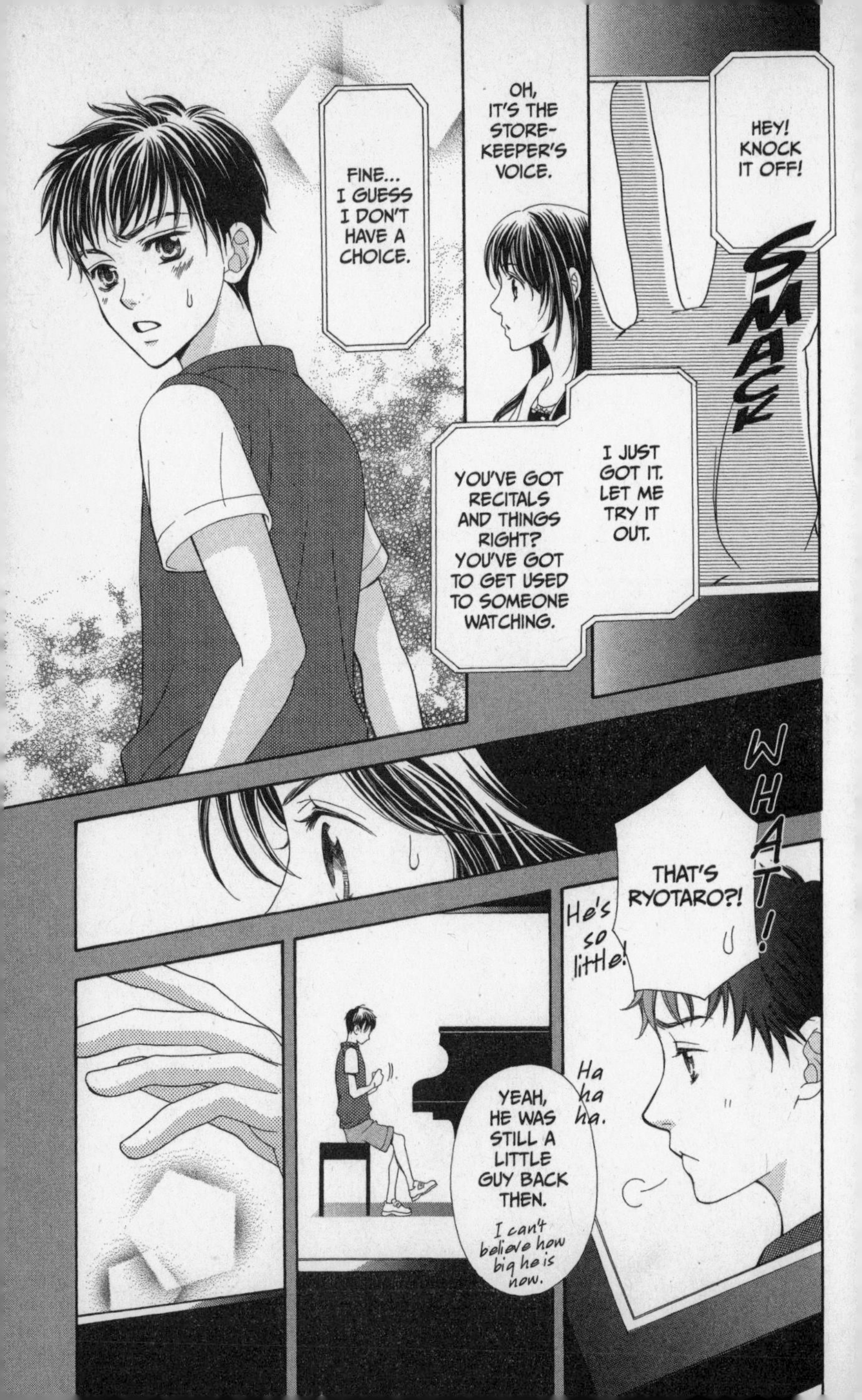
HEY! KNOCK IT OFF!
SMACK
OH, IT'S THE STORE-KEEPER'S VOICE.
I JUST GOT IT. LET ME TRY IT OUT.
YOU'VE GOT RECITALS AND THINGS RIGHT? YOU'VE GOT TO GET USED TO SOMEONE WATCHING.
FINE... I GUESS I DON'T HAVE A CHOICE.
WHAT!
THAT'S RYOTARO?!
He's so little!
Ha ha ha.
YEAH, HE WAS STILL A LITTLE GUY BACK THEN.
I can't believe how big he is now.

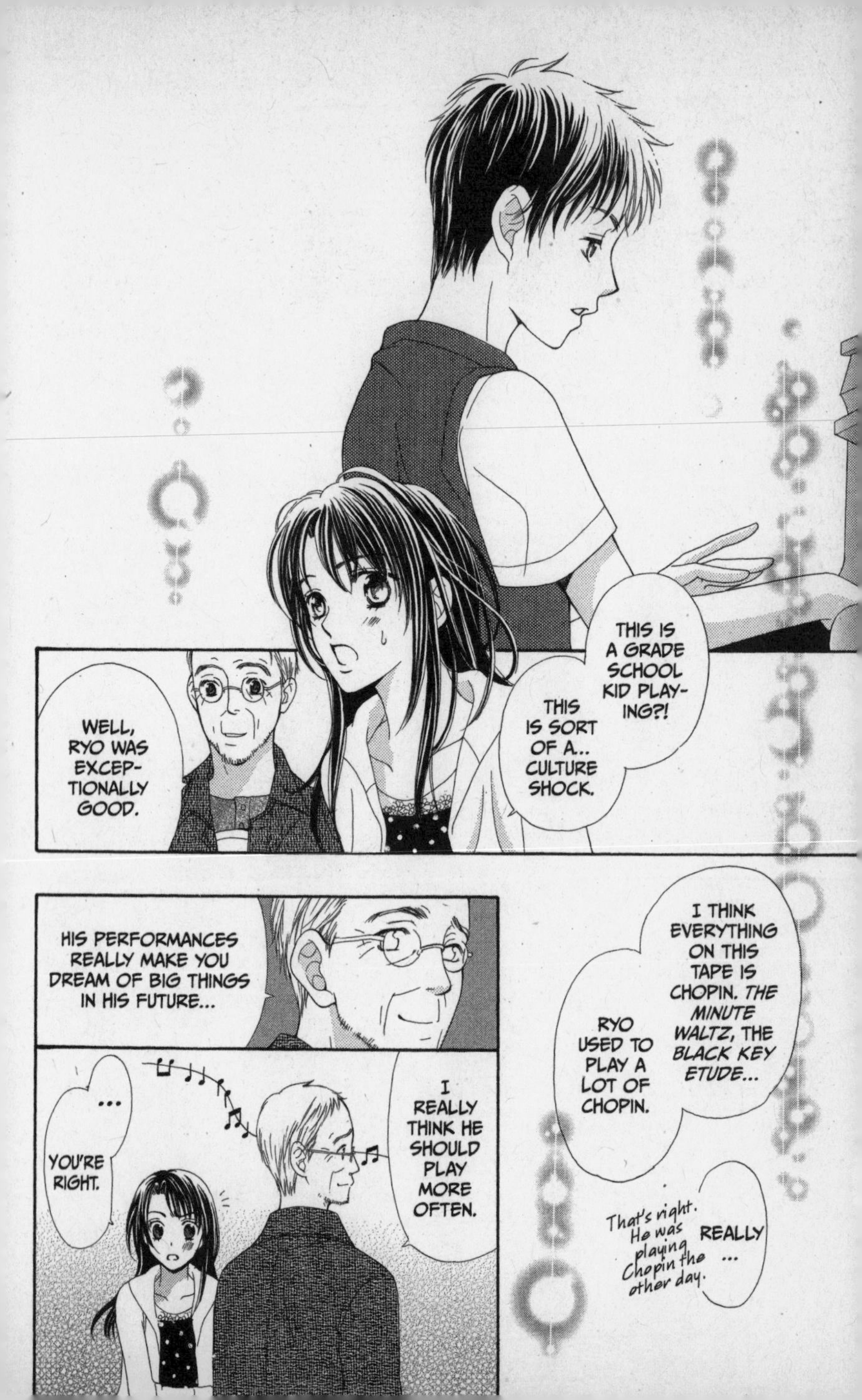
THIS IS A GRADE SCHOOL KID PLAYING?!
THIS IS SORT OF A... CULTURE SHOCK.
WELL, RYO WAS EXCEPTIONALLY GOOD.
I THINK EVERYTHING ON THIS TAPE IS CHOPIN. *THE MINUTE WALTZ*, THE *BLACK KEY ETUDE*...
RYO USED TO PLAY A LOT OF CHOPIN.
REALLY ...
That's right. He was playing Chopin the other day.
HIS PERFORMANCES REALLY MAKE YOU DREAM OF BIG THINGS IN HIS FUTURE...
I REALLY THINK HE SHOULD PLAY MORE OFTEN.
...
YOU'RE RIGHT.

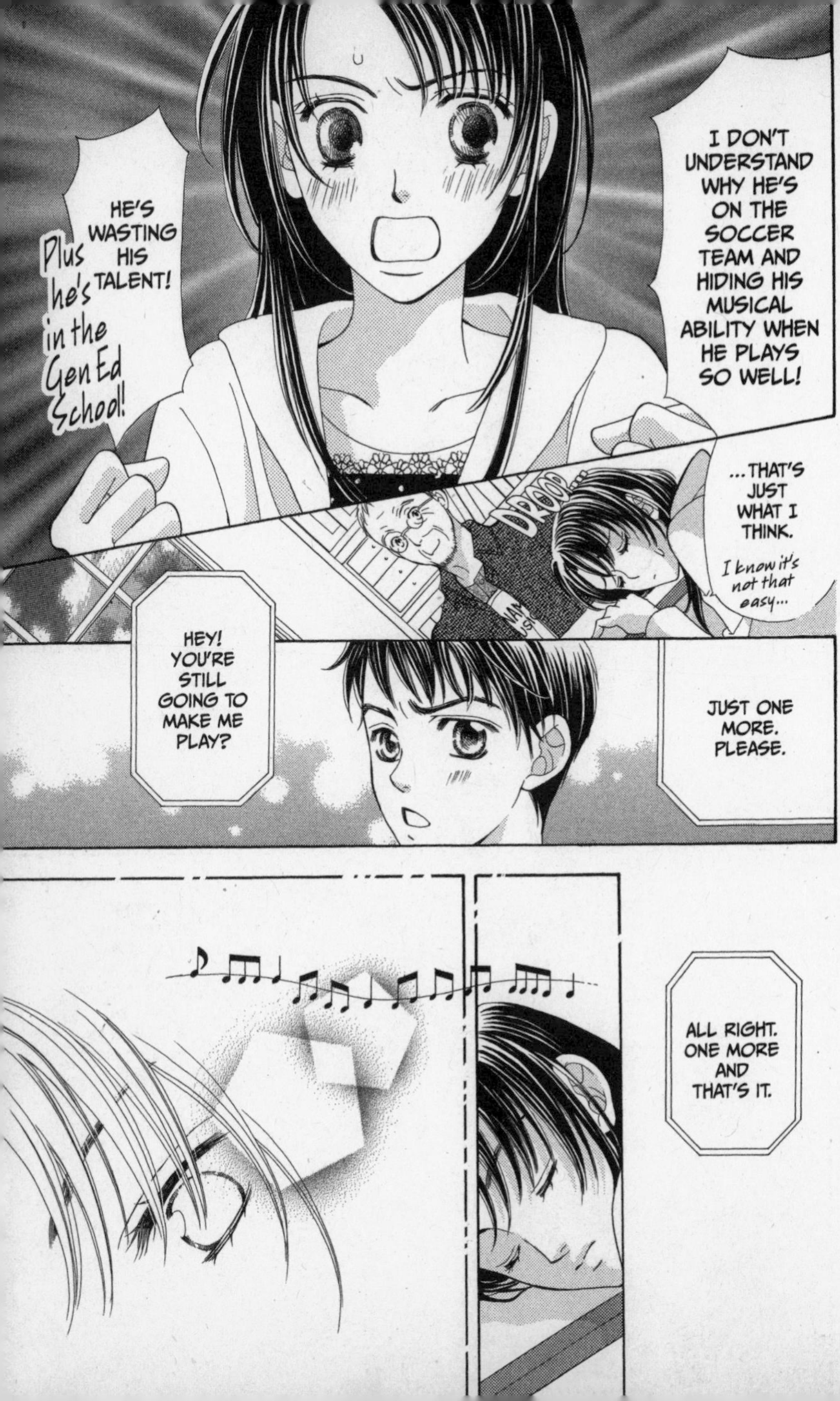
I DON'T UNDERSTAND WHY HE'S ON THE SOCCER TEAM AND HIDING HIS MUSICAL ABILITY WHEN HE PLAYS SO WELL!
HE'S WASTING HIS TALENT!
Plus he's in the Gen Ed School!
DROOP...
...THAT'S JUST WHAT I THINK.
I know it's not that easy...
JUST ONE MORE. PLEASE.
HEY! YOU'RE STILL GOING TO MAKE ME PLAY?
ALL RIGHT. ONE MORE AND THAT'S IT.

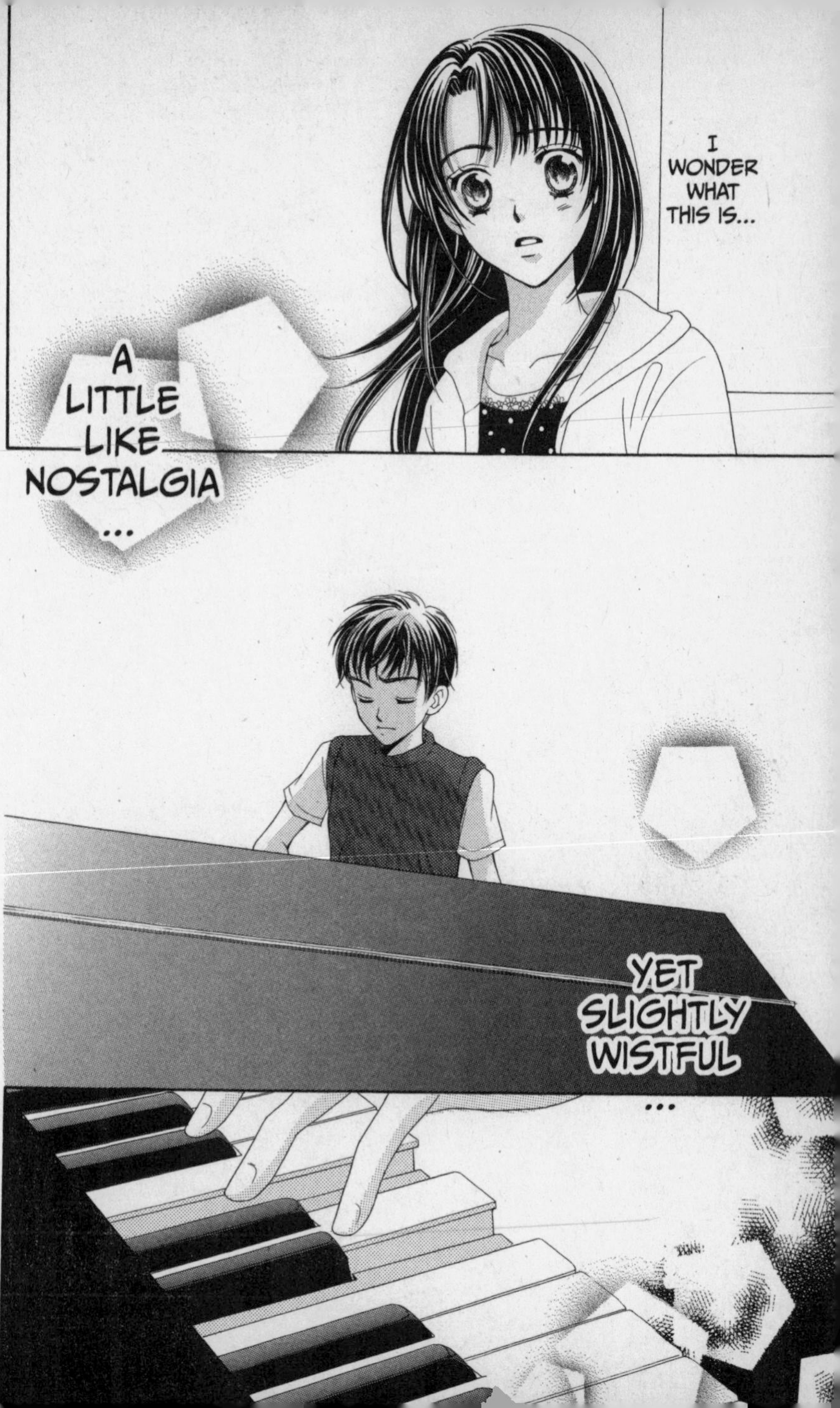
I WONDER WHAT THIS IS...
A LITTLE LIKE NOSTALGIA ...
YET SLIGHTLY WISTFUL ...

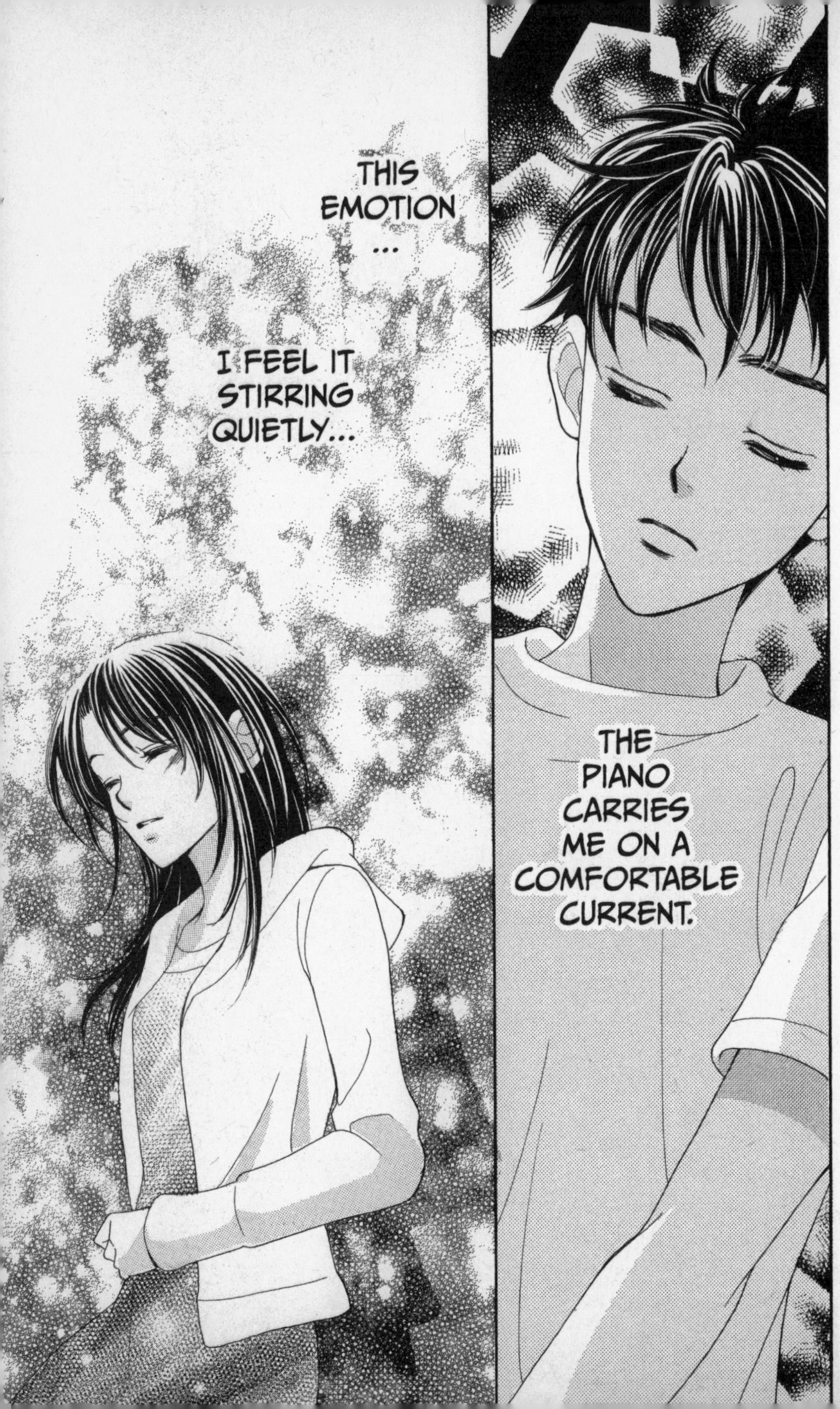
THE PIANO CARRIES ME ON A COMFORTABLE CURRENT.
THIS EMOTION ...
I FEEL IT STIRRING QUIETLY...

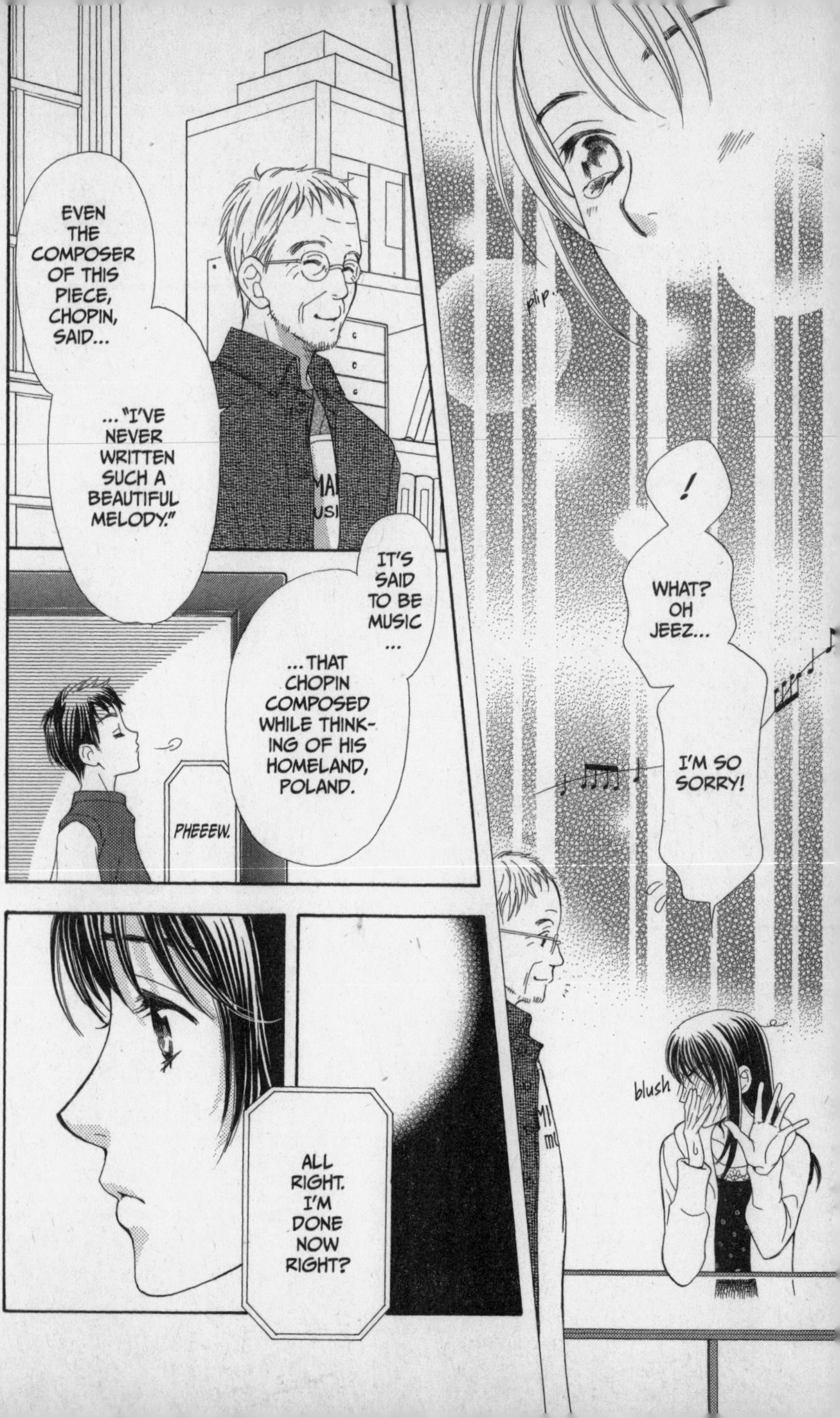
plip...
!
WHAT? OH JEEZ...
I'M SO SORRY!
blush
EVEN THE COMPOSER OF THIS PIECE, CHOPIN, SAID...
..."I'VE NEVER WRITTEN SUCH A BEAUTIFUL MELODY."
IT'S SAID TO BE MUSIC ...
...THAT CHOPIN COMPOSED WHILE THINKING OF HIS HOMELAND, POLAND.
PHEEEW.
ALL RIGHT. I'M DONE NOW RIGHT?

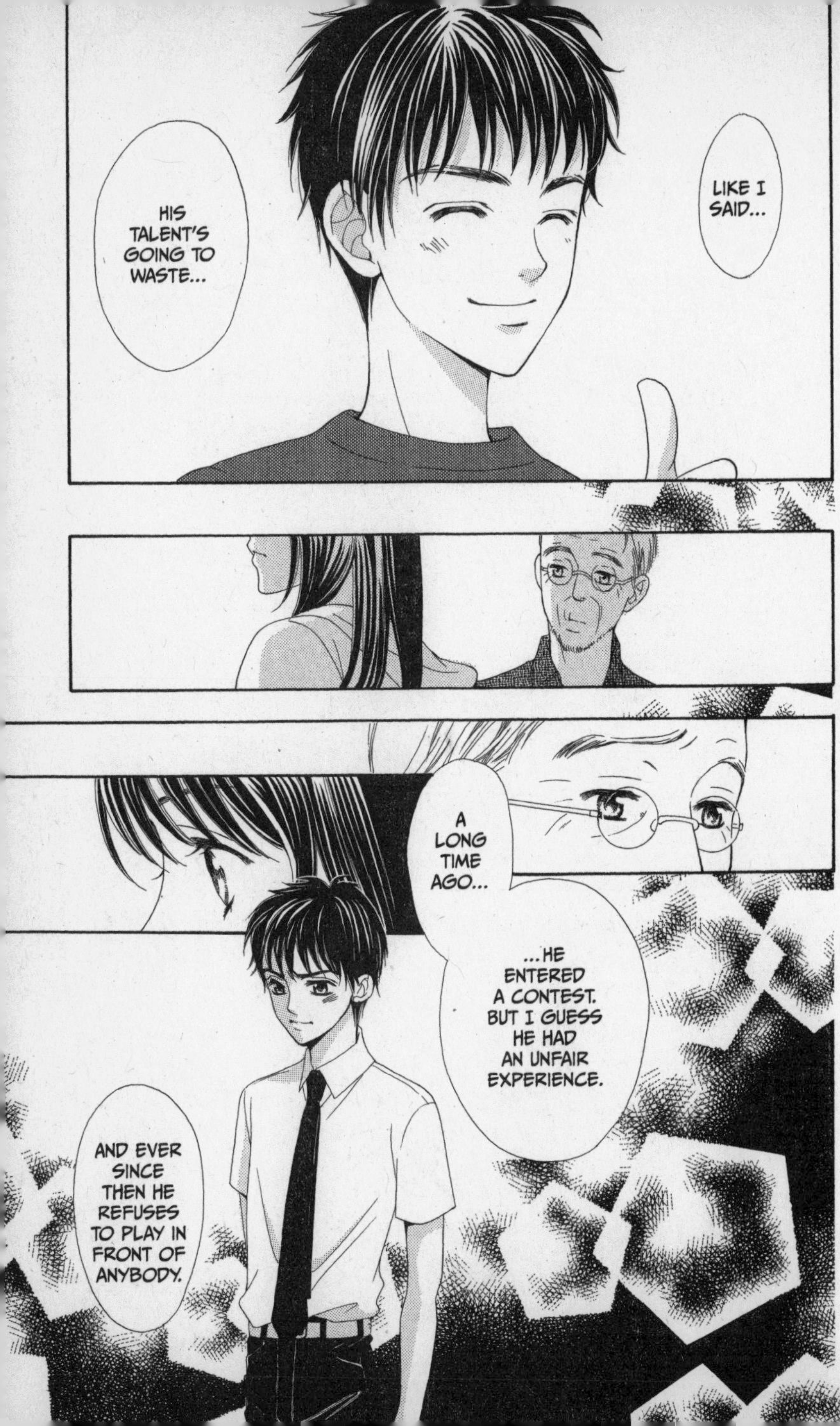
LIKE I SAID...
HIS TALENT'S GOING TO WASTE...
A LONG TIME AGO...
...HE ENTERED A CONTEST. BUT I GUESS HE HAD AN UNFAIR EXPERIENCE.
AND EVER SINCE THEN HE REFUSES TO PLAY IN FRONT OF ANYBODY.

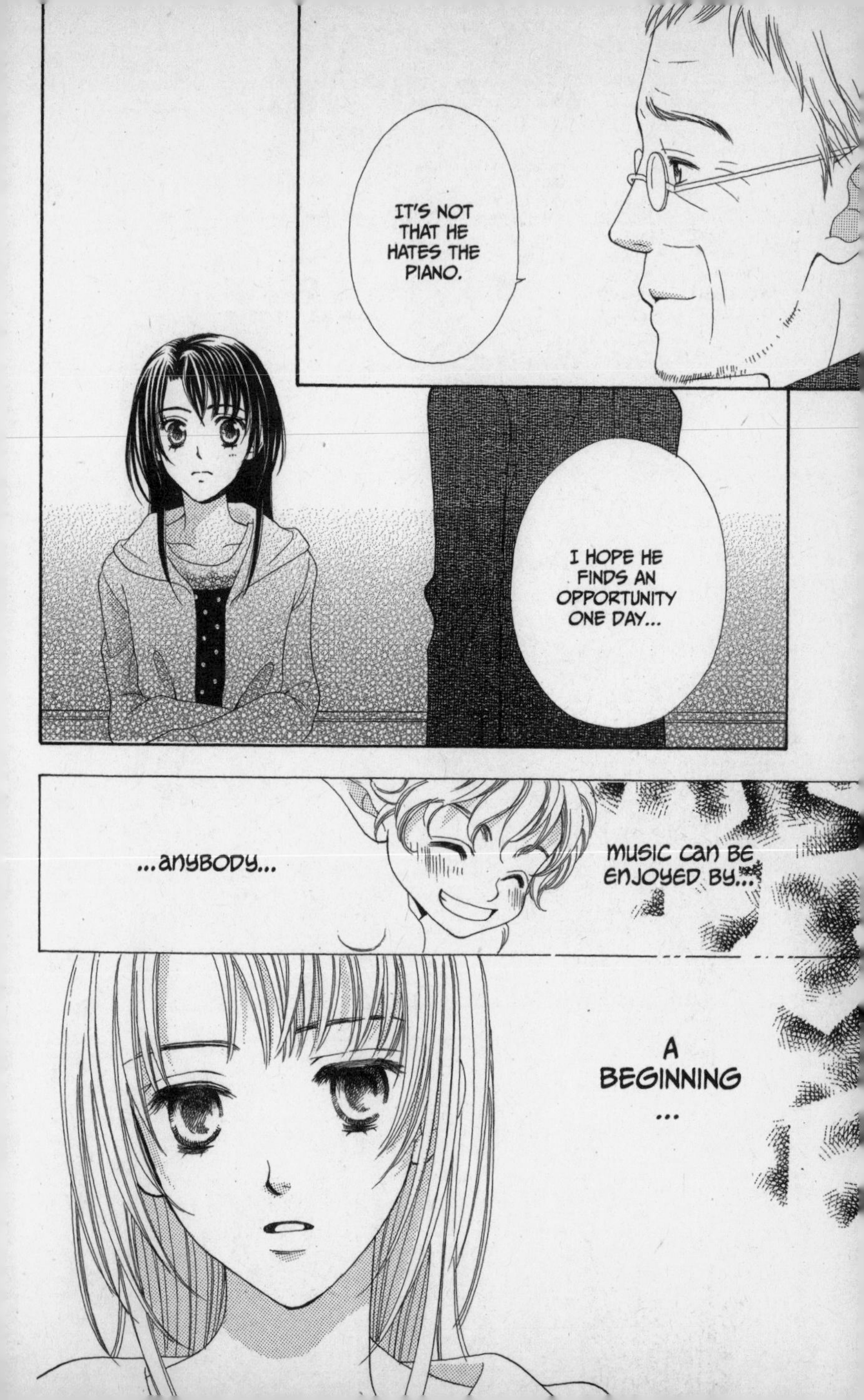
IT'S NOT THAT HE HATES THE PIANO.
I HOPE HE FINDS AN OPPORTUNITY ONE DAY...
music can be enjoyed by...
...anybody...
A BEGINNING ...

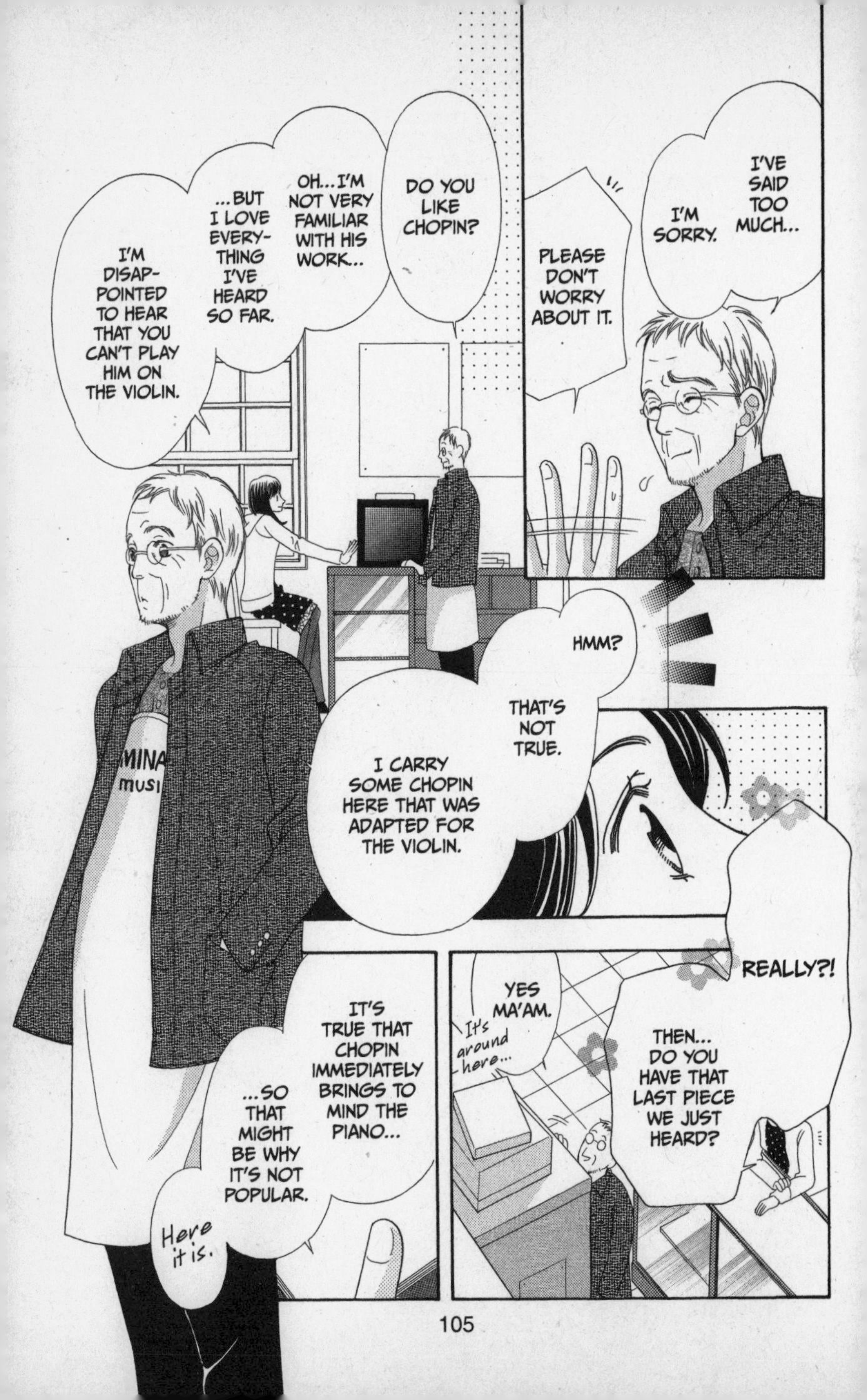
I'VE SAID TOO MUCH...
I'M SORRY.
PLEASE DON'T WORRY ABOUT IT.
DO YOU LIKE CHOPIN?
OH...I'M NOT VERY FAMILIAR WITH HIS WORK...
...BUT I LOVE EVERYTHING I'VE HEARD SO FAR.
I'M DISAPPOINTED TO HEAR THAT YOU CAN'T PLAY HIM ON THE VIOLIN.
HMM?
THAT'S NOT TRUE.
I CARRY SOME CHOPIN HERE THAT WAS ADAPTED FOR THE VIOLIN.
REALLY?!
THEN... DO YOU HAVE THAT LAST PIECE WE JUST HEARD?
YES MA'AM.
It's around here...
IT'S TRUE THAT CHOPIN IMMEDIATELY BRINGS TO MIND THE PIANO...
...SO THAT MIGHT BE WHY IT'S NOT POPULAR.
Here it is.

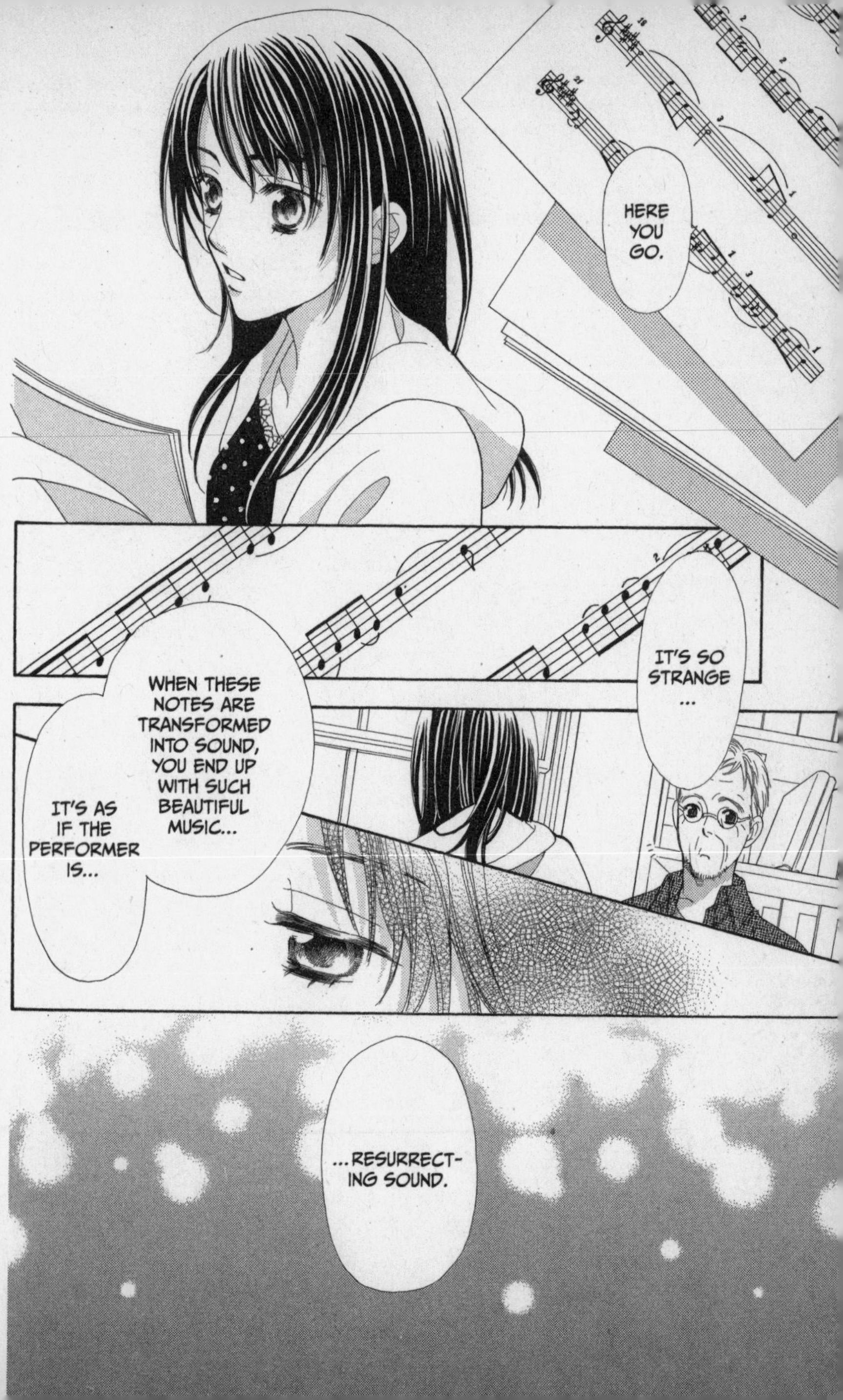
HERE YOU GO.
IT'S SO STRANGE...
WHEN THESE NOTES ARE TRANSFORMED INTO SOUND, YOU END UP WITH SUCH BEAUTIFUL MUSIC...
IT'S AS IF THE PERFORMER IS...
...RESURRECT-ING SOUND.

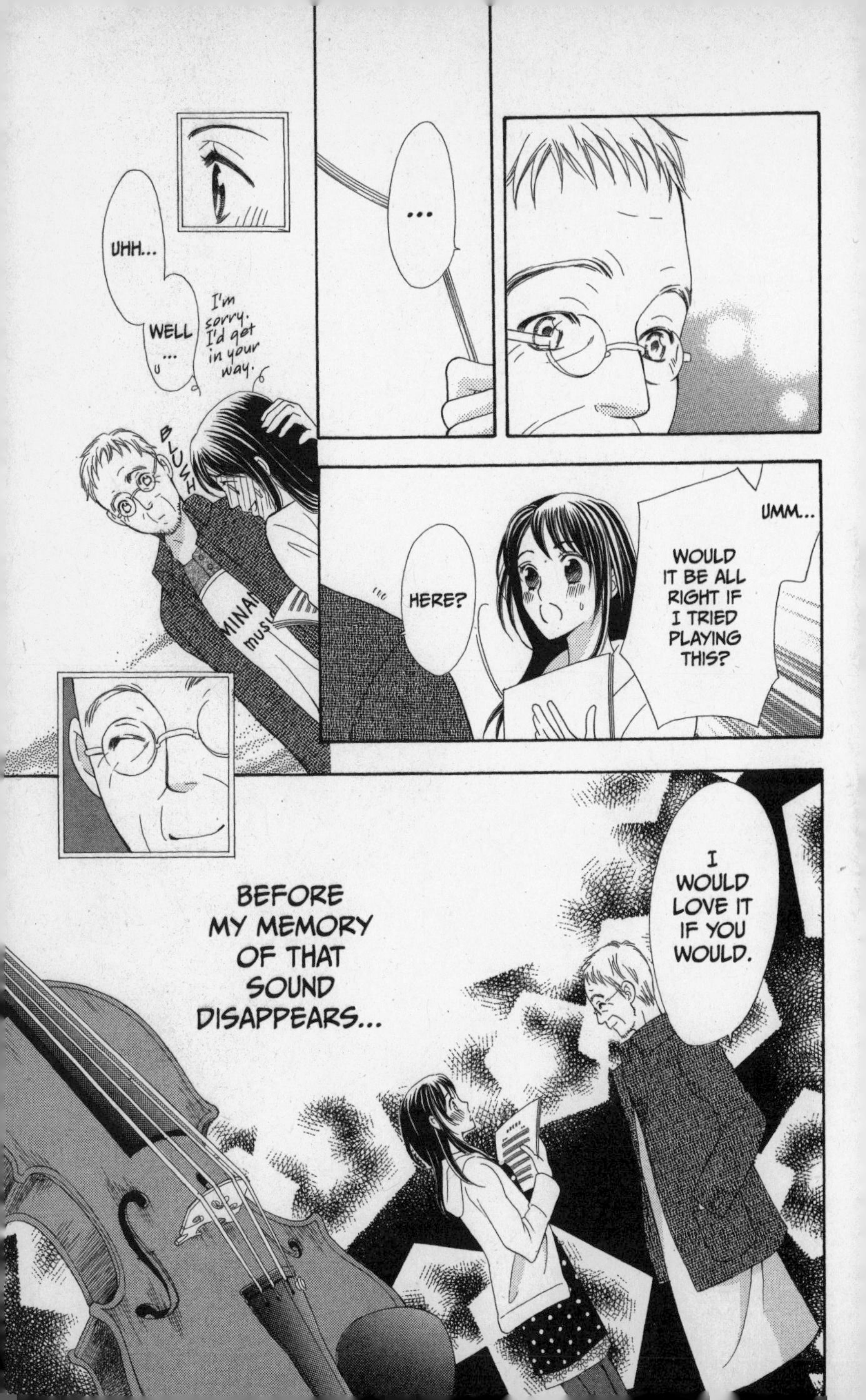
...
UHH...
WELL ...
I'm sorry. I'd get in your way.
BLUSH
UMM...
WOULD IT BE ALL RIGHT IF I TRIED PLAYING THIS?
HERE?
I WOULD LOVE IT IF YOU WOULD.
BEFORE MY MEMORY OF THAT SOUND DISAPPEARS...

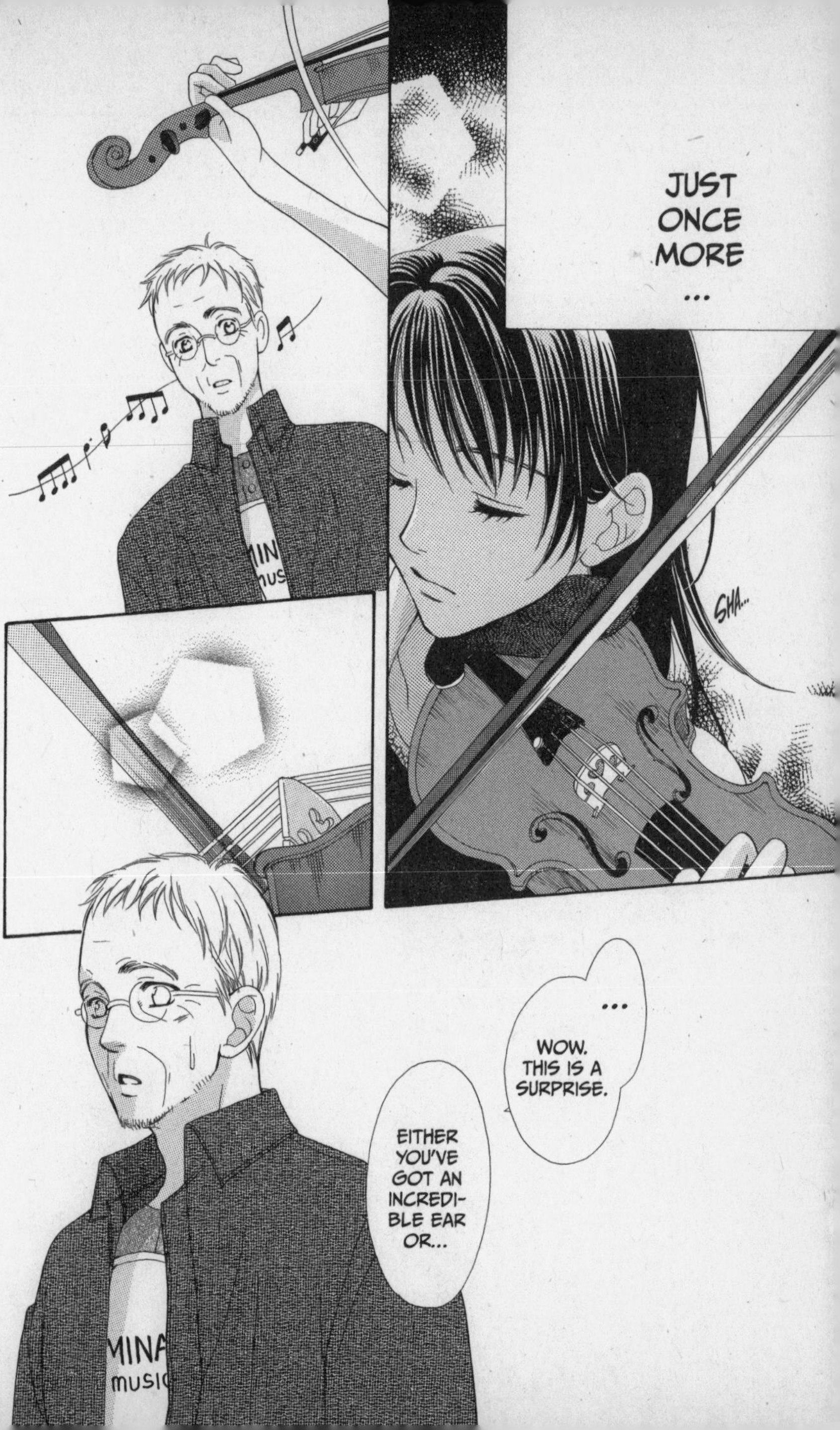
JUST ONCE MORE ...
SHA...
...
WOW. THIS IS A SURPRISE.
EITHER YOU'VE GOT AN INCREDIBLE EAR OR...

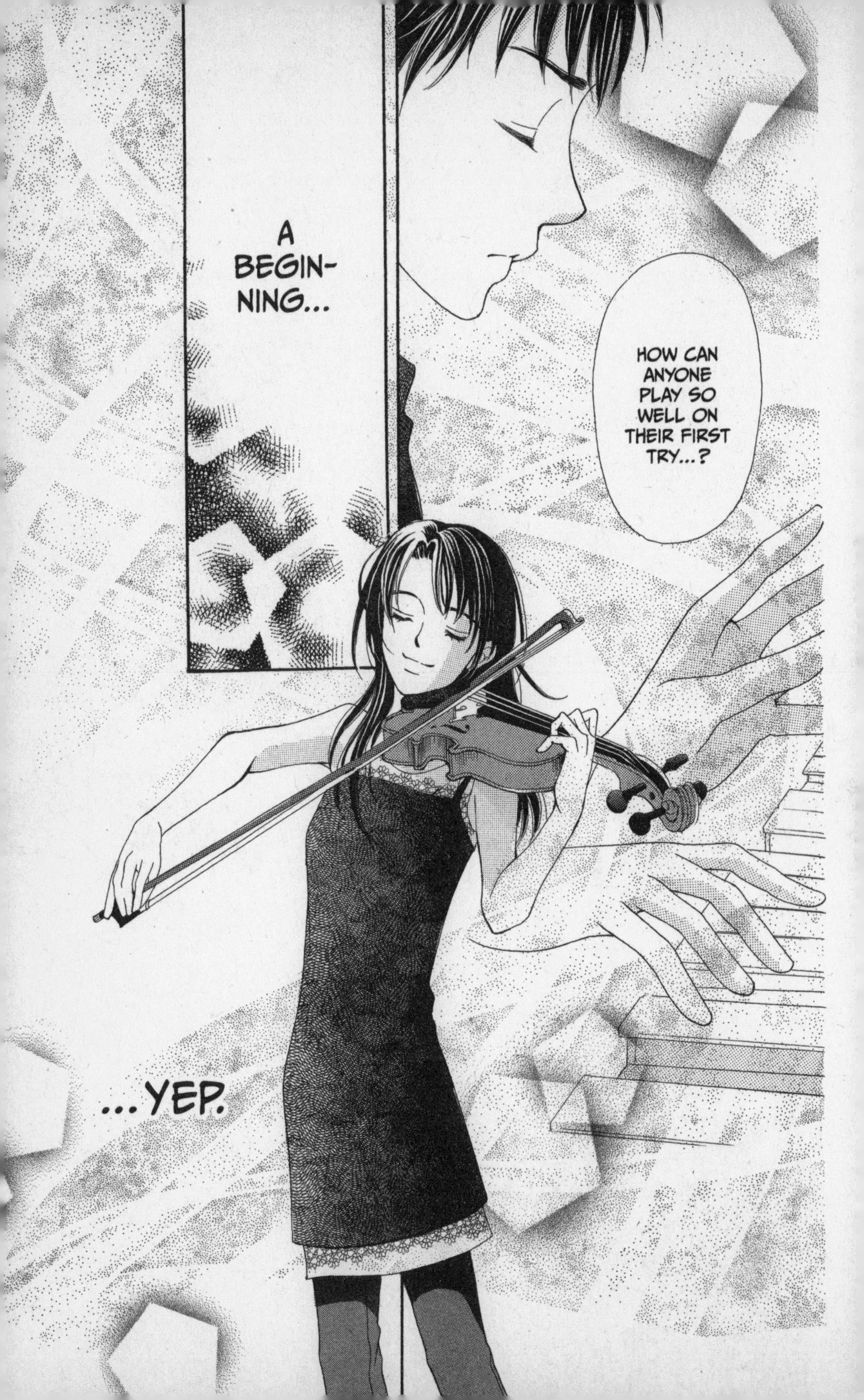
HOW CAN ANYONE PLAY SO WELL ON THEIR FIRST TRY...?
A BEGINNING...
...YEP.

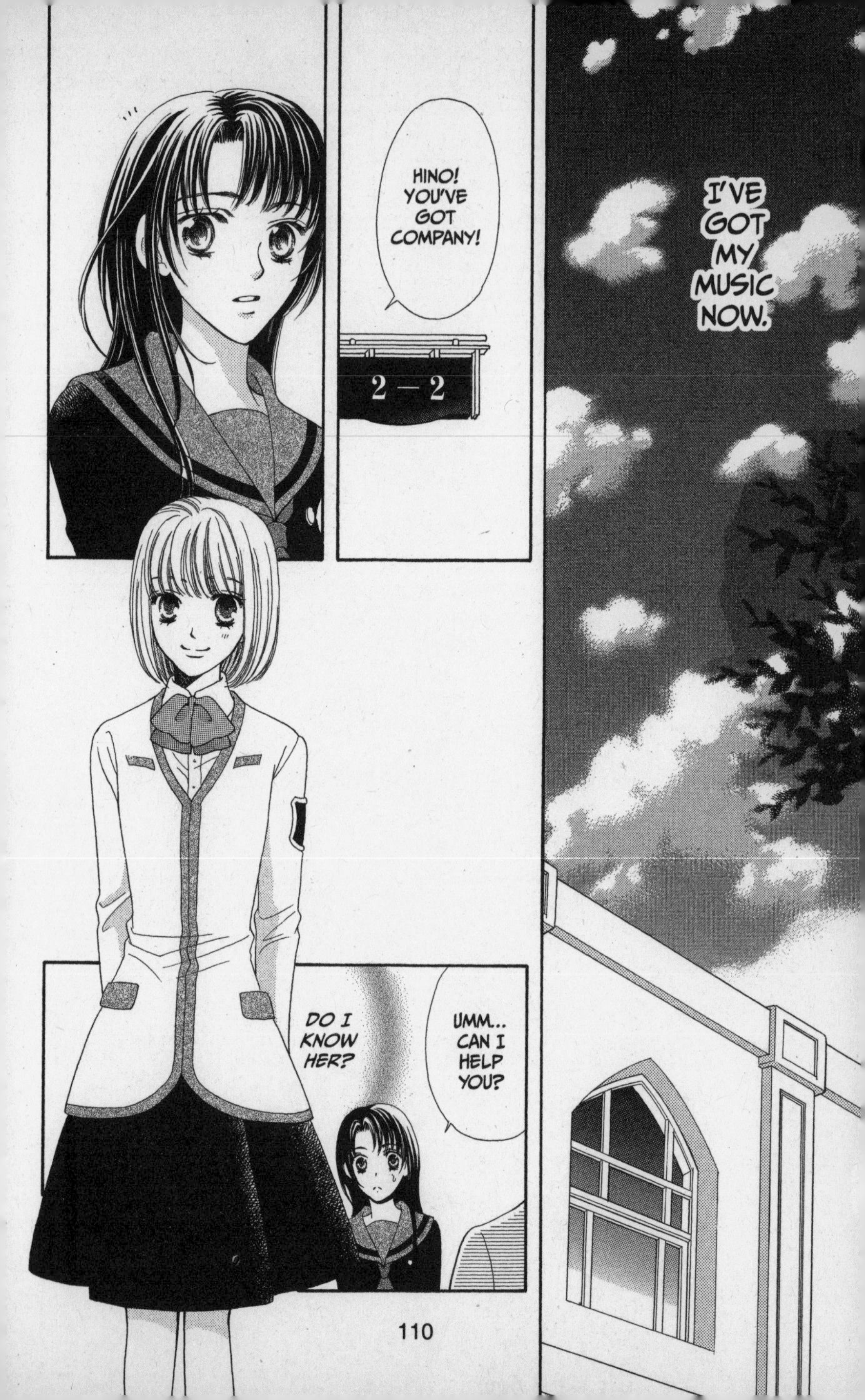
I'VE GOT MY MUSIC NOW.
HINO! YOU'VE GOT COMPANY!
2-2
UMM... CAN I HELP YOU?
DO I KNOW HER?

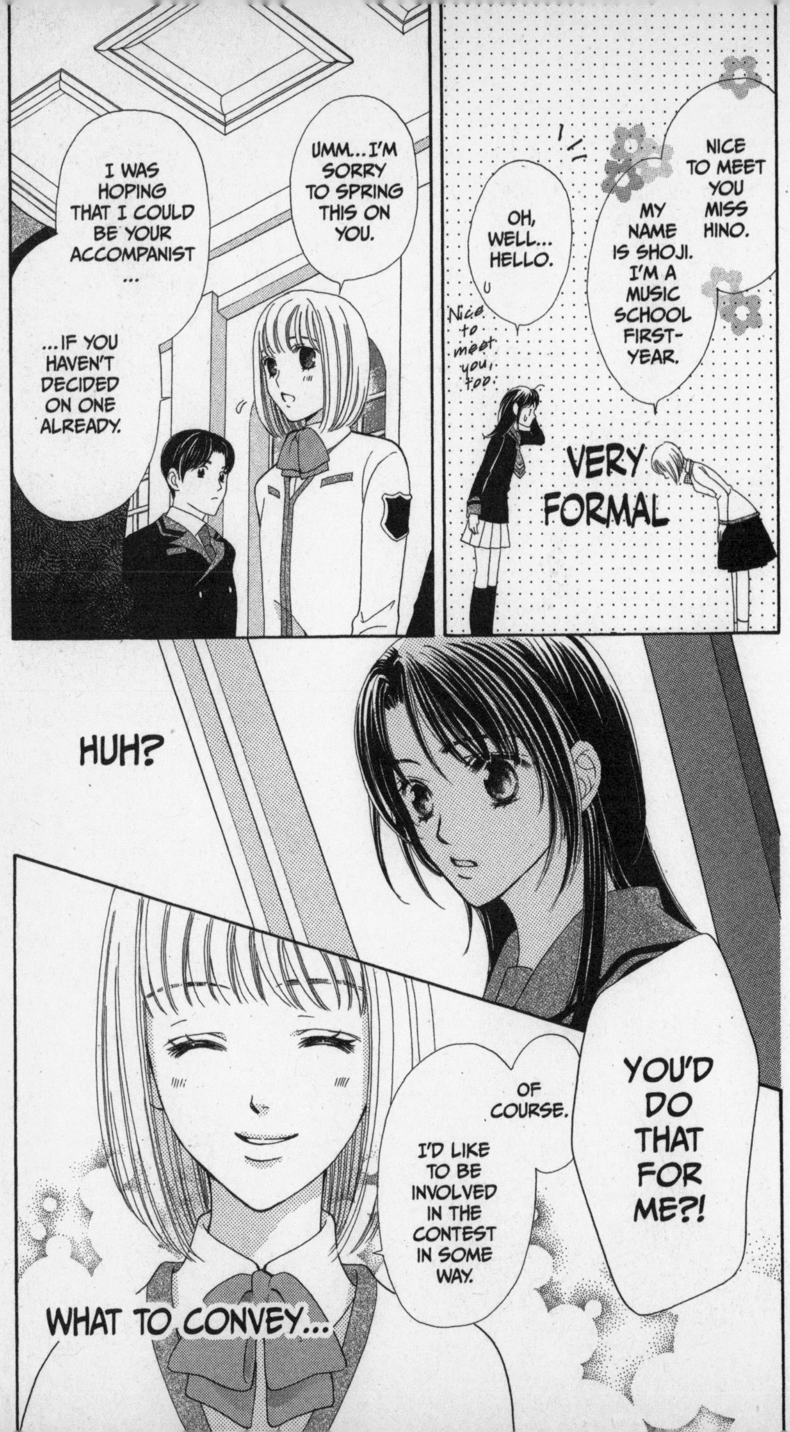
NICE TO MEET YOU MISS HINO.
MY NAME IS SHOJI. I'M A MUSIC SCHOOL FIRST-YEAR.
OH, WELL... HELLO.
Nice to meet you, too.
VERY FORMAL
UMM...I'M SORRY TO SPRING THIS ON YOU.
I WAS HOPING THAT I COULD BE YOUR ACCOMPANIST...
...IF YOU HAVEN'T DECIDED ON ONE ALREADY.
HUH?
YOU'D DO THAT FOR ME?!
OF COURSE.
I'D LIKE TO BE INVOLVED IN THE CONTEST IN SOME WAY.
WHAT TO CONVEY...

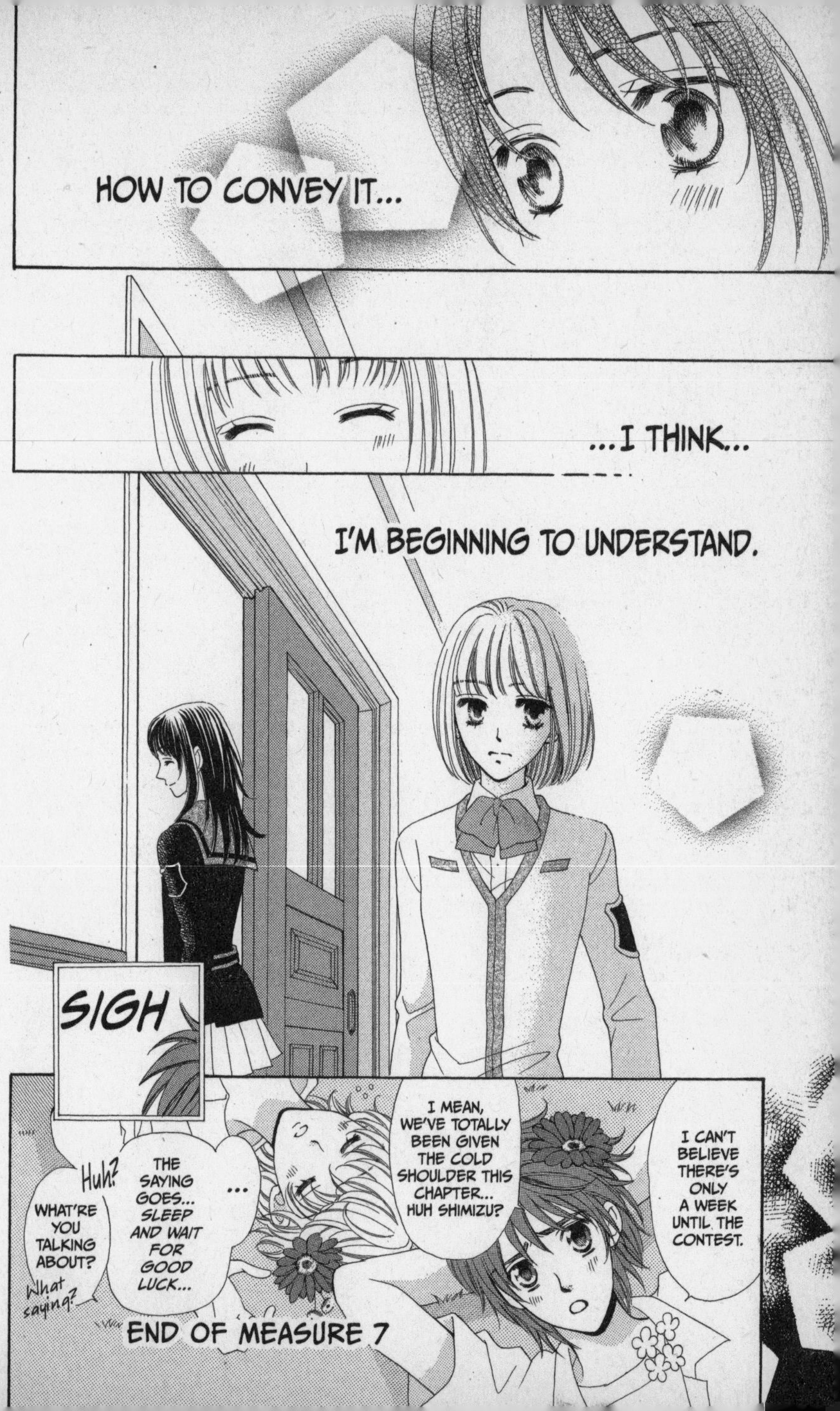
HOW TO CONVEY IT...
...I THINK...
I'M BEGINNING TO UNDERSTAND.
SIGH
I CAN'T BELIEVE THERE'S ONLY A WEEK UNTIL THE CONTEST.
I MEAN, WE'VE TOTALLY BEEN GIVEN THE COLD SHOULDER THIS CHAPTER... HUH SHIMIZU?
...
THE SAYING GOES... SLEEP AND WAIT FOR GOOD LUCK...
Huh? WHAT'RE YOU TALKING ABOUT?
What saying?
END OF MEASURE 7

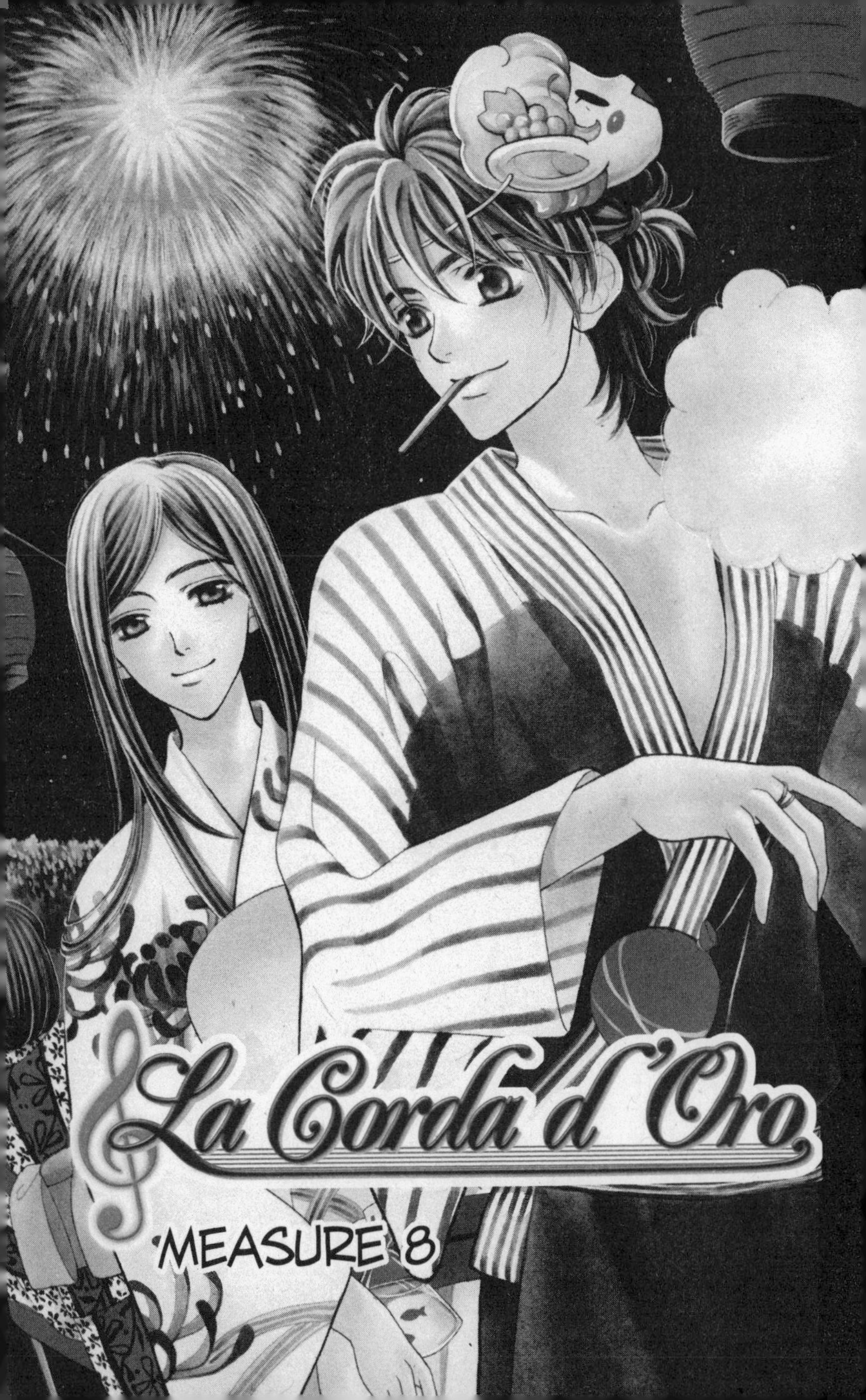
La Corda d'Oro
MEASURE 8

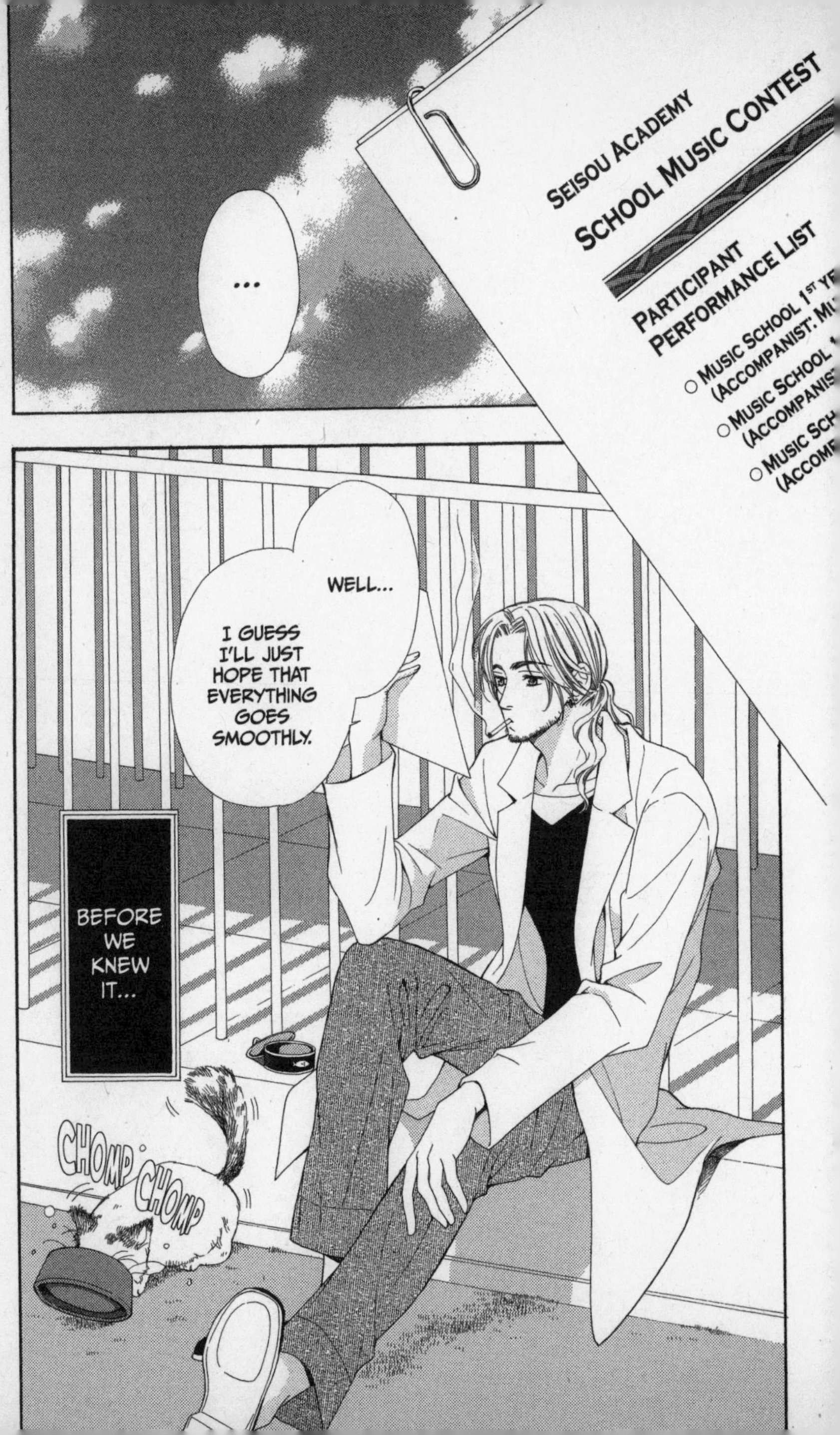
SEISOU ACADEMY
SCHOOL MUSIC CONTEST
PARTICIPANT PERFORMANCE LIST
...
WELL...
I GUESS I'LL JUST HOPE THAT EVERYTHING GOES SMOOTHLY.
BEFORE WE KNEW IT...
CHOMP CHOMP

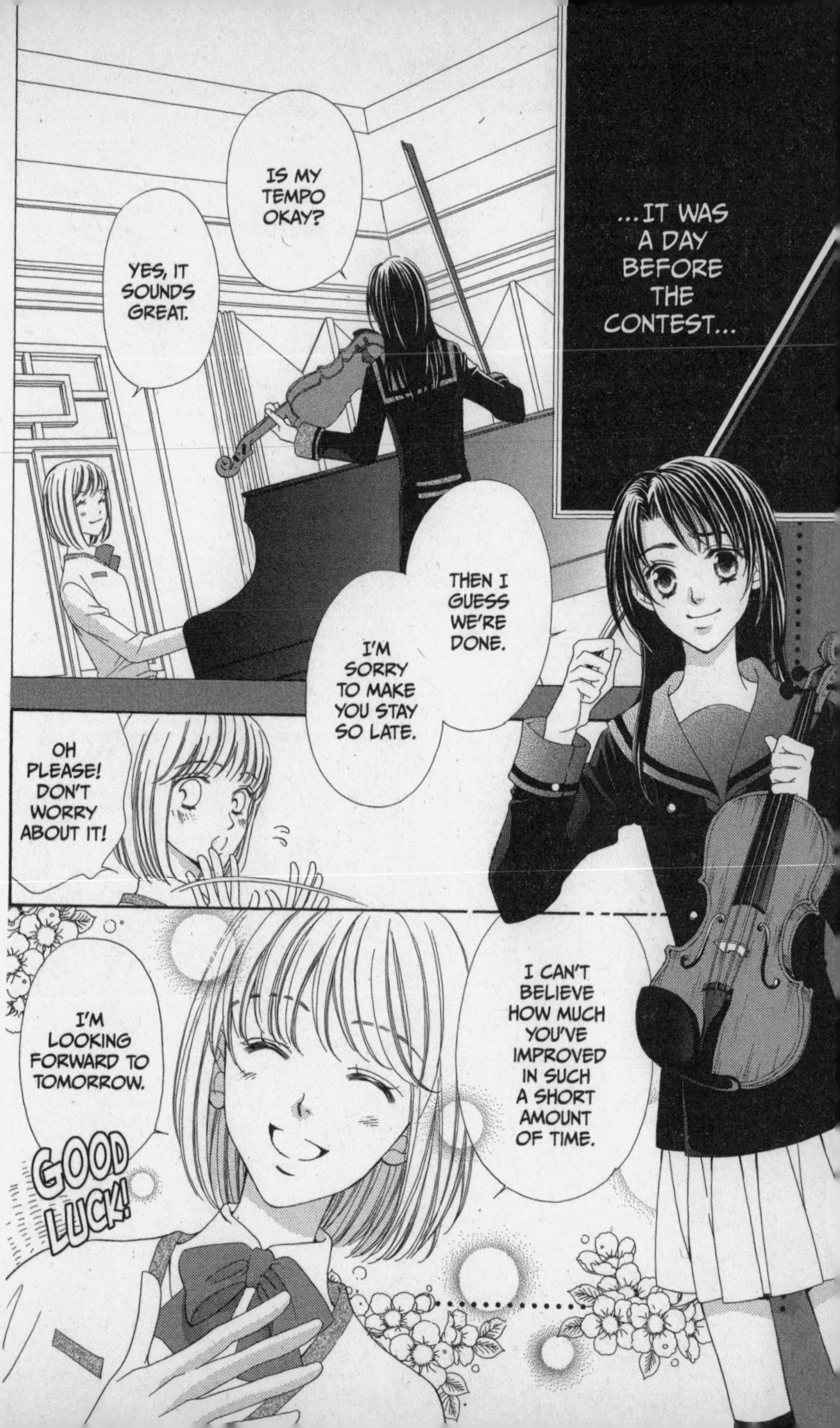
...IT WAS A DAY BEFORE THE CONTEST...
IS MY TEMPO OKAY?
YES, IT SOUNDS GREAT.
THEN I GUESS WE'RE DONE.
I'M SORRY TO MAKE YOU STAY SO LATE.
OH PLEASE! DON'T WORRY ABOUT IT!
I CAN'T BELIEVE HOW MUCH YOU'VE IMPROVED IN SUCH A SHORT AMOUNT OF TIME.
I'M LOOKING FORWARD TO TOMORROW.
GOOD LUCK!

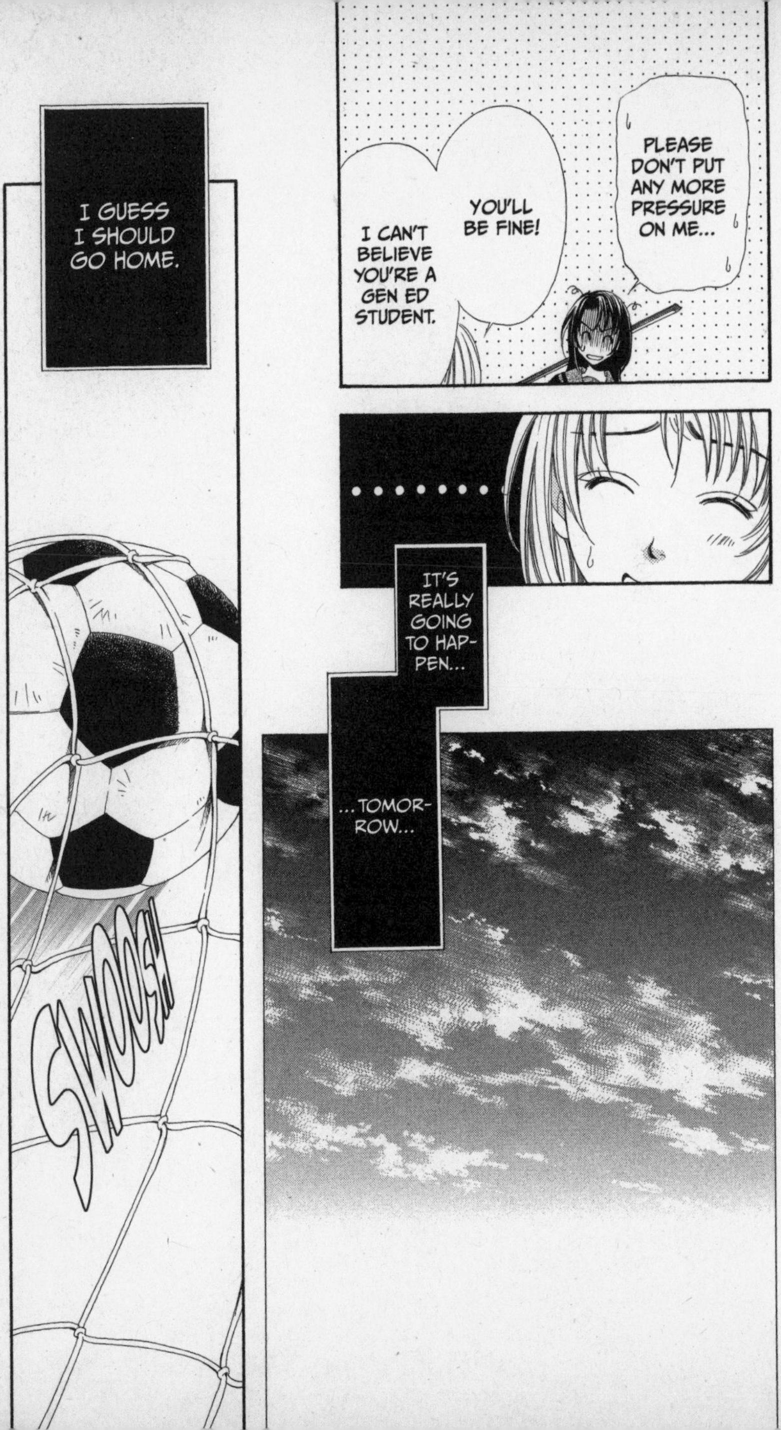
PLEASE DON'T PUT ANY MORE PRESSURE ON ME...
YOU'LL BE FINE!
I CAN'T BELIEVE YOU'RE A GEN ED STUDENT.
....
IT'S REALLY GOING TO HAP-PEN...
...TOMOR-ROW...
I GUESS I SHOULD GO HOME.
SWOOSH!

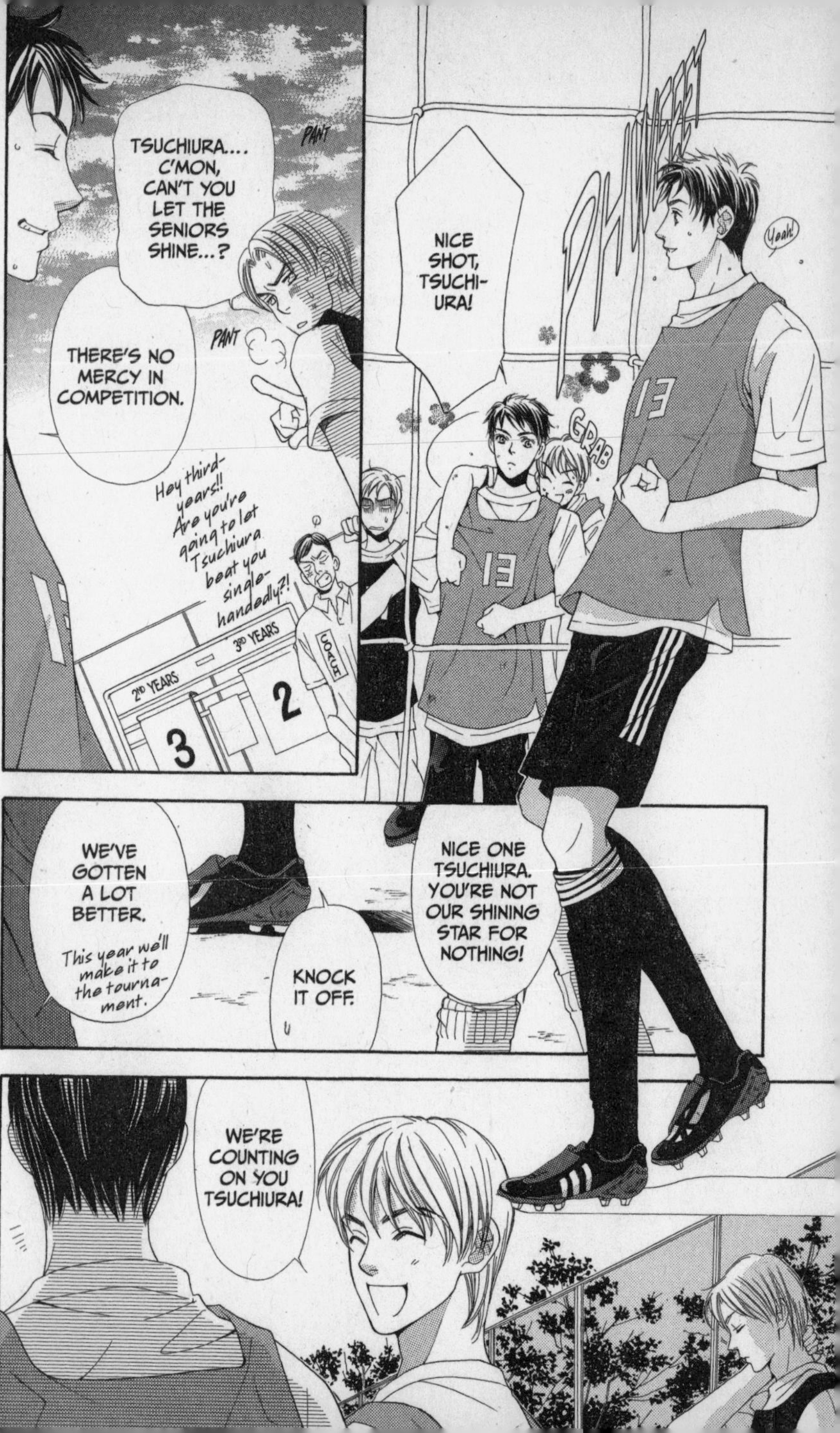
NICE SHOT, TSUCHIURA!
Yeah!
GRAB
TSUCHIURA.... C'MON, CAN'T YOU LET THE SENIORS SHINE...?
PANT
PANT
THERE'S NO MERCY IN COMPETITION.
Hey third-years!! Are you're going to let Tsuchiura beat you single-handedly?!
3RD YEARS
2ND YEARS
2
3
COACH
NICE ONE TSUCHIURA. YOU'RE NOT OUR SHINING STAR FOR NOTHING!
KNOCK IT OFF.
WE'VE GOTTEN A LOT BETTER.
This year we'll make it to the tournament.
WE'RE COUNTING ON YOU TSUCHIURA!

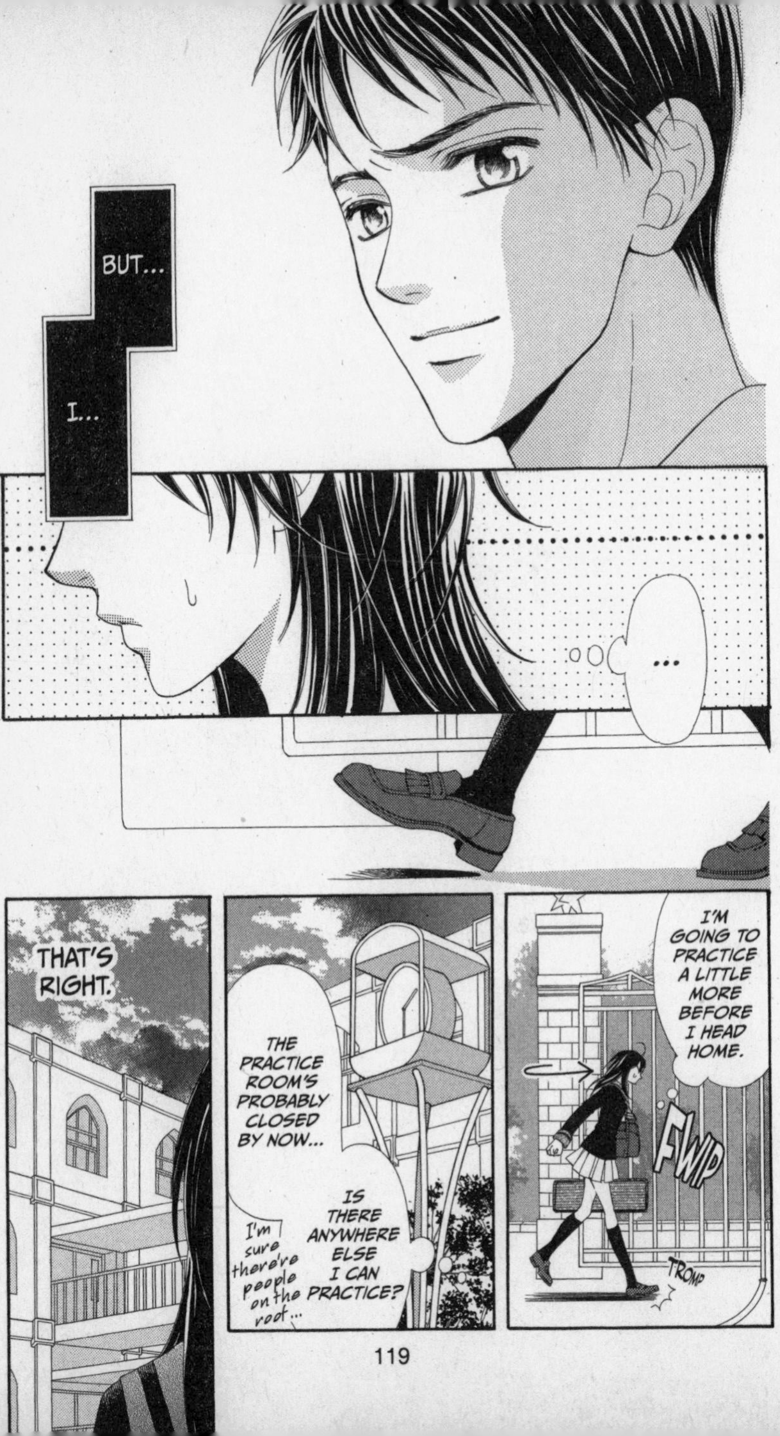
BUT...
I...
...
I'M GOING TO PRACTICE A LITTLE MORE BEFORE I HEAD HOME.
FWIP
TROMP
THE PRACTICE ROOM'S PROBABLY CLOSED BY NOW...
IS THERE ANYWHERE ELSE I CAN PRACTICE?
I'm sure there're people on the roof...
THAT'S RIGHT.

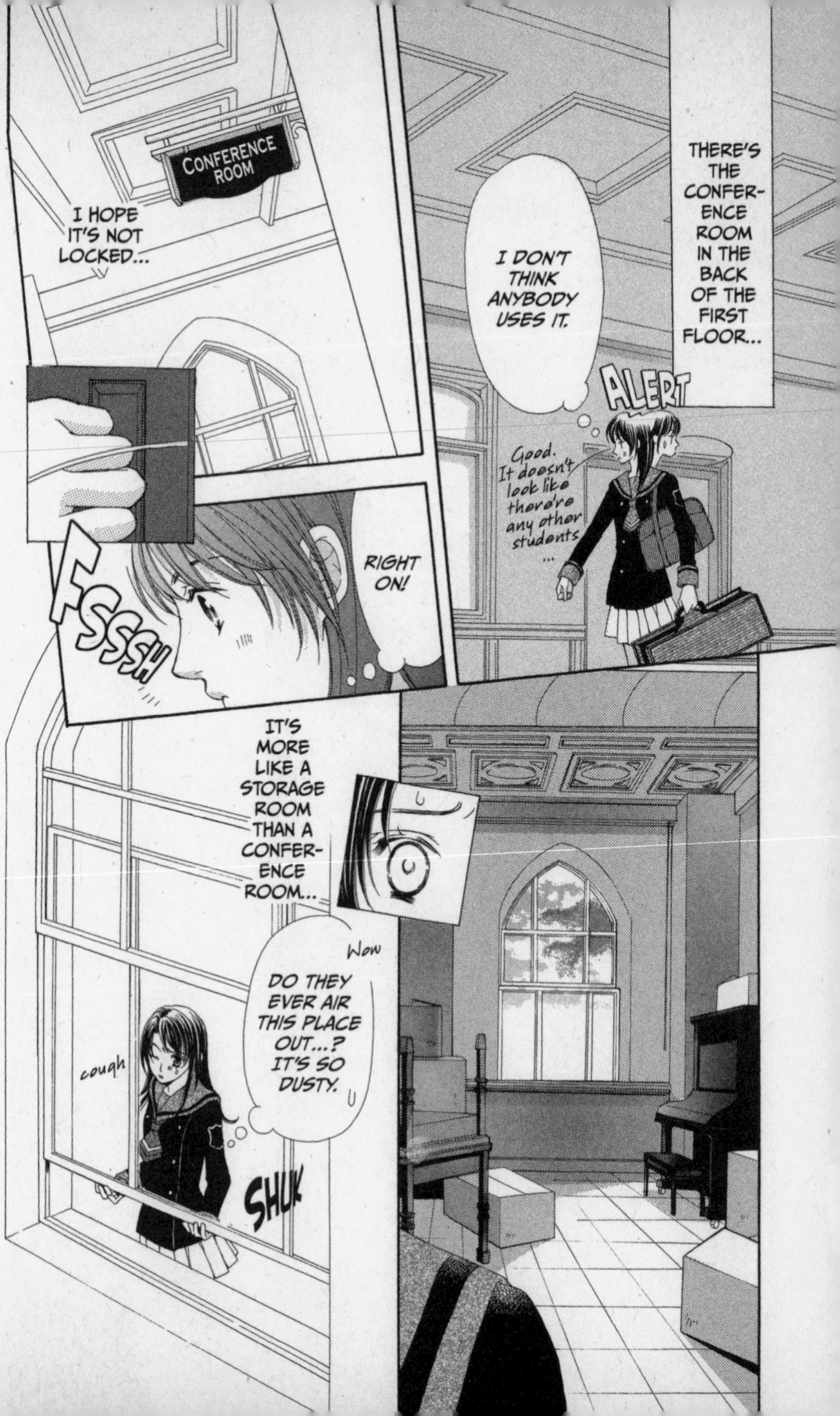
THERE'S THE CONFER-ENCE ROOM IN THE BACK OF THE FIRST FLOOR...
I DON'T THINK ANYBODY USES IT.
ALERT
Good. It doesn't look like there're any other students...
CONFERENCE ROOM
I HOPE IT'S NOT LOCKED...
FSSSH
RIGHT ON!
IT'S MORE LIKE A STORAGE ROOM THAN A CONFER-ENCE ROOM...
Wow
DO THEY EVER AIR THIS PLACE OUT...? IT'S SO DUSTY.
cough
SHUK

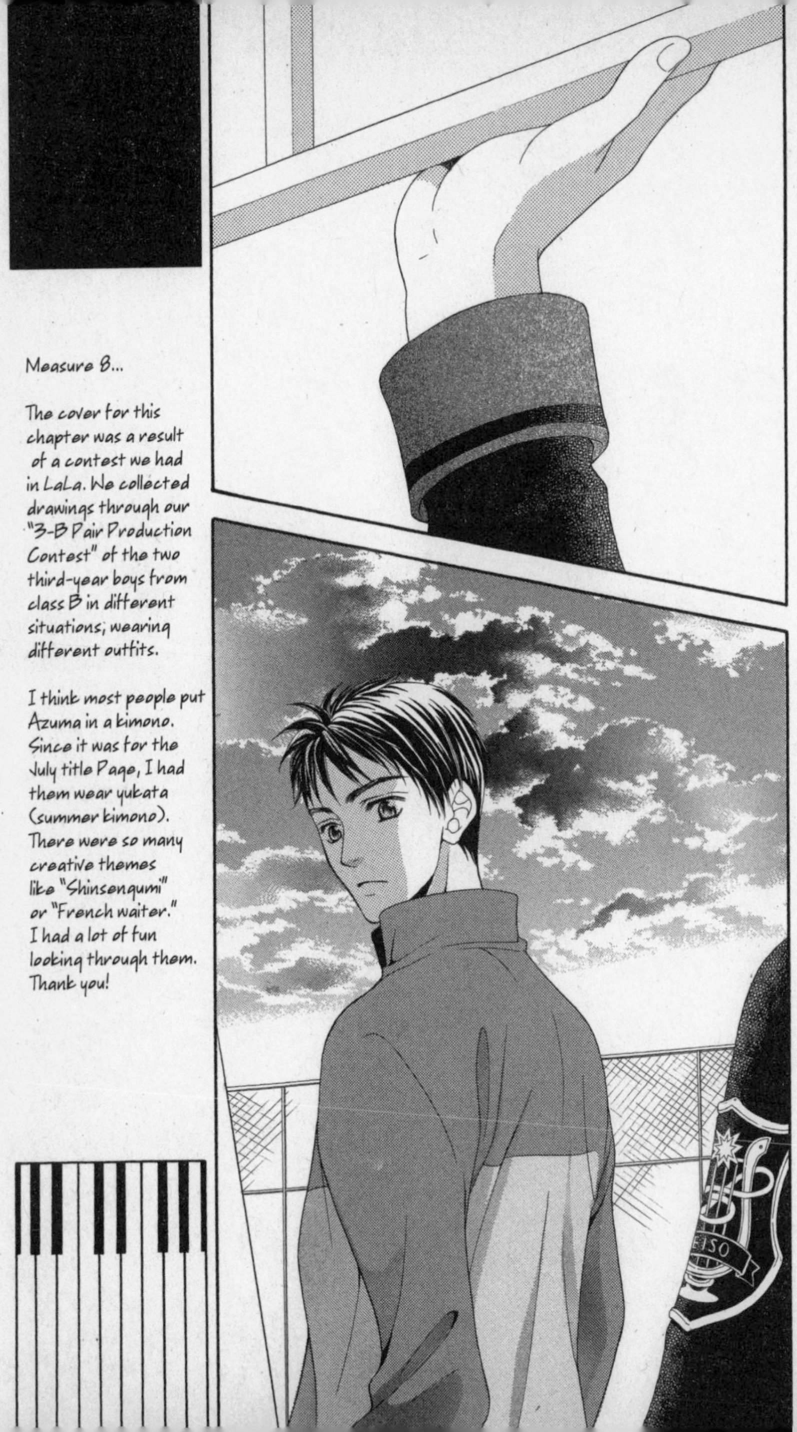

Measure 8...

The cover for this chapter was a result of a contest we had in LaLa. We collected drawings through our "3-B Pair Production Contest" of the two third-year boys from class B in different situations; wearing different outfits.

I think most people put Azuma in a kimono. Since it was for the July title Page, I had them wear yukata (summer kimono). There were so many creative themes like "Shinsengumi" or "French waiter." I had a lot of fun looking through them. Thank you!

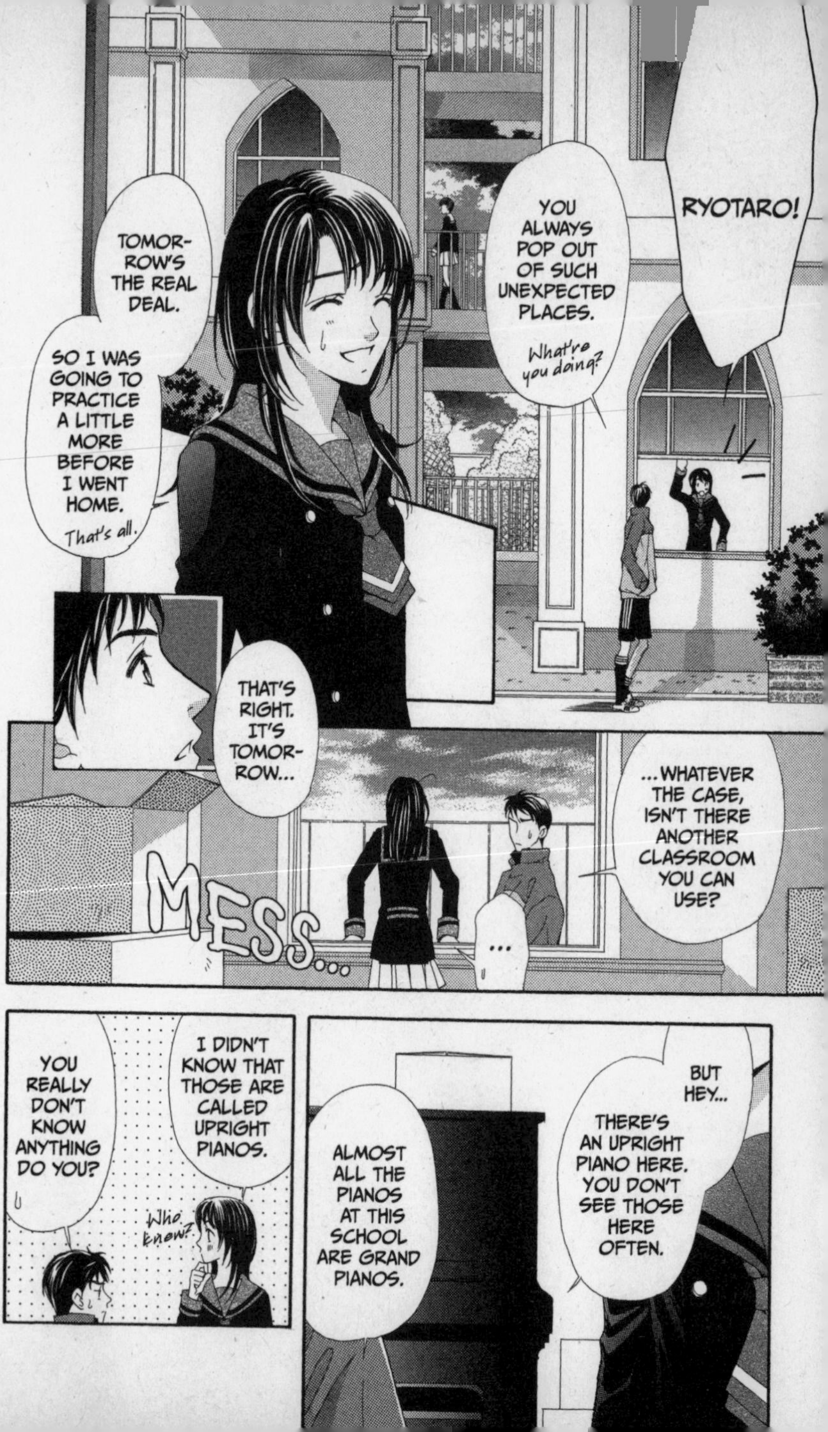

RYOTARO!
YOU ALWAYS POP OUT OF SUCH UNEXPECTED PLACES.
What're you doing?
TOMORROW'S THE REAL DEAL.
SO I WAS GOING TO PRACTICE A LITTLE MORE BEFORE I WENT HOME.
That's all.
THAT'S RIGHT. IT'S TOMORROW...
...WHATEVER THE CASE, ISN'T THERE ANOTHER CLASSROOM YOU CAN USE?
...
MESS...
BUT HEY...
THERE'S AN UPRIGHT PIANO HERE. YOU DON'T SEE THOSE HERE OFTEN.
ALMOST ALL THE PIANOS AT THIS SCHOOL ARE GRAND PIANOS.
I DIDN'T KNOW THAT THOSE ARE CALLED UPRIGHT PIANOS.
Who knew?
YOU REALLY DON'T KNOW ANYTHING DO YOU?

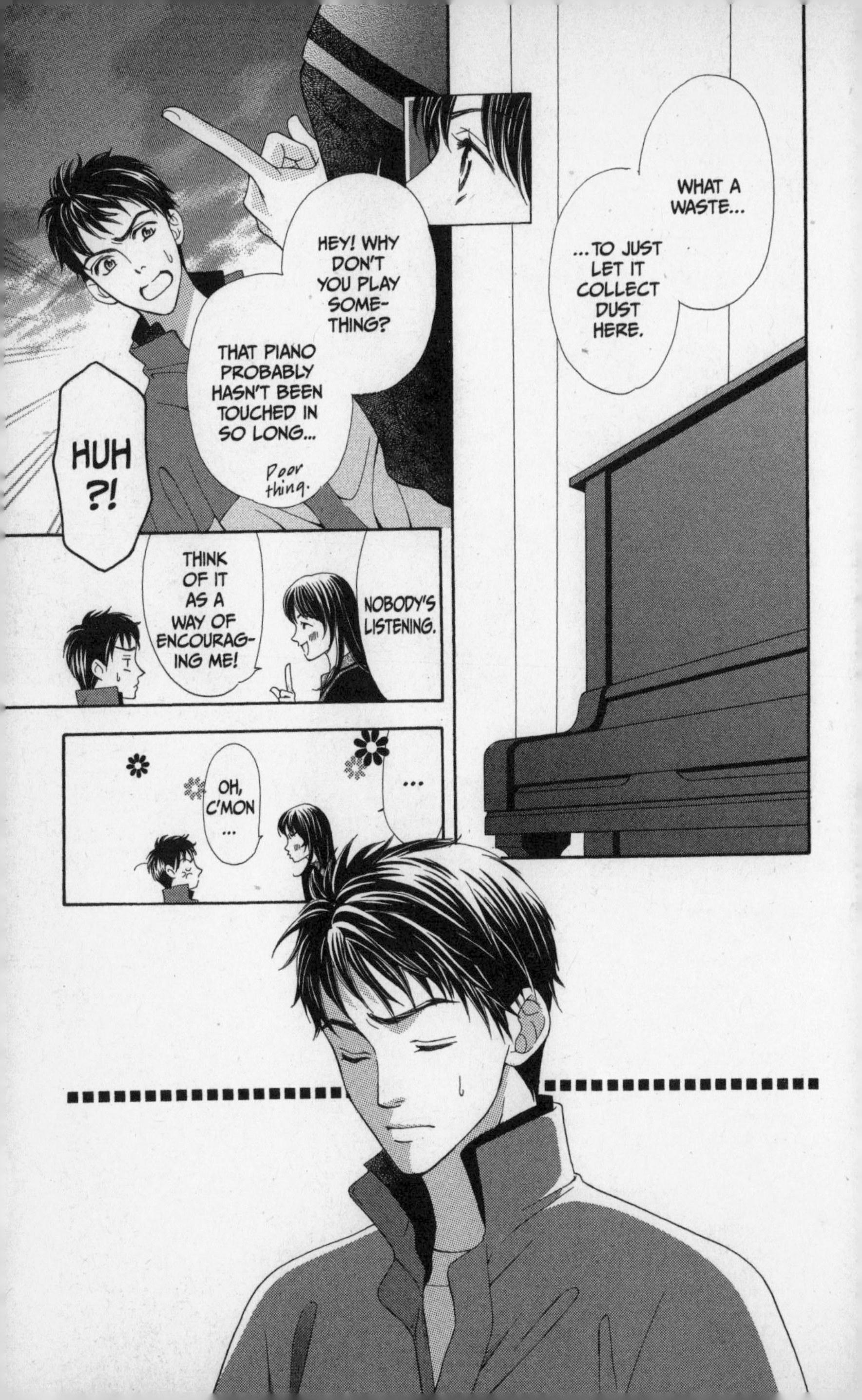
WHAT A WASTE...
...TO JUST LET IT COLLECT DUST HERE.
HEY! WHY DON'T YOU PLAY SOME-THING?
THAT PIANO PROBABLY HASN'T BEEN TOUCHED IN SO LONG...
Poor thing.
HUH ?!
NOBODY'S LISTENING.
THINK OF IT AS A WAY OF ENCOURAG-ING ME!
...
OH, C'MON ...

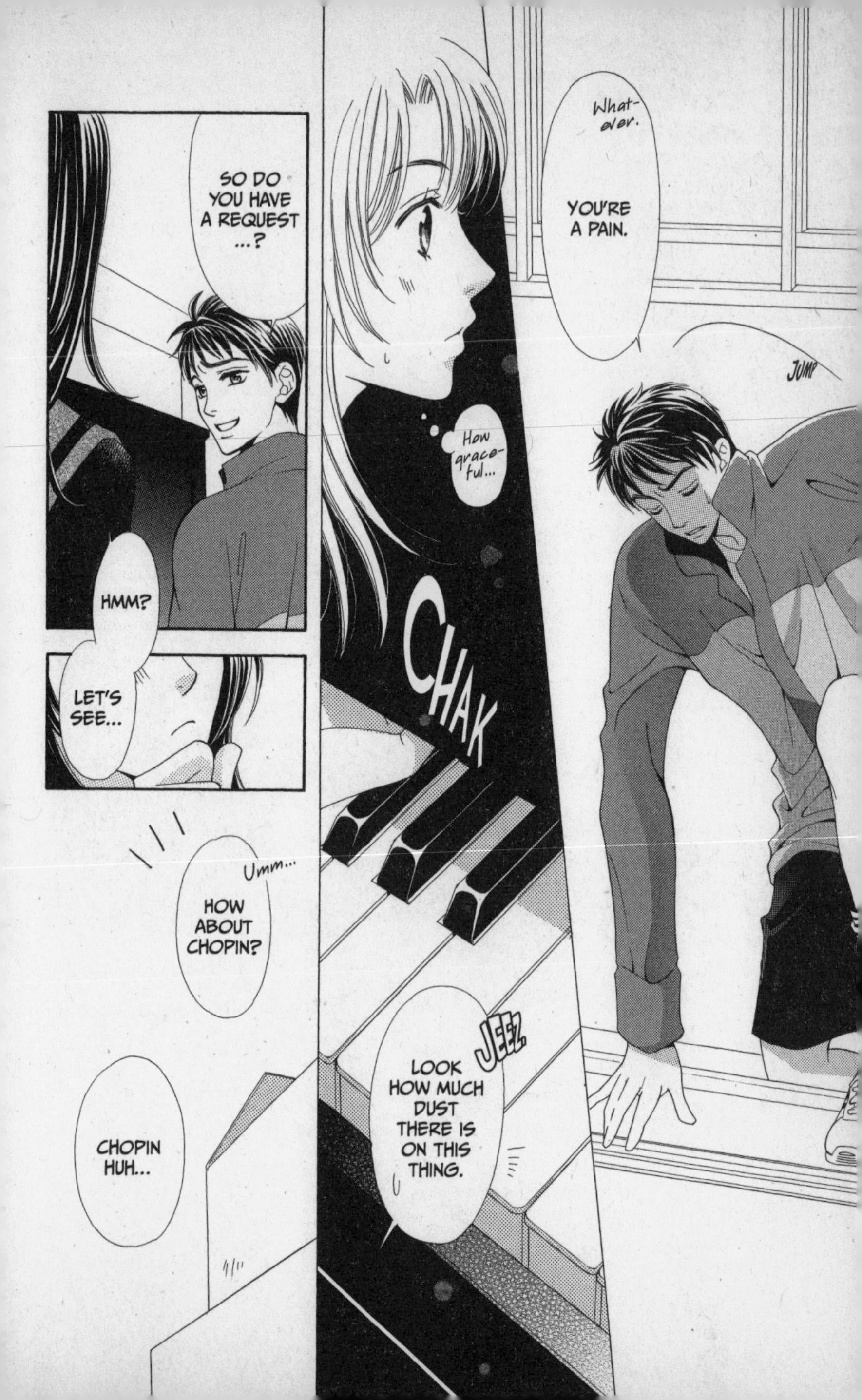
What-ever.
YOU'RE A PAIN.
JUMP
How graceful...
CHAK
JEEZ
LOOK HOW MUCH DUST THERE IS ON THIS THING.
SO DO YOU HAVE A REQUEST ...?
HMM?
LET'S SEE...
Umm...
HOW ABOUT CHOPIN?
CHOPIN HUH...

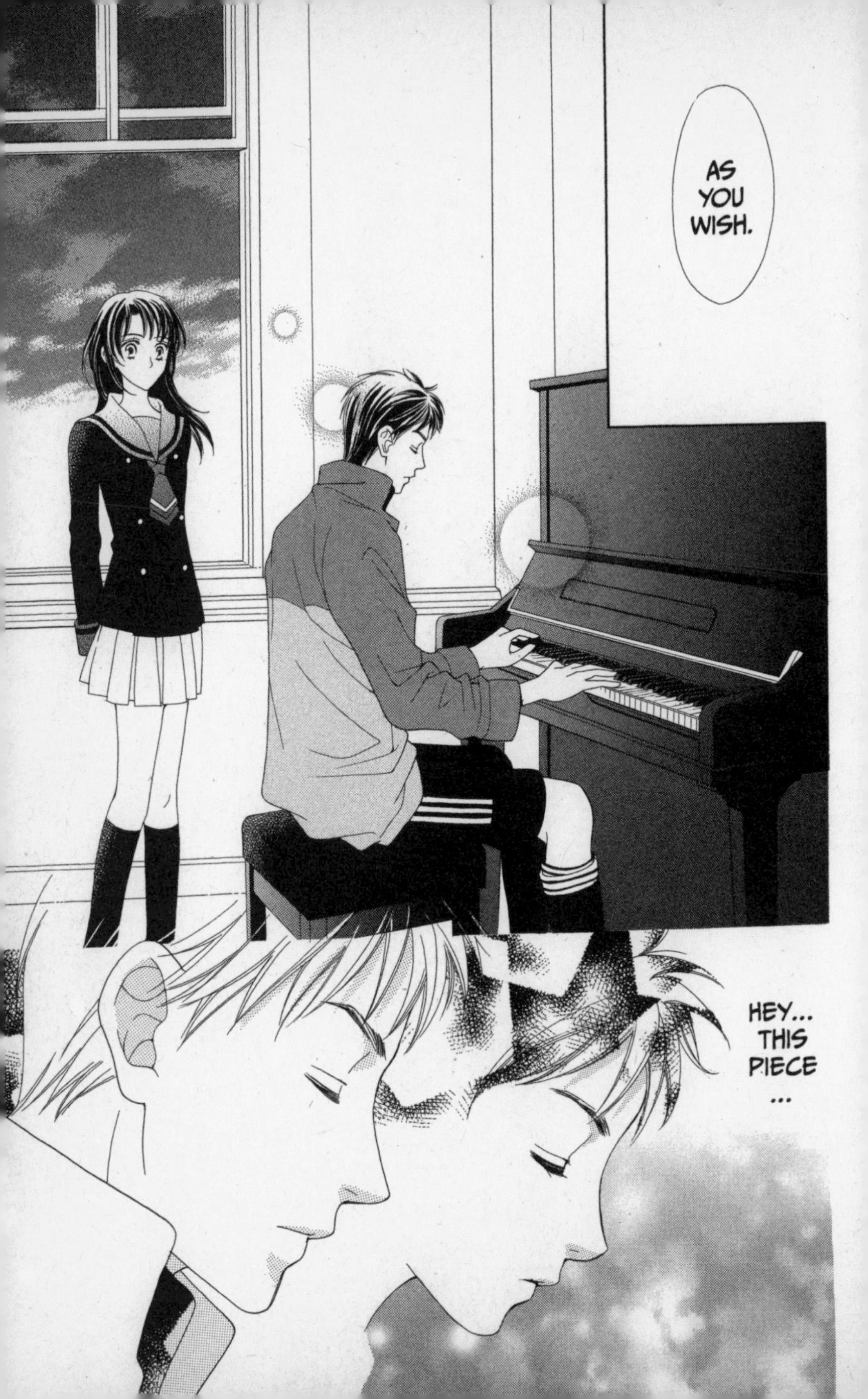
AS YOU WISH.
HEY... THIS PIECE ...

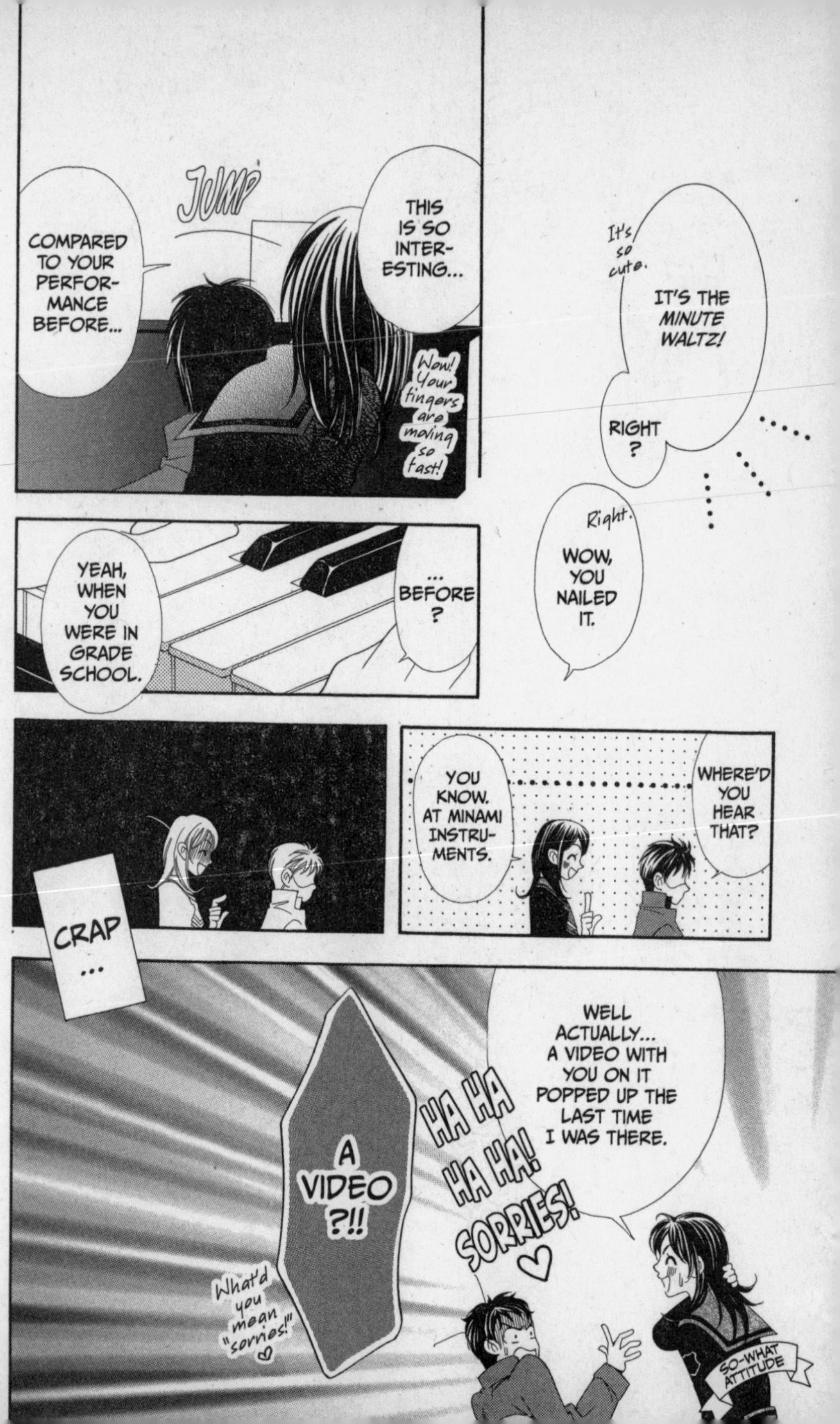
It's so cute.
IT'S THE MINUTE WALTZ!
RIGHT?
Right.
WOW, YOU NAILED IT.
THIS IS SO INTERESTING...
Wow! Your fingers are moving so fast!
JUMP
COMPARED TO YOUR PERFORMANCE BEFORE...
... BEFORE?
YEAH, WHEN YOU WERE IN GRADE SCHOOL.
WHERE'D YOU HEAR THAT?
YOU KNOW. AT MINAMI INSTRUMENTS.
CRAP...
WELL ACTUALLY... A VIDEO WITH YOU ON IT POPPED UP THE LAST TIME I WAS THERE.
HA HA HA HA! SORRIES! ♥
SO-WHAT ATTITUDE
A VIDEO?!!
What'd you mean "sorries!" ♥

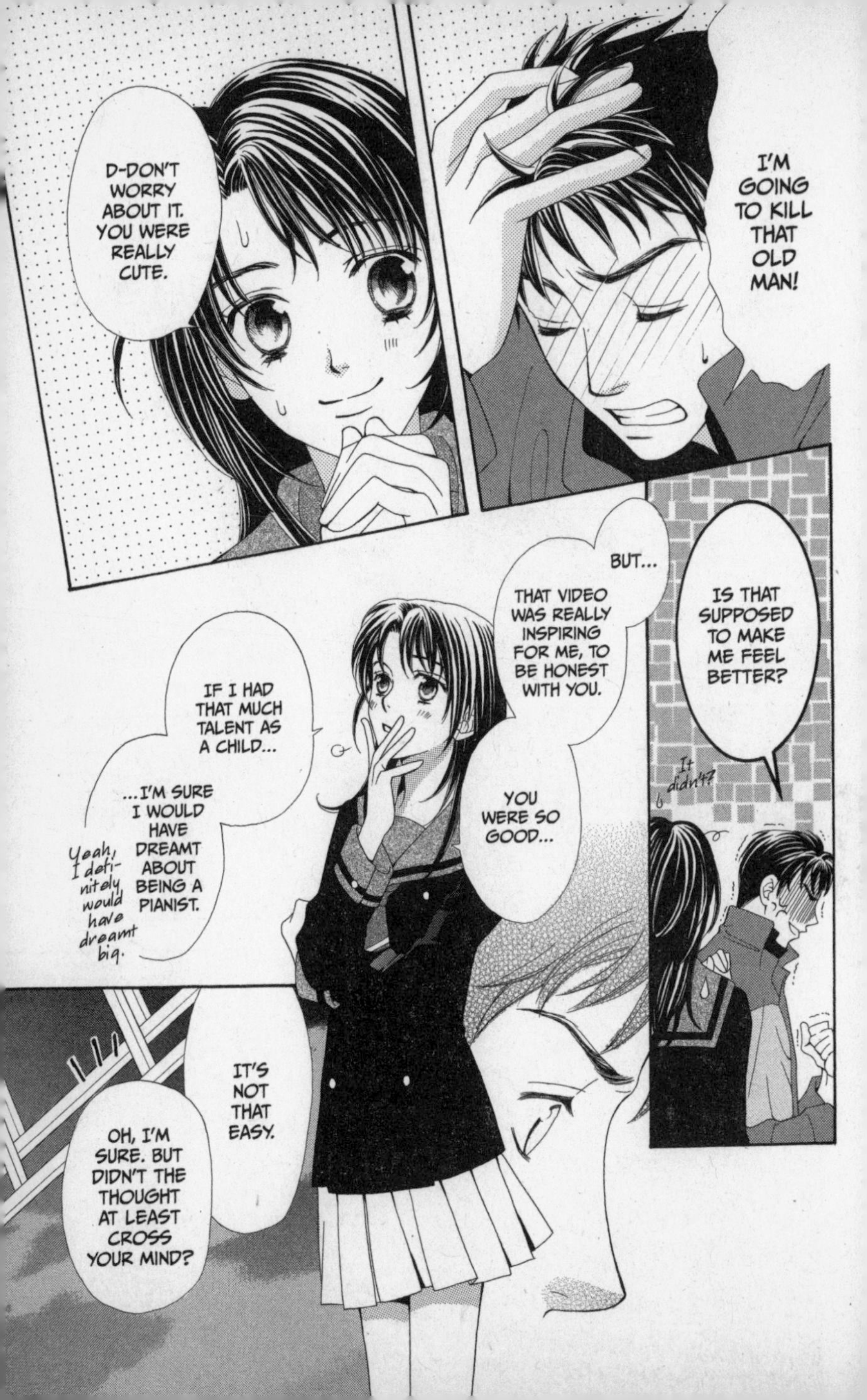
I'M GOING TO KILL THAT OLD MAN!
D-DON'T WORRY ABOUT IT. YOU WERE REALLY CUTE.
IS THAT SUPPOSED TO MAKE ME FEEL BETTER?
It didn't?
BUT...
THAT VIDEO WAS REALLY INSPIRING FOR ME, TO BE HONEST WITH YOU.
YOU WERE SO GOOD...
IF I HAD THAT MUCH TALENT AS A CHILD...
...I'M SURE I WOULD HAVE DREAMT ABOUT BEING A PIANIST.
Yeah, I definitely would have dreamt big.
IT'S NOT THAT EASY.
OH, I'M SURE. BUT DIDN'T THE THOUGHT AT LEAST CROSS YOUR MIND?

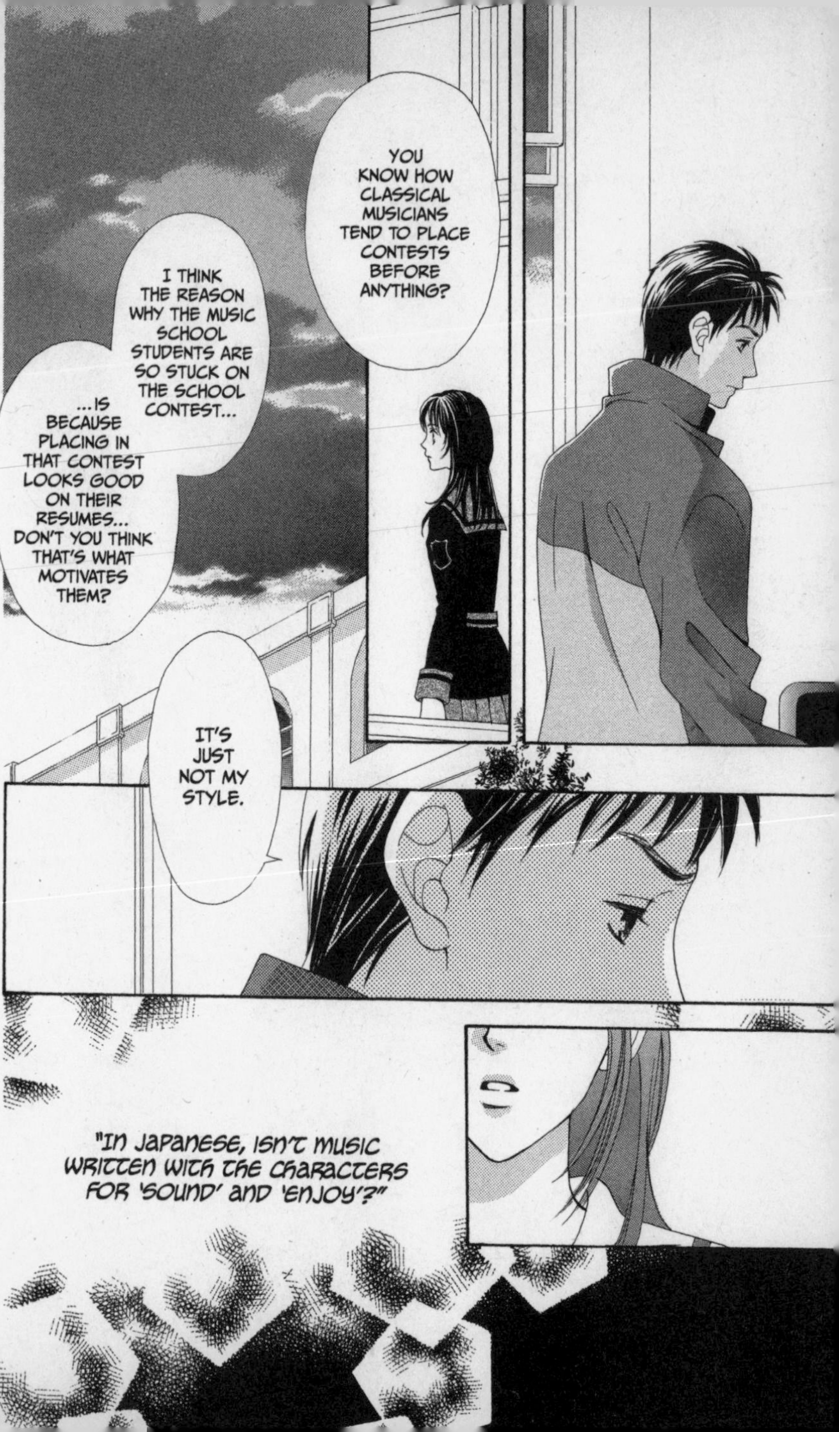
YOU KNOW HOW CLASSICAL MUSICIANS TEND TO PLACE CONTESTS BEFORE ANYTHING?
I THINK THE REASON WHY THE MUSIC SCHOOL STUDENTS ARE SO STUCK ON THE SCHOOL CONTEST...
...IS BECAUSE PLACING IN THAT CONTEST LOOKS GOOD ON THEIR RESUMES... DON'T YOU THINK THAT'S WHAT MOTIVATES THEM?
IT'S JUST NOT MY STYLE.
"In Japanese, isn't music written with the characters for 'sound' and 'enjoy'?"

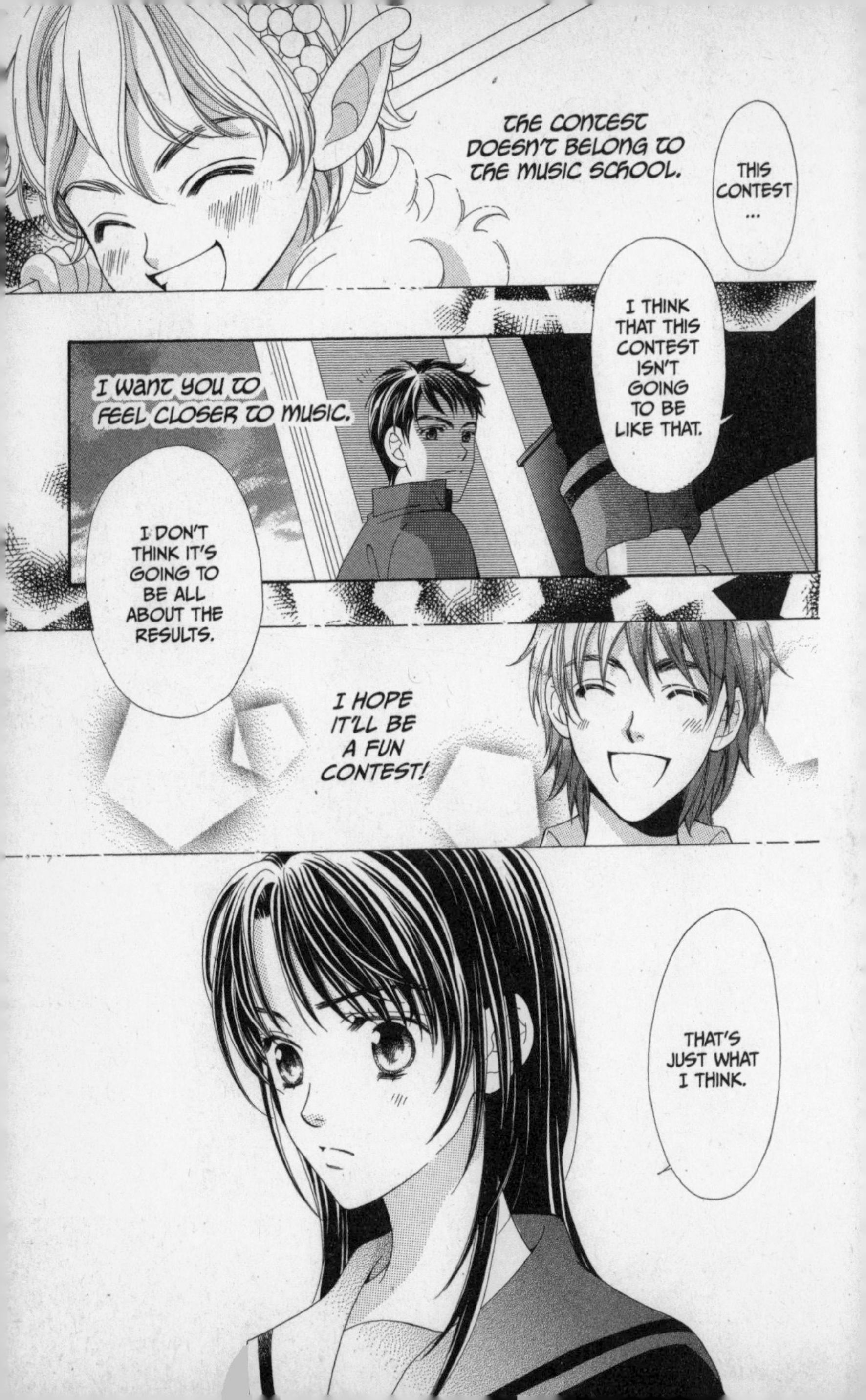
THIS CONTEST...
THE CONTEST DOESN'T BELONG TO THE MUSIC SCHOOL.
I THINK THAT THIS CONTEST ISN'T GOING TO BE LIKE THAT.
I WANT YOU TO FEEL CLOSER TO MUSIC.
I DON'T THINK IT'S GOING TO BE ALL ABOUT THE RESULTS.
I HOPE IT'LL BE A FUN CONTEST!
THAT'S JUST WHAT I THINK.

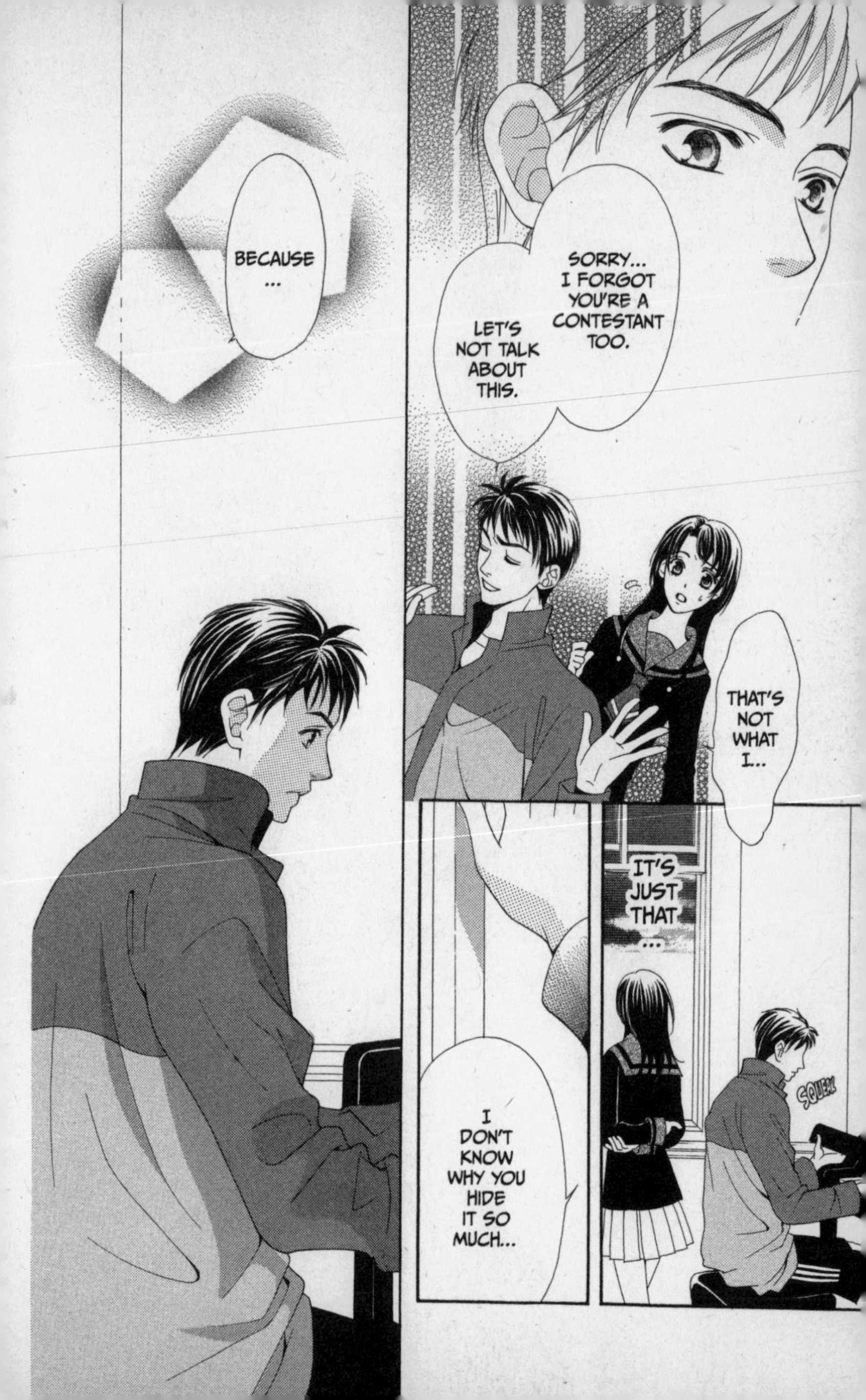
SORRY... I FORGOT YOU'RE A CONTESTANT TOO.
LET'S NOT TALK ABOUT THIS.
THAT'S NOT WHAT I...
IT'S JUST THAT...
SQUEAK
I DON'T KNOW WHY YOU HIDE IT SO MUCH...
BECAUSE...

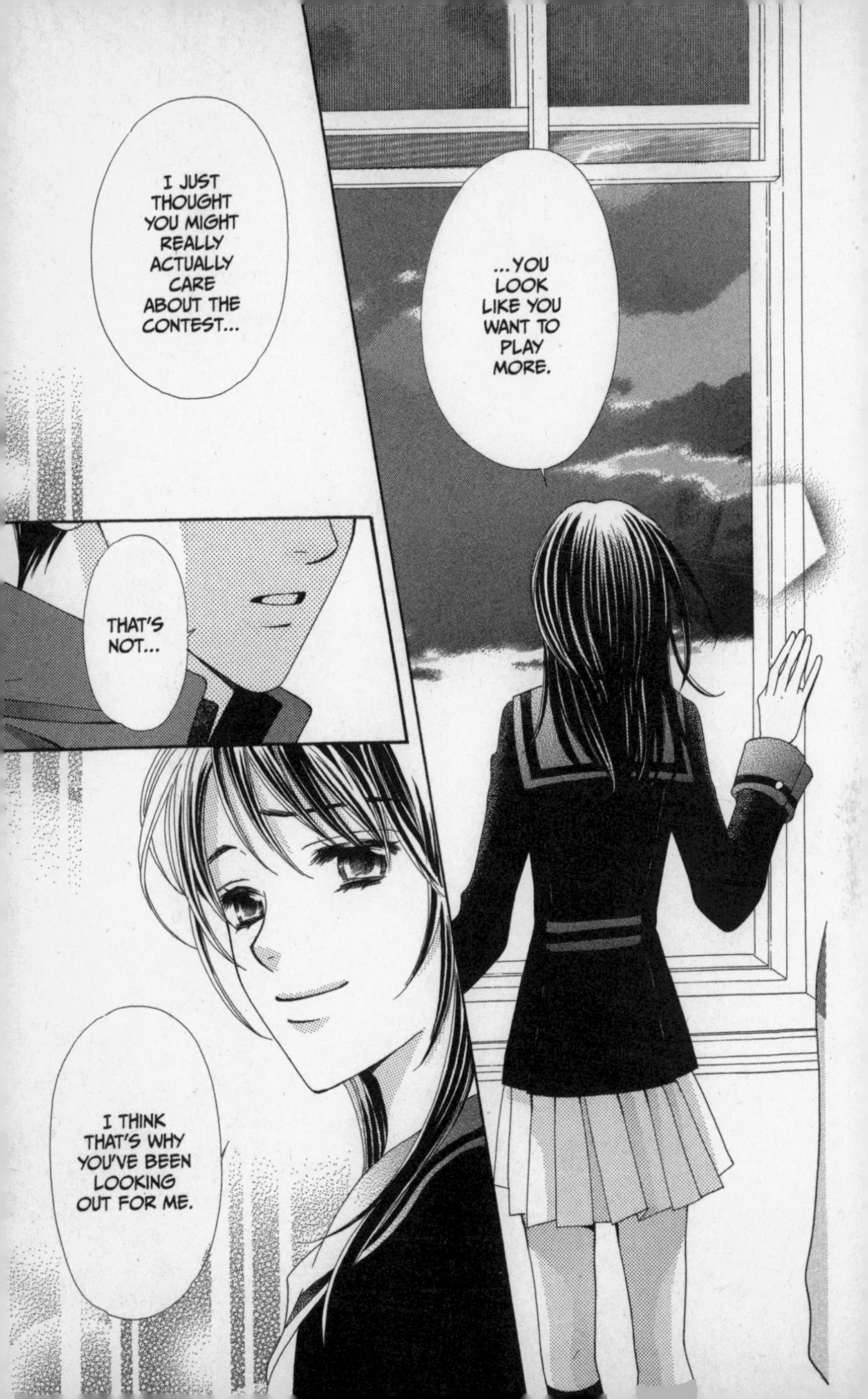
...YOU LOOK LIKE YOU WANT TO PLAY MORE.
I JUST THOUGHT YOU MIGHT REALLY ACTUALLY CARE ABOUT THE CONTEST...
THAT'S NOT...
I THINK THAT'S WHY YOU'VE BEEN LOOKING OUT FOR ME.

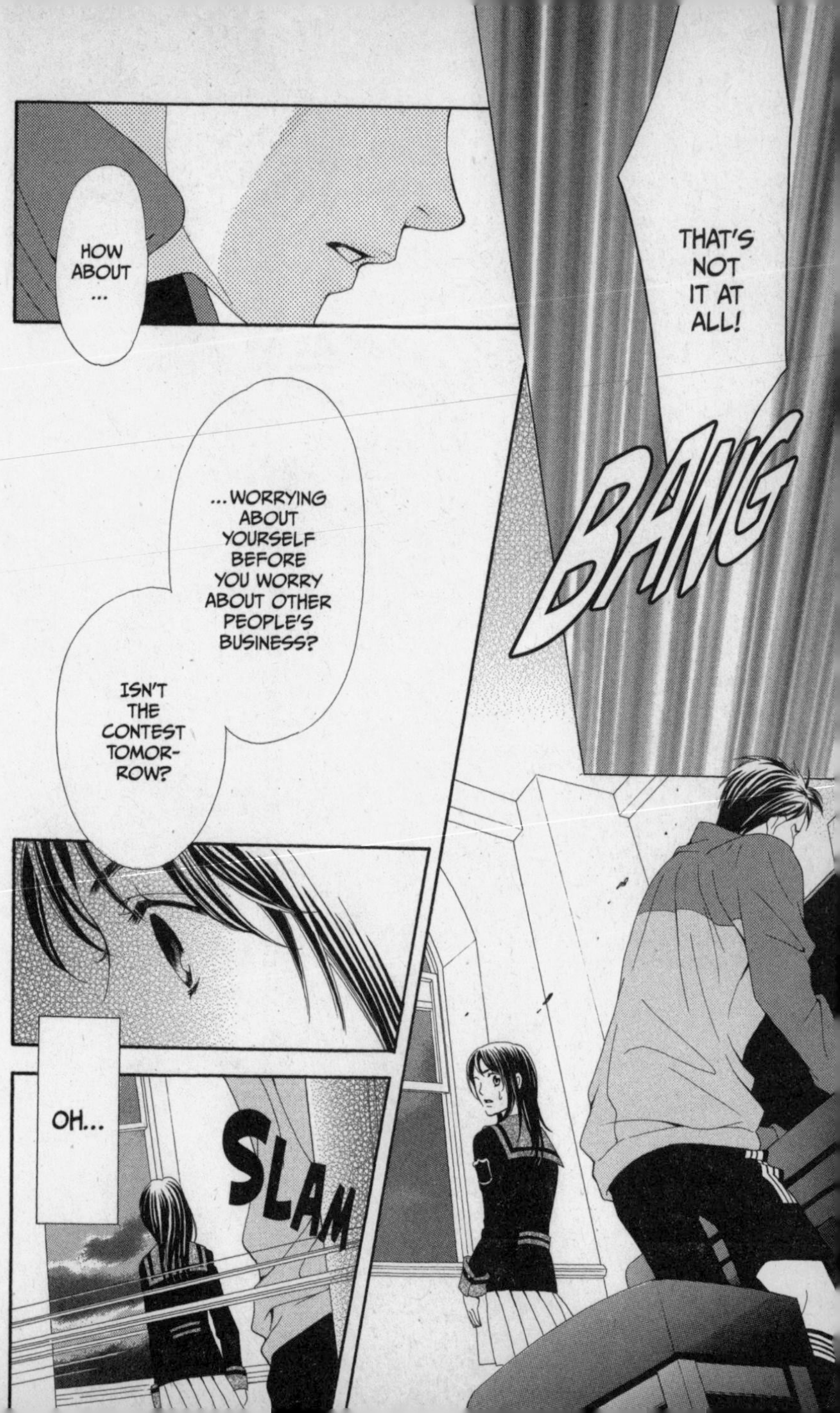
THAT'S NOT IT AT ALL!
BANG
HOW ABOUT ...
...WORRYING ABOUT YOURSELF BEFORE YOU WORRY ABOUT OTHER PEOPLE'S BUSINESS?
ISN'T THE CONTEST TOMOR-ROW?
OH...
SLAM

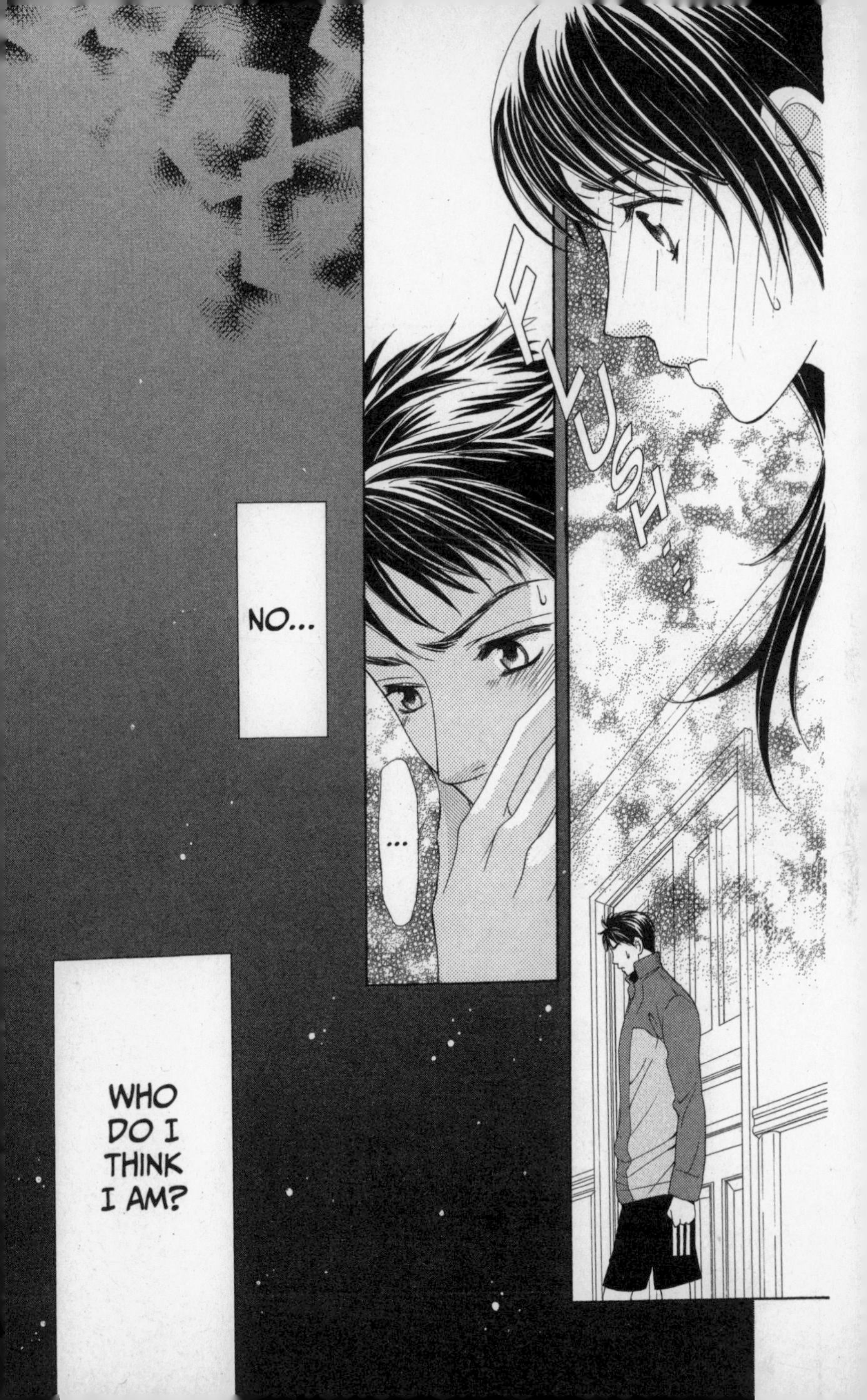
FLUSH...
...
NO...
WHO DO I THINK I AM?

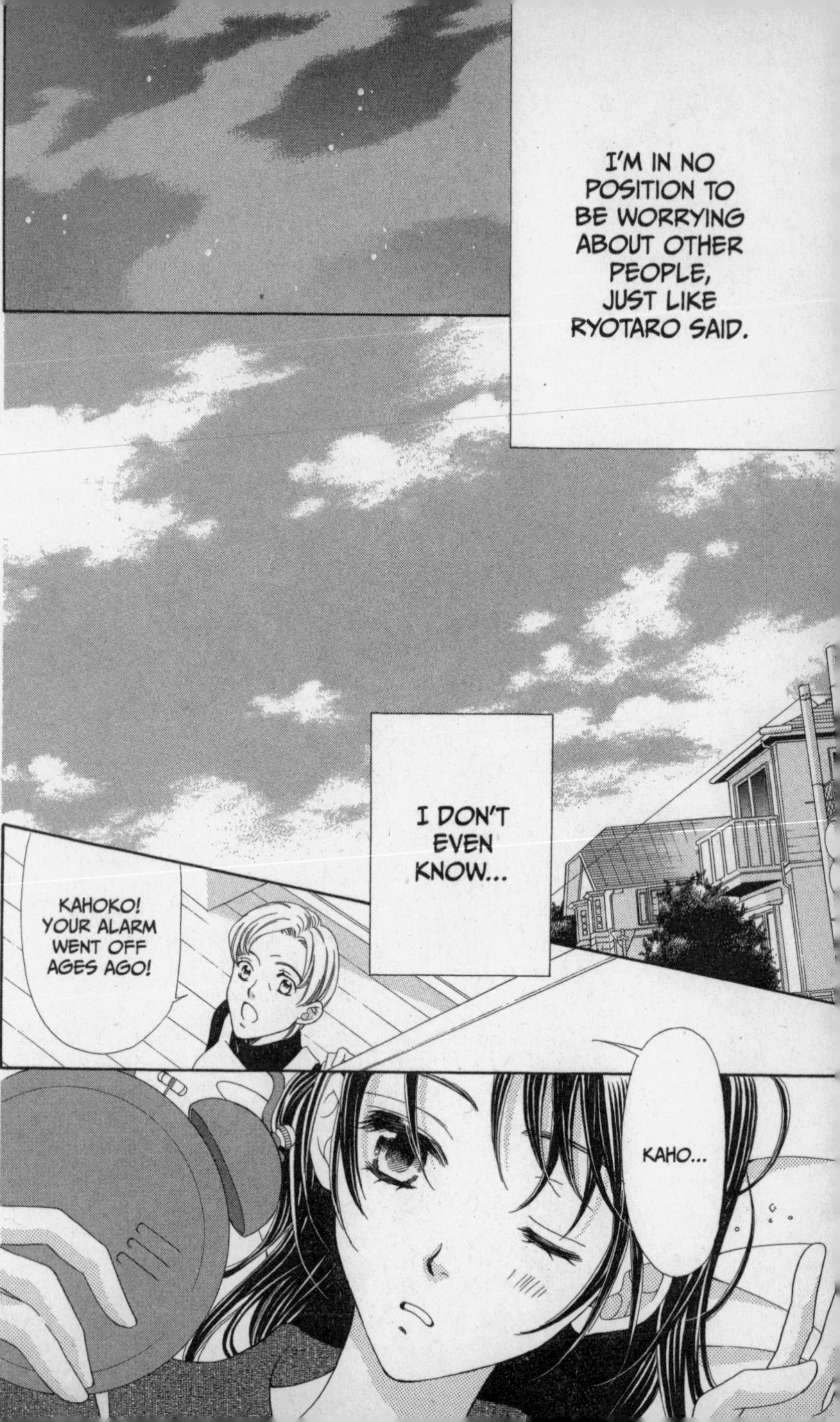
I'M IN NO POSITION TO BE WORRYING ABOUT OTHER PEOPLE, JUST LIKE RYOTARO SAID.
I DON'T EVEN KNOW...
KAHOKO! YOUR ALARM WENT OFF AGES AGO!
KAHO...

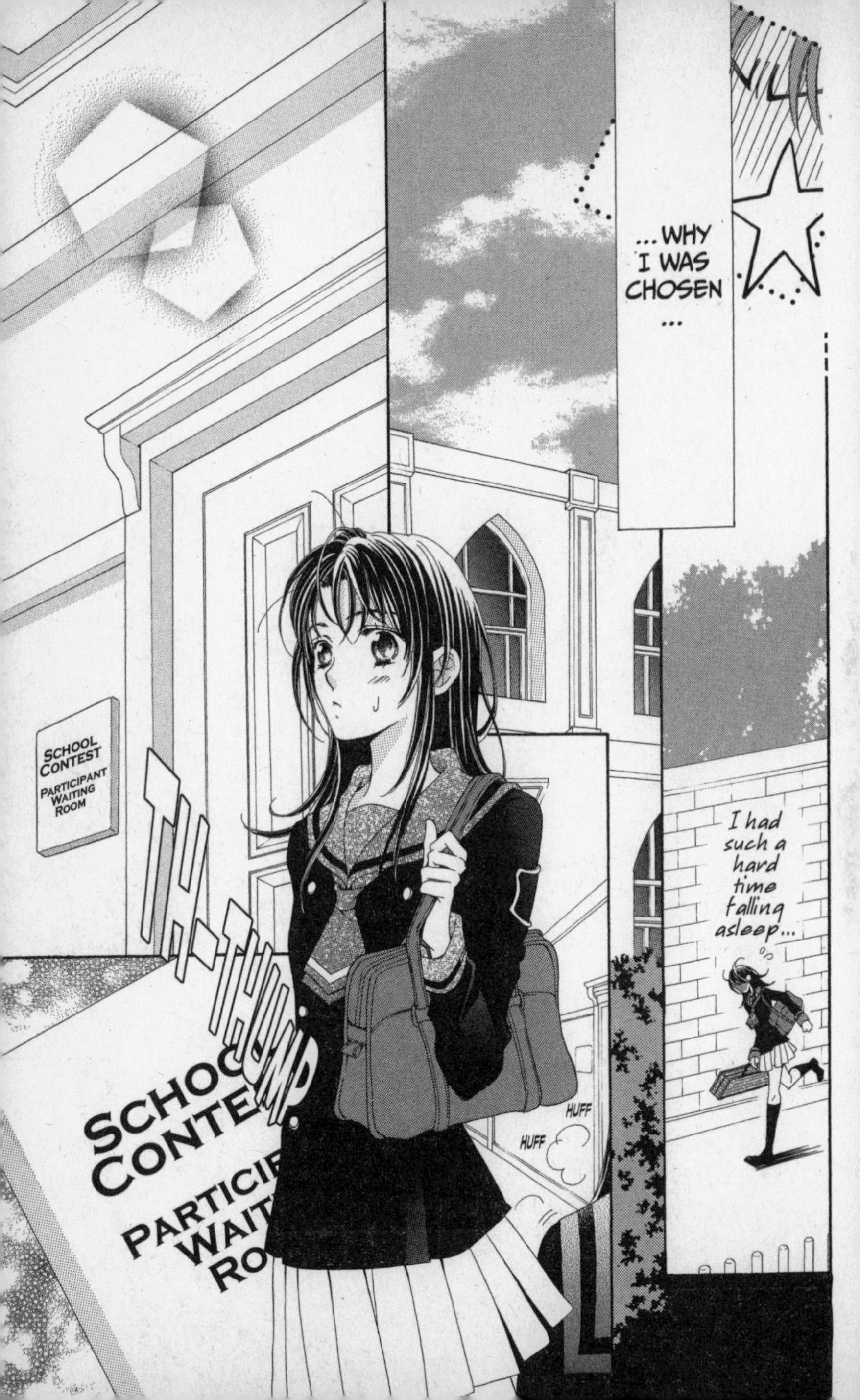
...WHY I WAS CHOSEN ...
I had such a hard time falling asleep...
HUFF
HUFF
SCHOOL CONTEST PARTICIPANT WAITING ROOM
TH-THUMP

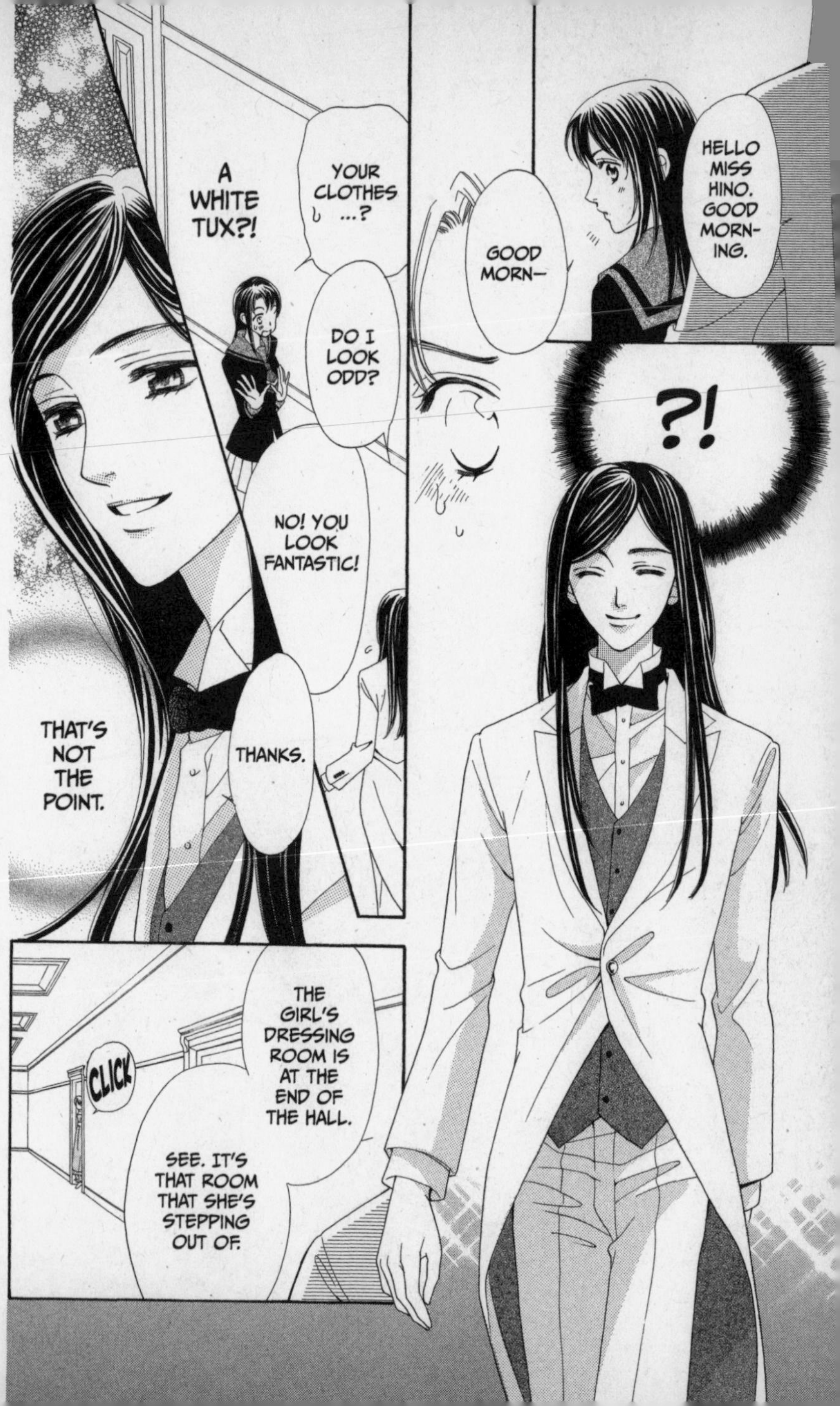
HELLO MISS HINO. GOOD MORNING.
GOOD MORN—
?!
YOUR CLOTHES ...?
A WHITE TUX?!
DO I LOOK ODD?
NO! YOU LOOK FANTASTIC!
THANKS.
THAT'S NOT THE POINT.
THE GIRL'S DRESSING ROOM IS AT THE END OF THE HALL.
CLICK
SEE. IT'S THAT ROOM THAT SHE'S STEPPING OUT OF.

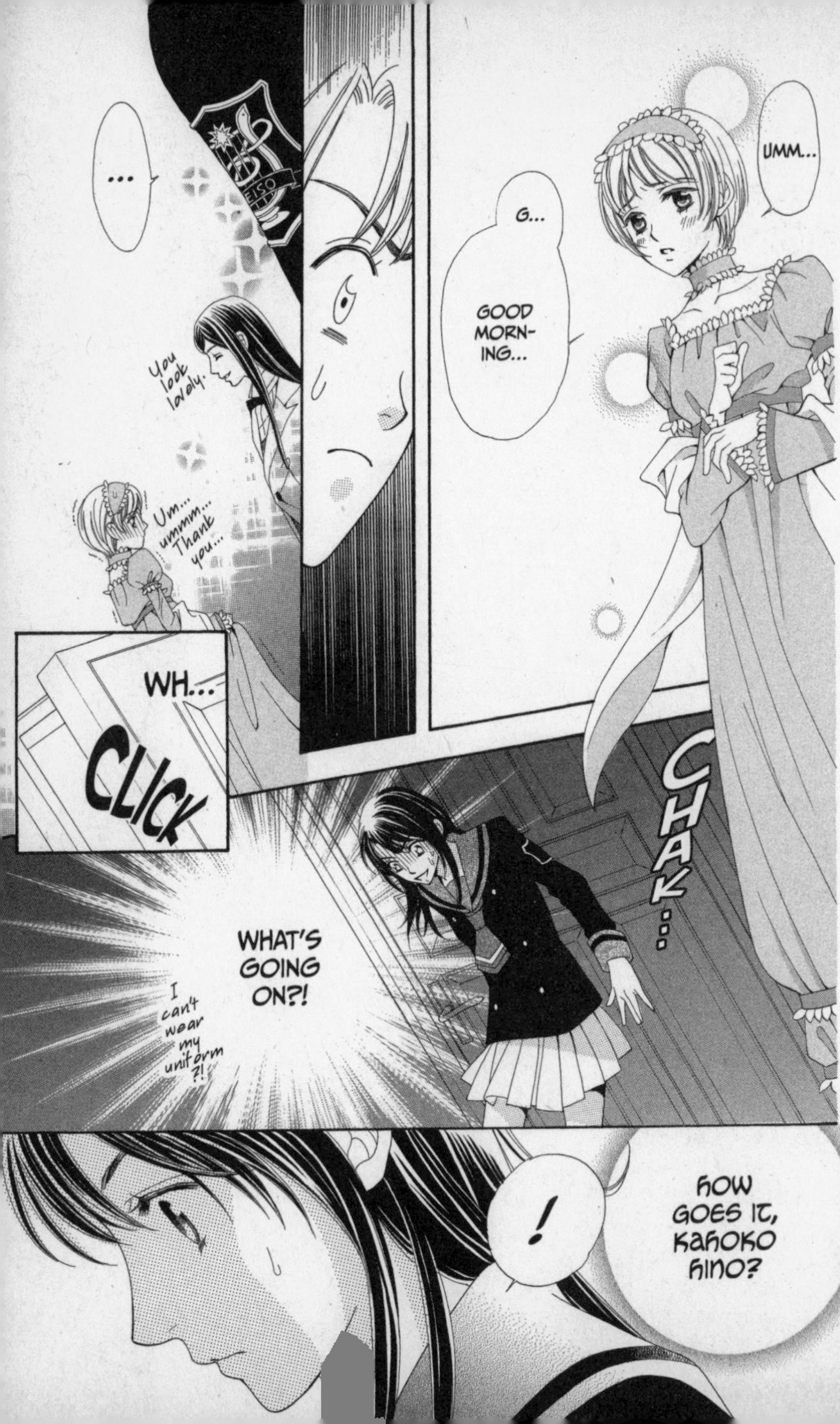
UMM...
G...
GOOD MORNING...
...
You look lovely.
Um... ummm... Thank you...
CHAK...
WH...
CLICK
WHAT'S GOING ON?!
I can't wear my uniform?!
HOW GOES IT, KAHOKO HINO?
!

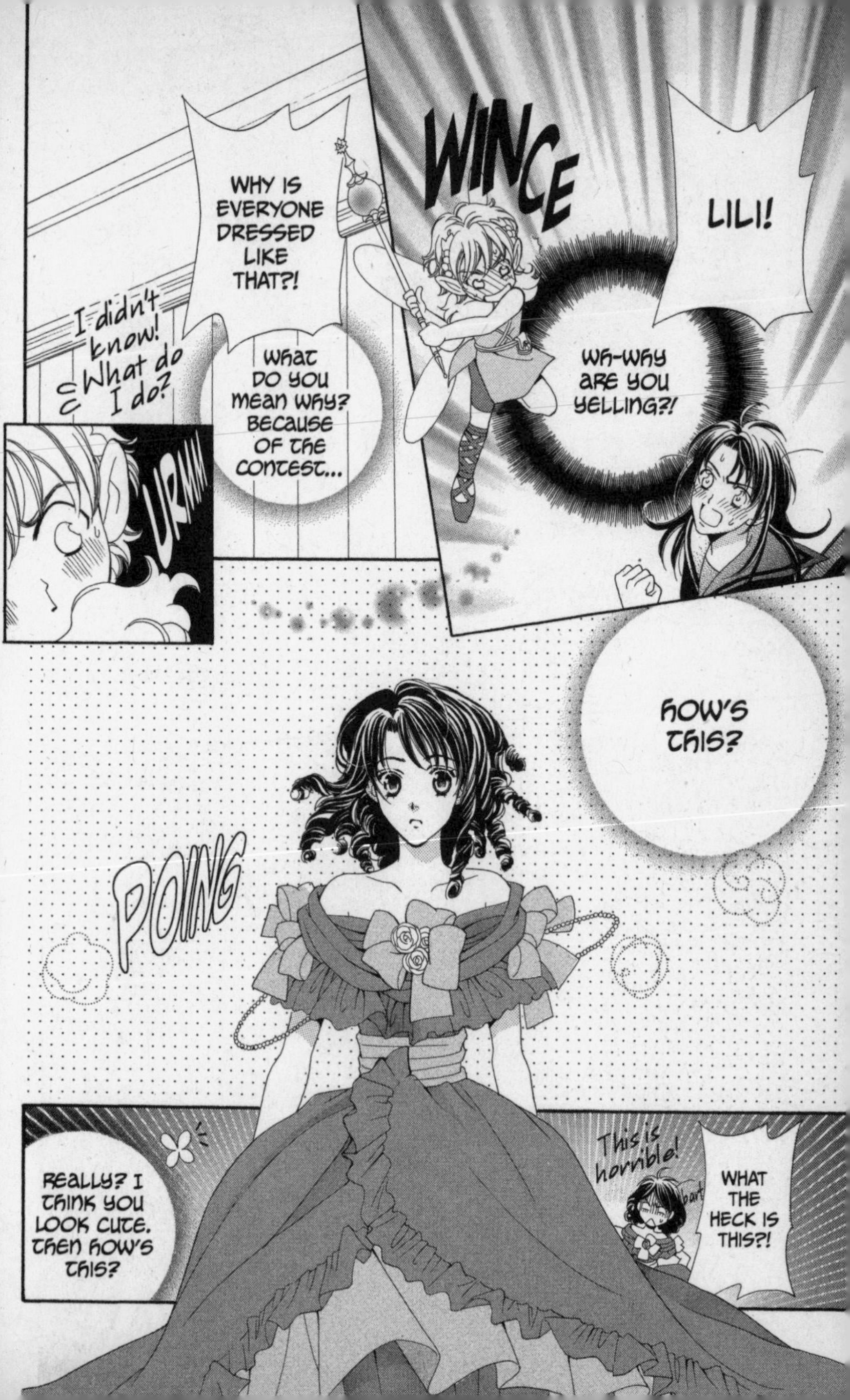
LILI!
WINCE
WH-WHY ARE YOU YELLING?!
WHY IS EVERYONE DRESSED LIKE THAT?!
WHAT DO YOU MEAN WHY? BECAUSE OF THE CONTEST...
I didn't know! What do I do?
URMM
HOW'S THIS?
POING
WHAT THE HECK IS THIS?!
This is horrible!
REALLY? I THINK YOU LOOK CUTE. THEN HOW'S THIS?

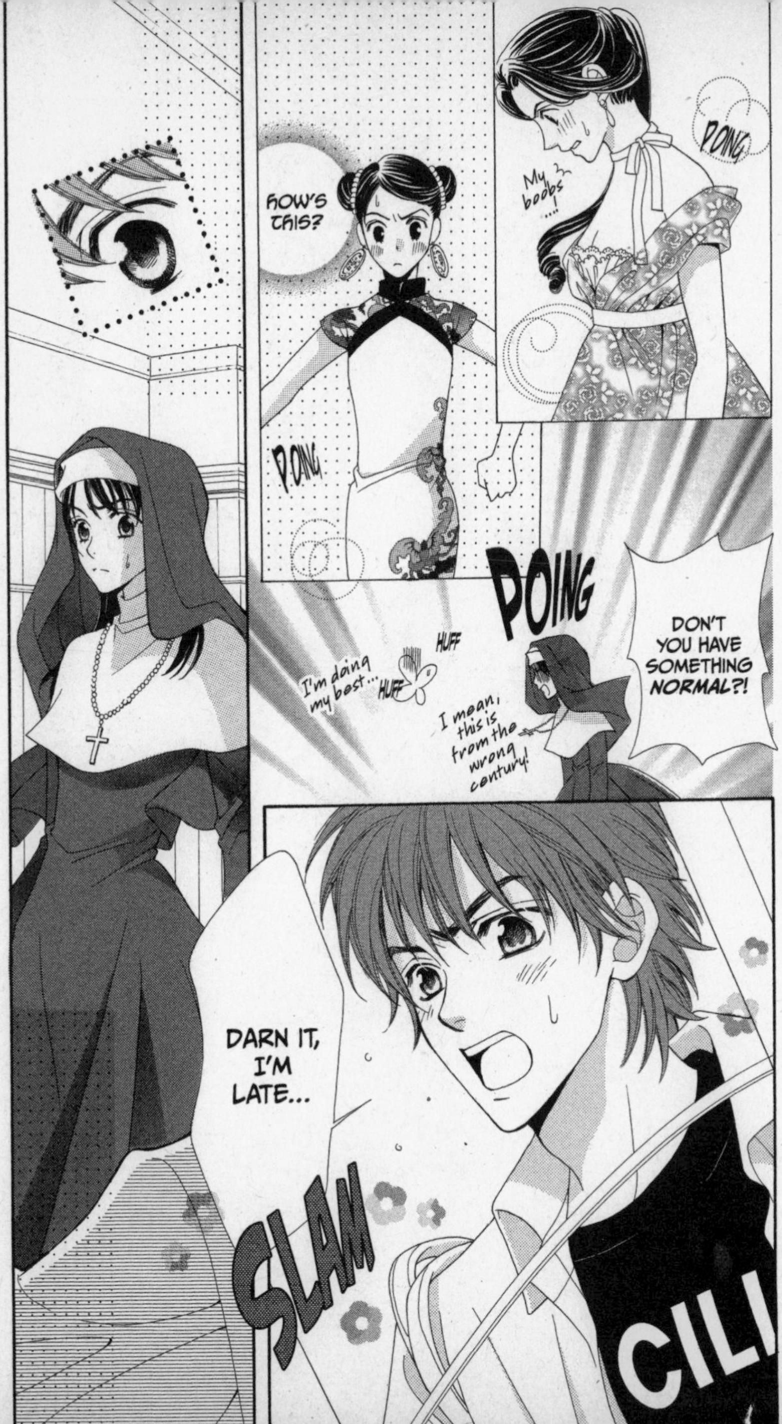

My boobs...!
POING
HOW'S THIS?
POING
DON'T YOU HAVE SOMETHING NORMAL?!
POING
I mean, this is from the wrong century!
HUFF
HUFF
I'm doing my best...
DARN IT, I'M LATE...
SLAM
CILI

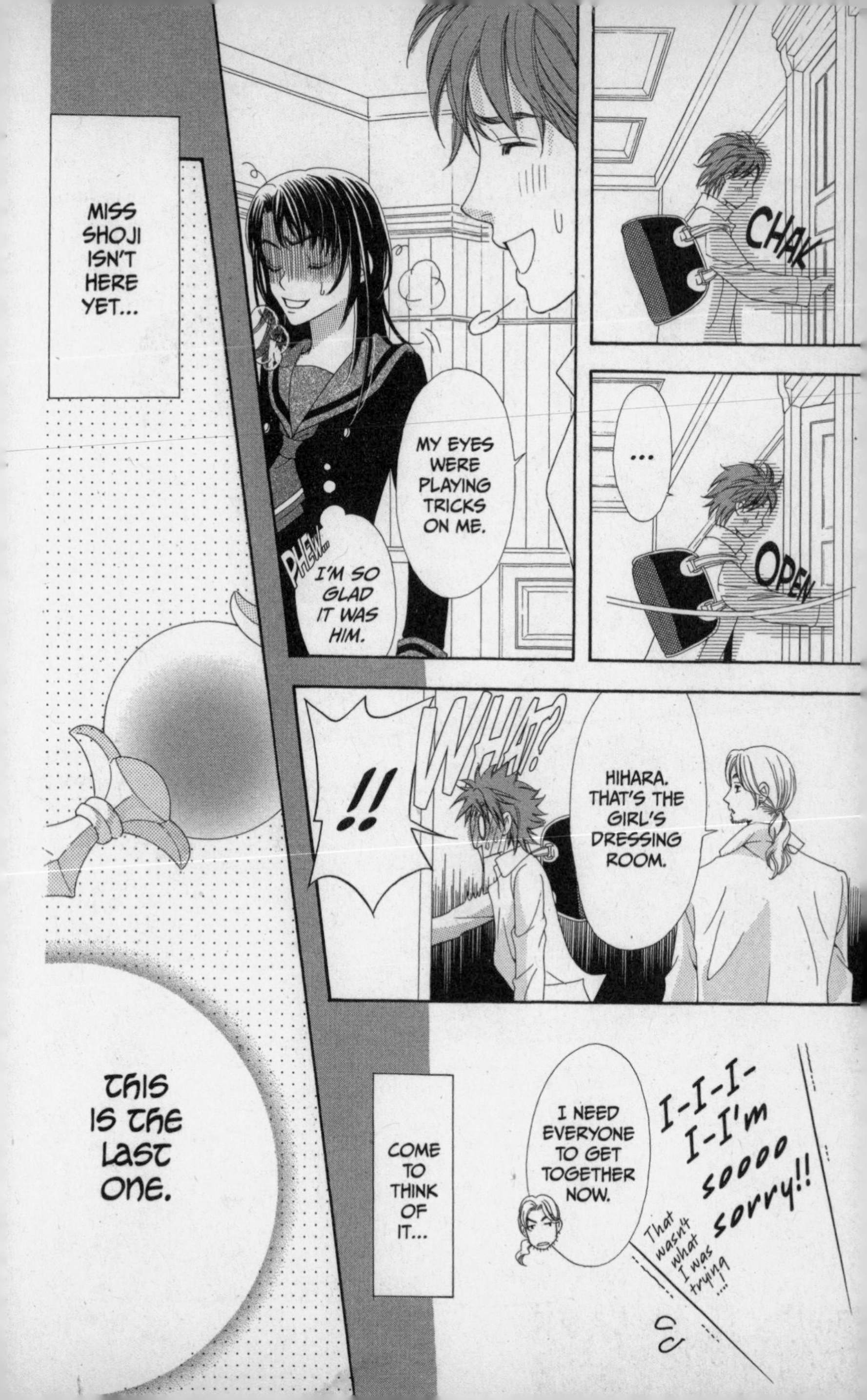
CHAK
...
OPEN
MY EYES WERE PLAYING TRICKS ON ME.
PHEW...
I'M SO GLAD IT WAS HIM.
MISS SHOJI ISN'T HERE YET...
HIHARA. THAT'S THE GIRL'S DRESSING ROOM.
WHAT?
!!
I-I-I-I-I'm soooo sorry!!
That wasn't what I was trying...!
I NEED EVERYONE TO GET TOGETHER NOW.
COME TO THINK OF IT...
THIS IS THE LAST ONE.

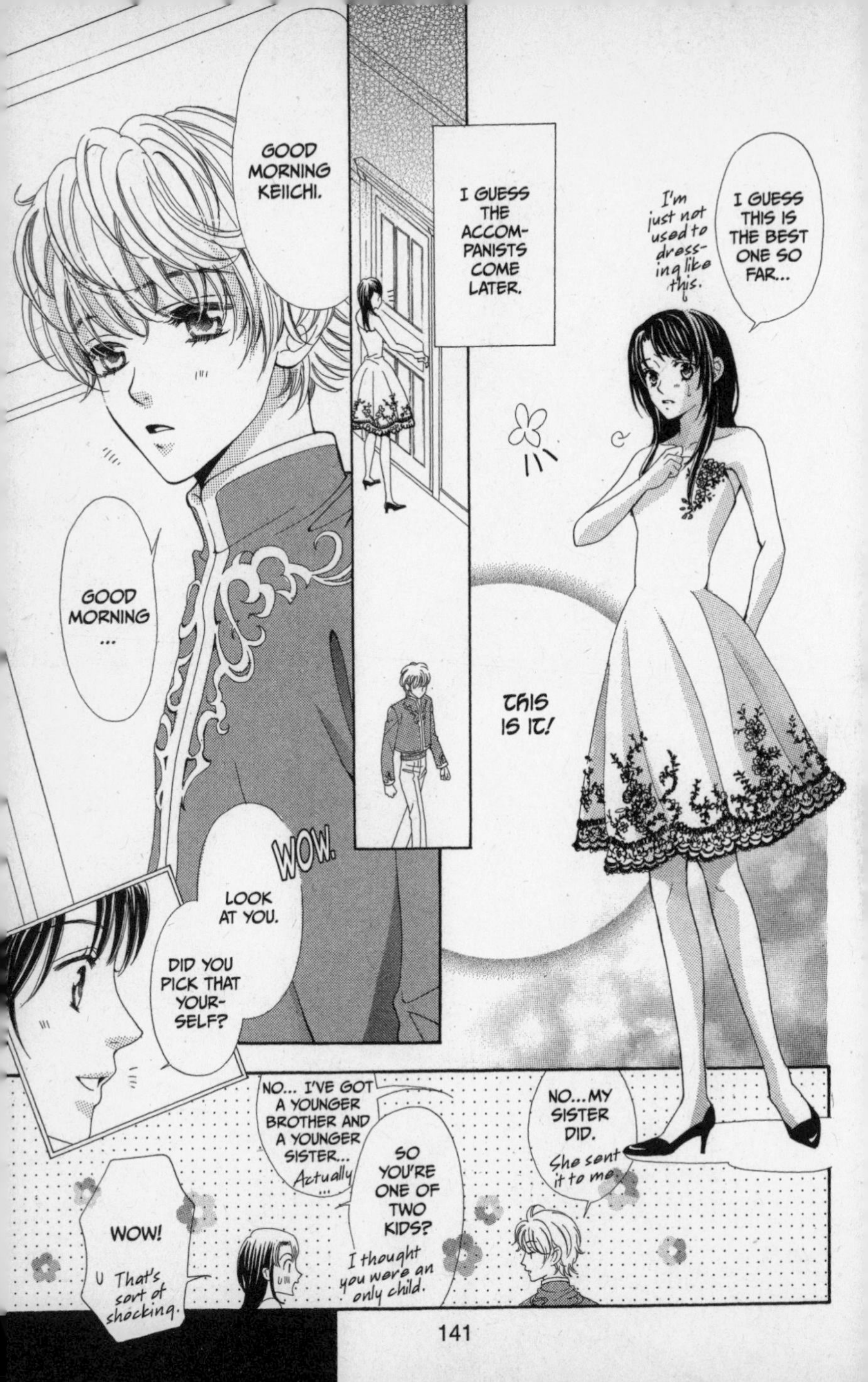

I GUESS THIS IS THE BEST ONE SO FAR...
I'm just not used to dress-ing like this.
THIS IS IT!
I GUESS THE ACCOM-PANISTS COME LATER.
GOOD MORNING KEIICHI.
GOOD MORNING ...
WOW.
LOOK AT YOU.
DID YOU PICK THAT YOUR-SELF?
NO...MY SISTER DID.
She sent it to me.
SO YOU'RE ONE OF TWO KIDS?
I thought you were an only child.
NO... I'VE GOT A YOUNGER BROTHER AND A YOUNGER SISTER...
Actually ...
WOW!
That's sort of shocking.

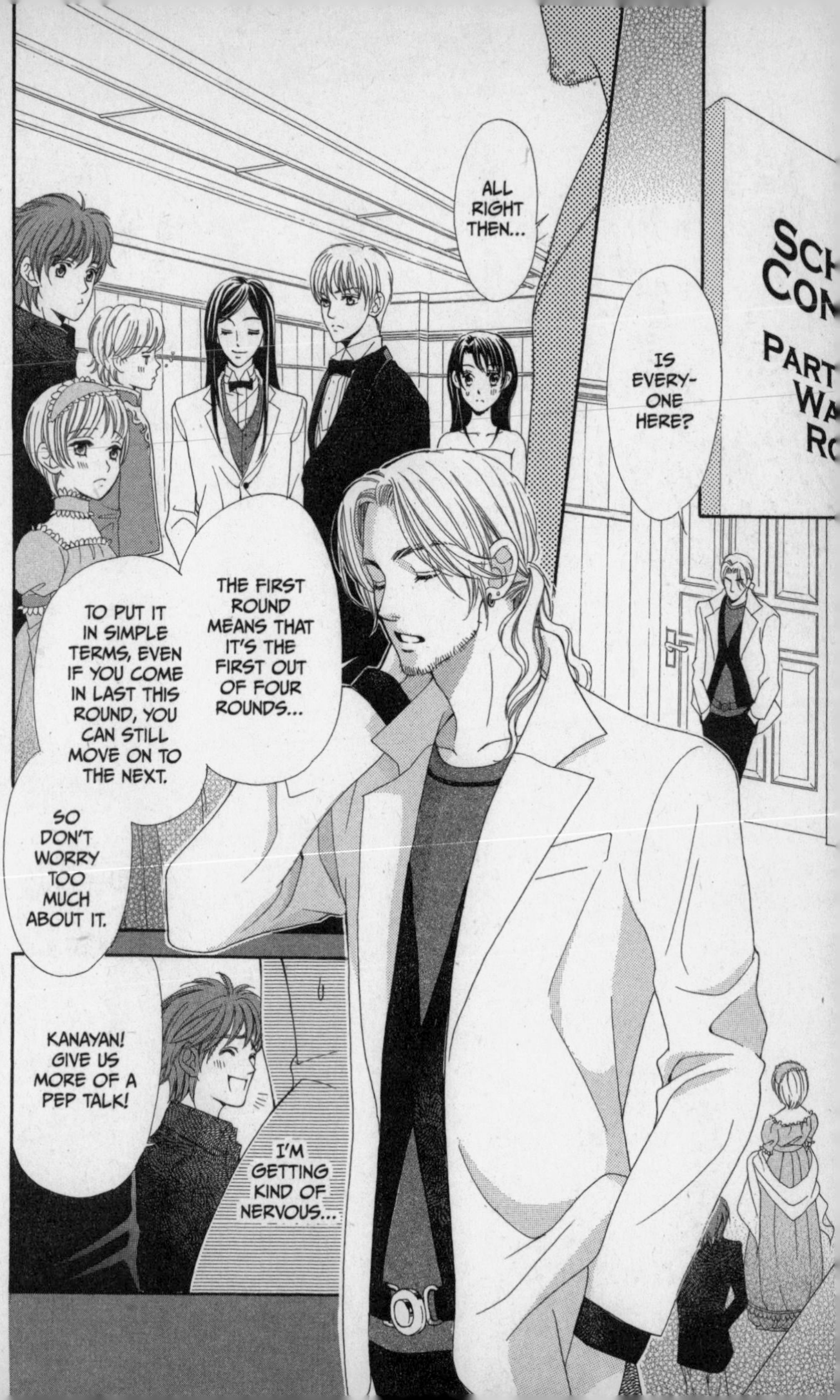
ALL RIGHT THEN...
IS EVERY-ONE HERE?
THE FIRST ROUND MEANS THAT IT'S THE FIRST OUT OF FOUR ROUNDS...
TO PUT IT IN SIMPLE TERMS, EVEN IF YOU COME IN LAST THIS ROUND, YOU CAN STILL MOVE ON TO THE NEXT.
SO DON'T WORRY TOO MUCH ABOUT IT.
KANAYAN! GIVE US MORE OF A PEP TALK!
I'M GETTING KIND OF NERVOUS...

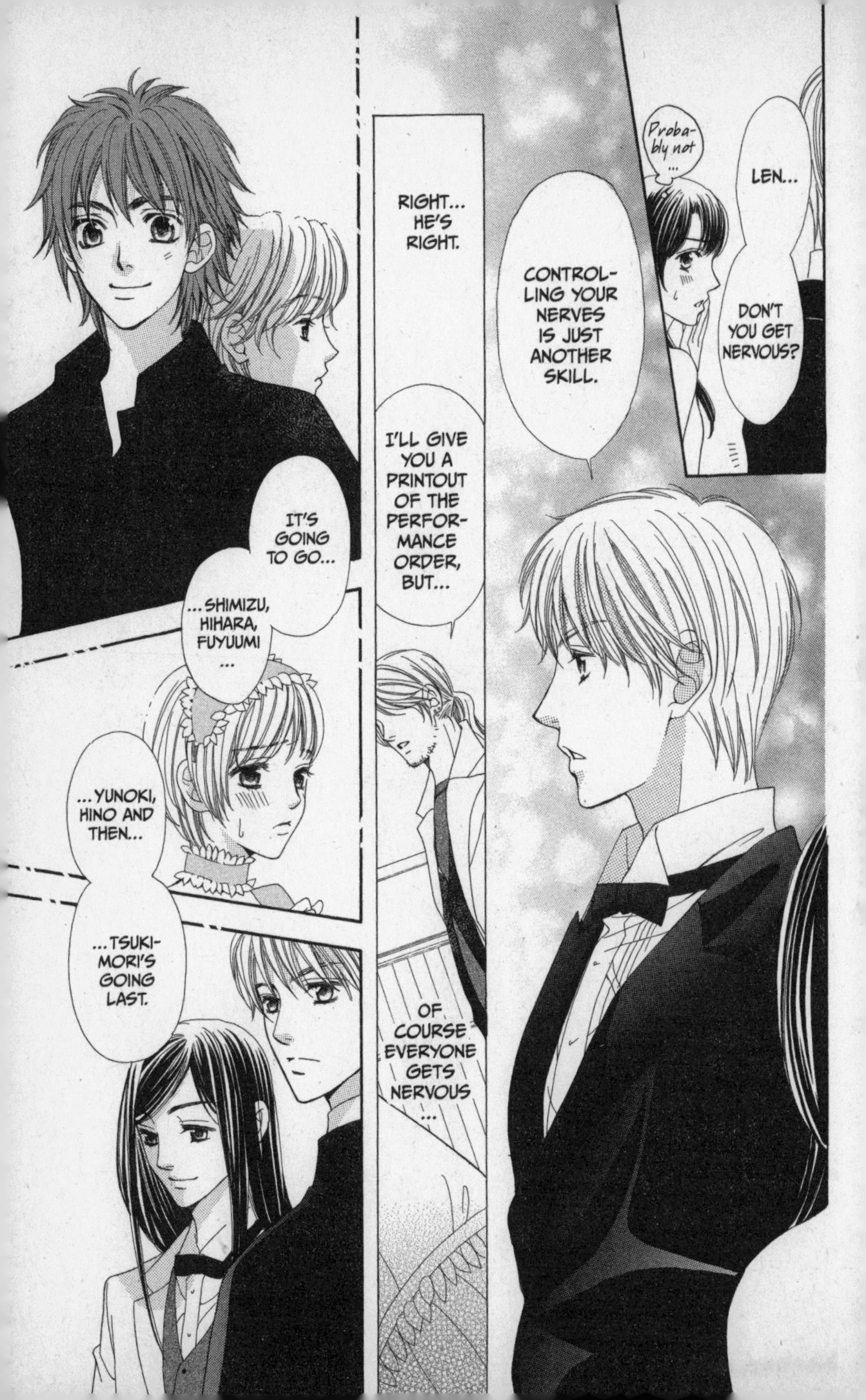
LEN...
DON'T YOU GET NERVOUS?
Proba-bly not ...
CONTROL-LING YOUR NERVES IS JUST ANOTHER SKILL.
RIGHT... HE'S RIGHT.
OF COURSE EVERYONE GETS NERVOUS ...
I'LL GIVE YOU A PRINTOUT OF THE PERFOR-MANCE ORDER, BUT...
IT'S GOING TO GO...
...SHIMIZU, HIHARA, FUYUUMI ...
...YUNOKI, HINO AND THEN...
...TSUKI-MORI'S GOING LAST.

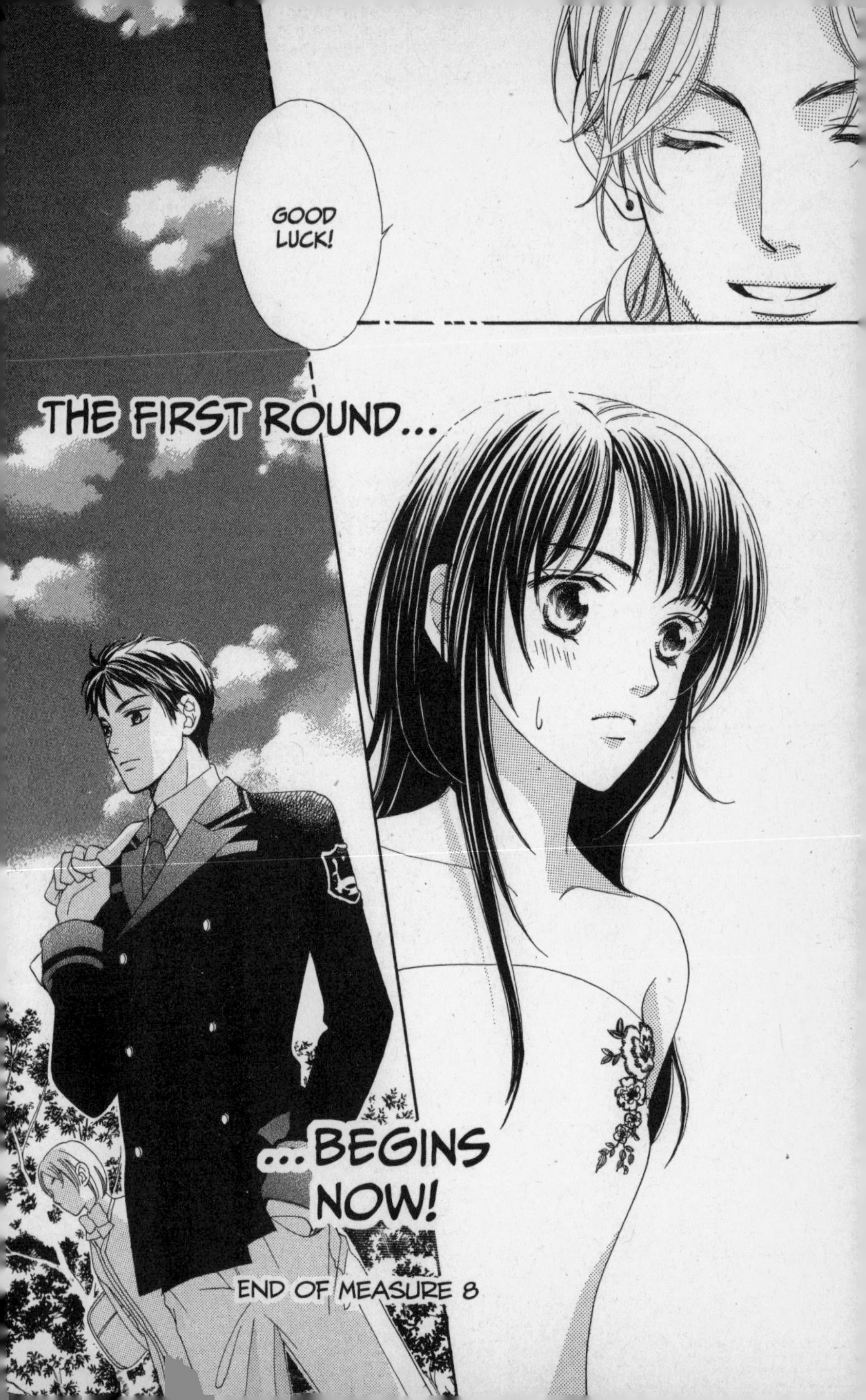
GOOD LUCK!
THE FIRST ROUND...
...BEGINS NOW!
END OF MEASURE 8

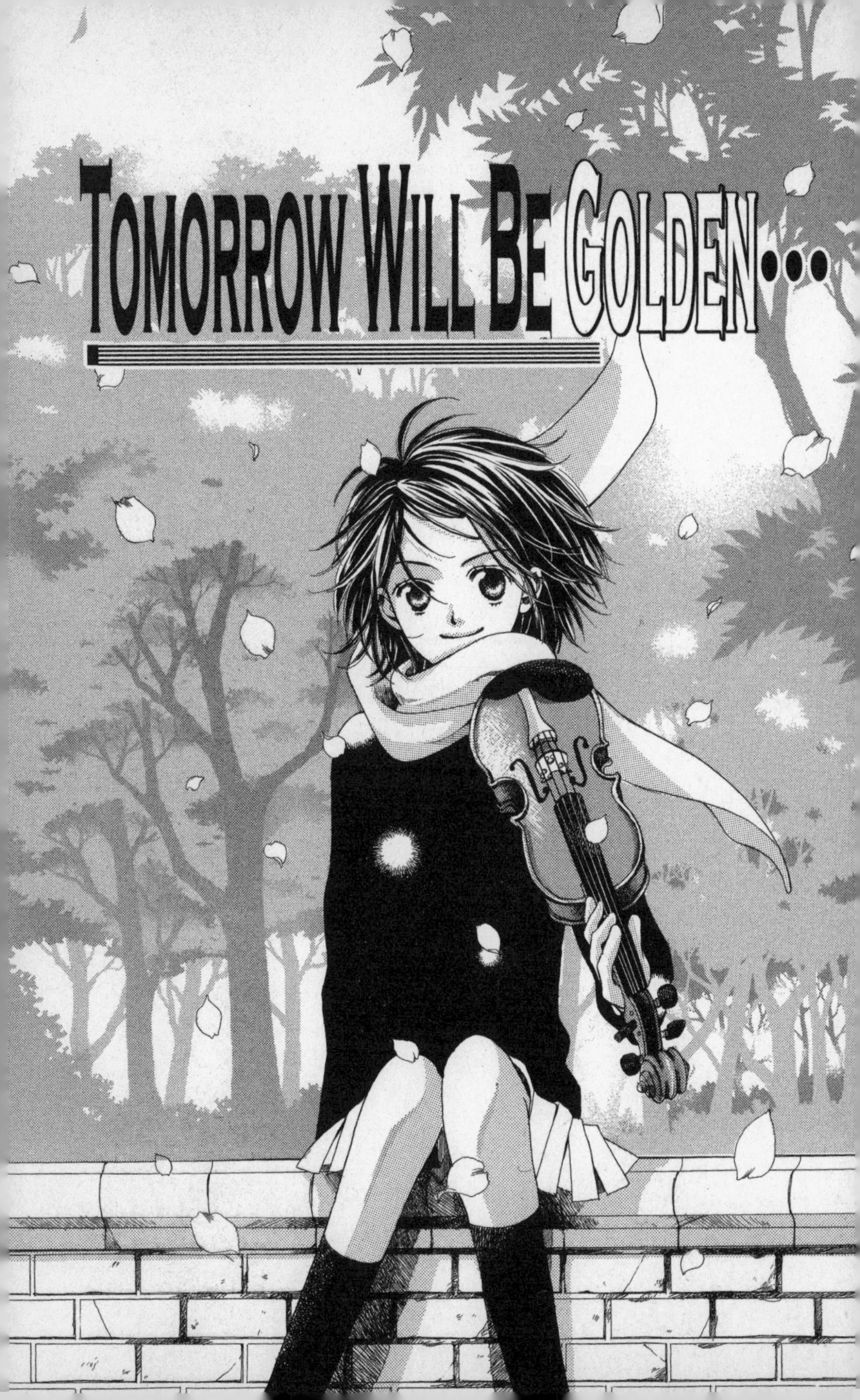
TOMORROW WILL BE GOLDEN...

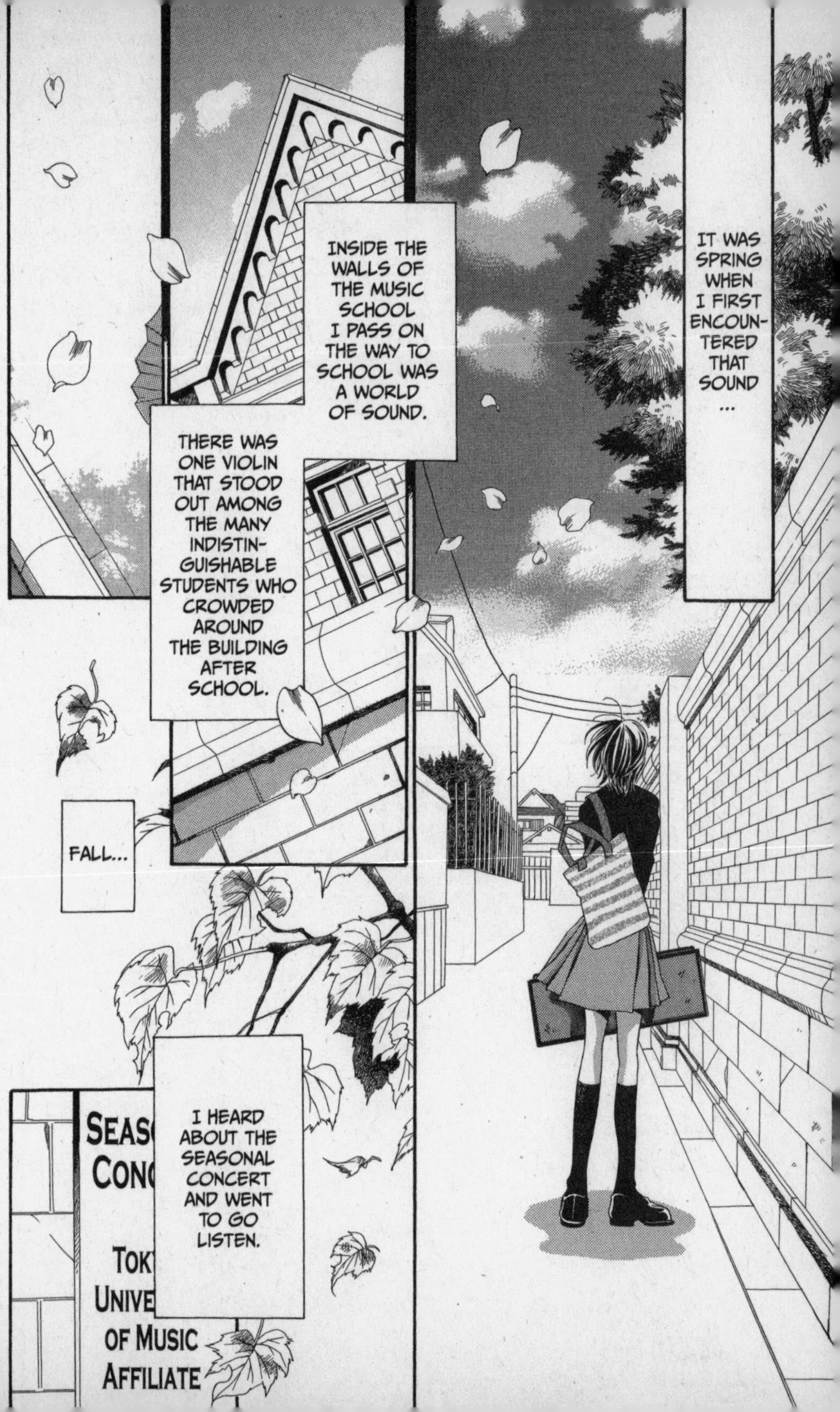
IT WAS SPRING WHEN I FIRST ENCOUN-TERED THAT SOUND ...
INSIDE THE WALLS OF THE MUSIC SCHOOL I PASS ON THE WAY TO SCHOOL WAS A WORLD OF SOUND.
THERE WAS ONE VIOLIN THAT STOOD OUT AMONG THE MANY INDISTIN-GUISHABLE STUDENTS WHO CROWDED AROUND THE BUILDING AFTER SCHOOL.
FALL...
I HEARD ABOUT THE SEASONAL CONCERT AND WENT TO GO LISTEN.
SEAS
CONC
TOKY
UNIVE
OF MUSIC
AFFILIATE

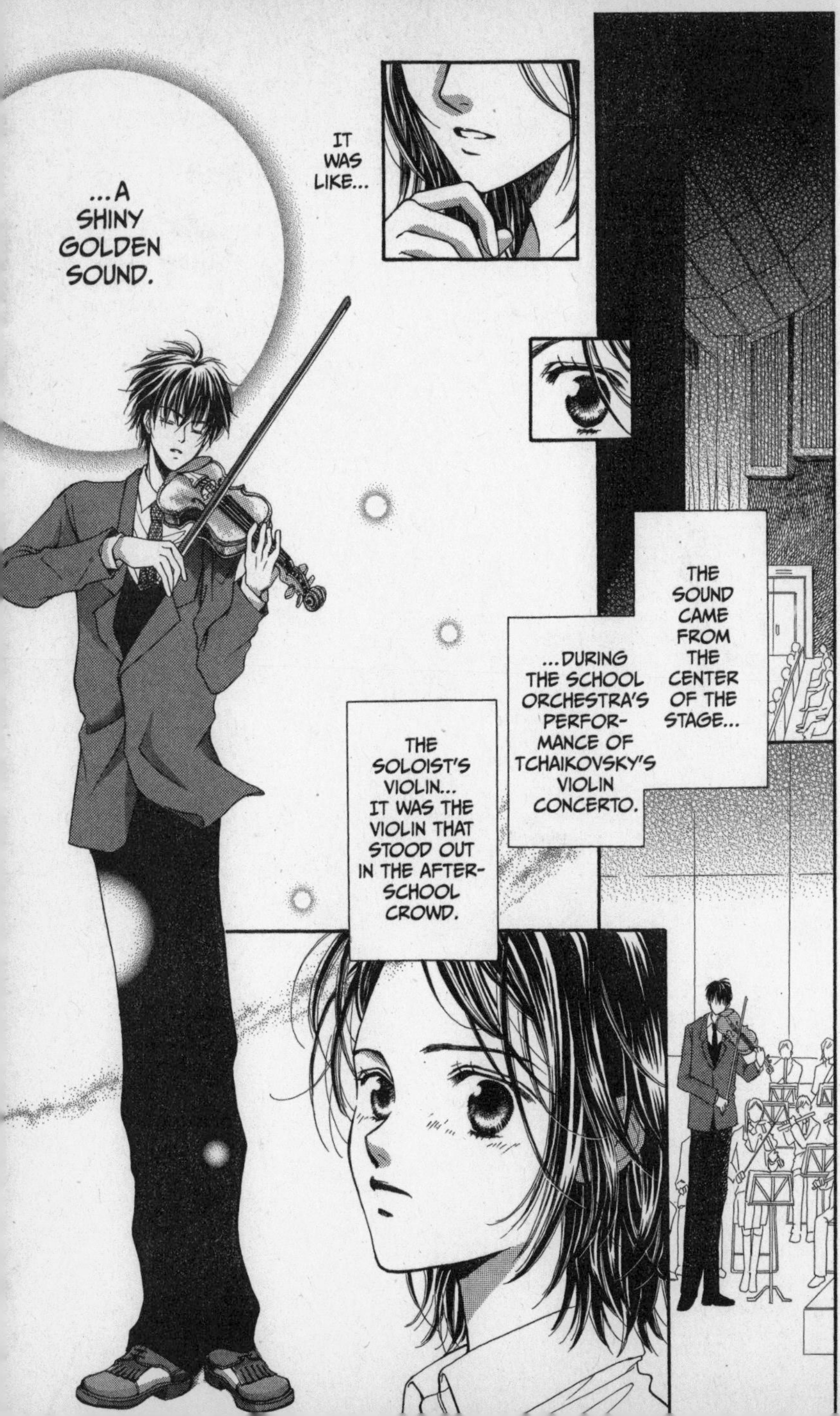
THE SOUND CAME FROM THE CENTER OF THE STAGE...
...DURING THE SCHOOL ORCHESTRA'S PERFOR-MANCE OF TCHAIKOVSKY'S VIOLIN CONCERTO.
THE SOLOIST'S VIOLIN... IT WAS THE VIOLIN THAT STOOD OUT IN THE AFTER-SCHOOL CROWD.
IT WAS LIKE...
...A SHINY GOLDEN SOUND.

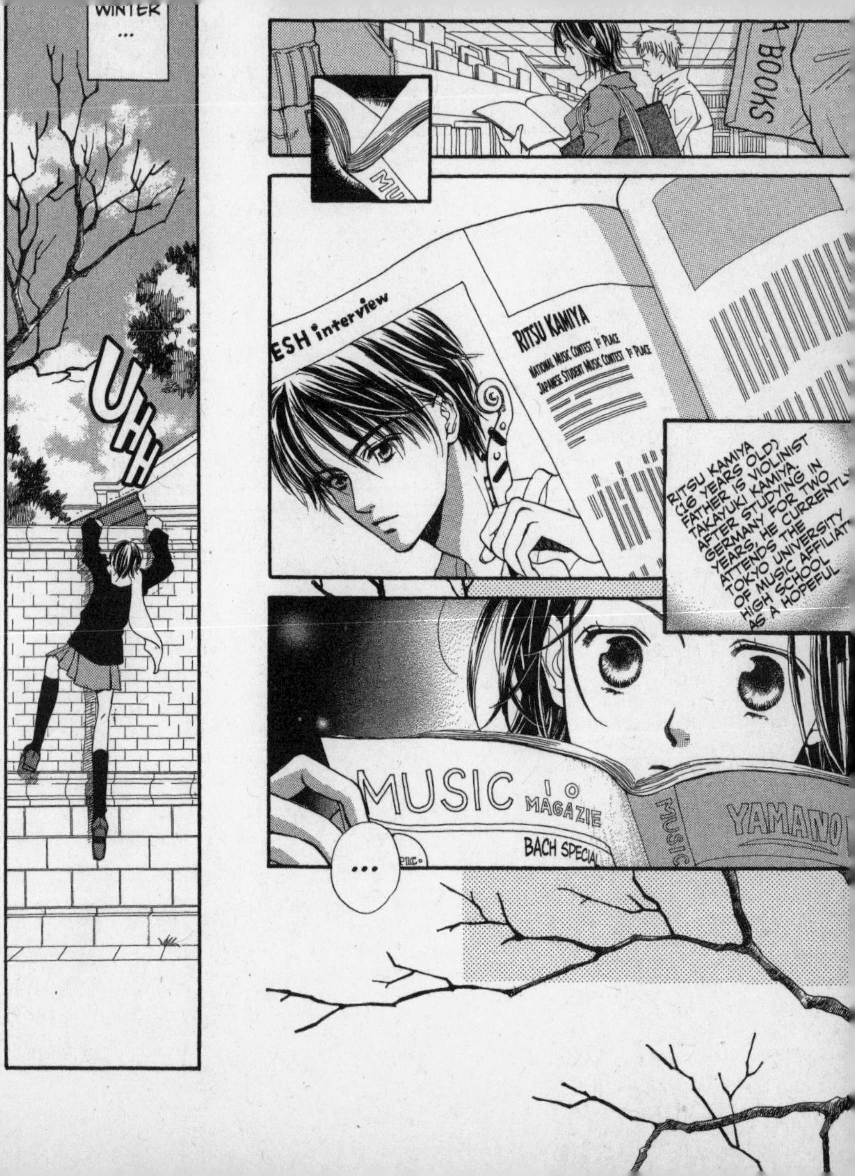
BOOKS
ESH interview
RITSU KAMIYA
NATIONAL MUSIC CONTEST 1st PLACE
JAPANESE STUDENT MUSIC CONTEST 1st PLACE
RITSU KAMIYA (16 YEARS OLD) FATHER IS VIOLINIST TAKAYUKI KAMIYA. AFTER STUDYING IN GERMANY FOR TWO YEARS, HE CURRENTLY ATTENDS THE TOKYO UNIVERSITY OF MUSIC AFFILIAT HIGH SCHOOL AS A HOPEFUL
MUSIC 10 MAGAZIE
BACH SPECIAL
MUSIC
YAMANO
...
WINTER ...
UHH

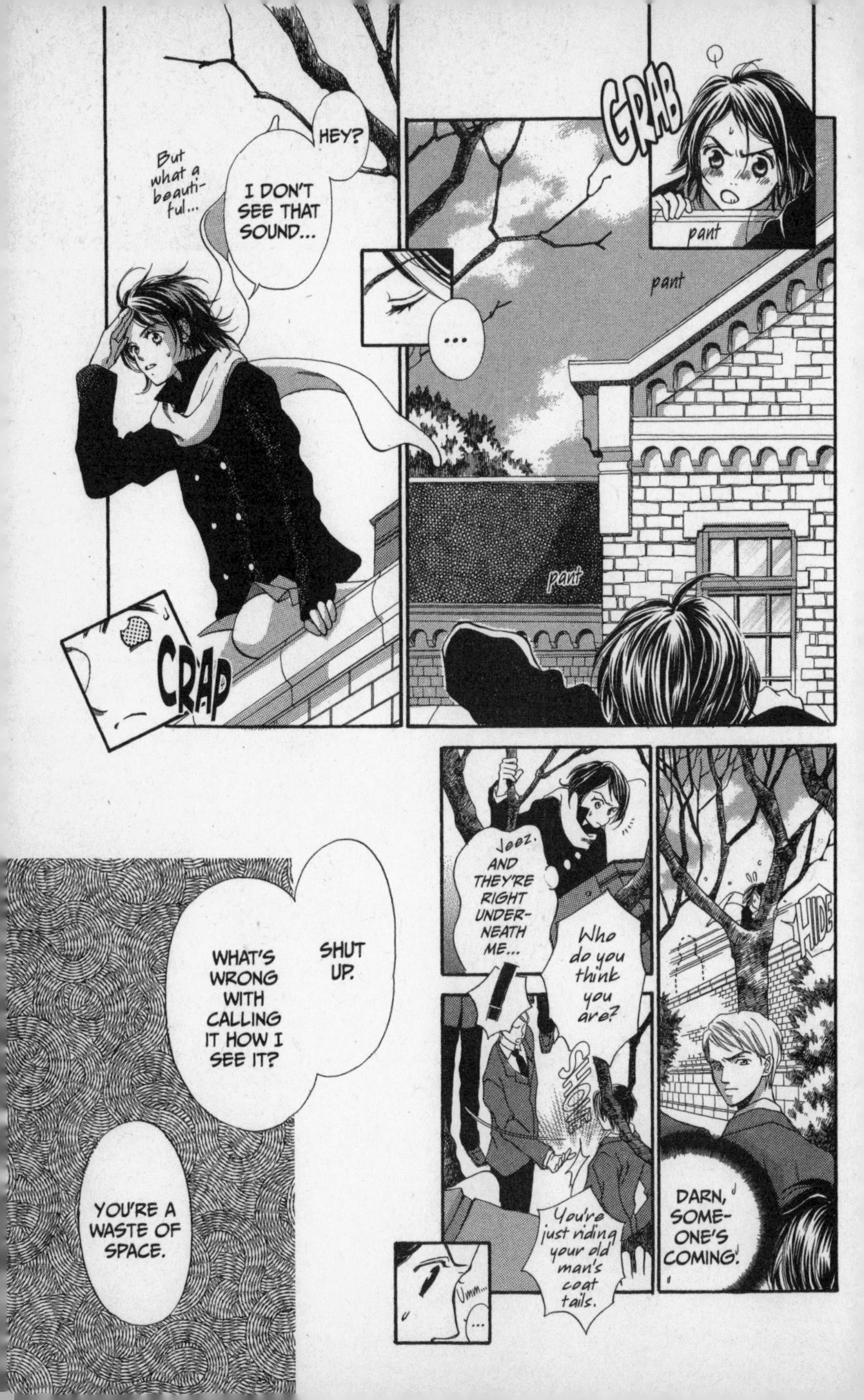
GRAB
pant
pant
...
pant
HEY?
I DON'T SEE THAT SOUND...
But what a beautiful...
CRAP
HIDE
DARN, SOMEONE'S COMING!
Jeez. AND THEY'RE RIGHT UNDERNEATH ME...
Who do you think you are?
!
SHOVE
You're just riding your old man's coat tails.
Umm...
...
SHUT UP.
WHAT'S WRONG WITH CALLING IT HOW I SEE IT?
YOU'RE A WASTE OF SPACE.

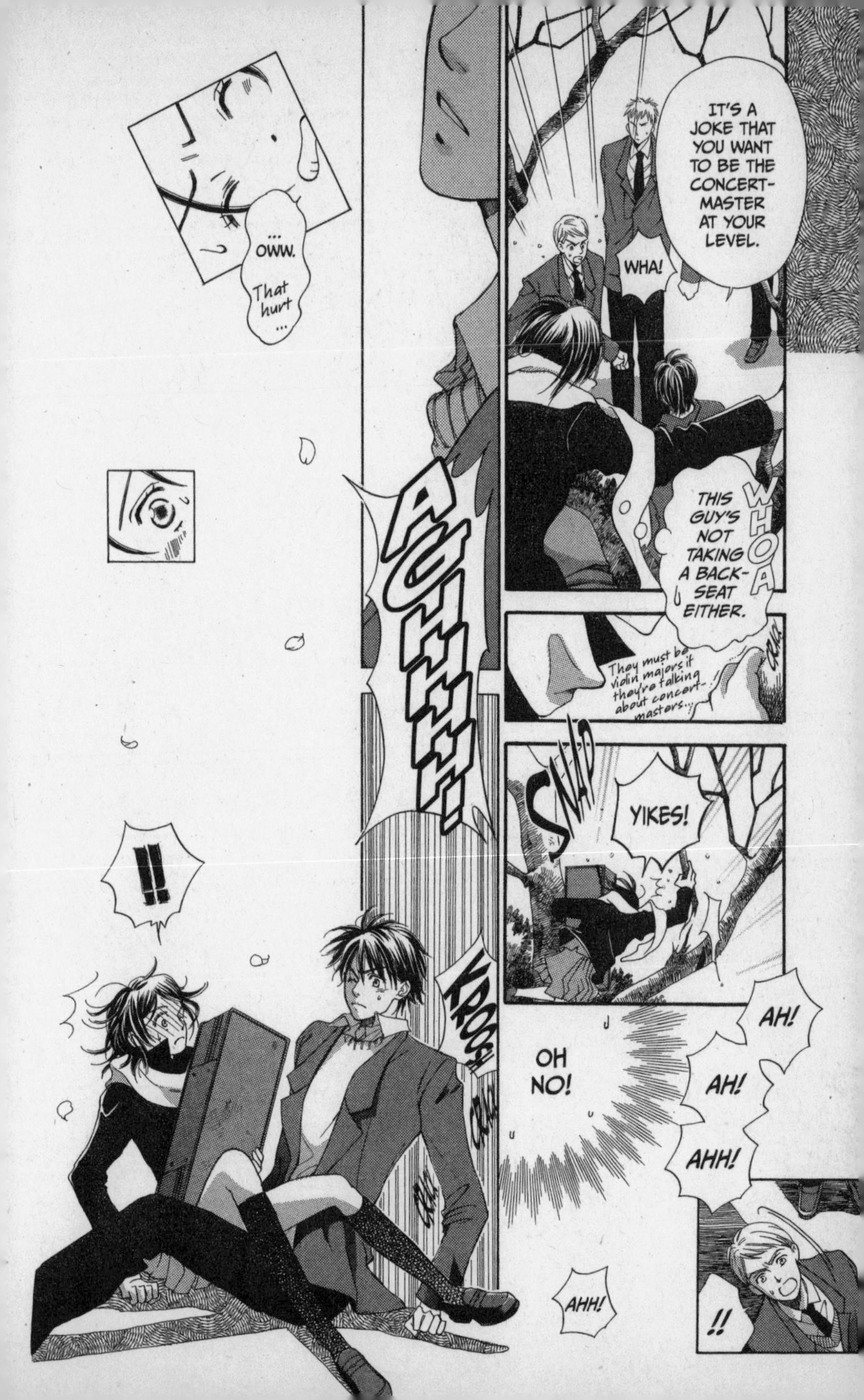
IT'S A JOKE THAT YOU WANT TO BE THE CONCERT-MASTER AT YOUR LEVEL.
WHA!
WHOA
THIS GUY'S NOT TAKING A BACK-SEAT EITHER.
CRACK
They must be violin majors if they're talking about concert-masters...
SNAP
YIKES!
AH!
AH!
AHH!
OH NO!
!!
AHH!
AUGHHH!
KROOSH
CRACK
CRACK
!!
...OWW.
That hurt...

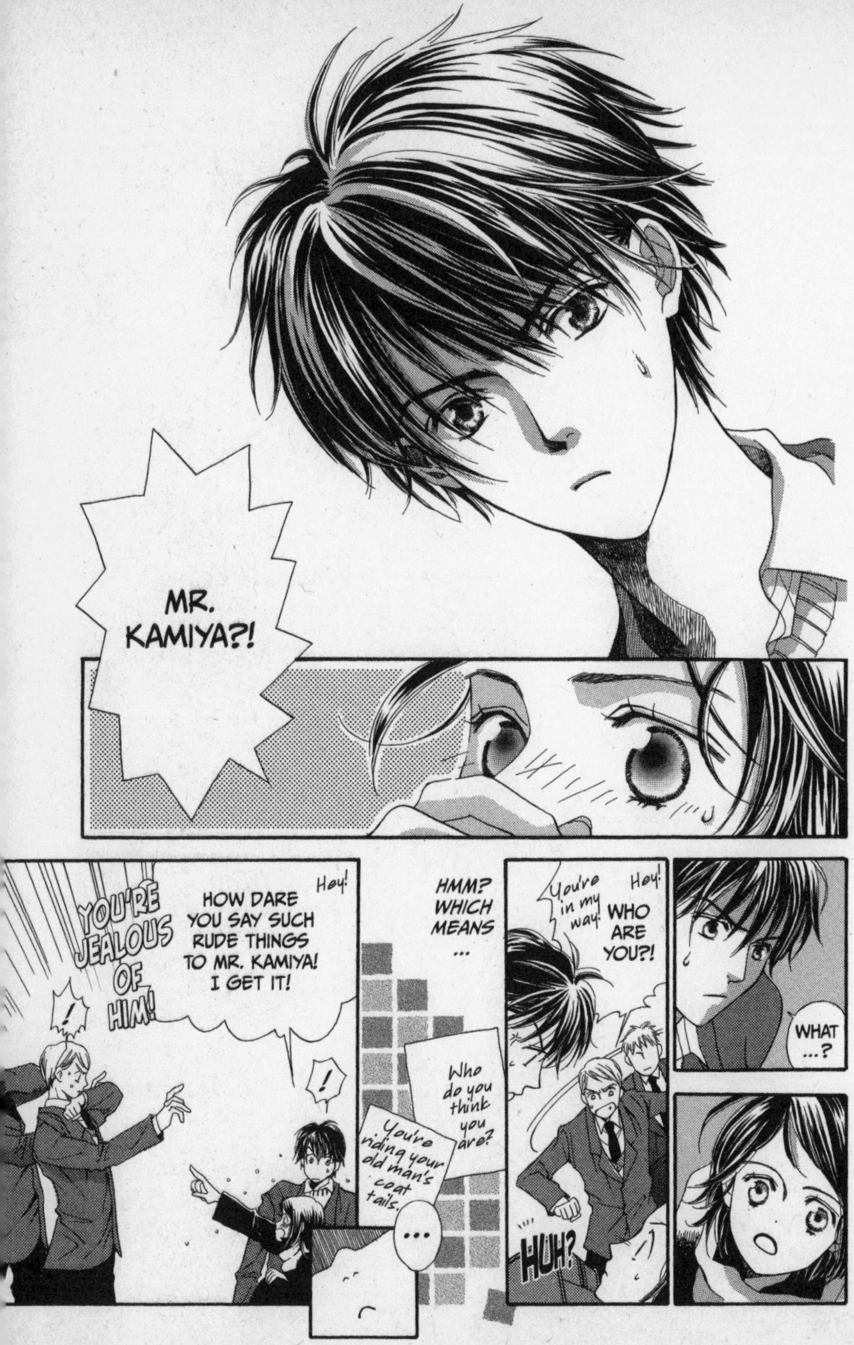
MR. KAMIYA?!
WHAT ...?
Hey!
WHO ARE YOU?!
You're in my way!
HUH?
Who do you think you are?
You're riding your old man's coat tails.
...
HMM? WHICH MEANS ...
Hey!
HOW DARE YOU SAY SUCH RUDE THINGS TO MR. KAMIYA! I GET IT!
YOU'RE JEALOUS OF HIM!
!
!

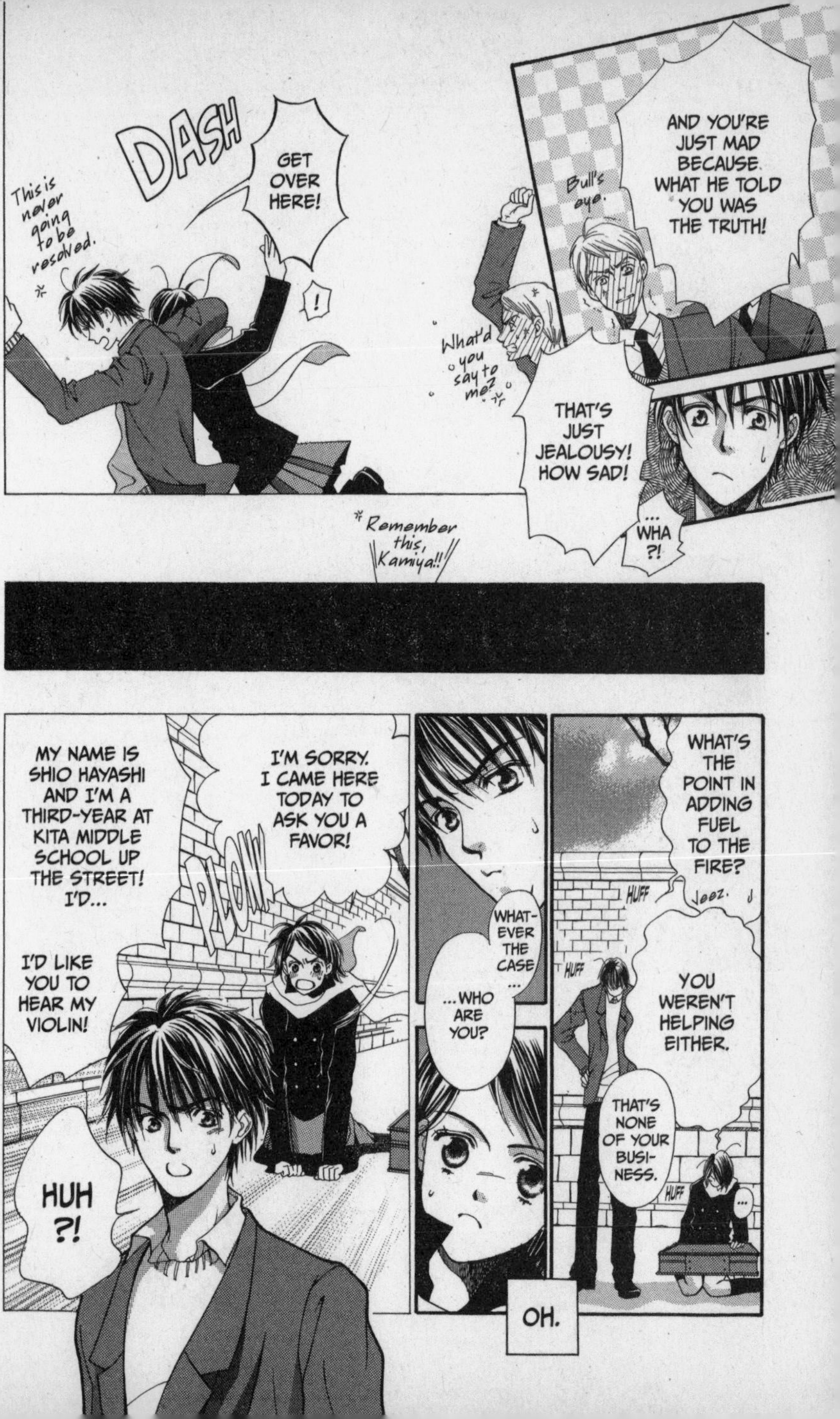
AND YOU'RE JUST MAD BECAUSE WHAT HE TOLD YOU WAS THE TRUTH!
Bull's eye.
What'd you say to me?
THAT'S JUST JEALOUSY! HOW SAD!
...WHA?!
DASH
GET OVER HERE!
!
This is never going to be resolved.
Remember this, Kamiya!!
WHAT'S THE POINT IN ADDING FUEL TO THE FIRE?
Jeez.
HUFF
HUFF
YOU WEREN'T HELPING EITHER.
THAT'S NONE OF YOUR BUSINESS.
HUFF
...
OH.
WHATEVER THE CASE...
...WHO ARE YOU?
I'M SORRY. I CAME HERE TODAY TO ASK YOU A FAVOR!
MY NAME IS SHIO HAYASHI AND I'M A THIRD-YEAR AT KITA MIDDLE SCHOOL UP THE STREET! I'D...
I'D LIKE YOU TO HEAR MY VIOLIN!
HUH?!

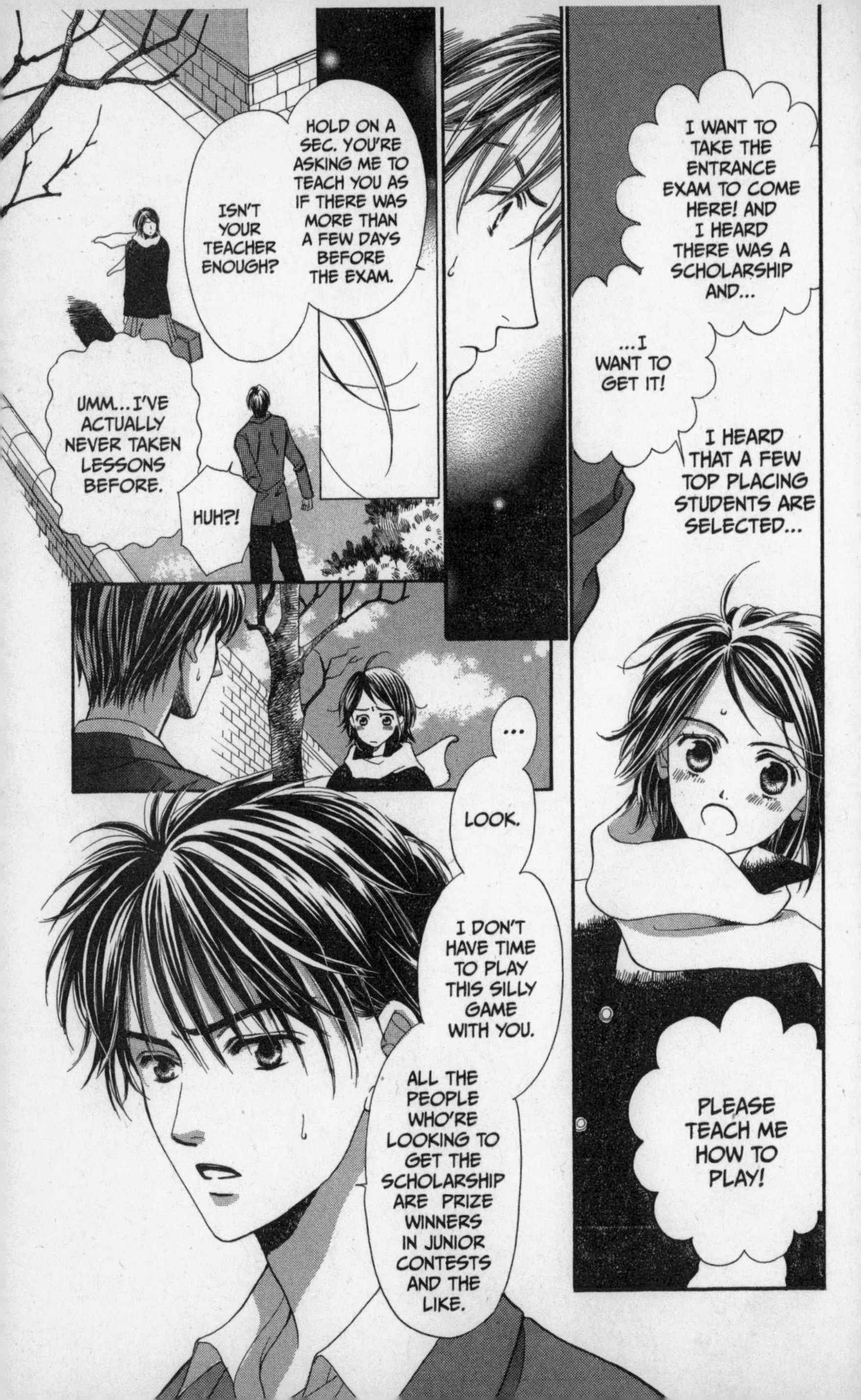
I WANT TO TAKE THE ENTRANCE EXAM TO COME HERE! AND I HEARD THERE WAS A SCHOLARSHIP AND...
...I WANT TO GET IT!
I HEARD THAT A FEW TOP PLACING STUDENTS ARE SELECTED...
PLEASE TEACH ME HOW TO PLAY!
HOLD ON A SEC. YOU'RE ASKING ME TO TEACH YOU AS IF THERE WAS MORE THAN A FEW DAYS BEFORE THE EXAM.
ISN'T YOUR TEACHER ENOUGH?
UMM...I'VE ACTUALLY NEVER TAKEN LESSONS BEFORE.
HUH?!
...
LOOK.
I DON'T HAVE TIME TO PLAY THIS SILLY GAME WITH YOU.
ALL THE PEOPLE WHO'RE LOOKING TO GET THE SCHOLARSHIP ARE PRIZE WINNERS IN JUNIOR CONTESTS AND THE LIKE.

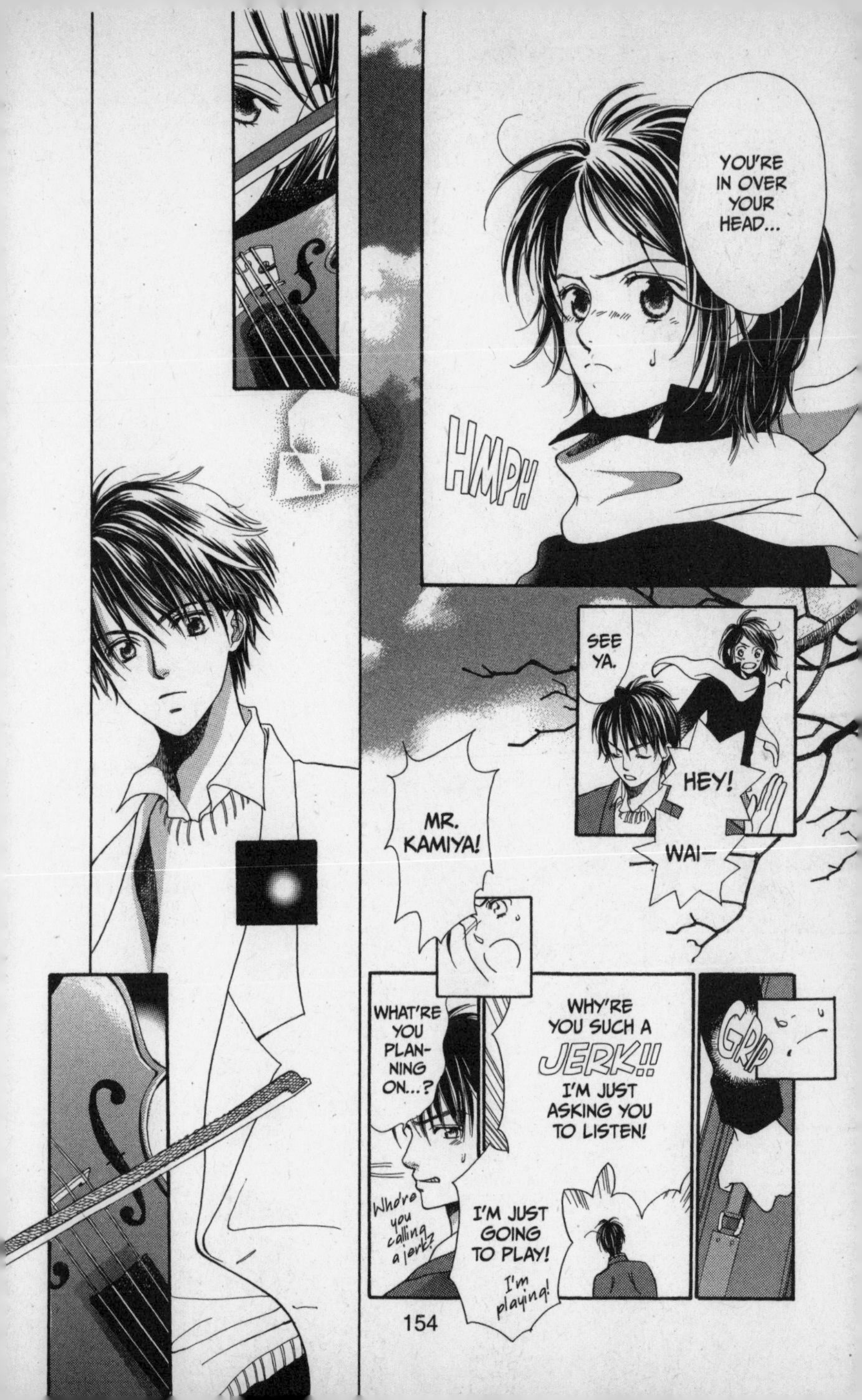
YOU'RE IN OVER YOUR HEAD...
HMPH
SEE YA.
HEY!
WAI–
MR. KAMIYA!
GRIP
WHY'RE YOU SUCH A JERK!! I'M JUST ASKING YOU TO LISTEN!
I'M JUST GOING TO PLAY!
I'm playing!
WHAT'RE YOU PLAN-NING ON...?
Who're you calling a jerk?

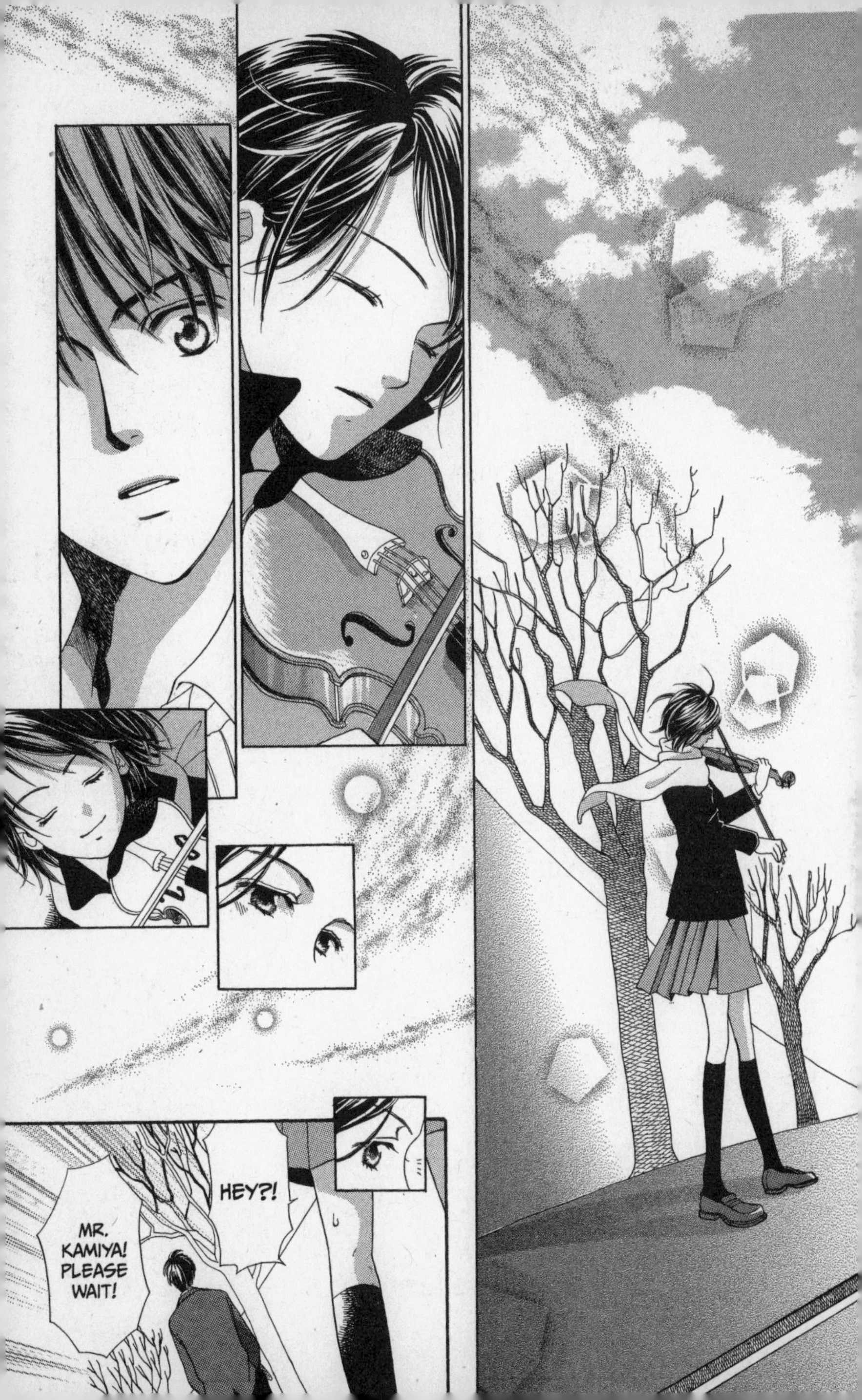
HEY?!
MR. KAMIYA! PLEASE WAIT!

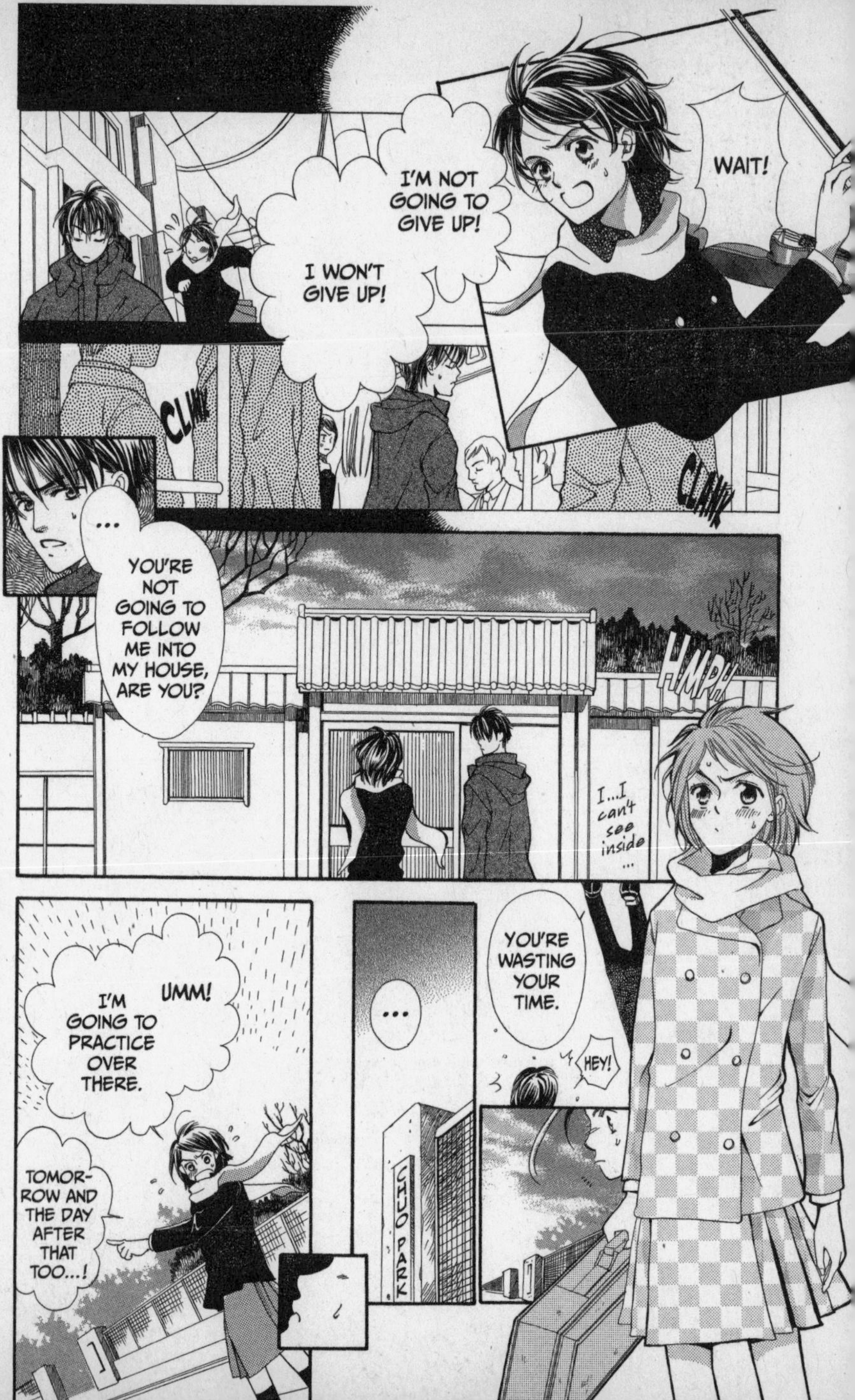
WAIT!
I'M NOT GOING TO GIVE UP!
I WON'T GIVE UP!
CLANK
CLANK
...
YOU'RE NOT GOING TO FOLLOW ME INTO MY HOUSE, ARE YOU?
HMPH
I...I can't see inside...
YOU'RE WASTING YOUR TIME.
HEY!
...
CHUO PARK
UMM!
I'M GOING TO PRACTICE OVER THERE.
TOMORROW AND THE DAY AFTER THAT TOO...!

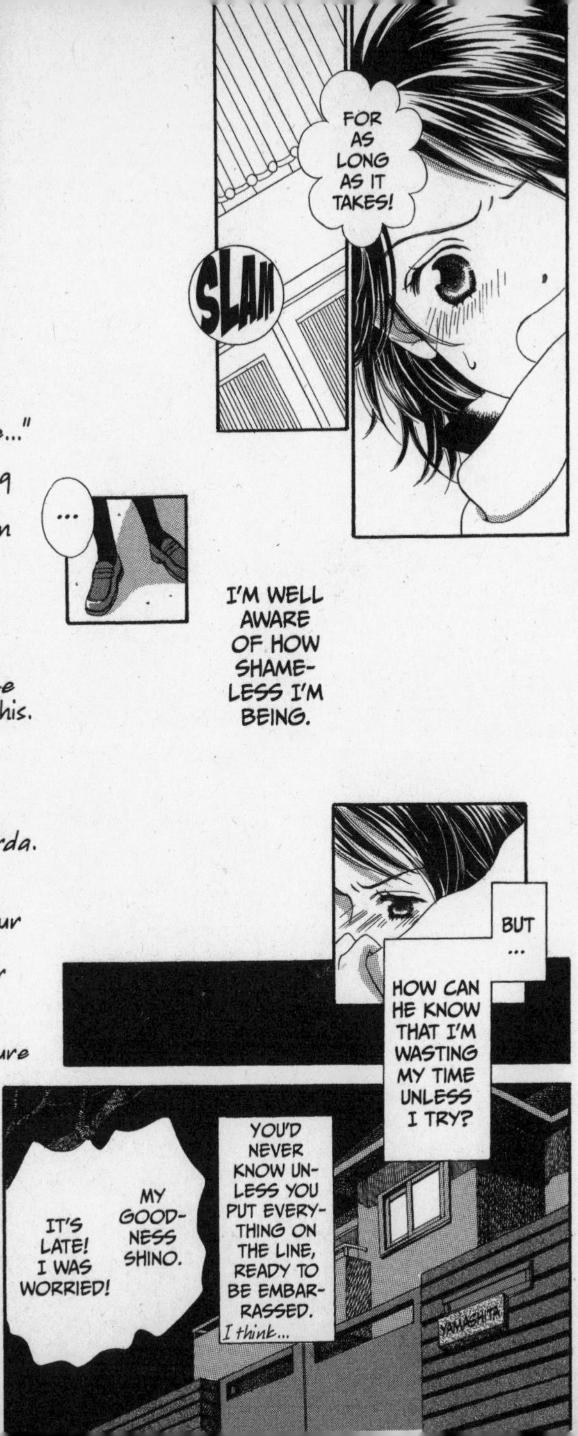
FOR AS LONG AS IT TAKES!
SLAM
...
I'M WELL AWARE OF HOW SHAME-LESS I'M BEING.
BUT ...
HOW CAN HE KNOW THAT I'M WASTING MY TIME UNLESS I TRY?
YOU'D NEVER KNOW UN-LESS YOU PUT EVERY-THING ON THE LINE, READY TO BE EMBAR-RASSED.
I think...
MY GOOD-NESS SHINO.
IT'S LATE! I WAS WORRIED!
YAMASHITA

"Tomorrow will be..."

It's embarrassing to look at my scripts from even a month ago, let alone... I'm at a loss for words...

I'm sorry to make you sit through this.

This is a violin-related story I wrote before I started La Corda. Yes...

Thank you for your time. I hope to see you again for volume 3.

♫2004 Yuki Kure

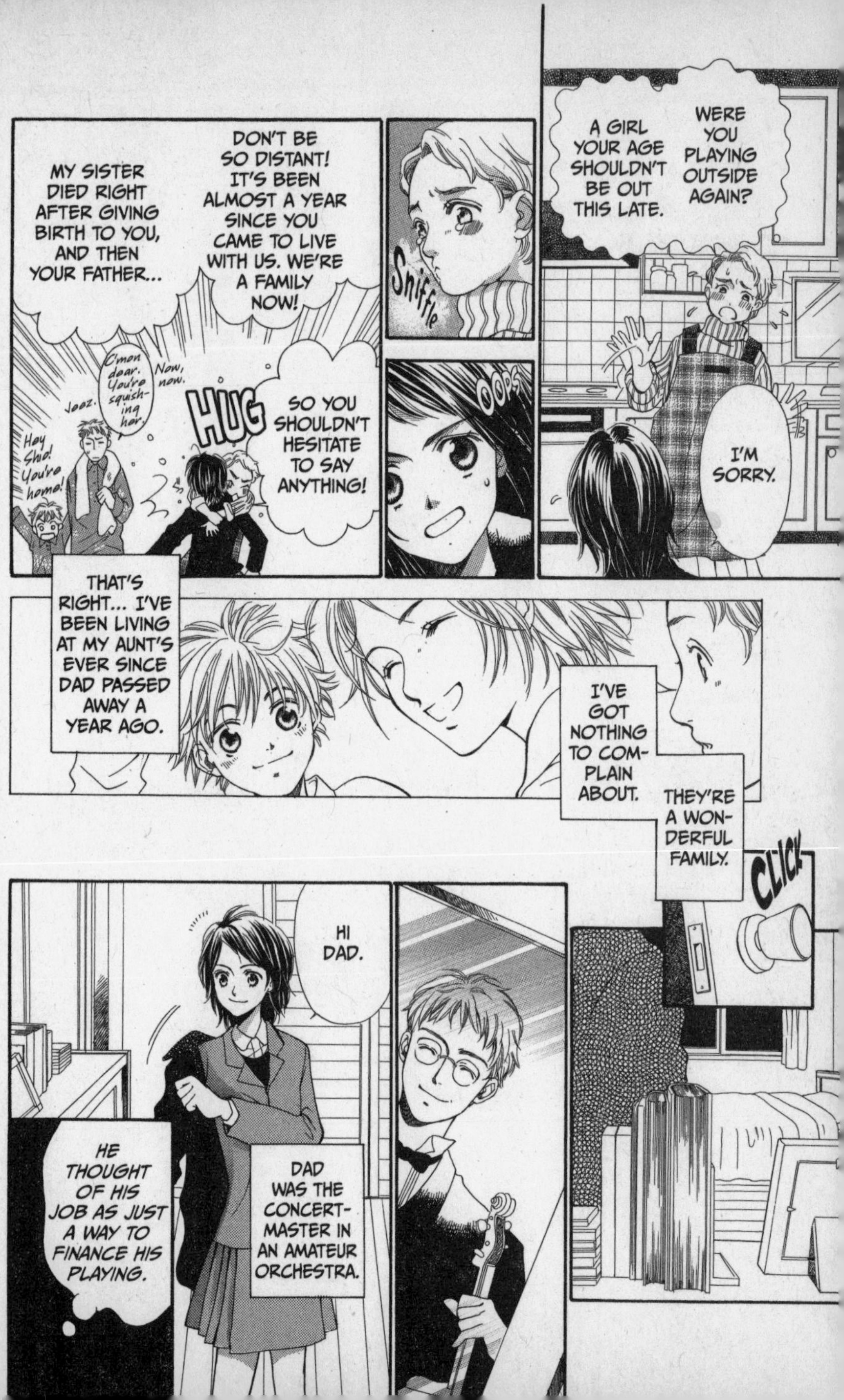
WERE YOU PLAYING OUTSIDE AGAIN?
A GIRL YOUR AGE SHOULDN'T BE OUT THIS LATE.
I'M SORRY.
Sniffle
OOPS
DON'T BE SO DISTANT! IT'S BEEN ALMOST A YEAR SINCE YOU CAME TO LIVE WITH US. WE'RE A FAMILY NOW!
MY SISTER DIED RIGHT AFTER GIVING BIRTH TO YOU, AND THEN YOUR FATHER...
SO YOU SHOULDN'T HESITATE TO SAY ANYTHING!
HUG
Now, now.
C'mon dear. You're squishing her.
Jeez.
Hey Shio! You're home!
THAT'S RIGHT... I'VE BEEN LIVING AT MY AUNT'S EVER SINCE DAD PASSED AWAY A YEAR AGO.
I'VE GOT NOTHING TO COMPLAIN ABOUT.
THEY'RE A WONDERFUL FAMILY.
CLICK
HI DAD.
DAD WAS THE CONCERT-MASTER IN AN AMATEUR ORCHESTRA.
HE THOUGHT OF HIS JOB AS JUST A WAY TO FINANCE HIS PLAYING.

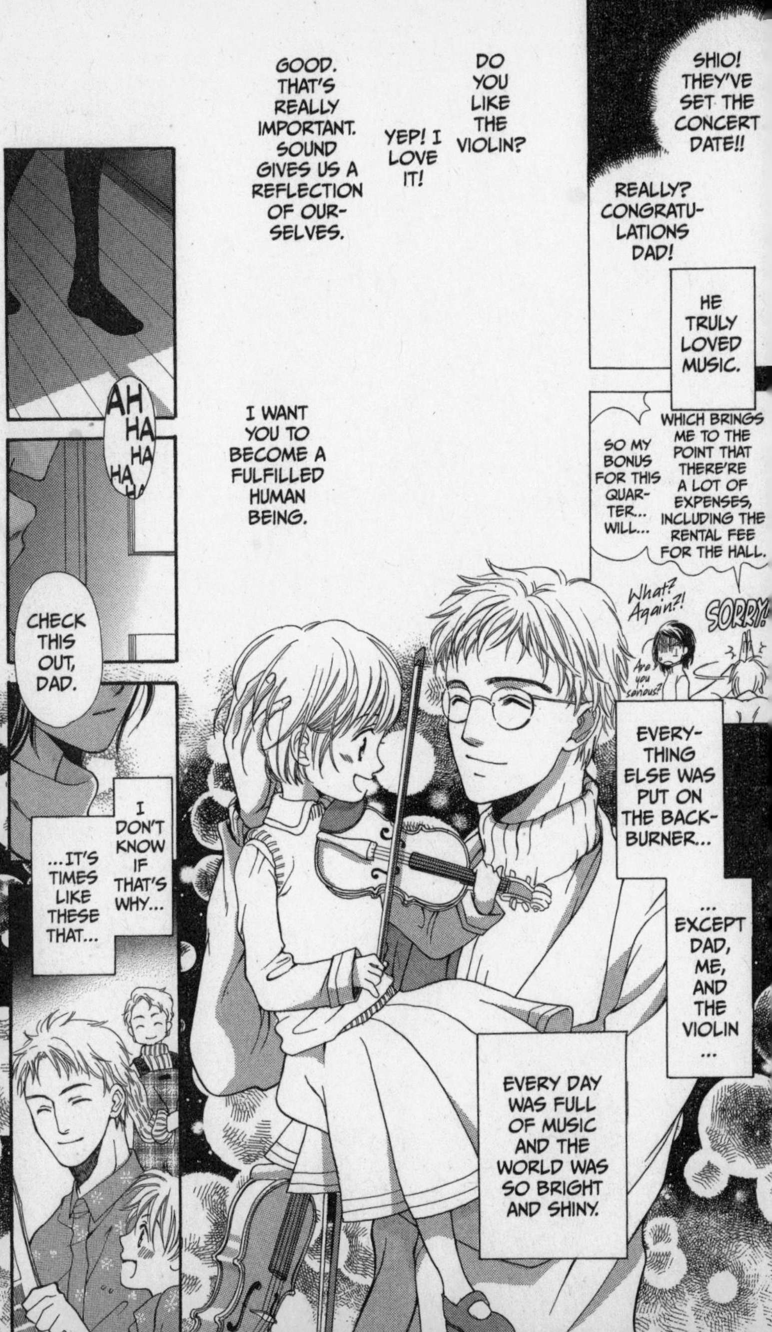
SHIO! THEY'VE SET THE CONCERT DATE!!
REALLY? CONGRATULATIONS DAD!
HE TRULY LOVED MUSIC.
WHICH BRINGS ME TO THE POINT THAT THERE'RE A LOT OF EXPENSES, INCLUDING THE RENTAL FEE FOR THE HALL.
SO MY BONUS FOR THIS QUARTER... WILL...
What? Again?!
SORRY!
Are you serious?
DO YOU LIKE THE VIOLIN?
YEP! I LOVE IT!
GOOD. THAT'S REALLY IMPORTANT. SOUND GIVES US A REFLECTION OF OURSELVES.
I WANT YOU TO BECOME A FULFILLED HUMAN BEING.
AH HA HA HA
CHECK THIS OUT, DAD.
EVERYTHING ELSE WAS PUT ON THE BACK-BURNER...
...EXCEPT DAD, ME, AND THE VIOLIN...
EVERY DAY WAS FULL OF MUSIC AND THE WORLD WAS SO BRIGHT AND SHINY.
I DON'T KNOW IF THAT'S WHY...
...IT'S TIMES LIKE THESE THAT...

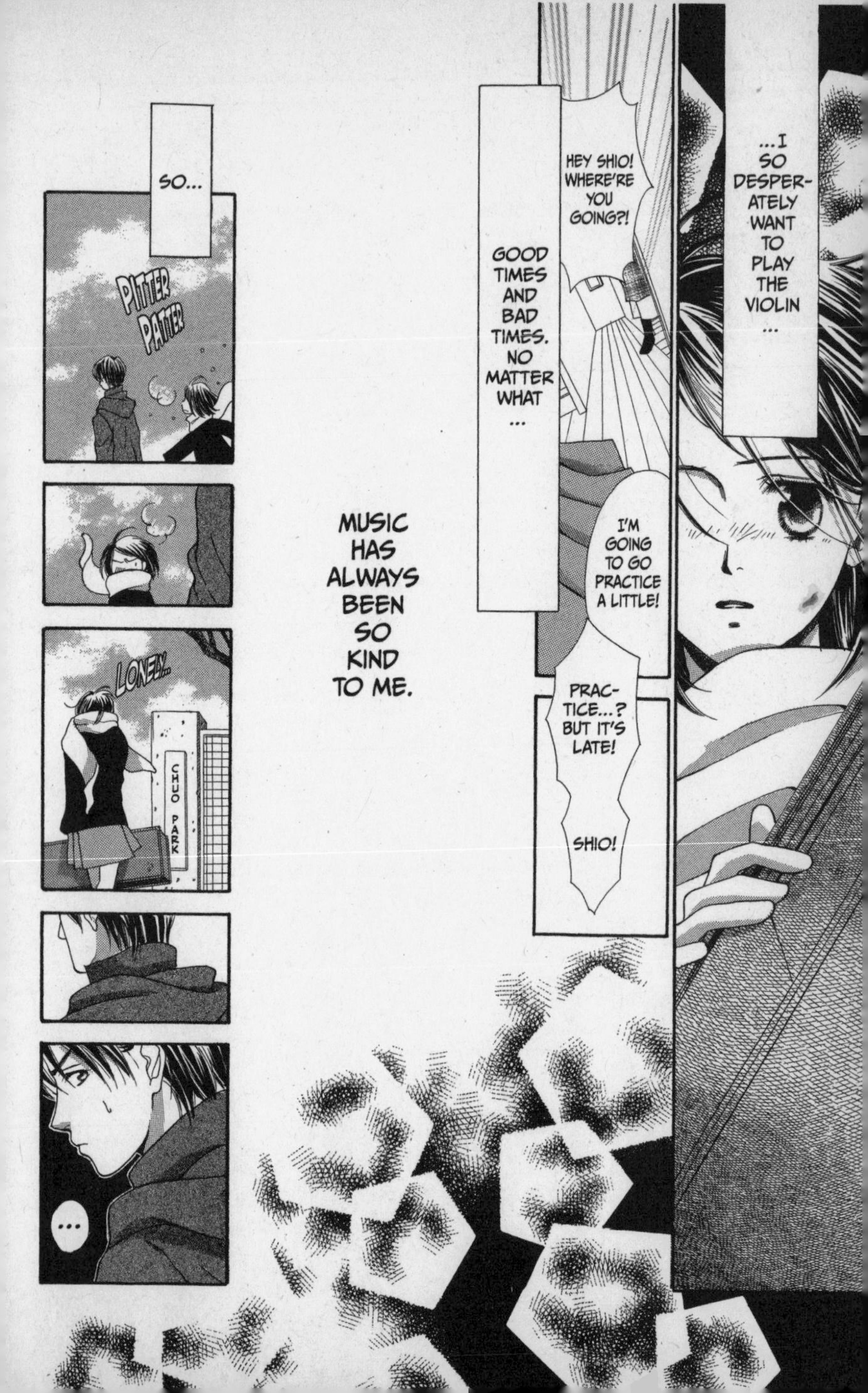
...I SO DESPERATELY WANT TO PLAY THE VIOLIN ...
HEY SHIO! WHERE'RE YOU GOING?!
GOOD TIMES AND BAD TIMES. NO MATTER WHAT ...
I'M GOING TO GO PRACTICE A LITTLE!
PRACTICE...? BUT IT'S LATE!
SHIO!
MUSIC HAS ALWAYS BEEN SO KIND TO ME.
SO...
PITTER PATTER
LONELY...
CHUO PARK
...

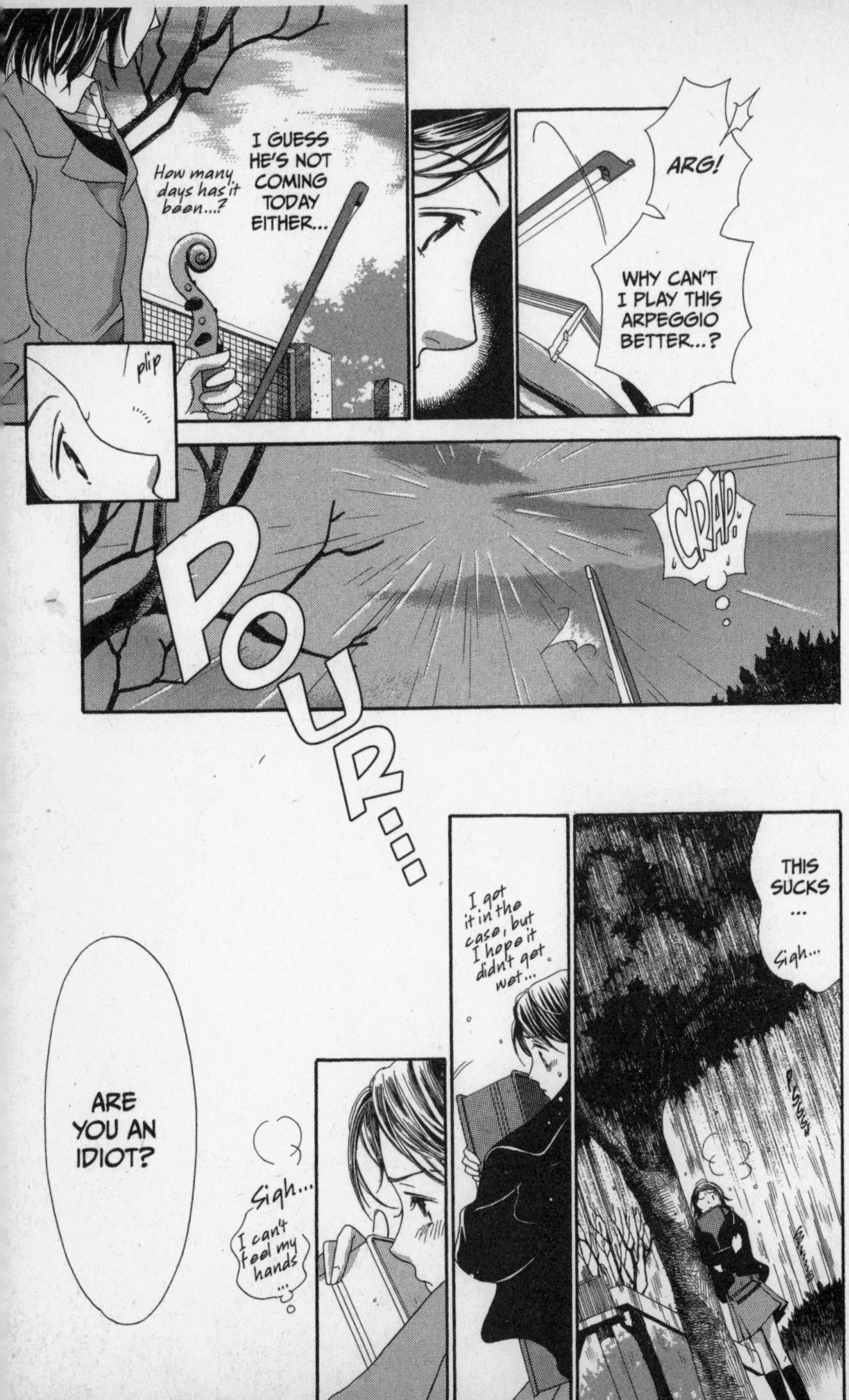
ARG!
WHY CAN'T I PLAY THIS ARPEGGIO BETTER...?
I GUESS HE'S NOT COMING TODAY EITHER...
How many days has it been...?
plip
CRAP!
POUR...
THIS SUCKS...
Sigh...
I got it in the case, but I hope it didn't get wet...
Sigh...
I can't feel my hands...
ARE YOU AN IDIOT?

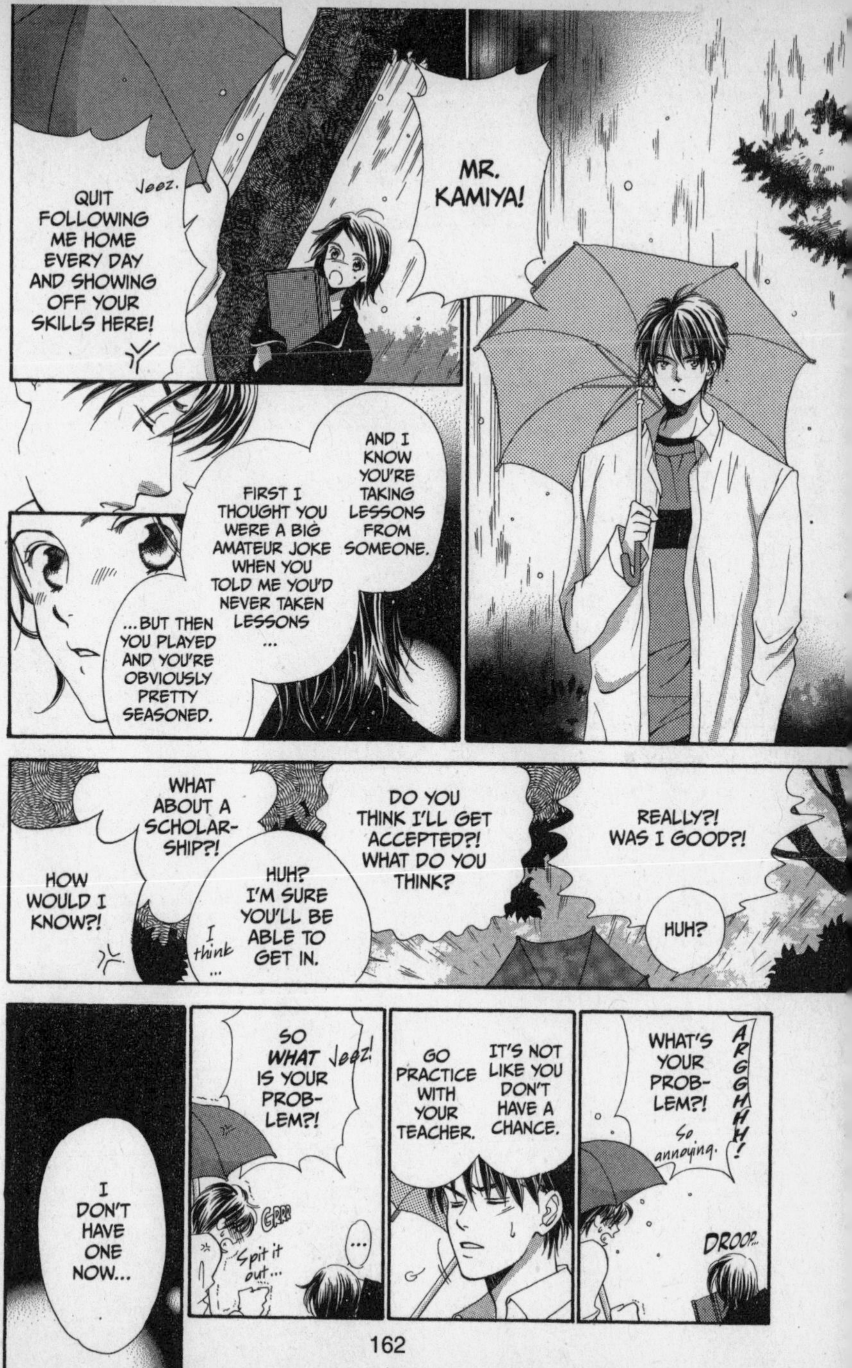
MR. KAMIYA!
Jeez.
QUIT FOLLOWING ME HOME EVERY DAY AND SHOWING OFF YOUR SKILLS HERE!
AND I KNOW YOU'RE TAKING LESSONS FROM SOMEONE.
FIRST I THOUGHT YOU WERE A BIG AMATEUR JOKE WHEN YOU TOLD ME YOU'D NEVER TAKEN LESSONS ...
...BUT THEN YOU PLAYED AND YOU'RE OBVIOUSLY PRETTY SEASONED.
REALLY?! WAS I GOOD?!
HUH?
DO YOU THINK I'LL GET ACCEPTED?! WHAT DO YOU THINK?
HUH? I'M SURE YOU'LL BE ABLE TO GET IN.
I think ...
WHAT ABOUT A SCHOLAR-SHIP?!
HOW WOULD I KNOW?!
ARGGHHH!
WHAT'S YOUR PROB-LEM?!
So annoying.
DROOP...
IT'S NOT LIKE YOU DON'T HAVE A CHANCE.
GO PRACTICE WITH YOUR TEACHER.
Jeez!
SO WHAT IS YOUR PROB-LEM?!
GRRR
Spit it out...
...
I DON'T HAVE ONE NOW...

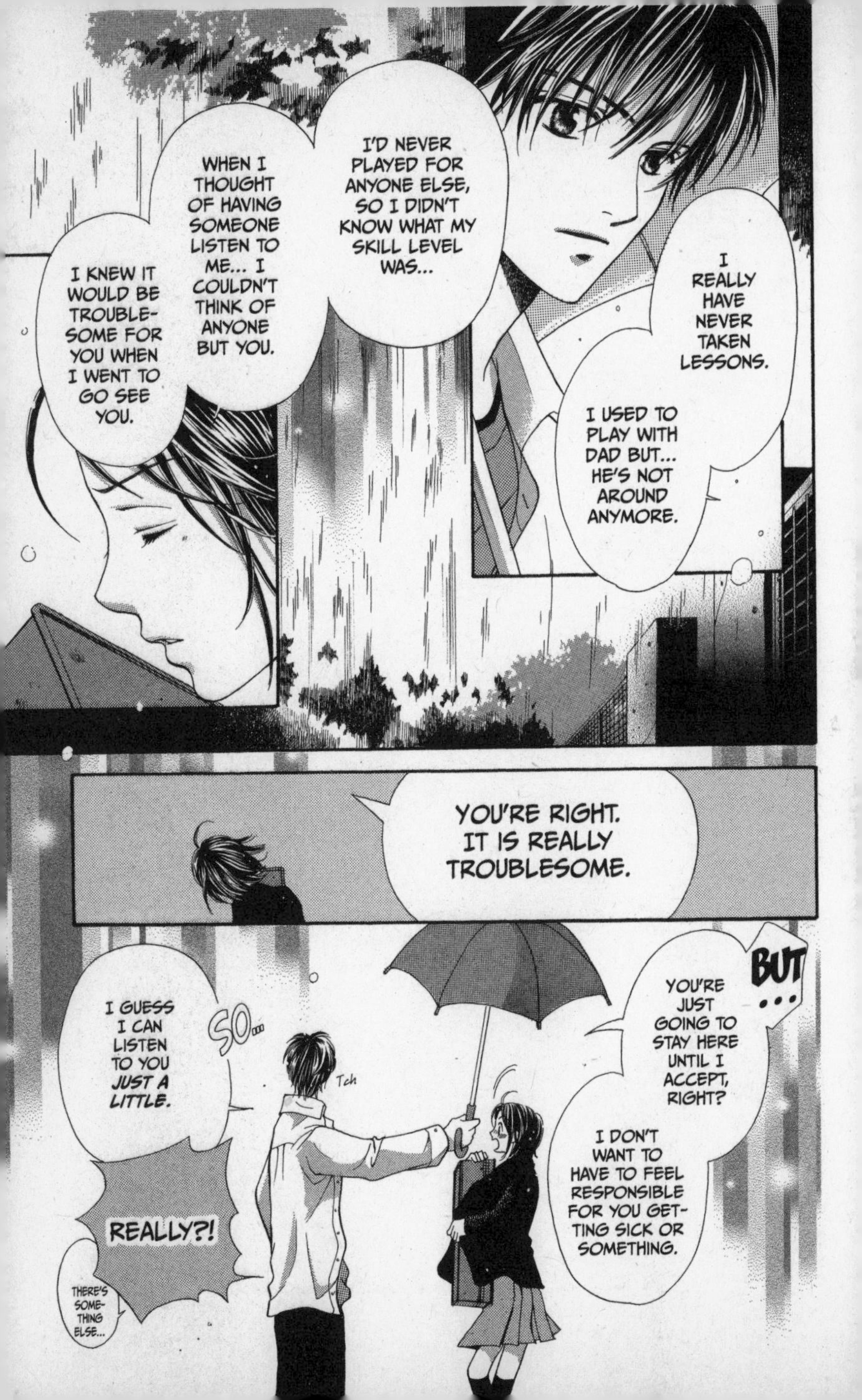
I REALLY HAVE NEVER TAKEN LESSONS.
I USED TO PLAY WITH DAD BUT... HE'S NOT AROUND ANYMORE.
I'D NEVER PLAYED FOR ANYONE ELSE, SO I DIDN'T KNOW WHAT MY SKILL LEVEL WAS...
WHEN I THOUGHT OF HAVING SOMEONE LISTEN TO ME... I COULDN'T THINK OF ANYONE BUT YOU.
I KNEW IT WOULD BE TROUBLE-SOME FOR YOU WHEN I WENT TO GO SEE YOU.
YOU'RE RIGHT. IT IS REALLY TROUBLESOME.
BUT...
YOU'RE JUST GOING TO STAY HERE UNTIL I ACCEPT, RIGHT?
I DON'T WANT TO HAVE TO FEEL RESPONSIBLE FOR YOU GET-TING SICK OR SOMETHING.
SO...
I GUESS I CAN LISTEN TO YOU *JUST A LITTLE.*
Tch
REALLY?!
THERE'S SOME-THING ELSE...

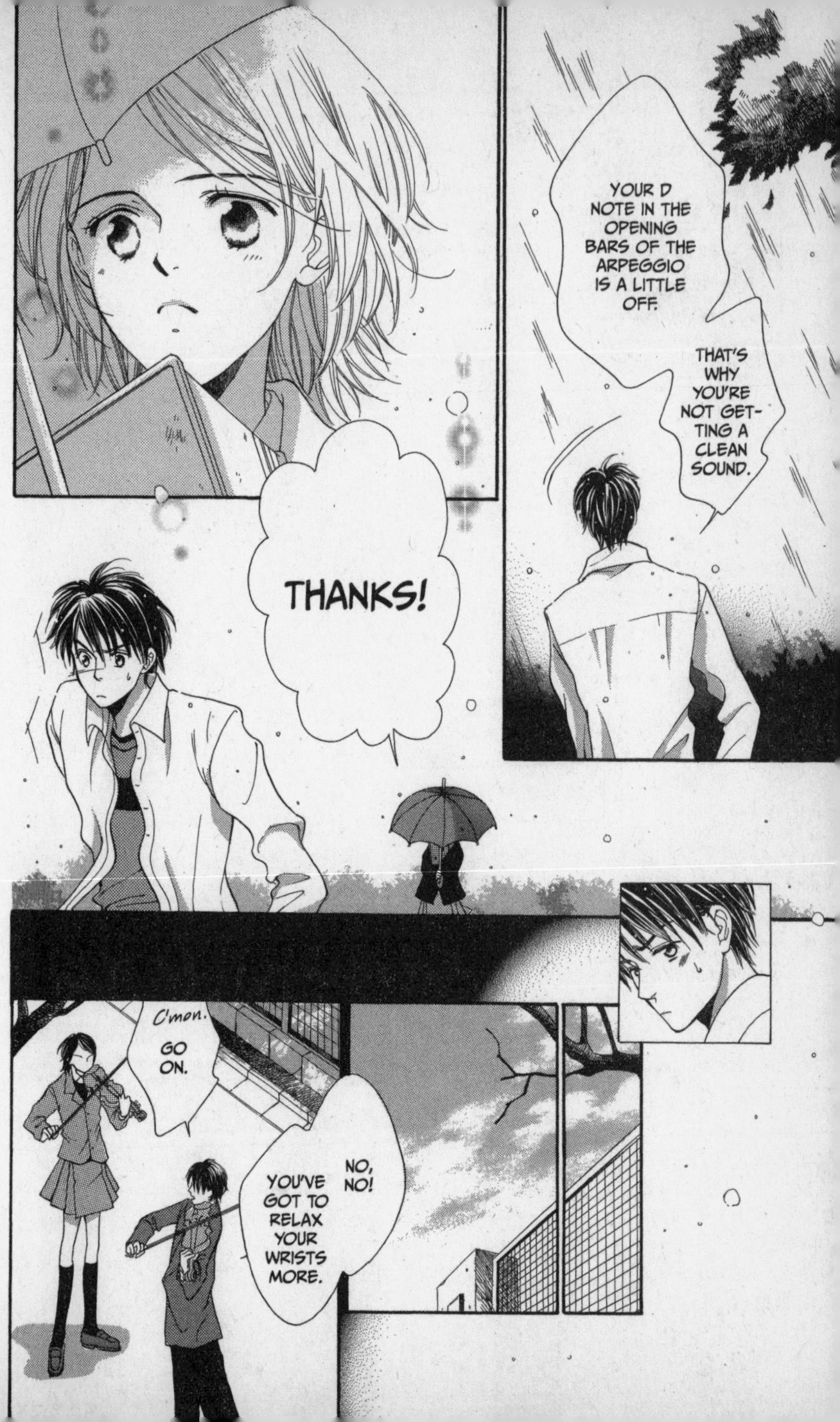
YOUR D NOTE IN THE OPENING BARS OF THE ARPEGGIO IS A LITTLE OFF.
THAT'S WHY YOU'RE NOT GET-TING A CLEAN SOUND.
THANKS!
C'mon.
GO ON.
NO, NO!
YOU'VE GOT TO RELAX YOUR WRISTS MORE.

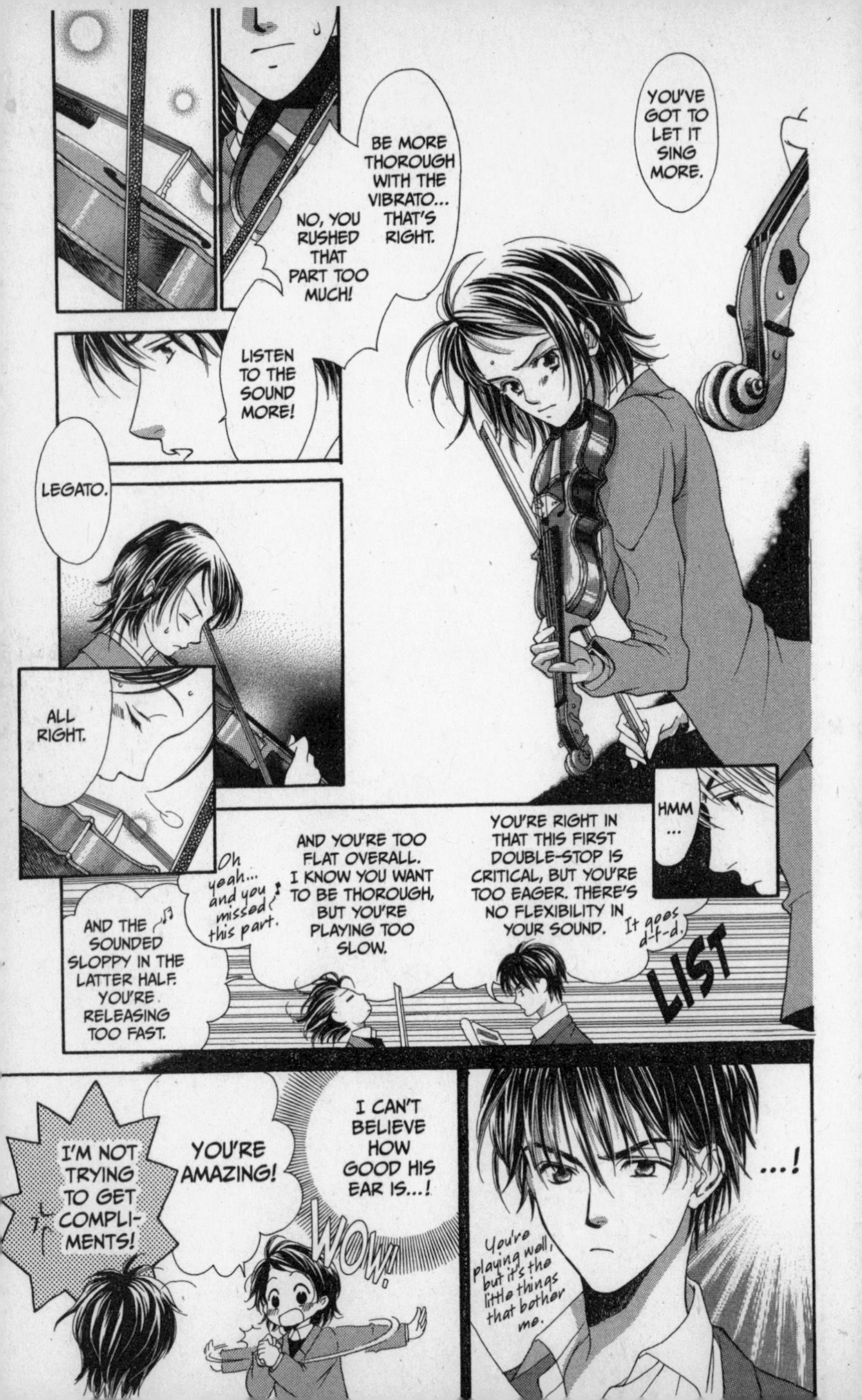
YOU'VE GOT TO LET IT SING MORE.
BE MORE THOROUGH WITH THE VIBRATO... THAT'S RIGHT.
NO, YOU RUSHED THAT PART TOO MUCH!
LISTEN TO THE SOUND MORE!
LEGATO.
ALL RIGHT.
HMM...
YOU'RE RIGHT IN THAT THIS FIRST DOUBLE-STOP IS CRITICAL, BUT YOU'RE TOO EAGER. THERE'S NO FLEXIBILITY IN YOUR SOUND.
It goes d-f-d.
LIST
AND YOU'RE TOO FLAT OVERALL. I KNOW YOU WANT TO BE THOROUGH, BUT YOU'RE PLAYING TOO SLOW.
Oh yeah... and you missed this part.
AND THE ♪ SOUNDED SLOPPY IN THE LATTER HALF. YOU'RE RELEASING TOO FAST.
...!
You're playing well, but it's the little things that bother me.
I CAN'T BELIEVE HOW GOOD HIS EAR IS...!
YOU'RE AMAZING!
WOW!
I'M NOT TRYING TO GET COMPLI-MENTS!

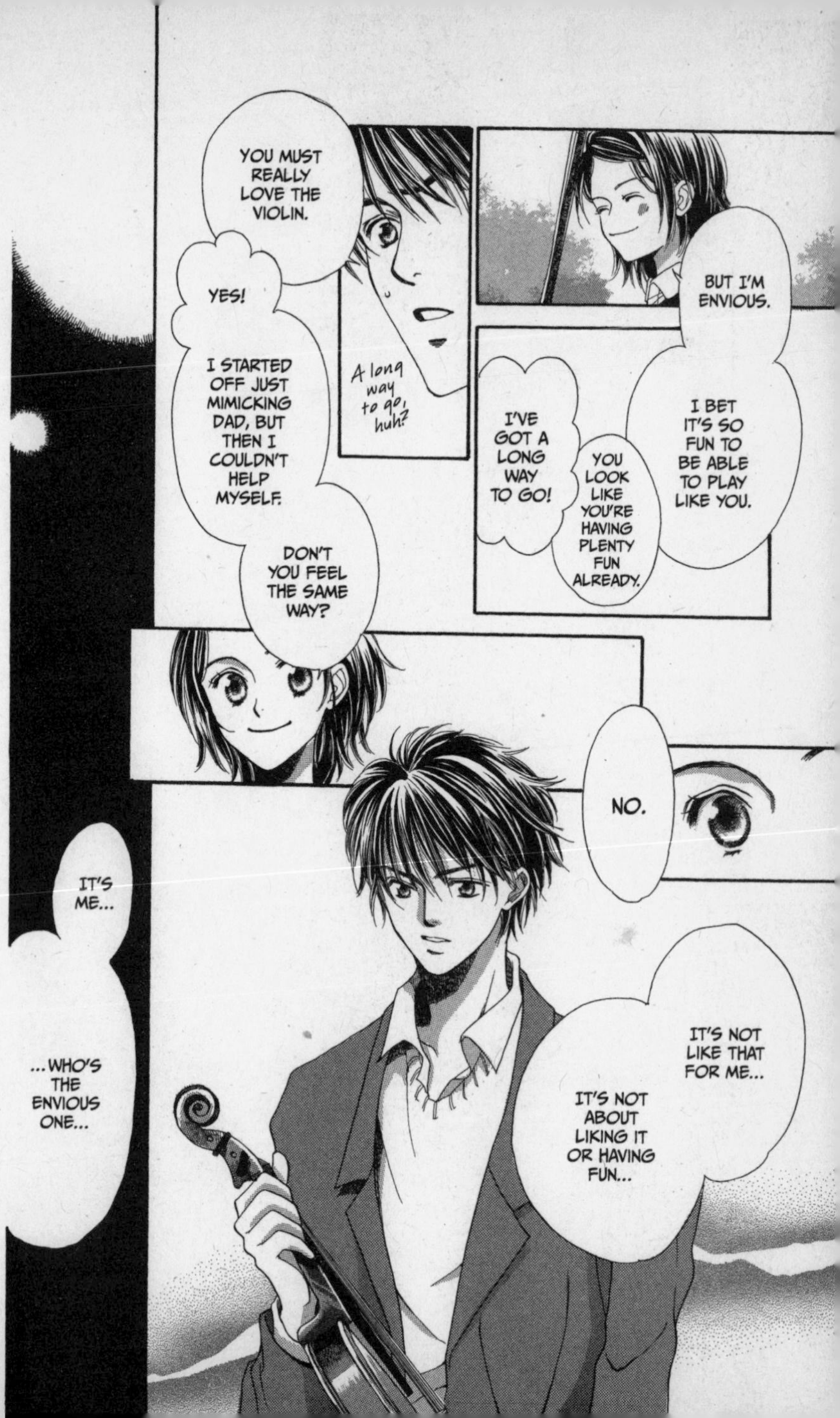
BUT I'M ENVIOUS.
I BET IT'S SO FUN TO BE ABLE TO PLAY LIKE YOU.
I'VE GOT A LONG WAY TO GO!
YOU LOOK LIKE YOU'RE HAVING PLENTY FUN ALREADY.
YOU MUST REALLY LOVE THE VIOLIN.
A long way to go, huh?
YES!
I STARTED OFF JUST MIMICKING DAD, BUT THEN I COULDN'T HELP MYSELF.
DON'T YOU FEEL THE SAME WAY?
NO.
IT'S NOT LIKE THAT FOR ME...
IT'S NOT ABOUT LIKING IT OR HAVING FUN...
IT'S ME...
...WHO'S THE ENVIOUS ONE...

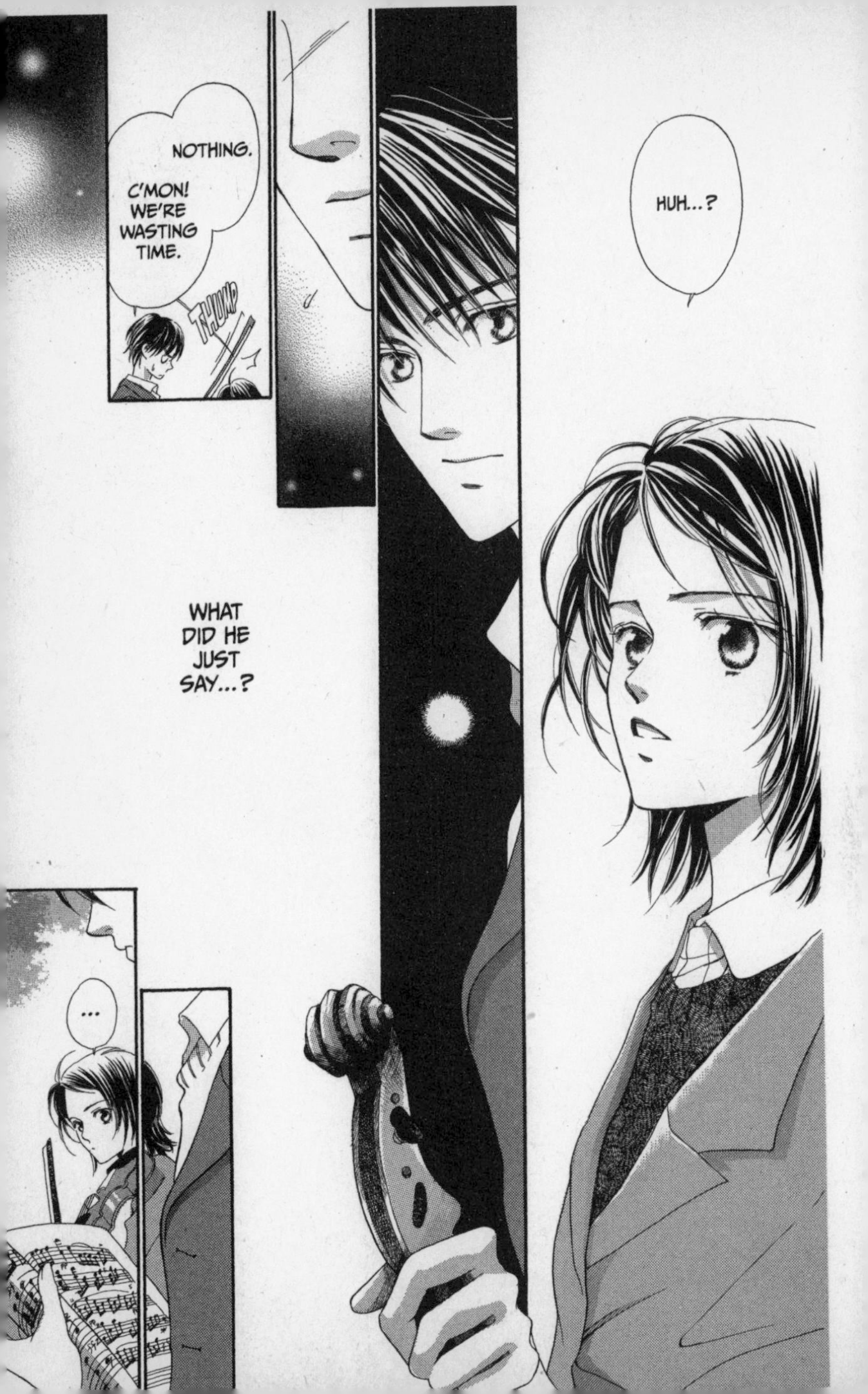
HUH...?
NOTHING.
C'MON! WE'RE WASTING TIME.
THUMP
WHAT DID HE JUST SAY...?
...

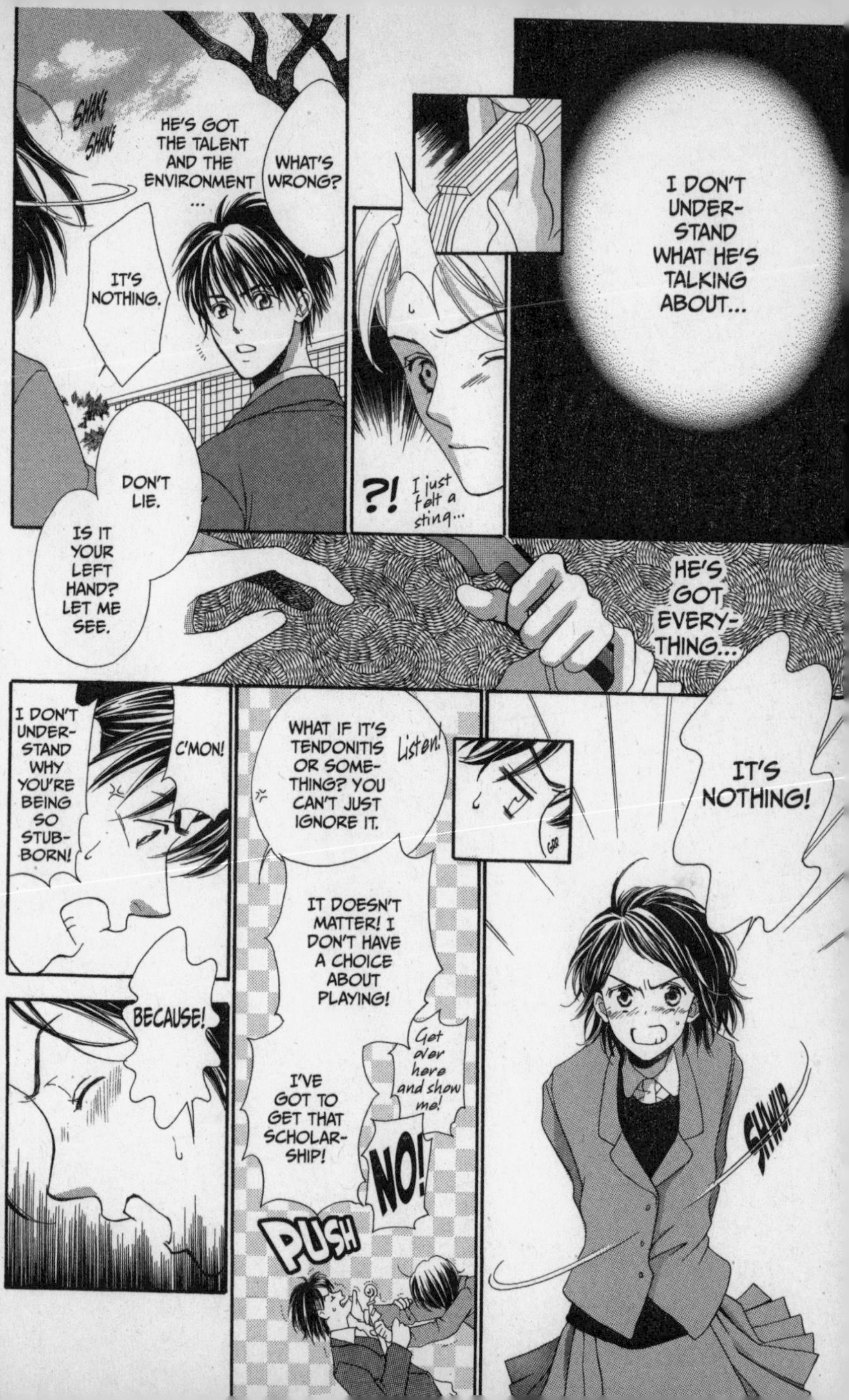
I DON'T UNDERSTAND WHAT HE'S TALKING ABOUT...
?!
I just felt a sting...
WHAT'S WRONG?
HE'S GOT THE TALENT AND THE ENVIRONMENT ...
SHAKE SHAKE
IT'S NOTHING.
DON'T LIE.
IS IT YOUR LEFT HAND? LET ME SEE.
HE'S GOT EVERYTHING...
IT'S NOTHING!
SHWIP
GRR
Listen!
WHAT IF IT'S TENDONITIS OR SOMETHING? YOU CAN'T JUST IGNORE IT.
IT DOESN'T MATTER! I DON'T HAVE A CHOICE ABOUT PLAYING!
Get over here and show me!
I'VE GOT TO GET THAT SCHOLARSHIP!
NO!
PUSH
C'MON!
I DON'T UNDERSTAND WHY YOU'RE BEING SO STUBBORN!
BECAUSE!

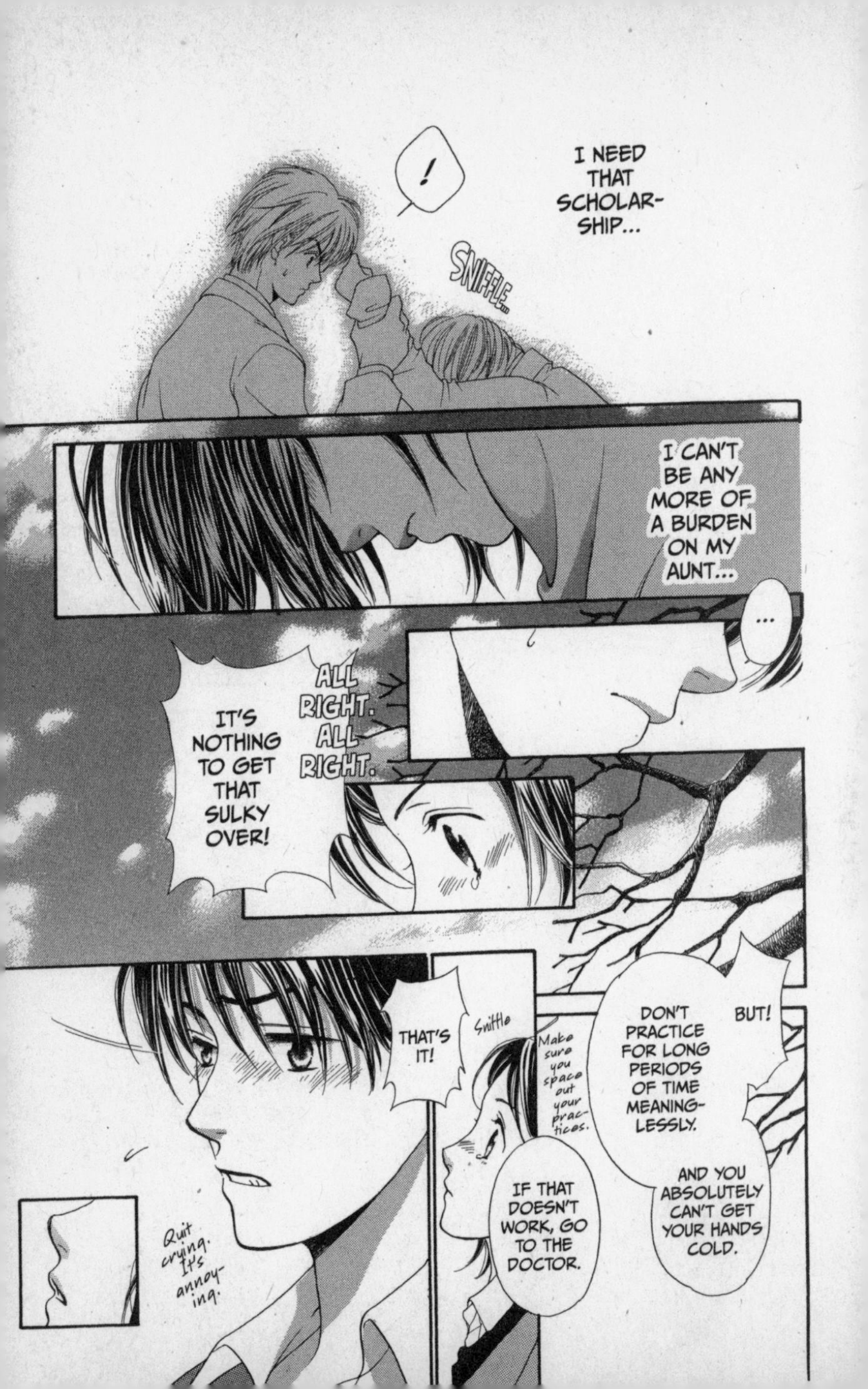
I NEED THAT SCHOLAR-SHIP...
!
SNIFFLE...
I CAN'T BE ANY MORE OF A BURDEN ON MY AUNT...
...
ALL RIGHT. ALL RIGHT.
IT'S NOTHING TO GET THAT SULKY OVER!
BUT!
DON'T PRACTICE FOR LONG PERIODS OF TIME MEANING-LESSLY.
Make sure you space out your prac-tices.
AND YOU ABSOLUTELY CAN'T GET YOUR HANDS COLD.
IF THAT DOESN'T WORK, GO TO THE DOCTOR.
Sniffle
THAT'S IT!
Quit crying. It's annoy-ing.

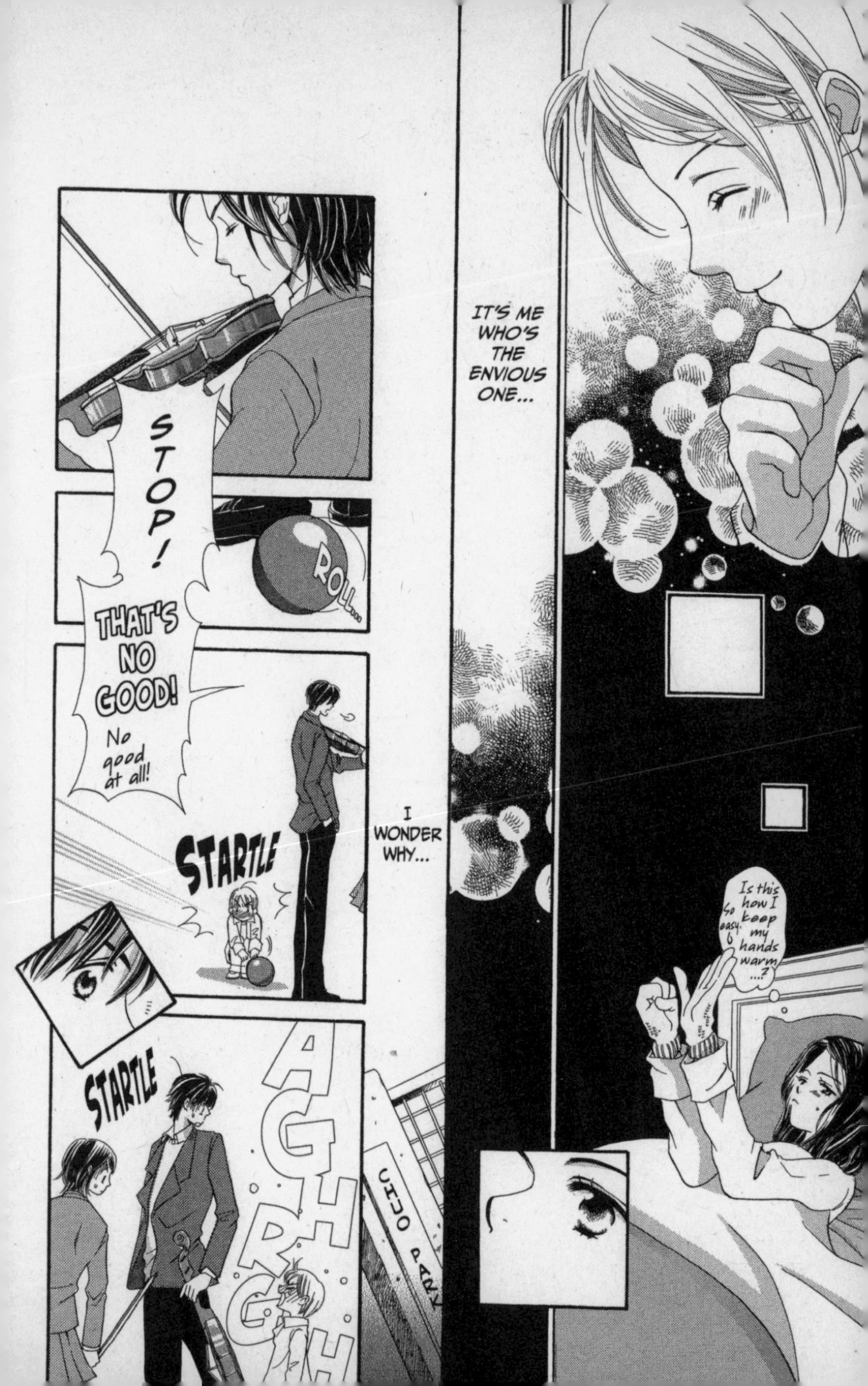
IT'S ME WHO'S THE ENVIOUS ONE...
Is this how I keep my hands warm...?
So easy.
STOP!
THAT'S NO GOOD!
No good at all!
ROLL...
I WONDER WHY...
STARTLE
STARTLE
AGHRGH
CHUO PARK

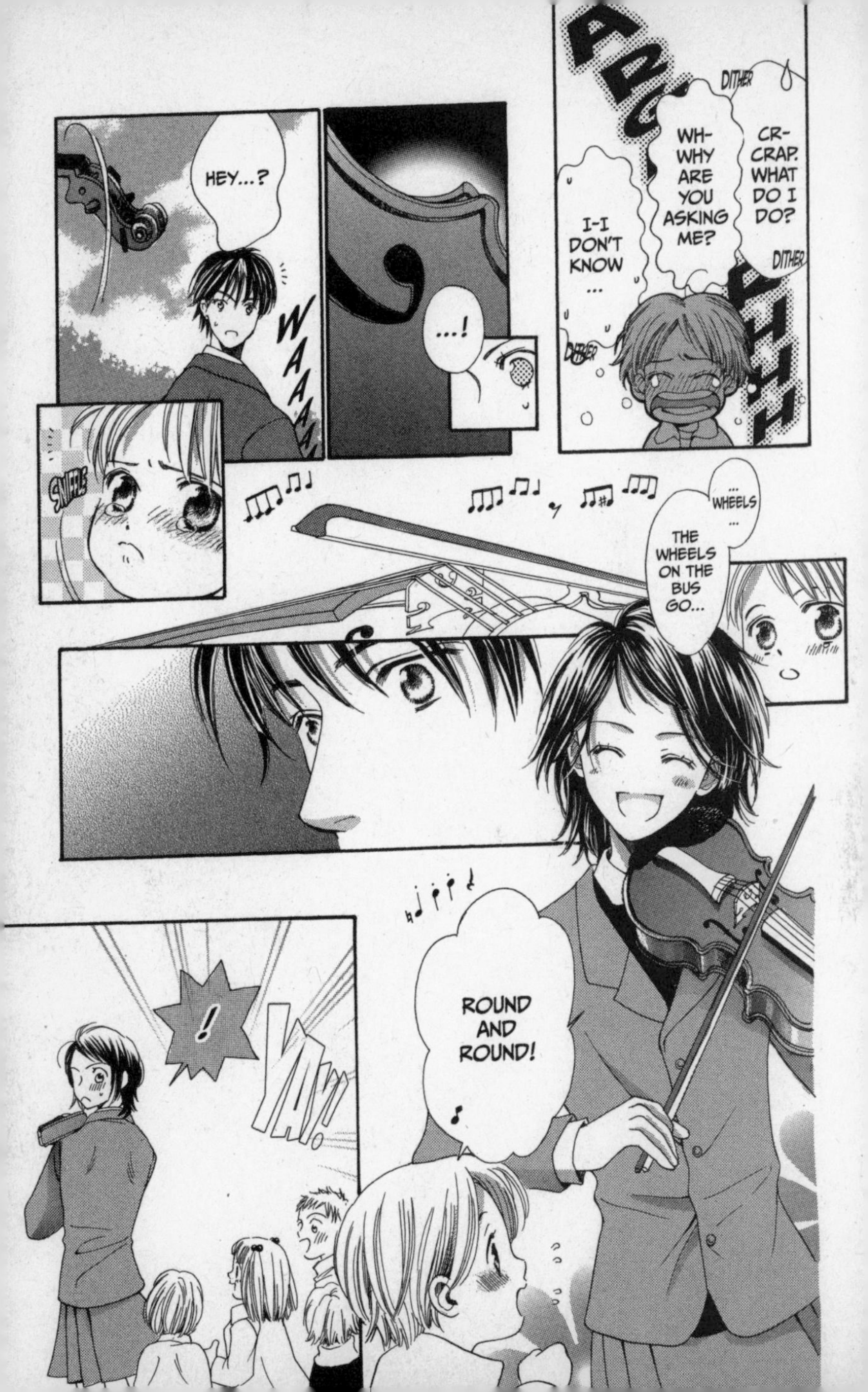
DITHER
CR-CRAP. WHAT DO I DO?
WH-WHY ARE YOU ASKING ME?
DITHER
I-I DON'T KNOW ...
DITHER
...!
HEY...?
SNIFFLE
... WHEELS ...
THE WHEELS ON THE BUS GO...
ROUND AND ROUND!
!

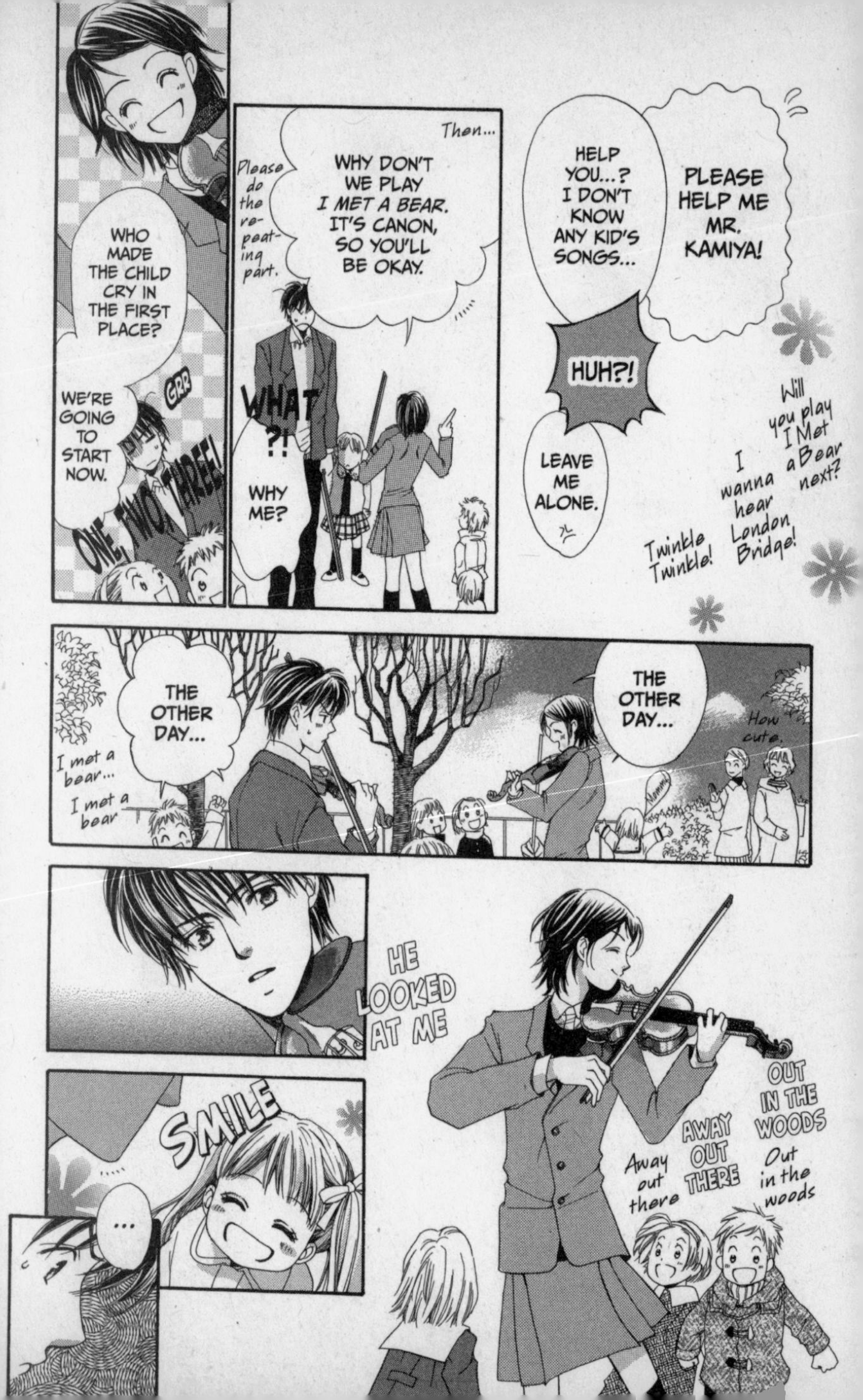
PLEASE HELP ME MR. KAMIYA!
HELP YOU...? I DON'T KNOW ANY KID'S SONGS...
HUH?!
LEAVE ME ALONE.
Will you play I Met a Bear next?
I wanna hear London Bridge!
Twinkle Twinkle!
Then...
WHY DON'T WE PLAY I MET A BEAR. IT'S CANON, SO YOU'LL BE OKAY.
Please do the re-peating part.
WHAT?!
WHY ME?
WHO MADE THE CHILD CRY IN THE FIRST PLACE?
GRR
WE'RE GOING TO START NOW.
ONE, TWO, THREE!
THE OTHER DAY...
How cute.
THE OTHER DAY...
I met a bear...
I met a bear
OUT IN THE WOODS
Out in the woods
AWAY OUT THERE
Away out there
HE LOOKED AT ME
SMILE
...

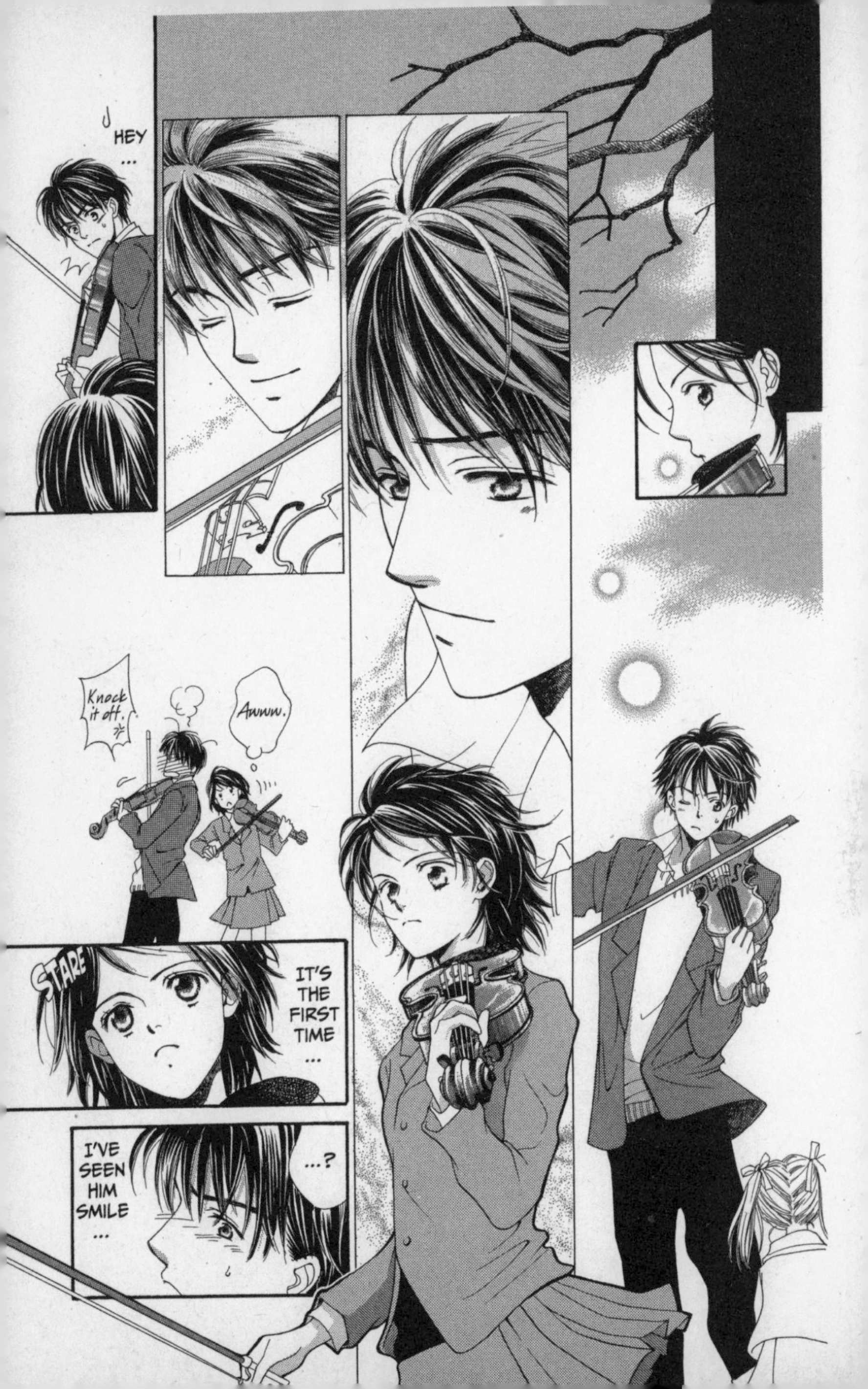
HEY ...
Awww.
Knock it off.
IT'S THE FIRST TIME ...
STARE
...?
I'VE SEEN HIM SMILE ...

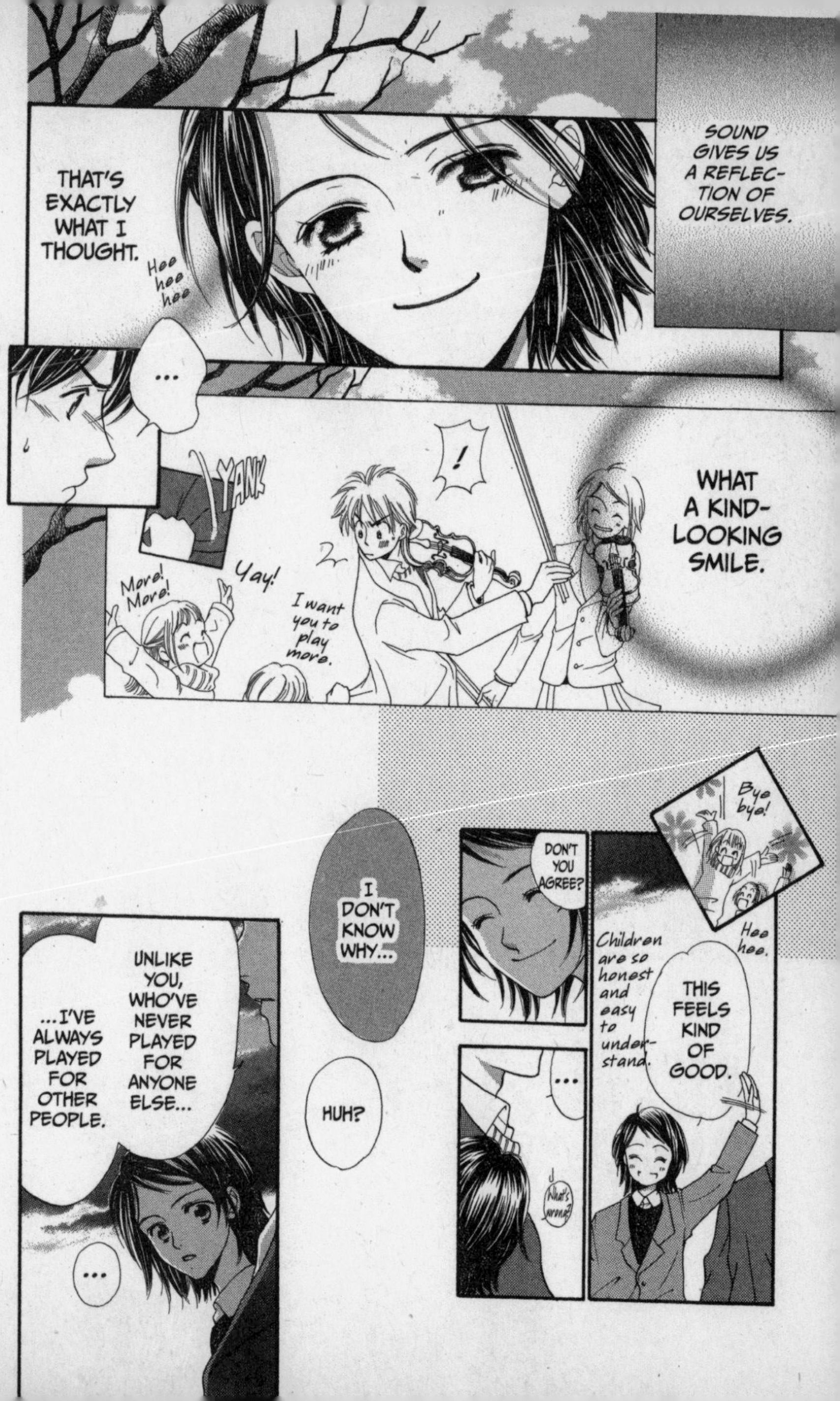
SOUND GIVES US A REFLECTION OF OURSELVES.
THAT'S EXACTLY WHAT I THOUGHT.
Hee hee hee
...
WHAT A KIND-LOOKING SMILE.
!
YANK
Yay!
I want you to play more.
More! More!
Bye bye!
DON'T YOU AGREE?
Children are so honest and easy to understand.
Hee hee.
THIS FEELS KIND OF GOOD.
...
What's wrong?
I DON'T KNOW WHY...
HUH?
UNLIKE YOU, WHO'VE NEVER PLAYED FOR ANYONE ELSE...
...I'VE ALWAYS PLAYED FOR OTHER PEOPLE.
...

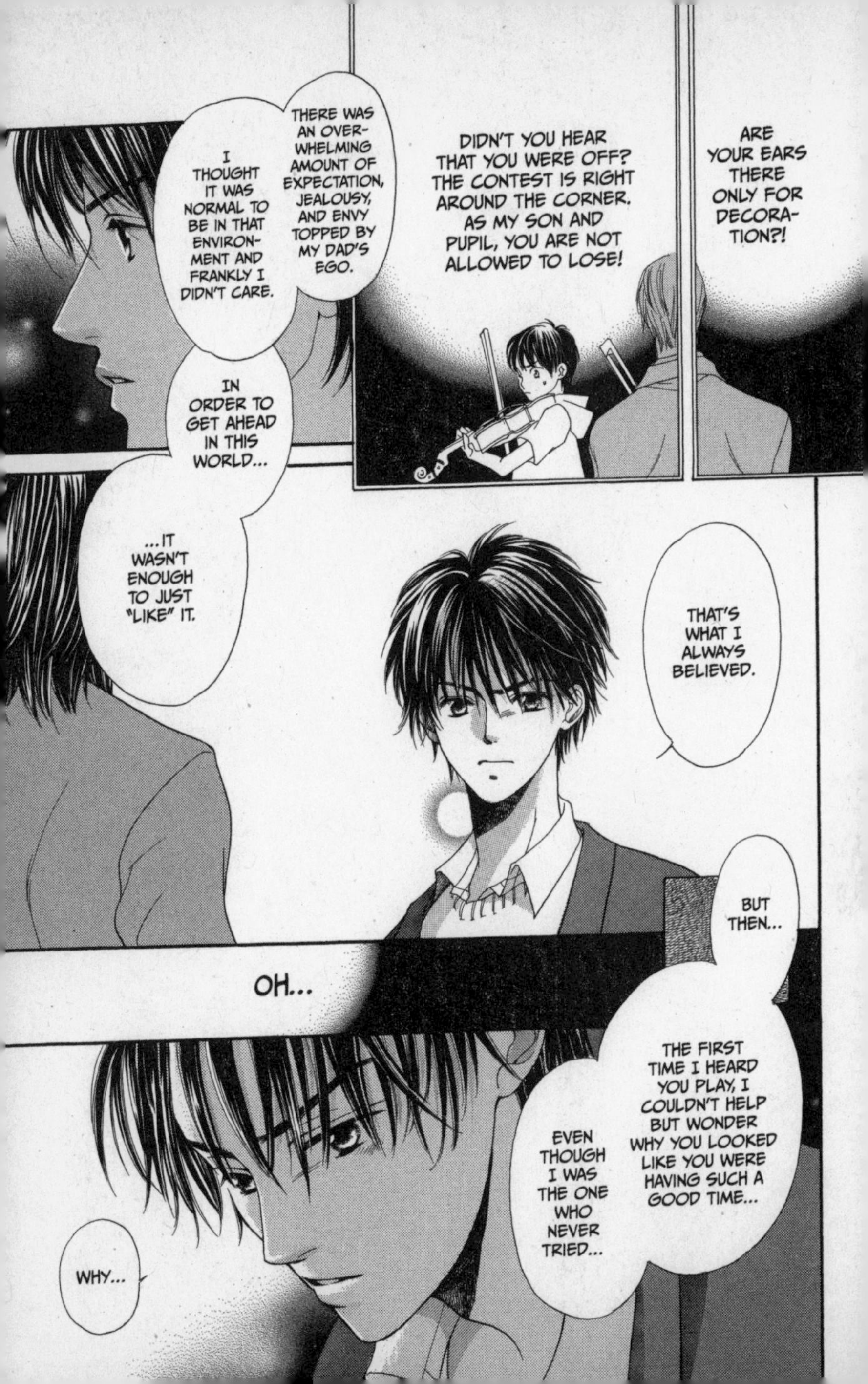
ARE YOUR EARS THERE ONLY FOR DECORATION?!
DIDN'T YOU HEAR THAT YOU WERE OFF? THE CONTEST IS RIGHT AROUND THE CORNER. AS MY SON AND PUPIL, YOU ARE NOT ALLOWED TO LOSE!
THERE WAS AN OVER-WHELMING AMOUNT OF EXPECTATION, JEALOUSY, AND ENVY TOPPED BY MY DAD'S EGO.
I THOUGHT IT WAS NORMAL TO BE IN THAT ENVIRON-MENT AND FRANKLY I DIDN'T CARE.
IN ORDER TO GET AHEAD IN THIS WORLD...
...IT WASN'T ENOUGH TO JUST "LIKE" IT.
THAT'S WHAT I ALWAYS BELIEVED.
BUT THEN...
OH...
THE FIRST TIME I HEARD YOU PLAY, I COULDN'T HELP BUT WONDER WHY YOU LOOKED LIKE YOU WERE HAVING SUCH A GOOD TIME...
EVEN THOUGH I WAS THE ONE WHO NEVER TRIED...
WHY...

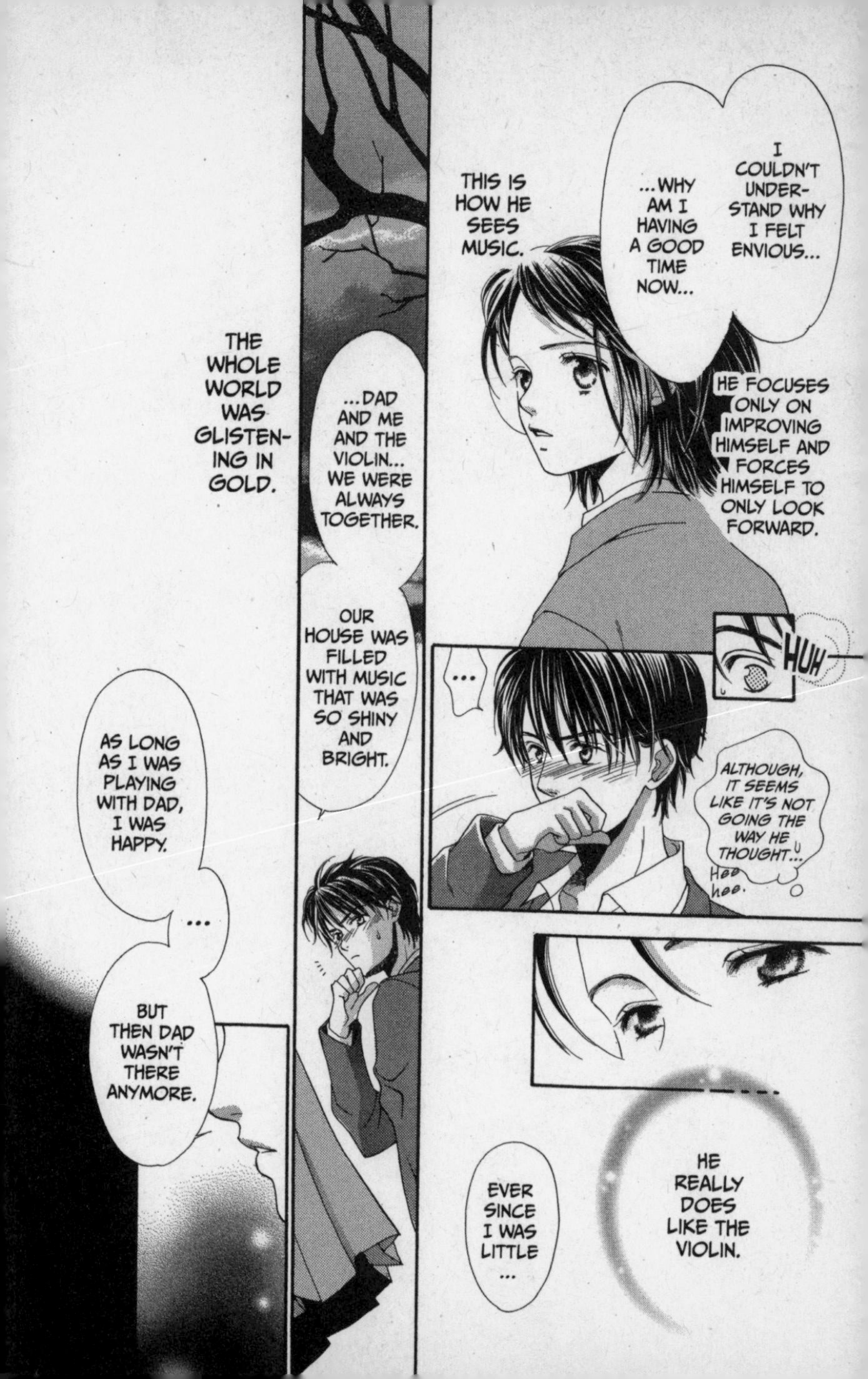
I COULDN'T UNDER-STAND WHY I FELT ENVIOUS...
...WHY AM I HAVING A GOOD TIME NOW...
THIS IS HOW HE SEES MUSIC.
HE FOCUSES ONLY ON IMPROVING HIMSELF AND FORCES HIMSELF TO ONLY LOOK FORWARD.
HUH
...
ALTHOUGH, IT SEEMS LIKE IT'S NOT GOING THE WAY HE THOUGHT...
Hee hee.
HE REALLY DOES LIKE THE VIOLIN.
EVER SINCE I WAS LITTLE ...
...DAD AND ME AND THE VIOLIN... WE WERE ALWAYS TOGETHER.
OUR HOUSE WAS FILLED WITH MUSIC THAT WAS SO SHINY AND BRIGHT.
THE WHOLE WORLD WAS GLISTEN-ING IN GOLD.
AS LONG AS I WAS PLAYING WITH DAD, I WAS HAPPY.
...
BUT THEN DAD WASN'T THERE ANYMORE.

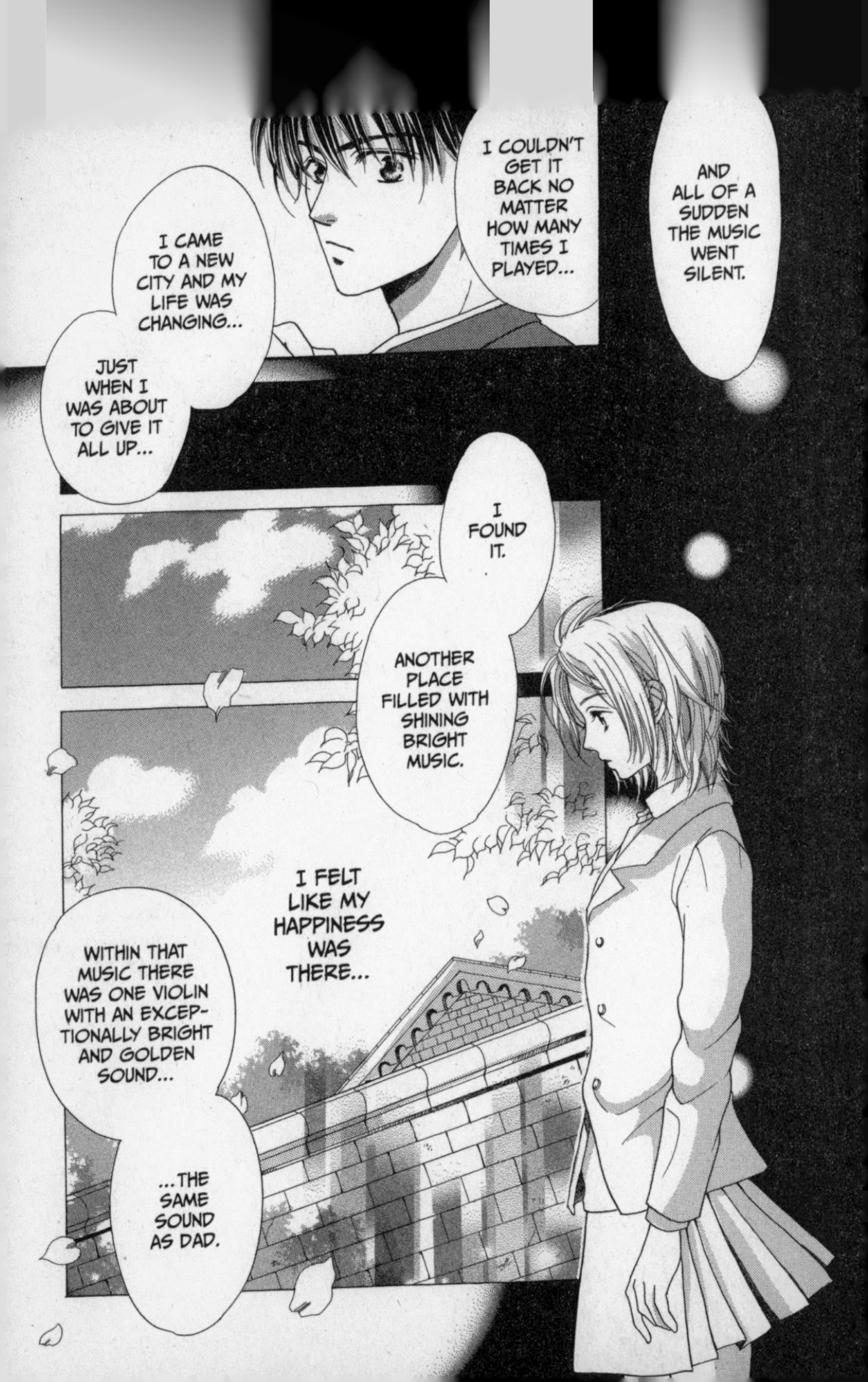
AND ALL OF A SUDDEN THE MUSIC WENT SILENT.
I COULDN'T GET IT BACK NO MATTER HOW MANY TIMES I PLAYED...
I CAME TO A NEW CITY AND MY LIFE WAS CHANGING...
JUST WHEN I WAS ABOUT TO GIVE IT ALL UP...
I FOUND IT.
ANOTHER PLACE FILLED WITH SHINING BRIGHT MUSIC.
I FELT LIKE MY HAPPINESS WAS THERE...
WITHIN THAT MUSIC THERE WAS ONE VIOLIN WITH AN EXCEP-TIONALLY BRIGHT AND GOLDEN SOUND...
...THE SAME SOUND AS DAD.

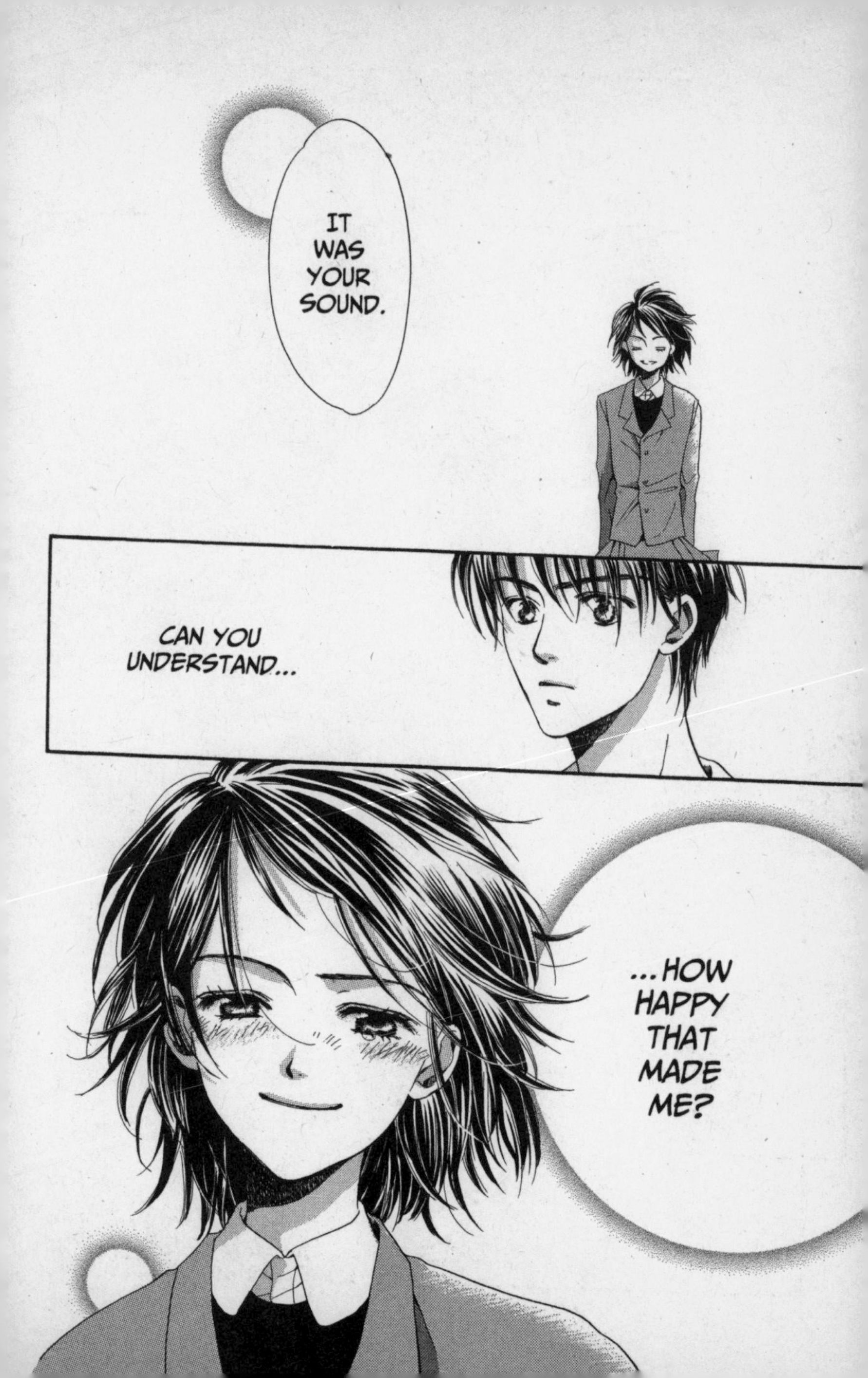
IT WAS YOUR SOUND.
CAN YOU UNDERSTAND...
...HOW HAPPY THAT MADE ME?

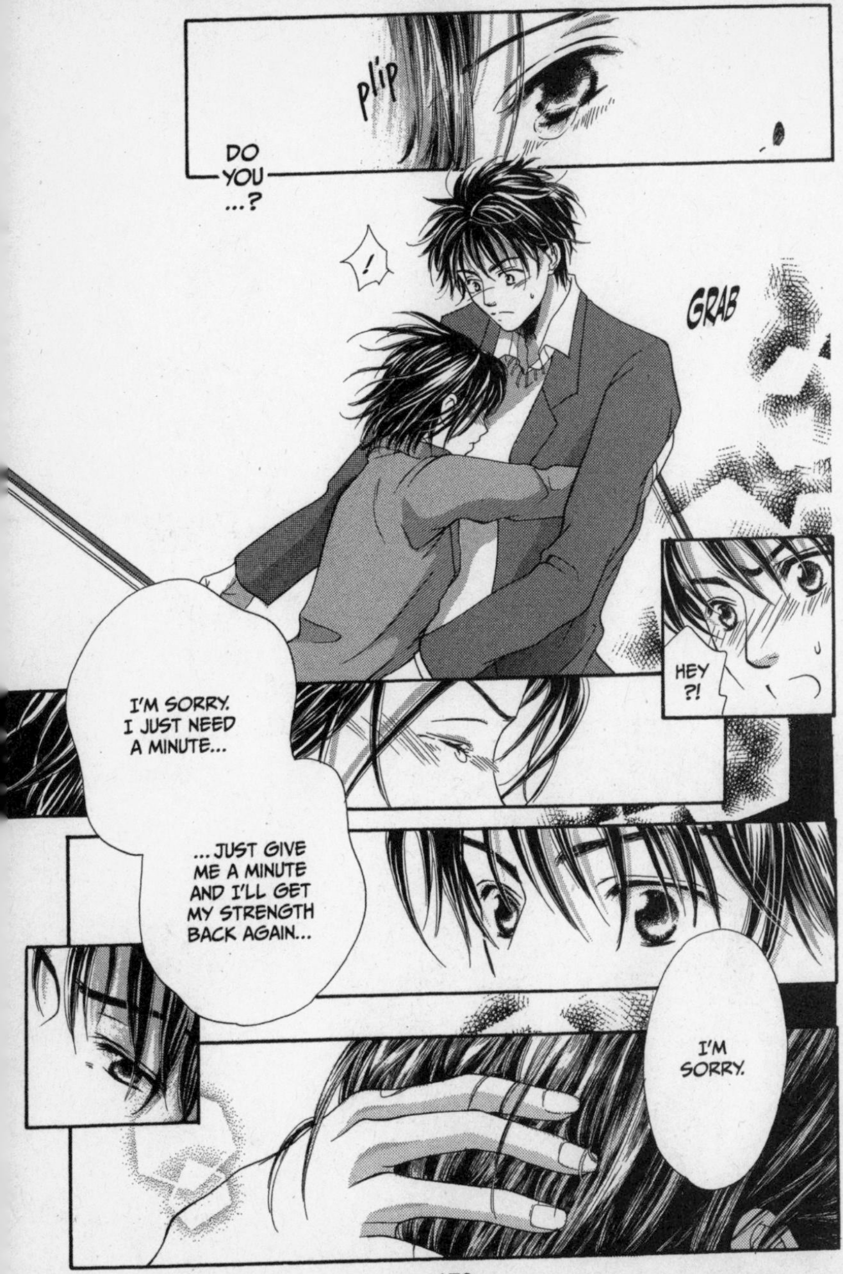
plip
DO YOU ...?
!
GRAB
HEY ?!
I'M SORRY. I JUST NEED A MINUTE...
...JUST GIVE ME A MINUTE AND I'LL GET MY STRENGTH BACK AGAIN...
I'M SORRY.

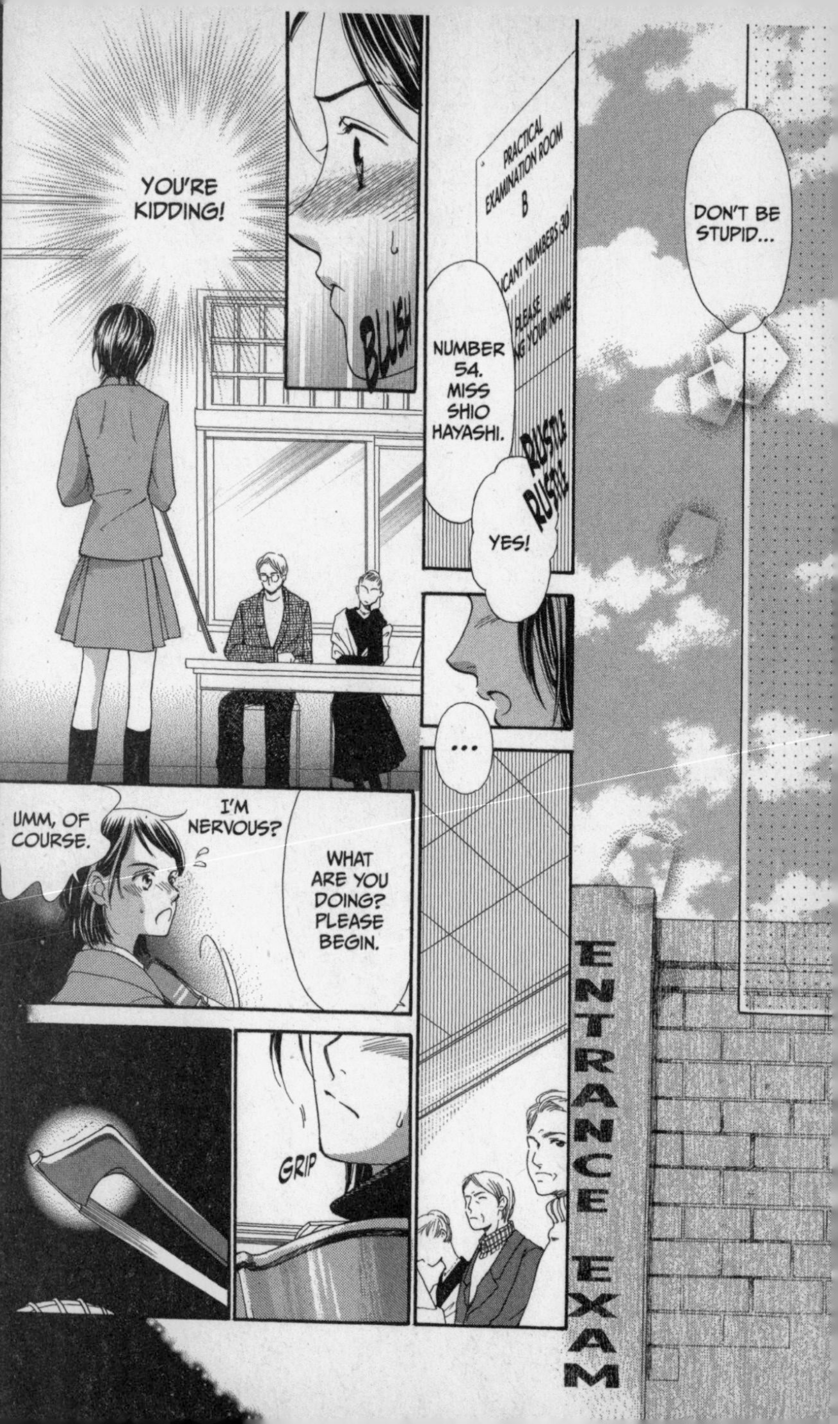
DON'T BE STUPID...
ENTRANCE EXAM
PRACTICAL EXAMINATION ROOM B
NUMBER 54. MISS SHIO HAYASHI.
RUSTLE RUSTLE
YES!
...
BLUSH
YOU'RE KIDDING!
WHAT ARE YOU DOING? PLEASE BEGIN.
I'M NERVOUS?
UMM, OF COURSE.
GRIP

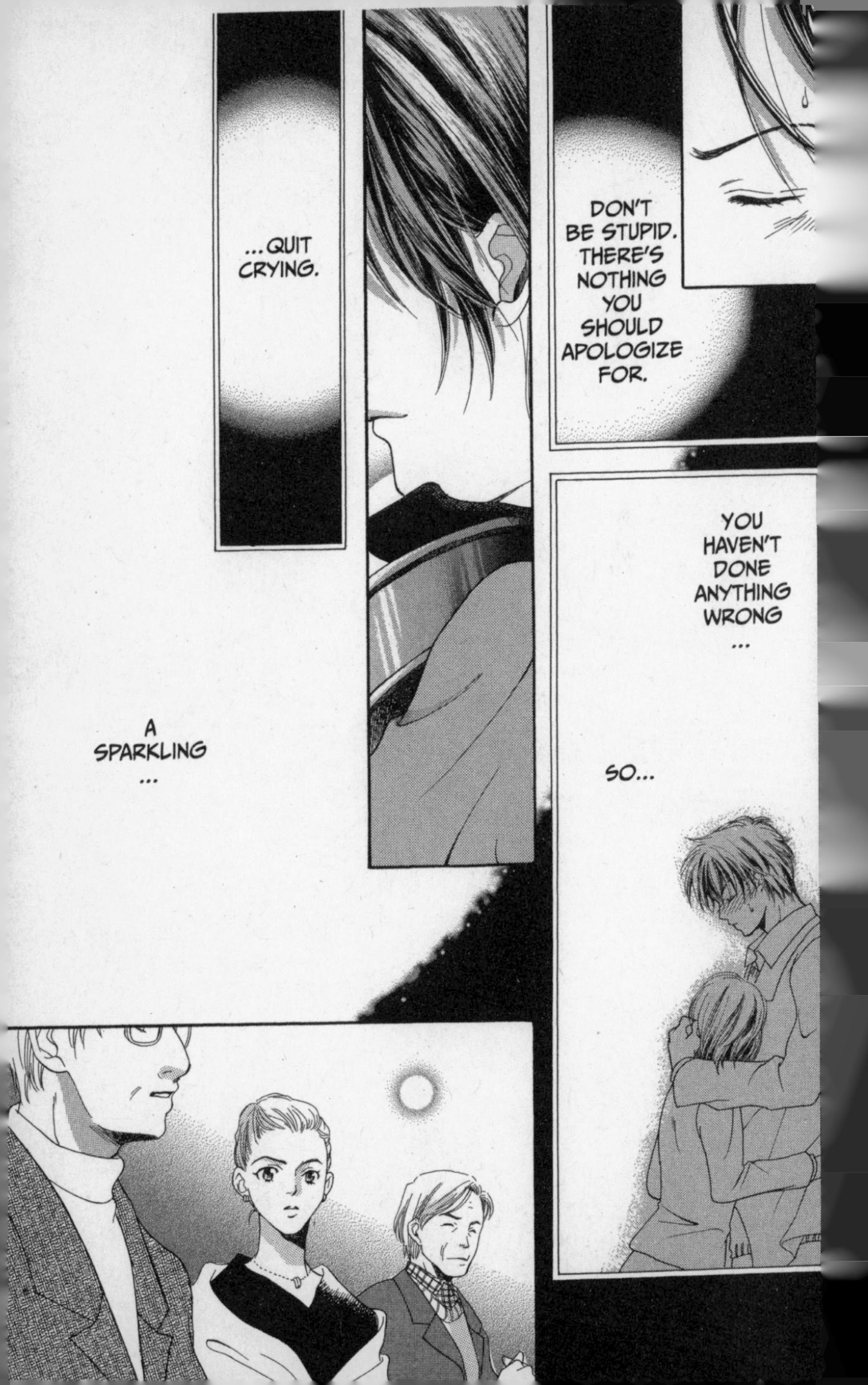
DON'T BE STUPID. THERE'S NOTHING YOU SHOULD APOLOGIZE FOR.
...QUIT CRYING.
YOU HAVEN'T DONE ANYTHING WRONG ...
SO...
A SPARKLING ...

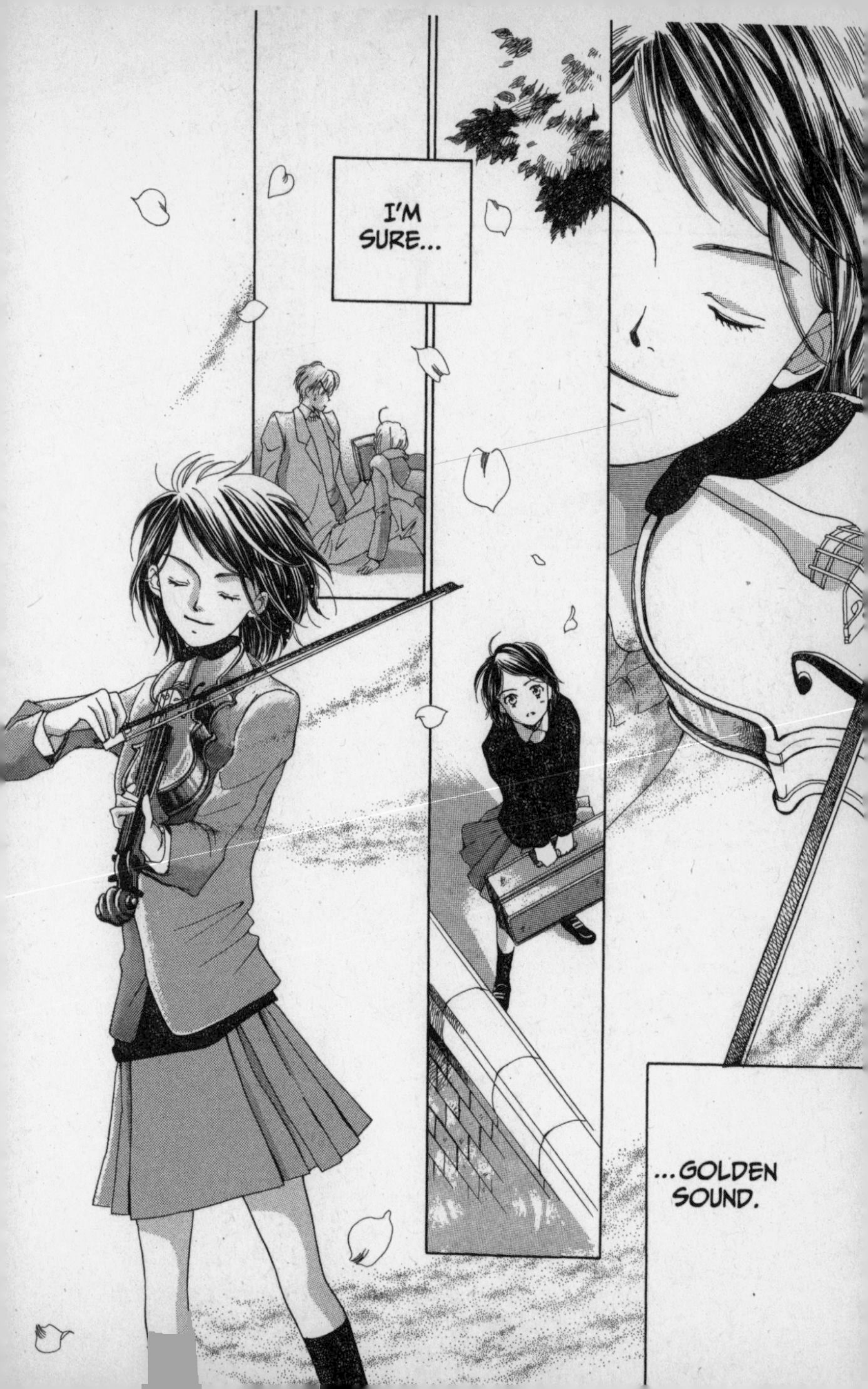
I'M SURE...
...GOLDEN SOUND.

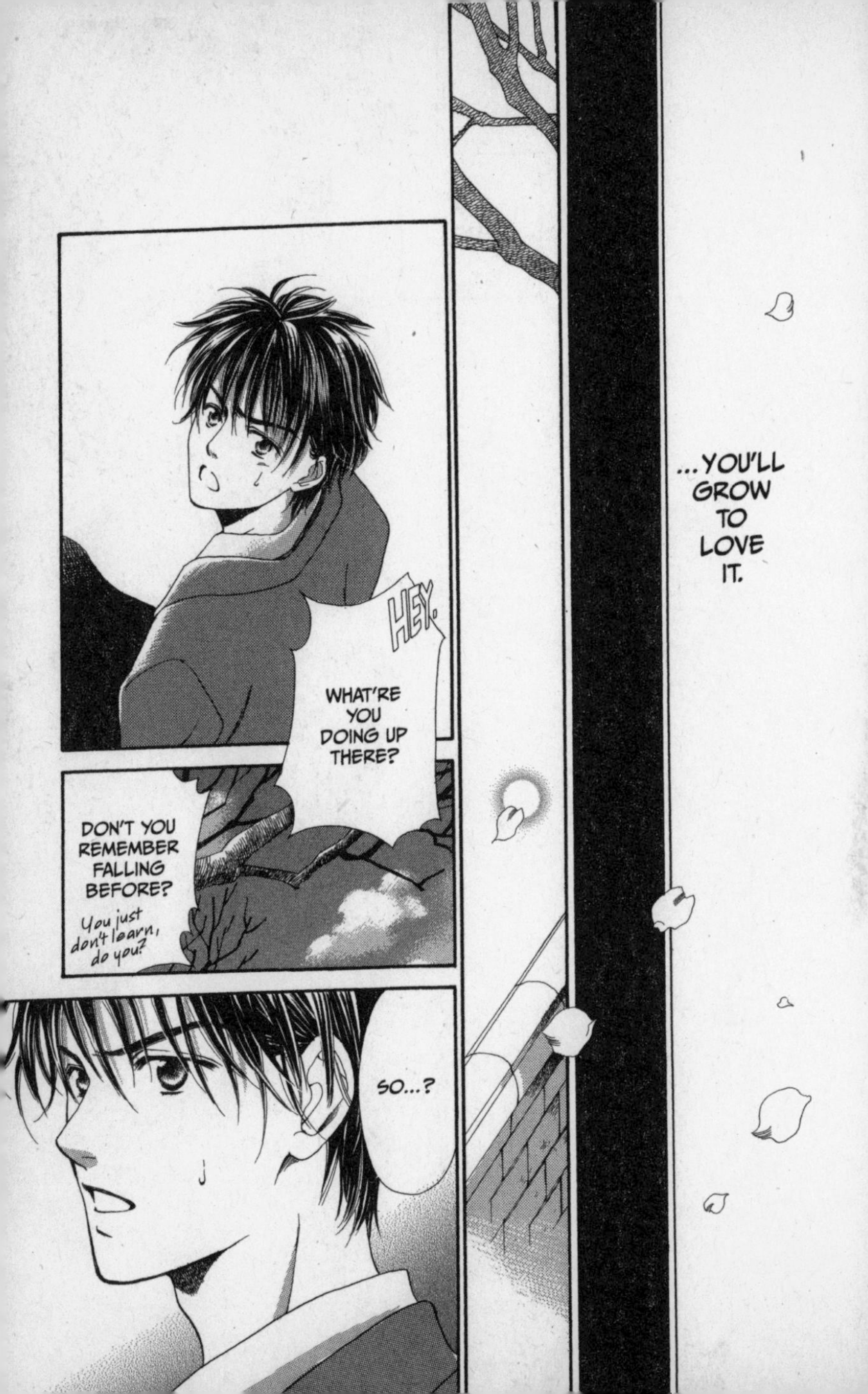
...YOU'LL GROW TO LOVE IT.
HEY.
WHAT'RE YOU DOING UP THERE?
DON'T YOU REMEMBER FALLING BEFORE?
You just don't learn, do you?
SO...?

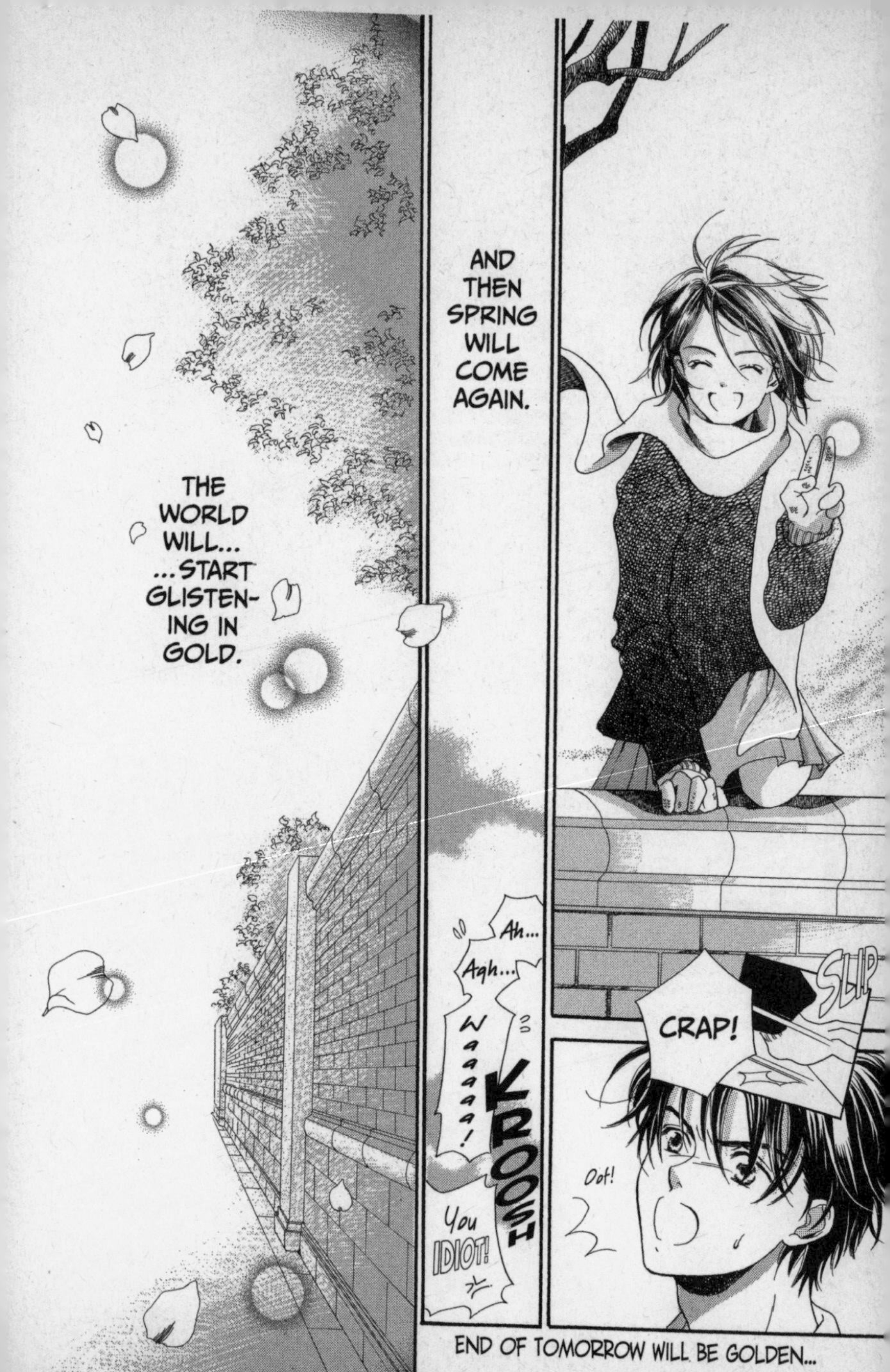
SLIP
CRAP!
Oof!
AND THEN SPRING WILL COME AGAIN.
Ah...
Agh...
Waaaaa!
KRROOOSH
You IDIOT!
THE WORLD WILL...
...START GLISTENING IN GOLD.

END OF TOMORROW WILL BE GOLDEN...

BACKSTAGE WITH THE JOURNALISM CLUB

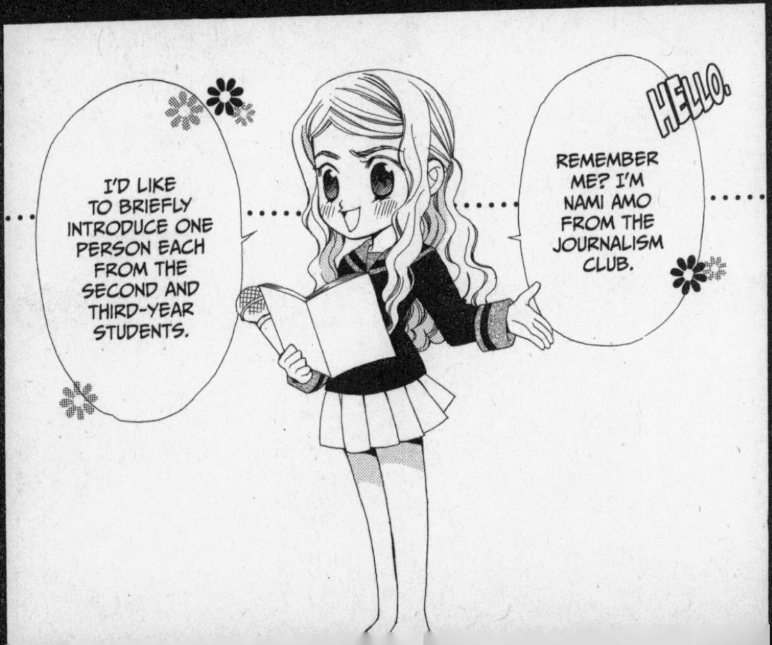
HELLO.
REMEMBER ME? I'M NAMI AMO FROM THE JOURNALISM CLUB.
I'D LIKE TO BRIEFLY INTRODUCE ONE PERSON EACH FROM THE SECOND AND THIRD-YEAR STUDENTS.

月森　蓮

LEN TSUKIMORI

Sneak shot →

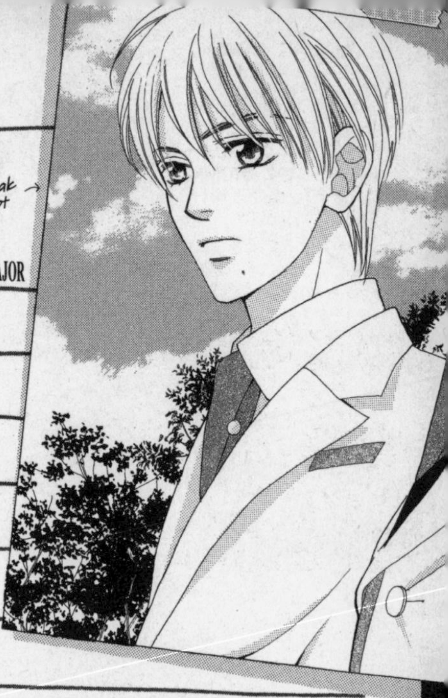

MUSIC SCHOOL SECOND YEAR CLASS A: VIOLIN MAJOR

BIRTHDAY: APRIL 24TH

ZODIAC SIGN: TAURUS

BLOOD TYPE: A

HEIGHT: 5'8"

FAMILY: FATHER, MOTHER, PATERNAL GRANDMOTHER AND MATERNAL GRANDFATHER

■ ALMOST EVERYBODY IN HIS FAMILY IS INVOLVED IN MUSIC. HIS BEST SUBJECT IS ENGLISH.

Although apparently not bad at German either.

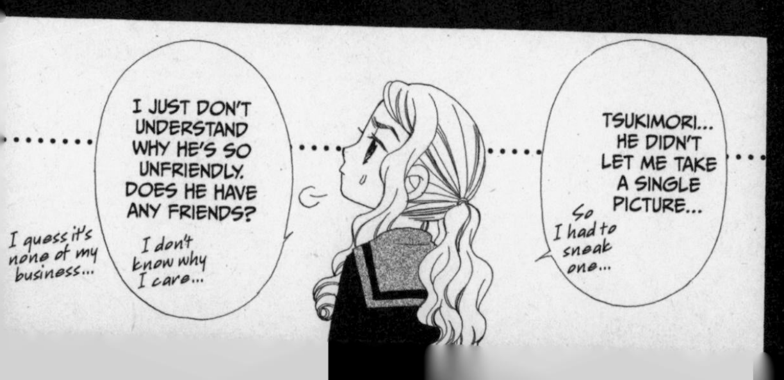
TSUKIMORI... HE DIDN'T LET ME TAKE A SINGLE PICTURE...
So I had to sneak one...
I JUST DON'T UNDERSTAND WHY HE'S SO UNFRIENDLY. DOES HE HAVE ANY FRIENDS?
I don't know why I care...
I guess it's none of my business...

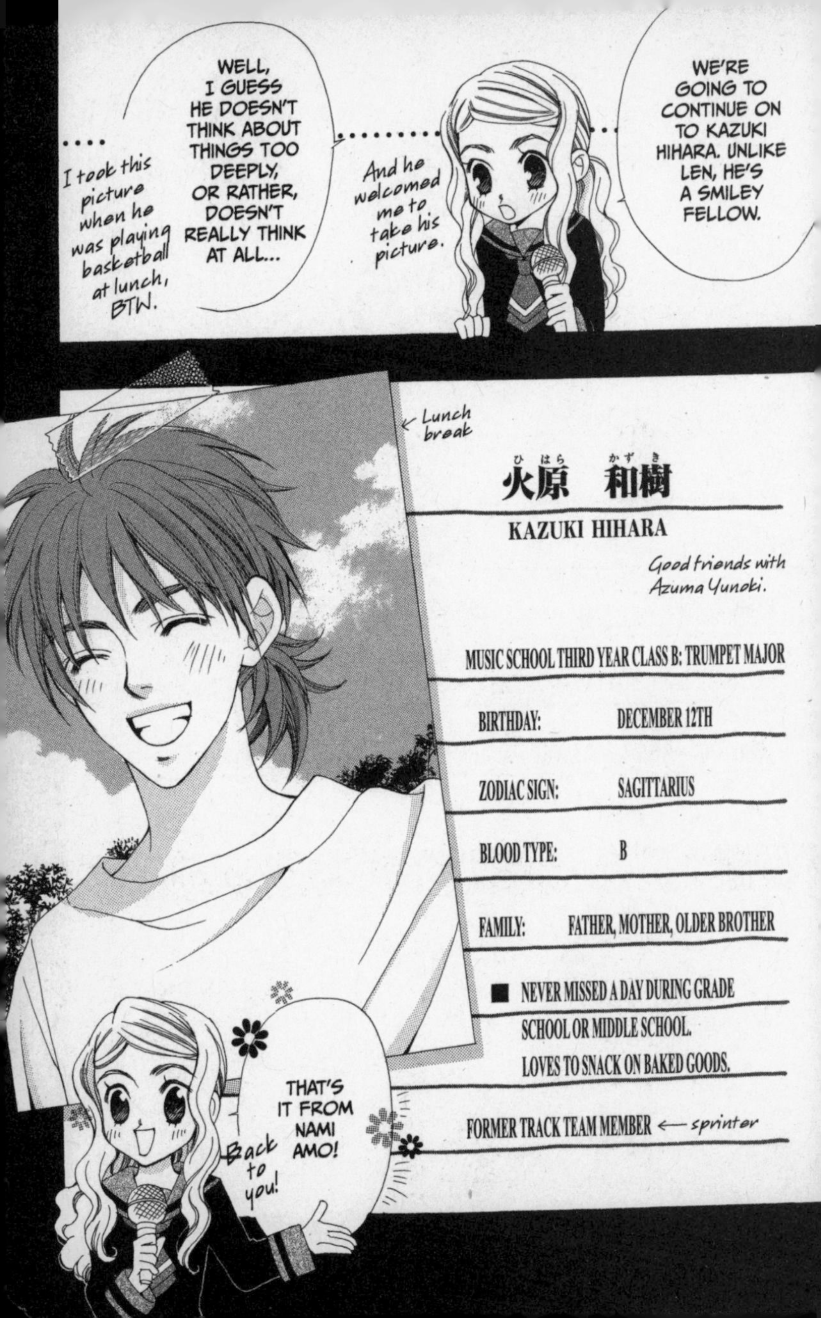

WE'RE GOING TO CONTINUE ON TO KAZUKI HIHARA. UNLIKE LEN, HE'S A SMILEY FELLOW.
And he welcomed me to take his picture.
WELL, I GUESS HE DOESN'T THINK ABOUT THINGS TOO DEEPLY, OR RATHER, DOESN'T REALLY THINK AT ALL...
I took this picture when he was playing basketball at lunch, BTW.
← Lunch break
ひはら かずき
火原 和樹
KAZUKI HIHARA
Good friends with Azuma Yunoki.
MUSIC SCHOOL THIRD YEAR CLASS B: TRUMPET MAJOR
BIRTHDAY: DECEMBER 12TH
ZODIAC SIGN: SAGITTARIUS
BLOOD TYPE: B
FAMILY: FATHER, MOTHER, OLDER BROTHER
■ NEVER MISSED A DAY DURING GRADE SCHOOL OR MIDDLE SCHOOL.
LOVES TO SNACK ON BAKED GOODS.
FORMER TRACK TEAM MEMBER ← sprinter
THAT'S IT FROM NAMI AMO!
Back to you!

Hello again.
I'd like you to thank you for
purchasing volume 2 of La Corda d'Oro.

Since Ryotaro plays such a central
part in this second volume, I was
honestly a little nervous that those
of you who are Len, Keiichi, Kazuki,
Azuma, etc. fans would be disappointed.
(I'm a big wimp.)

And there're some characters who
have yet to make an appearance...
(wry smile)
I'm sure they'll make an appearance
soon, so please be patient! Yes.

Last but not least, to all the readers
and all my editors who have been such
tremendous help, and Koei...Thank you so
very much. I truly appreciate everything.

Until next time.
2004 Yuki Kure

SPECIAL THANKS

A.IZUMI
A.OGURA
A.KASHIMA
N.SATOH
M.SHIINO
E.NAKANO
Y.OTSUKA
Y.KOMURO
S.MATSUOKA

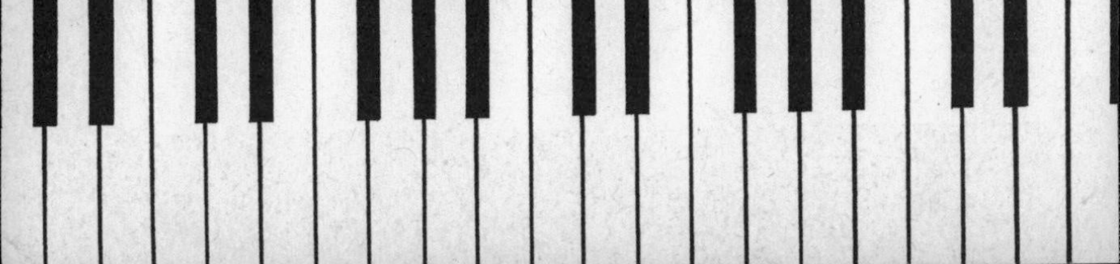

La Corda d'Oro End Notes

You can appreciate music just by listening to it, but knowing the story behind a piece can help enhance your enjoyment. In that spirit, here is background information about some of the topics mentioned in *La Corda d'Oro*. Enjoy!

Page 9, panel 1: Hanami
A gathering under the cherry blossom trees where people gather to enjoy food and drink and admire the cherry blossoms.

Page 11, panel 3: Sakura
Japanese for cherry blossoms, they symbolize samurai and the fragility of life.

Page 64, panel 4: Frédéric Chopin
1810-1849. Born to a French father and a Polish mother, Chopin grew up in Poland but moved to Paris in 1831 due to political unrest in his native country. He found quick acceptance in the finest circles, and became greatly talked about for his skills as a composer, his ill health, and his affair with controversial novelist George Sand. He composed exclusively for the piano and was known as a great improviser, preferring to create while playing rather than laboring with paper and pen.

Page 91, panel 3: Minuet
Introduced first at the opera, minuets are based on the 3/4 time and rhythm of the lively French social dances with which they share a name. In the late 17th century, minuets were adopted in suites, such as the suites by Johann Sebastian Bach and George Frideric Handel.

Page 91, panel 3: Humoresque
A character piece, usually for the piano, composed to express a mood or idea. Humoresques are usually more good-humored than humorous. The most famous humoresque was composed by the Czechoslovakian-born Antonin Dvorak, while he was living in New York City.

Page 91, panel 3: Thaïs "Méditation"
From the opera *Thaïs* by French composer Jules Massenet, "Meditation" is considered one of the world's great encore pieces, designed to allow the leader of the orchestra to show off his skills.

Page 91, panel 3: Romance No. 1 in G major
A concerto composed during 1800-1802 by Ludwig van Beethoven for the violin and orchestra.

Page 98, panel 3: The Minute Waltz
Composed around 1846 as part of Chopin's opus 64, *Trois Valses*, and dedicated "To Mme. la Comtesse Delphine Potocka." With this waltz, Chopin was trying to invoke the image of a dog chasing its tail, and even originally named the piece *Petit Chien* (small dog).

Page 98, panel 3: Black Key Etude
The fifth part of Chopin's Piano Etudes Opus 10, it is known as the "Black Key" etude because only one white key is used in the entire piece. It is a short yet difficult piece.

Page 147, panel 1: Tchaikovsky's Violin Concerto
Pyotr Ilyich Tchaikovsky's Violin Concerto in D major, Opus 35 is one of the most well-known of all the concertos, as well as being one of the most technically difficult. It was composed in 1878 in a Swiss resort while Tchaikovsky recovered from the depression brought about by his ill-advised marriage. It premiered in 1881 to less than favorable reviews, and one critic went so far as to quip that it "brought us face to face with the revolting thought that music can exist which stinks to the ear."

Page 150, panel 1: Concertmaster
The first violin chair is the concertmaster, responsible for leading the orchestra in tuning before concerts and rehearsal as well as many technical and managerial details. Concertmasters will sometimes also act in labor negotiations for the other players. The position is like an assistant conductor, although in the days when orchestras were smaller, the concertmaster was in fact the conductor.

Yuki Kure made her debut in 2000
with the story *Chijo yori Eien ni*
(Forever from the Earth), published
in monthly *LaLa* magazine.
La Corda d' Oro is her first manga
series published. Her hobby is
watching soccer games and
collecting small goodies.

LA CORDA D'ORO
Vol. 2
The Shojo Beat Manga Edition

STORY AND ART BY
YUKI KURE

ORIGINAL CONCEPT BY
RUBY PARTY

English Translation & Adaptation/Mai Ihara
Touch-up Art & Lettering/Gia Cam Luc
Design/Yukiko Whitley
Editor/Pancha Diaz

Managing Editor/Megan Bates
Editorial Director/Elizabeth Kawasaki
VP & Editor in Chief/Yumi Hoashi
Sr. Director of Acquisitions/Rika Inouye
Sr. VP of Marketing/Liza Coppola
Exec. VP of Sales & Marketing/John Easum
Publisher/Hyoe Narita

Kiniro no Corda by Yuki Kure © Yuki Kure, KOEI Co., Ltd. 2002
All rights reserved.
First published in Japan in 2004 by HAKUSENSHA, Inc., Tokyo.
English language translation rights in America and Canada arranged
with HAKUSENSHA, Inc., Tokyo.
New and adapted artwork and text © 2007 VIZ Media, LLC.
The LA CORDA D'ORO logo is a trademark of VIZ Media, LLC.
The stories, characters and incidents mentioned in this publication are entirely fictional.

No portion of this book may be reproduced or transmitted in any form or
by any means without written permission from the copyright holders.

Printed in Canada

Published by VIZ Media, LLC
P.O. Box 77010
San Francisco, CA 94107

Shojo Beat Manga Edition
10 9 8 7 6 5 4 3 2
First printing, January 2007

store.viz.com

PARENTAL ADVISORY
LA CORDA D'ORO is rated T for Teen and is recommended
for ages 13 and up. This volume contains mild violence.

Skip·Beat!™

by Yoshiki Nakamura

Kyoko won't let Sho get away with ruffling her feathers again!

Only $8.99 each

Skip·Beat! 4 — Yoshiki Nakamura

Skip·Beat! 3

Skip·Beat! 2 — Yoshiki Nakamura

Skip·Beat! 1 — Yoshiki Nakamura

In stores January 2, 2007!

 Shojo Beat — MANGA from the HEART

 THE REAL DRAMA BEGINS IN...

 RATED T TEEN SB VIZ MEDIA

Skip·Beat! © Yoshiki Nakamura 2002/HAKUSENSHA, Inc.
Covers subject to change.

On sale at:
www.shojobeat.com
Also available at your local bookstore and comic store.

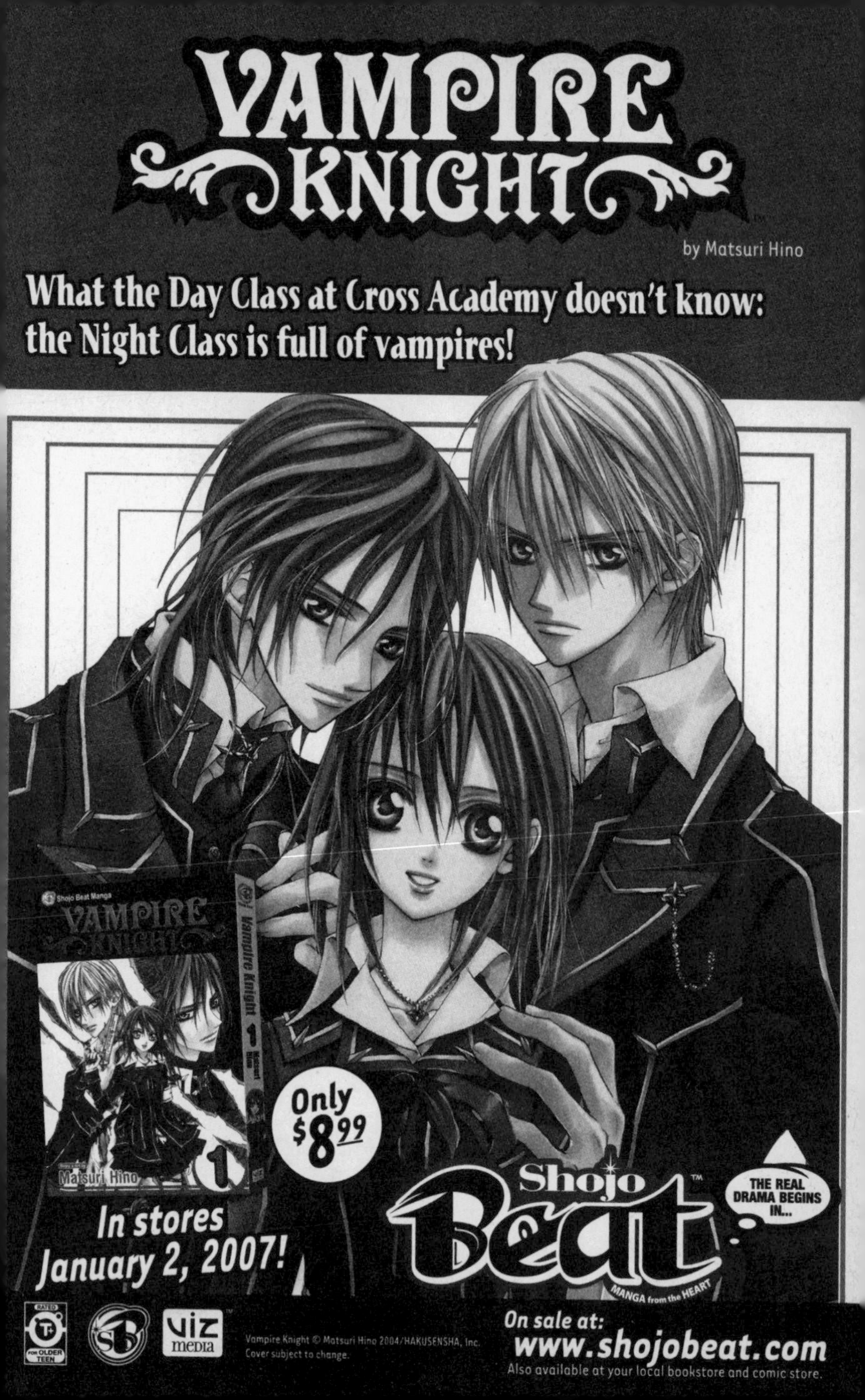
VAMPIRE KNIGHT™
by Matsuri Hino
What the Day Class at Cross Academy doesn't know: the Night Class is full of vampires!
Shojo Beat Manga
VAMPIRE KNIGHT
Vampire Knight 1 Matsuri Hino
Matsuri Hino
Only $8.99
In stores January 2, 2007!
Shojo Beat™
MANGA from the HEART
THE REAL DRAMA BEGINS IN...
RATED T+ FOR OLDER TEEN
VIZ media
Vampire Knight © Matsuri Hino 2004/HAKUSENSHA, Inc.
Cover subject to change.
On sale at:
www.shojobeat.com
Also available at your local bookstore and comic store.

PUNCH!™

by Rie Takada

In stores January 2, 2007!

Shojo Beat Manga

PUNCH!

2

Rie Takada

Shojo Beat Manga

PUNCH!

1

Rie Takada

Only **$8.99** each

Ruo's getting revenge on Elle by dating her boyfriend's little sister!

Shojo Beat™
MANGA from the HEART

THE REAL DRAMA BEGINS IN...

 VIZ media

 RATED T+ FOR OLDER TEEN

Punch! © 2006 Rie TAKADA/Shogakukan Inc.
Covers subject to change.

On sale at:
www.shojobeat.com
Also available at your local bookstore and comic store.

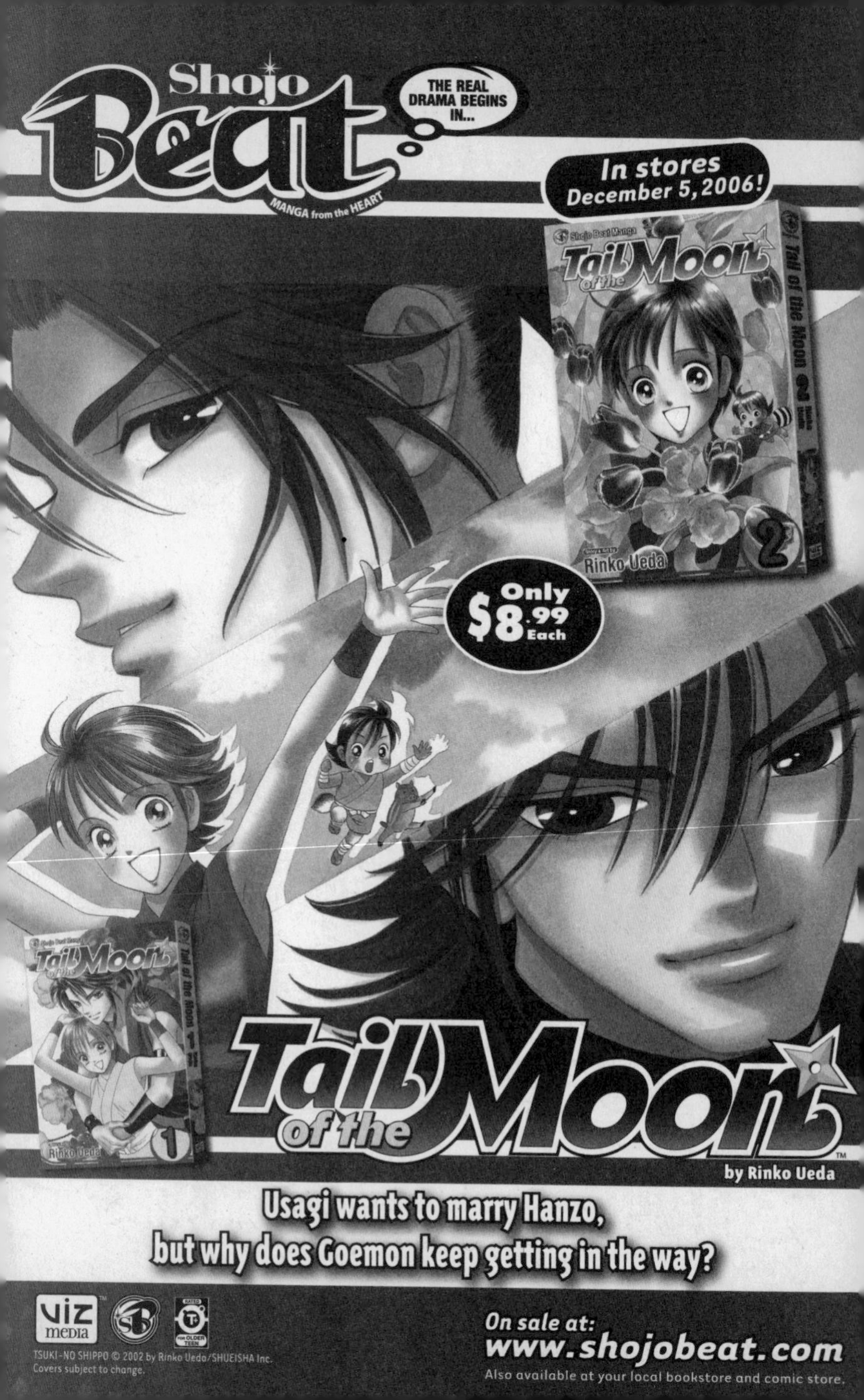
Shojo Beat
MANGA from the HEART
THE REAL DRAMA BEGINS IN...
In stores December 5, 2006!
Shojo Beat Manga
Tail of the Moon
Rinko Ueda
2
Only $8.99 Each
Tail of the Moon
Rinko Ueda
1
Tail of the Moon™
by Rinko Ueda
Usagi wants to marry Hanzo,
but why does Goemon keep getting in the way?
viz media
TSUKI-NO SHIPPO © 2002 by Rinko Ueda/SHUEISHA Inc.
Covers subject to change.
On sale at:
www.shojobeat.com
Also available at your local bookstore and comic store.

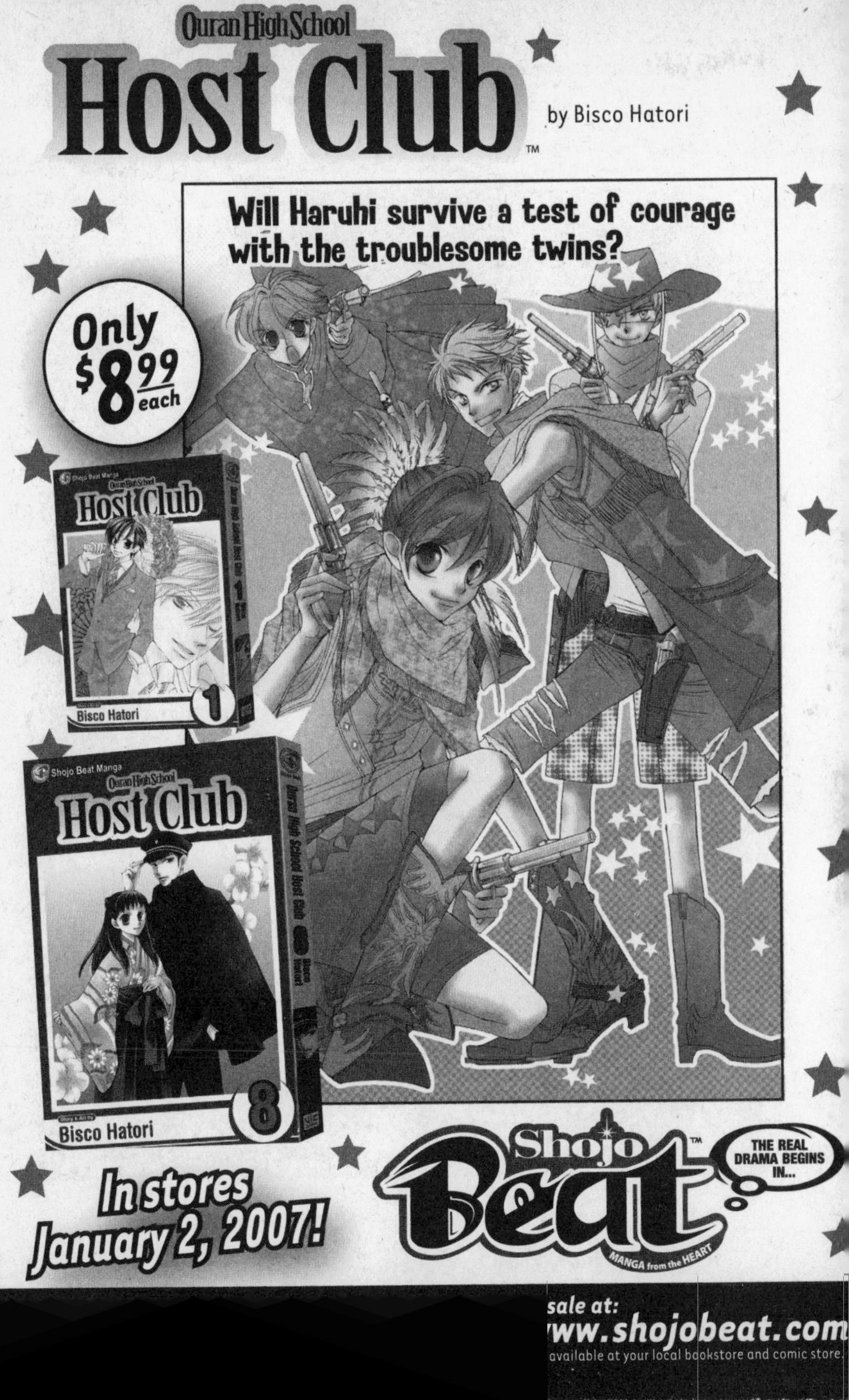
Ouran High School
Host Club™
by Bisco Hatori
Will Haruhi survive a test of courage with the troublesome twins?
Only $8.99 each
Shojo Beat Manga
Ouran High School
Host Club
Bisco Hatori
1
Shojo Beat Manga
Ouran High School
Host Club
Ouran High School Host Club
Story & Art by
Bisco Hatori
8
In stores January 2, 2007!
Shojo Beat™
THE REAL DRAMA BEGINS IN...
MANGA from the HEART
sale at:
ww.shojobeat.com
available at your local bookstore and comic store.

Tell us what you think about Shojo Beat Manga!

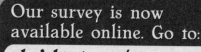

Our survey is now available online. Go to:

shojobeat.com/mangasurvey

Help us make our product offerings better!

FULL MOON WO SAGASHITE © 2001 by Arina Tanemura/SHUEISHA Inc.
Fushigi Yûgi: Genbu Kaiden © 2004 Yuu WATASE/Shogakukan Inc.
Ouran Koko Host Club © Bisco Hatori 2002/HAKUSENSHA, Inc.